Okanagan Women's Voices

Syilx and Settler Writing and Relations
1870s - 1960s

Okanagan Women's Voices

Syilx and Settler Writing and Relations 1870s - 1960s

Edited by
Jeannette Armstrong
Lally Grauer
Janet MacArthur

Library and Archives Canada Cataloguing in Publication

Title: Okanagan women's voices : Syilx and settler writing and relations, 1870s to 1960s /
edited by Jeannette Armstrong, Lally Grauer, Janet MacArthur.
Names: Armstrong, Jeannette C., editor. | Grauer, Lally, editor. | MacArthur, Janet H., editor.
Identifiers: Canadiana 2019020706X | ISBN 9781926886527 (softcover)
Subjects: LCSH: Okanagan Indians—British Columbia—Okanagan Valley (Region)—History. |
LCSH: Women— British Columbia—Okanagan Valley (Region)—History. |
LCSH: Frontier and pioneer life—British Columbia—Okanagan Valley (Region) |
LCSH: Okanagan Valley (B.C. : Region)—History.
Classification: LCC E99.O35 O43 2020 | DDC 971.1/500497943—dc23

Printed in Canada by Friesens

MIX
Paper from
responsible sources
FSC® C016245

Cover illustration: *spiƛəm* (Lewisia rediviva) is one of the four *captikʷł*
(syilx story) chiefs of the syilx people representing the power and enduring strength of the
female- *lax̌lax̌tkʷ*
~Jeannette Armstrong

Cover and Book Design: Ann Doyon

THEYTUS BOOKS
www.theytus.com
154 En'owkin Trail, Penticton, British Columbia, V2A 1E0

BRITISH COLUMBIA
ARTS COUNCIL
An agency of the Province of British Columbia

BRITISH
COLUMBIA
Supported by the Province of British Columbia

We acknowledge the financial support of
The Government of Canada through the
Department of Canadian Heritage for our
publishing activities. We acknowledge
the support of the Canada Council for the
Arts through the Creating, Knowing and
Sharing Program. We acknowledge the
support of the Province of British Columbia
through the British Columbia Arts Council.

Conseil des Arts
du Canada
Canada Council
for the Arts

Patrimoine
canadien
Canadian
Heritage

Contents

Isabel Christie MacNaughton (1915-2003)

Introduction

Jeannette Armstrong, Lally Grauer and Janet MacArthur

The writing and relations between Syilx women and settler women, largely of European descent, who came to inhabit the British Columbia southern interior in the latter part of the nineteenth and early twentieth centuries, is the focus of this book. Encounters in this contact zone between different peoples have been examined previously, but little has been written about the gender-specific relations among the women who lived here during this time. Jeannette Armstrong first had the idea that a book was needed to remedy the scarcity of women's voices, both Syilx and settler, in the history of the Okanagan, and brought on board her colleagues, Lally Grauer and Janet MacArthur. Armstrong and Grauer had collaborated before, notably on an anthology of poetry by Indigenous writers in Canada.[1] MacArthur's interest in Indigenous and settler autobiographical material brought her into the conversation. We decided upon a work that would make available Syilx and settler women's writing and storytelling, much of it discovered in local archives and not previously published. In the course of our research, we narrowed our focus to seven women writers, Susan Moir Allison (1845-1937), Josephine Shuttleworth (1865-1950), Eliza Jane Swalwell (1868-1944), Marie Houghton Brent (1870-1968), Hester Emily White (1877-1963), Mourning Dove (1886-1936) and Isabel Christie MacNaughton (1915-2003). Some of these women knew each other, or knew of each other; some had close relations. The body of work they produced is compelling for cultural, historical and literary reasons. Our compilation of their writing speaks to the many changes in the way British Columbia history has been studied in recent decades, and is part of the movement for the representation of diverse voices. *Okanagan Women's Voices* incorporates life writing (correspondence, journals, memoirs), translations of Syilx *captikʷɬ* (traditional stories), journalism, popular history, as well as poetry, drama, and fiction.

i

The Land

In Canada, the land of the Okanagan-Similkameen has often been thought of as an inaccessible, sparsely-peopled hinterland, an "interior" space walled in by geography. For a long time its history did not garner as much attention as that of the Pacific coast or the earlier-settled and more populated east. With this book we hope to contribute, alongside others who have gone before us and whom we frequently cite, toward remedying that situation.[2] For the Syilx, this land always been the center.

The Syilx people (often called the Okanagan or, in the United States, the Okanogan), identified by their common *nsyilxcn* language, had established a sustainable way of life for tens of thousands of years in what is now the south central interior of British Columbia and the northern interior of Washington State. To the Syilx, this land provided a diverse abundance to many villages along the water systems of their territory. Traveling south from north of Revelstoke, British Columbia, near Mica Creek, the Syilx found a wealth of fishing, hunting, root and berry crops, and trade was easily accessible by canoe through the great Columbia River and Arrow Lakes system that spanned territory in what is now Canada and the United States. As well, from *nkʼmapəlqs* or Nkamapulks, Head of the Lake, at the northernmost arm of the Okanagan Lake, waterways took the Syilx down the Okanagan Lake and the Okanagan river, and along the Kettle, the Similkameen, the Methow and the Sanpoil rivers south to their interior confluences with the mother Columbia River. On well-used trails through established huckleberry, deer, elk, moose and caribou harvest areas, the Syilx travelled east from their villages on the Slocan Lake, Trout Lake and the western shores of the Kootenay Lake area in British Columbia, and west through the Okanagan and Similkameen to the summit of the Cascade Mountain Range. These are the people with whom explorers, fur traders, miners, and settlers met when they entered the watersheds of the Columbia River in the nineteenth century.

Although we did not set out to cover specific geographical areas, our research and particular interests led us to the writing of women writers of Syilx descent from many different parts of Syilx land: Marie Houghton Brent, from the head of the Okanagan Lake and the Kelowna area; Eliza Jane Swalwell, from the central Kelowna area of Okanagan Lake; Josephine Shuttleworth from the lower Penticton area of the Okanagan Valley; and Mourning Dove, from the *nsyilxcn* peoples' great Kettle Falls fishery in what is now the state of Washington. Her family also lived, harvested and worked throughout Syilx territory in British Columbia.

We want to honour these women for their writing and for how they understood the land, the language and the Syilx experience of the land's *tmixʷ*, or the apprehension of all life forms as living spirit. This belief, among other things, underpinned a philosophy of reciprocity between people and the land, the animals, and all living things that created the fabric of life and ensured its continuance. The land is, for them, not just a setting for their stories but a source of power, a book marked everywhere by stories, an ongoing teacher. Their writing and storytelling show how that understanding continued into and was translated in the settlement period of the 1860s on. From her position within a Syilx and settler intermarriage, Josephine Shuttleworth shares her legacy of *captikʷ ł* or traditional stories that elaborate and explain relationships to the land as well as to incoming settlers. Eliza Jane Swalwell allows us insight into her Syilx relationship to the land together with her story as the daughter of one of the first ranchers in the Kelowna region, George William Simpson. Marie Houghton Brent, the child of a Syilx and a settler, understood the importance of Syilx identity and took advantage of her education to disseminate the story of her great-grandfather, *xʷistsmx̌ayqn*, Walking Grizzly, or Chief Nkwala and his line. Mourning Dove wrote to communicate elements of Syilx language, story and culture, including Syilx relationship to the land, in *Cogewea: The Half-Blood, Coyote Stories,* and stories she recorded in the Okanagan such as "House of Little Men."

To varying degrees, the settler women writers in this volume were able to connect to Syilx beliefs and understandings. Susan Allison, who lived on the west side of Okanagan Lake but was settled mainly in the Similkameen, near what is now Princeton, British Columbia, for nearly sixty years, became attuned to "something very real" within Syilx beliefs and philosophy and much of her writing implies their vitality and legitimacy. Hester White, in her occasional matter-of-fact recounting of Syilx stories, shows her respect for both story and storytellers, who were often Syilx people she grew up with in the Osoyoos area south of what is now Penticton. Isabel Christie MacNaughton also grew up in the southern Okanagan near Okanagan Falls, British Columbia. Her renditions of her neighbour Josephine Shuttleworth's *captikʷ ł* suggest Shuttleworth's powerful influence and MacNaughton's receptivity.

Trails, Boundaries, Inroads

The settlers, nevertheless, came with a very different conception of the land from the Syilx. Initially guided by Indigenous people on the trails in and out of what they called the "upper country," surveyors, trailblazers, mapmakers, and pre-emptors set the boundaries of what was named British Columbia according to the European gaze. Competing American and British colonial aspirations were resolved in 1846 by the establishment of the 49th parallel as a boundary between British North America and the United States, which profoundly disrupted the Syilx way of life and relations to the land. The fur trade rapidly diminished in the Okanagan, as Hudson's Bay Company brigades found alternative routes "north of the line" to the one established in 1810 travelling up the Columbia and Okanogan rivers and through the Okanagan valley to Kamloops. With the gold rushes of the late 1850s and early 1860s, people flooded into mining boom sites in the southern part of the province often via inland routes in American territory. To consolidate British interests, Governor James Douglas and others were eager to create wagon roads that would carry settlers and government agents into the southernmost interior valleys. Trailblazing work began for a wagon road over the Hope Mountains, as the settlers called them, just east of Hope. Susan Allison's husband John Fall Allison received commissions from Governor Douglas to find and improve suitable trails into the Similkameen and beyond, beginning in 1860s (Ormsby xxvii-xxviii). This work contributed to the creation of the route known as the Dewdney Trail built over five years from Hope to Wild Horse Creek in the east Kootenays under the auspices of Edgar Dewdney (Allison's brother-in-law after 1864) and Walter Moberly. The "old Hope Trail" (which follows much of the Dewdney Trail) was used for decades by those travelling from the lower mainland to the Similkameen and then on to the Okanagan and the Kootenays. From Hope to the forks of the Similkameen and Tulameen Rivers where the Allisons lived generally required two nights of camping out.

Many stopped at the Allisons' homestead.

The dependency of settlers on Indigenous people's knowledge and assistance is often revealed in the accounts of early travel in this volume. Susan Allison and Hester White, writing after the extension of rail travel and the advent of the car, look back to their early years or their childhoods in the Okanagan of the late nineteenth century, remembering the magic of the pack trail and wagon road. Both write vividly of deeply satisfying camping days and nights on the trail.

While settlers began to superimpose their view of the land as suitable for exploitation for profit and the movement of goods, remapping and renaming took place. The Syilx, like other Indigenous peoples in British Columbia, were squeezed into small parcels of land and their movement and agency were increasingly restricted. Reserves on Syilx land were established by W.G. Cox for Governor James Douglas in 1860, and by late 1865, Hester White's father J.C. Haynes, acting as an agent of government, had greatly reduced them. Women writers in this volume register the great changes which occurred in land usage that affected relations between Syilx and settlers. As early as the 1890s, Susan Allison writes about settlers' mistreatment of the Syilx. Marie Houghton Brent and Eliza Jane Swalwell address and convey increasing geographical, legal and cultural confinement of the Syilx in their respective works, "The Indians of the Okanagan Valley" (1935) and "Girlhood Days in the Okanagan" (1939). Further south in Syilx territory, the Colville reservation was established in 1872, and then drastically reduced by 1882. In *Cogewea, The Half-Blood* (1927), Mourning Dove endeavours to illuminate and reveal some of the devastating effects on Syilx land and people. She also responded as an activist and spokesperson on the Colville reservation in the early 1930s.

By 1948, when Hester White wrote her series of articles entitled "The Pioneer Trail," she suggests the history of settlement in the Okanagan is already forgotten and overlaid by highways and businesses. Her series, looking back with some nostalgia to the old trails, also attempts to imagine a pre-settlement Syilx land. Yet in doing so, her writing is already covering over, erasing, and renaming the Syilx relationship to land and the severe consequences of settlement for the Syilx.

Nevertheless, trails divagate, diverge and converge within

and among these texts, and inroads are made into regions the authors had not consciously charted. Finding these texts and placing them together has led us to new perspectives and understanding. Contradictions and changing perspectives may be found in an author's material. Over time, Allison's writing registers increasing anxiety over what settler remapping has meant for Syilx friends and relations. Writings may reveal multiple cultural influences and diverse conditions under which writing took place, as in Marie Houghton Brent's varying voices and genres in her writing about "Indians" in the pages of the Okanagan Historical Society's annual report, in her own jottings and reminiscences of childhood days at a convent in Kamloops, or in her transcription of *captik*ʷɬ about coyote. Eliza Jane Swalwell, while pointing in her reminiscences to the insidious effects of colonialism, nevertheless looks back fondly to the days of ranching before the establishment of roads, cars and orchards. The contiguity of the voices in this volume can reveal very different underlying philosophies or similar concerns and points of view. They do not fall neatly into what we may think of as "Indigenous" or "settler" perspectives. Marie Houghton Brent is just as admiring of her settler father's achievements as Hester Emily White is of hers. Susan Allison's numerous accounts of the Syilx or the stories of Josephine Shuttleworth as written down by Isabel Christie MacNaughton can be understood to reveal both Syilx and settler description and nuance.

Changing Relations

There is no doubt that the "invasion" of settlers in the Okanagan after the gold rush to the Fraser River and the Cariboo from 1858 on, to take a word employed by both Marie Houghton Brent and Hester Emily White, had a devastating impact on Syilx people and culture, which continues to this day. These women's voices give ample and important evidence on the subject of white hegemony, of the privilege of white women and the exploitation of women of Syilx heritage in the domestic sphere, of the wide gap in education and opportunity for Syilx versus settler, and of the poverty faced by many Syilx women throughout their lives. Some of the texts, such as Hester Emily White's writing about Matilda Kruger, suggest a complicated pattern of openness to and refusal of settler-Syilx relations. One area kept silenced was relationships between settler men and Syilx women. In her published writing, Susan Allison could only obliquely refer to her husband's Syilx wife, Nora Yacumtecum, and her sons' mixed heritage children. Hester White tried her best to erase any record of her father J.C. Haynes's relationship with Julie Abraham, a Syilx woman. This attitude has continued to be prevalent in the Okanagan region. As researchers, we found such silence surrounding the entwined personal journeys of Syilx and early settlers. The Okanagan Historical Society (OHS), which published its first report in 1926 and has been an invaluable resource for this text,[3] only began to acknowledge this history in 1996 with their publication of Jean Barman's essay "Lost Okanagan: In Search of the First Settler Families." Many of these relations have been kept out of the public domain to this day, unknown in some of the archives and museums we visited. Putting these women's writings together gave us an opportunity to respectfully recognize and consider some of these relationships. Negotiating the complexity of these relationships within a colonial society is evident not only in writing by settlers Allison and White in this volume, but also by Syilx women Brent and Swalwell. At the same time, the records provided by the women's voices in this text indicate that Syilx culture was sustained and found ways to continue through changing relations: for example, Swalwell puts forward political problems and solutions, Shuttleworth incorporates settlement into traditional *captikʷɬ*, and both Brent and Mourning Dove often and insistently voice Syilx history and story.

Collaborations and Approaches

Throughout this project, the three of us have maintained a focus on the connections formed among settler women and Syilx women as well as Syilx people in general. Our emphasis has been less on the opposing life trajectories of Syilx and settler women and more on their intersections. One of our questions as we approached our research was whether or not there was a trace in the archives of some "spaces between" where Indigenous and non-Indigenous women interacted, adapted, and accommodated each other in various ways, developing friendships, respect, understanding, and collaboration. What kinds of relationships were possible, permitted, made inroads or traversed boundaries? As we talked about these texts with one another, we began looking for places where dialogue took place and seeing a fluidity in these writings: evidence of adaptability on the part of both Syilx and settler, and shifting perspectives and negotiations.

We also learned to adapt to each other as editors over the many years of working together in research and writing, accommodating changes and challenges in our own and each other's lives: raising children and other family obligations; achieving a PhD; juggling the demands of researching, university service and teaching; and adjusting to retirement and the demands of new projects. Our individual approaches brought into focus different aspects of the women's documents we collected; thus, we thought it would be important to convey our perspectives in the three essays in this volume, which, we hope, also model how multiple perspectives create a sense of the past. As a knowledge keeper, researcher, elder, and fluent speaker of *nsyilxcn*, Armstrong has access to a history and an understanding of Syilx ontology and epistemology that makes an inestimably important contribution to our understanding of the narratives, people, and events recounted by both Indigenous and non-Indigenous women writers in this volume. Without Armstrong's Syilx perspective, it would have been impossible for us to get a sense, for example, of the complex interplay between Josephine Shuttleworth and Isabel Christie MacNaughton. Shuttleworth probably understood the *captikʷł* she told MacNaughton to be central and subtly transmitted Syilx teachings about how to get on with each other and the natural world, while MacNaughton saw them first as "legends" and then as "folk-tales." Armstrong's analysis allows us to understand that, between the two of them, the stories' vigour and potential meanings were nevertheless transmitted and captured. Her essay "Standing Between" positions the Syilx writers in this volume and their writing within a Syilx cultural context. Armstrong has long been a vibrant and moving creative and critical voice not only in national and global activism on behalf of Indigenous people but also for sustainable life on the planet. Her unflagging energies, commitment, and patience have been essential to this project.

Lally Grauer, who has done long hours of archival research for many projects in Indigenous studies, brings a comprehensive knowledge of contact history between Indigenous people and settlers to bear on the gathering of much of the unpublished material that appears in this volume. At times, her recovery and transcription of documents made us rethink our perspectives on the material as a whole. Her career in teaching Indigenous and Canadian literatures, working to develop an Indigenous studies program, and hosting numerous Indigenous writers on campus in her work as a university teacher, have familiarized her with Indigenous and settler discourse throughout Canada. Grauer's essay "Crossing Lines" traces a network of relations between many of the women writers and storytellers in this volume and revisits, from the context of their relationships with settler women, the work of Marie Houghton Brent and Josephine Shuttleworth which Jeannette Armstrong discusses in the first part of this work.

Janet MacArthur's longstanding research and writing on the ways in which personal and cultural trauma are represented in literature and autobiographical forms provides a perspective in this work on how the extreme experience of colonialism took its toll on the Syilx. Her essay explores how a settler with an awareness of this, Susan Allison, was "unsettled," grappling with conflicting feelings about the settler enterprise and an ambivalence that placed her in an in between position hard to convey publicly to a white audience. In her discussion in her essay "Something Very Real," MacArthur also makes use of feminist critical and cultural theory, postcolonial studies, particularly the recent body of work known as settler studies, and critical race theory, all staples of the critical dialogue today in the humanities about settlement history. Her work also asserts connections between Allison's attempts to reconcile herself with the dark side of settler colonialism and the attempts of contemporary Canadians to come to terms with the past.

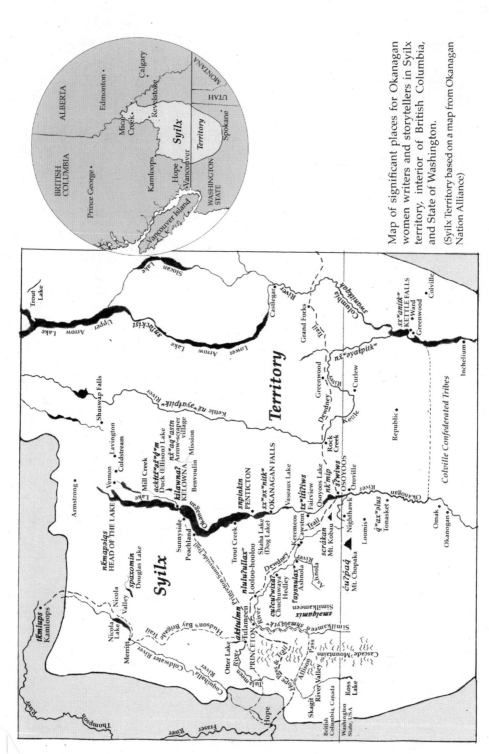

Map of significant places for Okanagan women writers and storytellers in Syilx territory, interior of British Columbia, and State of Washington.

(Syilx Territory based on a map from Okanagan Nation Alliance)

A Note to the Reader

As much as possible, we have tried to reproduce the voices of the women writers and storytellers in this volume. We have generally preserved their diverse standards of spelling, grammar, and punctuation, which occur particularly in the manuscripts here published for the first time, as well as in reprinted publications. While we have kept the texts as close to the originals as possible, we have corrected a few obvious typos. Occasionally paragraph breaks, commas, semicolons, or periods have been added in the interests of readability.

To the best of our ability we have determined dates for our selections in this anthology. Some pieces were published, others appear here for the first time, as indicated in the women's headnotes. A date following a work in roman type indicates its date of publication. If a date is italicized, it indicates the date of composition of an unpublished work. Two dates, one italicized and the other roman, indicate a date of composition and its later publication. Sometimes you will find two dates italicized. They will signify a date of the unpublished work's composition and its later date of completion.

Kruger, Marie Houghton Brent, Hester Emily White, and Isabel Christie MacNaughton. Your expertise has been essential to our work. Linda Armstrong at the En'owkin Centre on the Penticton Indian Reserve did everything she could to aid us in our research, with her usual speed and efficiency: thank you. Robin Irwin of the Princeton and District Museum and Archives warmly supported this work with her expertise and willingness to discuss her knowledge of regional history. Thanks also to Amanda Snyder, curatorial manager of the Kelowna Museum for her support. Art and Linda Martens of Hedley were gracious hosts and shared their interests in the Allisons of the Similkameen. Our thanks to Barbara Bell at the Vernon Museum and Archives in Vernon, British Columbia, for facilitating our investigation of the papers of Marie Houghton Brent and William Brent. We salute Tara Hurley, archivist at the Kelowna Public Archives, located at the Okanagan Heritage Museum in Kelowna, for her enthusiastic help and encouragement. Jeanne Boyle, archivist at the Penticton Museum and Archives, has provided endlessly helpful and patient assistance concerning Hester Emily White's papers. We enjoyed many conversations over restorative cups of tea, and her abiding interest in our project has been a great encouragement. Gayle Cornish, former curator and archivist at the Osoyoos and District Museum and Archives, made available a collection of letters from Hester Emily White to Katie Lacey, then uncatalogued, which helped bring Hester White to life; you are an inspiration to local researchers. Kara Burton, curator and director at the Osoyoos Archives, enabled access to files concerning Isabel Christie MacNaughton, particularly the Okanagan Society for the Revival of Indian Arts and Crafts.

As always, the staff at the BC Archives were very helpful. Carey Pallister, archivist at The Sisters of St. Ann Archives at the BC Museum, was an astute guide to the files of the St. Ann's Academy in Kamloops where Marie Houghton Brent attended school. We owe a great debt to Barry George, volunteer at the Okanogan County Historical Society and Museum in Washington, who put us on the track of Matilda Kruger's life in the United States. Thanks to Cheryl Gunselman, University of Washington for providing Marie Houghton Brent's letters to Ella Clarke.

We greatly appreciate the contribution made by research assistants who helped with initial investigation when the project was in gestation as well as ongoing research, transcription of documents, obtaining of permissions and copy-editing, including Kim Boehr, the late Kelly Curtis, Morgan Mayer, Brian Grootendorst, Sheryl Newton, and Dallas Good Water. Jan Gattrell and Sajni Lacey, your kind and patient advice on our bibliographic matters was beyond helpful. Kudos to Jane Ritchie for her map: she has skilfully indicated the geographical and literary terrain of our authors, patiently accommodating all our requests. Our publishers, Theytus Books, have our deepest respect and appreciation. We are grateful to Graham Angus, so capably taking the helm at Theytus and getting our book back on track for publication. Thanks to Ann Doyon for her dedicated and meticulous attention to design and composition, and for cheering us on through lockdown and isolation. Ann and Graham have taken extraordinary measures to track down and obtain photos that enhance our work, particularly photos of Eliza Jane Swalwell and of Matilda Kruger. We are very thankful to Peter Simpson, nephew of Eliza Jane Swalwell, for permitting us to use his family photos of her.

Jeannette Armstrong's acknowledgements

Limlmt to my dear friends and colleagues. Lally Grauer for her leadership and Janet MacArthur who asked so many good questions. Lally, thank you for your patience with me. Janet, thank you for excitement over the details I had to share. Ladies, I will miss our much enjoyed research breakfasts and afternoon teas. I am deeply grateful for colleagues and friends in the Colville Confederated Tribe and Wenatchee Valley College for including me in events and information sharing related to Mourning Dove. I am indebted to my family members whose support and love I could do nothing without.

Janet MacArthur's acknowledgements

Warm thanks to my long-time friend Lally Grauer for her cheery, kind, and mindful coordination of this project, particularly on our shared journey to the underworld of documentation, copyediting and indexing. Thank you to Jeannette Armstrong for her wisdom, friendship, and her work of all kinds that has helped my "transculturation" so much, and for the chance to get to En'owkin Center where I always feel a deep peace and optimism. Thanks to useful insight given me when I gave conference papers at the Association of Canadian College and University Teachers of English (ACCUTE) and B.C. Studies meetings on settler life writing. My gratitude is also extended to University of British Columbia, Okanagan and others who gave me very useful feedback: Daniel Keyes, Jennifer Gustar, Margaret Reeves, Jodey Castricano. and two perspicacious blind vettors for UBC Press. Special thanks to Jodey Castricano for seeing "something very real" in Allison's spirituality. I am also grateful to Bryce Traister Dean of the Faculty of Creative and Critical Studies at UBC Okanagan, for a research intensive work assignment in 2018-2019. Finally, I owe a debt of gratitude to my two daughters, Clare Nicolson and Larissa MacArthur, and to Neil MacArthur for the family that continues to ground my work in all venues.

Lally Grauer's acknowledgements

Jeannette Armstrong and Janet MacArthur, your combined eloquence and many talents have contributed so much to this work; without you it would not have been possible. Jeannette, thank you for your steady faith in the project and in me, and for opening up glimpses of different worlds and ways of understanding. Janet, I have so appreciated your incisive insights, your sharp editing eye and even sharper wit. We have shared so many laughs. I am indebted to my colleagues, students and the administration at Okanagan University College and the University of British Columbia, Okanagan campus, for their ongoing interest and support over the years. Special thanks to Sheryl Newton for her constructive input and assistance throughout the years. My colleague and dear friend Allison Hargreaves's steady encouragement and thoughtful conversations about the writing process and everything else under the sun have been a tremendous support. Thanks to Maggie Berg for endorsing the "slow" production of this book and her always cheerful reinforcement. I am grateful to Germaine Warkentin, Professor Emerita of the University of Toronto, for replying with lightning speed to pleas for help in tracking down out-of-print histories of Canada. Historian Robert Hayes, friend and fellow-researcher, you have been generous with your knowledge of the Okanagan settler community in many conversations; thank you. I have enjoyed discussions with my neighbours Jean and Jack Dangerfield about the complicated process of gathering and editing family reminiscences. Dear friends Katherine Farris, Elizabeth Merritt, and Jane Ritchie—my partner in other publishing efforts— thank you for giving kind and patient ear to my tribulations and applauding the breakthroughs in this long process. It has meant so much to me. To my neighbour Louise Hewitt, you have been an unwavering supporter, making my life easier in so many ways. To Leila Bell-Irving Grauer for your always astute, constructive advice and encouragement, my grateful appreciation.

Standing Between

Jeannette C. Armstrong

The distances between cultures in the Okanagan and Similkameen in the latter half of the 19th century, while as wide as land, culture, and class can divide, were traversed for us by some extraordinary women who lived those times. Indigenous women during the earlier fur trade period "occupied an influential position as 'women in between' two groups of men. . ." (Van Kirk 75). However, an uneasy dynamic in the early settlement period began to grow following the relatively reciprocal status quo that had been established between the two groups during the fur trade period. During early settlement times, some women of Syilx Okanagan descent, rather than being "between" two groups of men, were women who stood between two worlds, the expanding frontier world of the settler and the shrinking Indigenous world of the Syilx Okanagan people. Few Syilx Okanagan voices exist to counterbalance the overwhelming number of settler voices recounting those times. The voices of those Syilx women, whose own standing within the Syilx secured a privileged view from between the two worlds, offer us a unique glimpse into those times. Their lives, their voices, and their stories are gifts they have left to us.

The focus of this essay is to draw on the historical writings, letters, memoirs, stories and literature of four Syilx women who lived during the early generations of settlement by non-Syilx in the Okanagan. The words and stories left by these women provide glimpses into a sense of their own standing in the social and cultural distances being intersected, as well as reflect the growing disquiet between Syilx and settler. Standing as these women were between two societies, the unique views revealed in their writing provide a way to read those times beyond the primarily non-Syilx and male dominated views of history. The spaces occupied by these Okanagan women appear filled with a sense of striving to close the widening divide through engaging a deeper conversation between the Syilx and settler.

This essay discusses the writing of two daughters of marriages attended school in Alberta. Among the many stories she collected in childhood and retold in English, some were provided to her by members of the Nk'Mip community (Hines 7-8).[2] While living directly across the border along the Kettle River, she wrote passionately of her frustration at the plight of her relatives' treatment on the Canadian side of the border during the great flu epidemic of 1918-19 (*Mourning Dove* 189).

The lives these women lived and their words and stories, published and unpublished, are each a remarkable and important legacy to the historical record. They provide a personal and gendered perspective on early settler and Syilx intersections. In addition, the writings provide a distinctive and informed Syilx view of settler and Syilx relations. These women grace us with their reach into today's times. Although Syilx and settler relations remain fraught with many of the same tensions today, these extraordinary women give me pride and courage to follow in their footprints in the writing of this essay for this long overdue collection, itself a collaboration between Syilx and settler.

Historical Context

Prior to contact, a tradition of the Salish Interior people, of whom the Syilx are one group, was to establish political stability with neighbouring tribes through intermarriage to ensure peace and wealth through good inter-areal trade relations (Anastasio 150). The Syilx Okanagan people maintained that tradition after contact. Such strategic intertribal marriages of members of prominent families, in significant practice during the fur trade period, were still in practice in the early settlement periods. The practice, referred to in the oral narratives, customs and language of the Syilx people as the creation of *snaqsilx*, [3] is in essence the creation of family bonds to insure peaceful land-use and trade rights. However, such marriages,[4] as Marie Houghton Brent comments, were based on the consent of the woman as well as the two families. She made it clear that Okanagan women "were not bought or sold as chattels" ("Indians" 122). In some ways the practice parallels the arranged marriages once common in the European aristocracy for many of the same reasons.

During the early fur trade, the practice was extended by the Syilx chiefs to sanction strategic marriages of daughters, nieces, and granddaughters to the men who represented positions significant to the political and trade opportunities provided throughout Syilx territory. Although many such marriages were not formalized within European custom, all were formal marriages within Syilx custom. Intermarriages between Syilx women with European trade personnel, as well as with the Metis and Iroquois guides who were pack train workers and builders of the trade forts during the fur trade era, were common throughout Syilx territory. Marriages between Syilx and settler would have established a solid network of kinship ties between the two separate communities. For the Syilx, the bonds created would have represented a responsibility for insuring peaceful relations between the two.

After the fur trade ended and settlement became more widespread, the women and daughters of settler and Syilx marriages stood as observers of the changing attitudes in the Okanagan. Most stories of those times, witnessed directly by Syilx people, survive solely as oral narrative in the *nsyilxcn* language. The view into those times that these women provide, as injustices began to surface in the taking of lands for settlement and as tensions between Syilx and settler arose, give vehicle to the largely absent voice of the Syilx people in written history across the immense divides of language, culture, and political differences. The legacy of words left by these remarkable women allows us into their individual lives to bring forward the moments they chose to share in different ways. Their lives, positions, and stories allow us a more complex view of the nature of the relationship between settler and Syilx than has typically been transmitted through settler history. Moreover, it is important to note that the four women featured in this essay are direct lineal descendants of Chiefs of the Syilx. The important legacy they left, incredibly, in English, of a time when little ended up in print, provides us with a glimpse into the experiences shared by the many other Syilx women who had intermarried with or were close kin of the settler.

Oral stories as well as written accounts establish that during the fur trade, the gold rush, and the early settlement period, many Syilx accompanied or worked as guides on the pack-trains, as goods moved between the trade establishments. As most contemporary Syilx recall, even into their parents' generation, one of the common trade practices of the Chiefs of Salishan tribes was to be multilingually fluent in adjacent tribal languages in order to facilitate good relations and trade. Many Syilx, in particular the daughters, sisters, nieces, and granddaughters of Chiefs would also have been fluent during the fur trade and early settlement times in the three predominant trade languages, French,[5] English, and Chinook.[6] Fluency in those languages would have been just as important to the Syilx as a way to try to ensure good, respectful relations between themselves and those they saw as guests in their lands. Women often travelled with their fathers or husbands in the elevated role of interpreters and teachers of language on the brigades during the fur trade period. Syilx women who travelled with family members or as fur trader brides would have been fluent in the trade languages and would have acted as interpreters or *suxʷnmicin*[7] between the Syilx and men of the fur trade.

Pack trains were vital during the early settler period as the only way to move people and goods before there were trains or roads for wagons. Many women such as Josephine Shuttleworth were engaged on these pack trains, and Nora Yacumtecum, a Similkameen Syilx woman, ran her own pack train (see the essay "Something Very Real" in Part Two of this volume). These women, often daughters, sisters, nieces, and granddaughters of influential Syilx families, were most often fluent in the languages of both settler and Syilx. In "My School Days," Marie Houghton Brent points out that her cousin Mary Laurence, the daughter of Theresa Laurence who herself was engaged on pack trains at the beginning of settlement in the Okanagan (Rivère 70), was fluent in the four languages mentioned above, as was Brent herself. Both written accounts and oral historical accounts make clear that the relations and communications facilitated by such women in the Okanagan and Similkameen regions of the Columbia gave them something of a privileged standing in the fur trade times. Such a position seems to have held during early settlement times in the lives of these four women. In a significant way they represent the ancient privileged role within Syilx culture as interpreter or *suxʷnmicin* between cultures. Certainly, there is no hint in their writing and stories of a self-perception as inferior or underprivileged in any way, either as Syilx women or as descendants of the Syilx. Instead what shows through is that these women demonstrate that they understood that they had "position," allowing them to share an important view from within their "standing" as women between cultures. They were women privileged in their roles who clearly spoke from their positions of insiders to both settler and Syilx worlds.

Josephine

Josephine Shuttleworth (1865-1950), daughter of *k'łpaqcinxn* or Chief Francois of *snpinktn* (Penticton) was a storyteller of *captikʷł*,[8] the oral stories of her people. She lived her married life on land pre-empted by her settler husband near what is now Okanagan Falls, rather than in a reserve community. She was therefore probably more known by settler residents of the valley than by her Syilx people through her settler family ties, as well as through the translated and published stories she had shared. Using the art of oral story, Shuttleworth bridged the silence between the two cultures through her Syilx position as interpreter of Syilx culture to her settler family and friends, and consequently her stories left a rich legacy to both cultures. The telling of the stories to her family and the sharing of the stories with her non-native friends and their insertion into the settler minds who read them as story, opened for them a window into the Syilx connection with the land as peopled with beloved Syilx animal story characters. A legacy in itself is how her stories, during her life, mediated the gaps between the settlers—those who were her friends and family, and as well the members of the wider public in the Okanagan, British Columbia and Canada— and the Syilx as a people of this land. Her story legacy continues with the many grateful Syilx readers and their re-interpretations of the stories right to our modern times.

Shuttleworth was a close friend to Isabel Christie MacNaughton of Okanagan Falls. Buddie, as Isabel was known locally, collected her stories as told in the Syilx language and translated into English by Shuttleworth's daughter Louise. In "More Indian Tales," which MacNaughton published in the *Penticton Herald*, she writes "During a recent story-telling hour at the home of Mrs. Josephine Shuttleworth many interesting facts about the life of the Indians of long ago, in the days before the white traders had crossed the mountains, were told" (3). MacNaughton published a variety of the stories in the *Penticton Herald* in the late 1930s, which were photocopied by her for her scrapbook collection held at the Oliver and District Historical Society and some of which were reprinted over the years in various Okanagan Historical Society reports. Anthony Walsh, a white school teacher at the Inkameep Indian Day School, contacted MacNaughton in 1938 after reading some of the stories published in the newspaper to find out if she might be interested in making children's plays out of the stories. They arranged to meet at the Christie farm house and Walsh brought along with him Elizabeth Renyi, a writer of short plays, to assist them in turning several of the stories into plays to be performed by his school children at Inkameep (Walsh, "Developing" 4). They collaborated to create eight plays (4) which Walsh had the Inkameep children perform. The success of the plays, some based on Shuttleworth's stories, formed the foundation of an intriguing body of work, which the Inkameep children performed locally, regionally and on CBC radio (see "Crossing Lines" in Part Three of this volume).

It is my intent that through this essay Shuttleworth be rightly acknowledged and credited for her part as Syilx storyteller and for the different ways in which her Syilx stories moved others. Shuttleworth's voice and ways of telling are the source which moved her relatives and friends, including MacNaughton, to render them into English and publish them. Then their transformation by the three collaborators into theatre performed by the children of Inkameep reached and moved a regional, then provincial and national audience, and now they move us in these times. However, through the stories Shuttleworth shared, we can also explore and acknowledge her position of standing between two cultures and perhaps find some of her intent from that place, separated as she was from her community, although never from her Syilx culture and the Syilx *captikʷł* world.

Shuttleworth's friendship with MacNaughton also allowed for a unique blending of voice between the two women, providing a view into their relationship as well as Shuttleworth's relationship with her non-Syilx community. Without question, the influence of MacNaughton is to be read into all of her renditions of the stories translated into English: as well, some do deviate from generally accepted versions. For example, in the story "When Coyote Changed the Lives of the Valley Indians," reprinted in this volume, significant events in the storyline differ noticeably from the many other versions of this very well-known story

7

still told and retold by many Syilx people. The storyline covers Coyote bringing salmon to the Okanagan. In the version re-told by Shuttleworth and written by MacNaughton, Coyote leaves no salmon at Omak, Osoyoos or Okanagan Falls. In this version Coyote takes them all back downriver with him, leaving only other kinds of fish, a condition said to be true even at the time of MacNaughton's rendering of the story.

As a story, the outcomes seem logical; however, in reality all three places were well-known to be abundant salmon harvesting areas during Shuttleworth's own lifetime, which she must have known, as the photo of her and daughter Louise drying salmon implies. (See Shuttleworth headnote). All other versions of the story collected by ethnographers such as Charles Hill-Tout in 1911, James Teit in 1927, Leslie Spier (in Walter Cline et al.) in 1938, Verne Ray in 1939, Randy Bouchard in 1975, and in those told by all contemporary Syilx storytellers, the storyline has Coyote leaving salmon at all three places, and not leaving any at the Similkameen river where no salmon go beyond Coyote Falls.

Maggie Victor (*xʷałqnmalqs*), born in 1887, daughter of Chief Edward and grandniece of Chief Francois,[9] clearly explains that salmon were speared all along the Okanagan River. She tells Eric Sismey that "Fishing camps were colorful in a festive way. Cousins, aunts and uncles, families we had not seen for a year were greeted with gossip and news. They joined us with singing, dancing and feasting" ("Maggie" 140). She also mentions that this was before the dams on the river were built. Writing about the early days in an instalment of her series for the *Penticton Herald*, "The Pioneer Trail," settler Hester White also mentions

> [W]e find the Okanagans, 200 of them, camped beneath the pines on the flat near *Sa-ha-nit-que* [*sx̌ʷanitkʷ*] meaning "falls,"[10] now Okanagan Falls. They are ready, with willow traps, baskets, and drying racks, to catch and dry the beautiful blue-green Steween [*sc'win*, early sockeye salmon] . . . from the stream. (July 3, 1947)

In my own family narrative, my father, born in 1907 on the Penticton Reserve, described the salmon fishing camp gatherings at Okanagan Falls during his youth, before McIntyre Dam blocked the salmon passage.

It is difficult to accept that Shuttleworth, as a Chief's daughter,

8

would have altered what is one of the most known stories among the Syilx. She was born around the time of Canada's Confederation in 1867. Only a few years earlier in 1859, the first Syilx Okanagan roadblock took place. Oblate missionary Father Pandosy and his group were stopped by the Chief of Penticton, Capot Blanc (*paqɬpica?*). After intervention by Theresa, the wife of Cyprien Laurence, who happened to be the Chief's niece, they were allowed to pass through and were escorted by Francois, who was later to become Chief of Penticton. Pandosy went on to establish the mission at L'Anse au Sable in what is now Kelowna, and Chief Francois later became his close friend.[11] This story points to the prominent standing and power of Syilx women such as Theresa, whom Marie Houghton Brent writes is the daughter of the famous *xʷistsmx̌ayqn* (Walking Grizzly), known by settlers as Chief Nkwala, and a sister to his son, young Chief Nkwala ("Indian Lore").

Shuttleworth recounts the memory of her father in an article written down by MacNaughton entitled "Chief Francois, Who Died at 105, Was Notable Old Figure." She says that "Many and many another tale was told around Chief Francois' campfire" (3). There is no doubt he was a knowledgeable storyteller, and that Shuttleworth, who accompanied him on those journeys, would also have been. Her husband Harry Shuttleworth, whom she met through the pack train, was eligible to marry into a Chief's family, as he was himself a descendant of the Syilx, being the grandson of a Colville Chief[12] and the son of Henry Hardinge Digby Shuttleworth, heir of a titled English landowner in Lancashire, England. Henry Digby Shuttleworth was reported to have spoken Interior (Montana) Salish, Okanagan and the Nicola languages in addition to English and French (Sismey, "Shuttleworths" 136). Although there is no record to confirm this, his wife would have been fluent in those languages and most probably have been the one to teach Henry Digby the Indigenous languages. This would have been a great influence on their children as settlers. Their son Harry almost certainly was able to communicate in at least the *nsyilxcn* language with his wife Josephine, adding a significant layer to her settler knowledge. Josephine's daughter Louise was a fluent speaker, an indication that both her parents were also fluent.

From within the Penticton community history, we know

that Shuttleworth maintained close ties with her three sisters, Mary McLean, wife of Roderick McLean, officer in charge for the Hudson's Bay Company at Keremeos; Angeline Eneas, wife of Penticton Chief Gideon Eneas; as well as Ellen Alec, wife of Penticton Chief Jack Alec. Shuttleworth would have been schooled in the Syilx cultural knowledge and she would have had great authority from her influential family in regard to her "standing" in both Syilx and settler cultures. She was not just fluent in the *nsyilxcn* language, but would have been educated by her father in the *captikʷł* stories and the information contained in them. She carried the Syilx Chief's family responsibility to transfer knowledge to succeeding generations, which she accomplished in her legacy of storytelling.

However Shuttleworth's *captikʷł* stories may have been changed, either in translation or by embellishments, the melding of Shuttleworth's and MacNaughton's voices through story presents a model to help us to reflect on relationships between Syilx and settler during those times. A good example is "The Cranes Herald Spring," reprinted in this section. The content of the story is clearly Shuttleworth's and typical of *captikʷł* literature, offering only select key components to trigger the listener to create his or her own detail. However, the poetic voice of MacNaughton is also very much present in the descriptive imagery in her rendering of the story. The story is enriched and made fresh as a result of both voices.

A different example may be found in other stories. The character of Coyote, animated through key imagery in a story like "Folk Lore of the Days When Animal People Dwelt Here," is extremely lively and comical in the *nsyilxcn* language, and so it is a challenge to render it justice in English. However, that MacNaughton captures that energy in her rendition speaks not just to the ability of the translator, but also to MacNaughton's literary imagination, her close listening to voice tone and pacing, and her key observation of the dramatizing hand gestures typical of a great oral storyteller. The story MacNaughton transcribed and published most eloquently reveals the rapport and trust linking MacNaughton and Shuttleworth in that space between cultures that Shuttleworth opened through Syilx story.

The personality and character of Shuttleworth also comes

through in these writings from her position of standing between. Another story of hers published by MacNaughton in the *Penticton Herald*, "How Coyote Lost His Deer Meat and Created a Thirst, " is excerpted here:

> [A]s the Coyote was walking along on his way, he saw a teepee smoke rising. . . . When he went inside he saw an old man sitting with his back to the fire, making rope. . . .
>
> "Ahem! Ahem!" went Coyote. He coughed so that the old man would know he was there—a custom, he said, that would continue through the ages and sure enough, it has done [among the Syilx]. Then he picked up the poker and began to fix the fire, but still the old man paid no attention to him.
>
> As if he was not in the room at all the man arose from his work, took a piece of fat deer meat from one of the racks and roasted it over his fire.
>
> "Surely that is for me" thought Coyote. But the old man ate most of the meat himself, and when he had finished he put the meat away and sat down to work again. (3)

This *captikʷł* uses a device described by David C. Rubin in his study of oral traditions as "scripts"[13] (24). In my research I have described *captikʷł* script as an important element of Syilx oral story ("Constructing" 109-13). This story contains an entering-homes script which trusts the audience will expect that Coyote will be acknowledged and given food, as is absolutely required by custom among the Syilx. We can assume that MacNaughton would not have understood what was being implied by the interaction between Coyote and the old man. A Syilx listener would have understood its significance to the story as a social teaching. Shuttleworth would have surmised that and would have explained it to MacNaughton. So we may ask whether Shuttleworth told the story as a form of social comment about settler customs. We might assume she is making an indirect point about the settler custom of requiring an invitation to enter a home, since immediately after Coyote enters the old man's home in the story, another such *captikʷł* script is explained for an audience lacking familiarity with Syilx cultural customs. Shuttleworth explains that Coyote coughed so that "the old man would know he was there" emphasizing its importance as a customary observance of Syilx protocol when entering a home, and also implying the custom that one does not speak "at" a person, especially at an old man's back. A signal like a cough alerts the person to face you so then you may then speak "to" the person. Shuttleworth as storyteller would have known that captikʷł were told either to offer direct teachings or to make an indirect point to the listener when they have displayed socially rude behaviour. Indirect points are implied by captikʷł and are left up to the listeners to infer and understand.

Whether or not the meanings I suggest were intended by Shuttleworth, her choice to tell such stories allows us a glimpse into her view of what she would have considered inferior settler customs (generosity of shelter and food is one of the highest virtues among the Syilx) and shows her consideration of the relationship she had with MacNaughton. She chose not to quiet her Syilx story voice into submission as a part of her assimilation into settler society. She was not ashamed of her people's culture and customs, as might be expected in those times when settler culture and customs were perceived as superior. In fact, she would have been proud to hold the knowledge of the stories and would have seen them as a way to impress Syilx thought upon her listener to help the settler appreciate cultural difference.

The strength of her Syilx pride is also seen in the depth of the relationship between herself and MacNaughton, through the impact she left on her friend. This becomes more clear in MacNaughton's "Tribute" poems to Shuttleworth, printed in Part Three of this volume, especially in the words from "Portrait of a Lady in an Old Orchard" that describe "The welcoming grace of her smile, / And the soft dark light of her eyes" (2). The poem allows us to see the depth of that relationship and the space between that Shuttleworth walked softly across with her legacy of story.

Eliza Jane

Eliza Jane Swalwell (1868-1944) published "Girlhood Days in the Okanagan" in 1939 in the eighth report of the Okanagan Historical Society. The selection, although presented as a memoir, is also an attempt to bridge the vast divide between the two cultures that she was a part of. On first reading the memoir my immediate response was the recognition that this was an important document. I recognized that the narrative style is clearly a blend between the dry style of narrative common to many peoples' historical reminiscences of that period and the highly descriptive Okanagan historical oral narrative genre of recounting significant events I have written about and identified as *sma?may?*.[14] I was struck by the way in which her voice included a view of those times from a distinctly insider view of the relations between Syilx and settler.

The writing provides a clear insight into Swalwell's awareness of the role she held in being a daughter of Syilx and settler. In her own words she saw herself as "standing between two races" (35). Her family circumstance was a reflection of the practice of marriage between the daughters of Chiefs and new settlers as she writes that her mother was the sister of Chief Pantherhead of the village at Westbank. She grew up in a time of early settlement tensions in the Okanagan and her concern with the widening divide between settlers and her Indigenous community is expressed clearly in her comments. Her mother would have definitely had a deep influence on the way she approached voicing that concern.

The way Swalwell opens the narrative is in the classical Syilx *sma?may?* historical accounting manner. She provides information from her personal experience this way: "I remember this valley when everything was in a wild state, before there was any wagon road and everything had to be brought in by packtrain" (34). While the published narrative is intended for local public historical interest and provides information on early settler living practices, values, and attitudes, it also does not try to mask the depth of her feelings about her Syilx landscape. At the same time, in what can only be described as political writing, Swalwell provides an opinion regarding the corruption behind the loss of land rights by the Indians of British Columbia under what she calls the failed "Consolidated Land Act of 1874."[15] It proposed to consolidate reductions of reserves and to open lands to pre-emption for settlers, including huge tracts of land that had been previously designated as "Reserves" by Governor Douglas (Thomson, "History" 115) and the Chiefs of the Okanagan. The result was to ignite hostilities toward the settler so that in 1877 (Thomson, "History" 131) a council of war was held at the Head of the Lake (*nk'mapəlqs*) near Vernon by the Syilx Chiefs and their allies the Secwépemc (Shuswap), causing the formation of the first

Indian Reserve Commission[16] to quiet the situation (Armstong et al, *We Get Our Living* 51).

Clearly, Swalwell does not take a position of neutrality on the plight of her relatives. She writes, "Standing as I do between the two races, I could never see that intellectually the Indians are not the equals of the whites" (37). Her derisive points about white cultural strictures and government politics made through her explanation of land injustices are blunt and well informed.

She makes an indirect point through a side story about a judge sentencing a Syilx who is unaware of settler laws and is following Syilx marriage customs which she describes as "quite correct and proper, according to Indian customs and usages" (37). She suggests the hypocrisy of whites in the depiction of the Judge who in chastising states that "the Government had been generous in the allotment of Indian Reserves" and in return Indigenous people should "refrain from breaking the law and give no trouble" (37).

She follows the story with a lengthy, well-informed explanation of land injustices to back up her implications of hypocrisy. The provincial government had certainly not been generous; as she points out, Indigenous people in British Columbia "have been treated with less consideration than in any other part of Canada" (37). As well, she is critical of aspects of the Christian non-Syilx culture and emphatically states, "It seems to me the whites are too much bound and limited, too much enslaved by their written creeds and confessions of faith. The Indians are free of that, and consequently they are closer to nature and reality" (36).

Swalwell also shares her own closeness to nature as she writes her response to the Okanagan landscape in her description of an early morning ride as an "exquisite pleasure. . . to ride over this green and gracious pasture land" (36). She provides an insight into her personal experience and conveys the depth of her feelings toward the land in these words, "On such occasions I have sometimes seen things, or rather sensed something, so serene and beautiful that it left me weak and weeping as I sat in the saddle" (36). She attributes this "responsiveness to certain beautiful aspects of nature" as most likely coming from her indian mother (36). Her writing about her feelings toward the land, connected to the reverence for nature and originating with her Syilx mother, is a way of "placing" herself as Syilx at heart.

Through this one surviving example of Swalwell's contribution to our storied past, we are gifted with a view of her own sense of where she stood, as a part of the Syilx land and all of its people. We get a glimpse into her sense of responsibility in her position of standing between the two cultures. We are also gifted with her courageous voice, one of few voices during her time, besides that of Marie Houghton Brent, to document in the public pages of the reports of the Okanagan Historical Society her views on both the injustices of the whites and the strength and beauty of Syilx culture.

Marie

Marie Houghton Brent (1870-1968) was the great granddaughter of *xʷistsmx̌ayqn* (Walking Grizzly) or Chief Nkwala, famed chief during the fur trade era. The fact was central in her life and influenced her in many ways evident in the writing that she left. Part of the text of a letter or drafted speech, dated September 1923, to "the President, Officers and Members of the Okanagan Historical Society & Natural History" perhaps in preparation for its inaugural meeting, survives in handwritten notes and demonstrates his importance to her:

> Before we begin, may we pause a moment & see who was here first; in this place—on the old battlegrounds of ages past the Blackfoot used to come to fight the Okanagans—Old Niquala, Nicola called after him, Chief of all the Okanagans, made his headquarters. His word was law, no other existing & that before him of his father, grandfather, great grandfather & great, great grandfather. This is as far back as we know, there was no American [boundary] line at the time. This old man stopped all fights between the tribes & made peace between the Indians and the white man.

Brent may have been influenced by the stance her great grandfather took of making peace. She writes that her own mother Sophie Nkwala died in the early 1870s when Brent was very young and that she was raised in most part by her great aunt Theresa Nkwala (see "Indian Lore" in this section). Theresa would have imparted the oral education of the type the Syilx

15

Okanagan use to imbed essential family teachings, values and histories. Brent's great aunt was the same Theresa Laurence[17] who, a decade earlier, had acted as cultural interpreter to convince her uncle Capot Blanc, the Chief at Penticton, to allow Father Pandosy to pass through their land on their way north to establish a mission in the Okanagan.

Most particularly, in the Chief's families, the rigorous oral education would have been related to passing on a deep responsibility to the Syilx people through learning, remembering, and perpetuating their Chief's family history. In "Indian Lore," Brent writes about early childhood spent with her great aunt who instilled the story of their family and the responsibility to act as interpreter between the two cultures:

> In an Indian tribe they pick one sober child with a good memory and train them to remember the story of their family and their ancestors. I was chosen for this. It was my great grandfather's daughter that taught me.
>
> . . . .
>
> I now lived with my grandfather's sister.[18] My great aunt was from Colville. She was married to a Frenchman direct from France. Her name was Teresa N'kwala and his name. . . in French was Cyprienne Laurent. My great aunt spoke French too.
> My Grand Aunt taught me as a child the following tradition, which she in turn learned from her father, the old Chief N'kwala. (105)

Brent would also have understood the important role of being cultural and political "interpreter" for her people to other cultures. Her mother had been married to a prominent settler and Brent had to have been aware of the "interpreter" responsibility her mother and therefore she herself had in that world. This is evident in Brent's article written for the Okanagan Historical Society in 1935, "The Indians of the Okanagan Valley," presenting strong arguments on the good character and worth of her Syilx people. In her memoir "My School Days," she tells the story of her separation from her family at the Head of the Lake (near today's Vernon) to attend school in Kelowna:

One day I remember an elderly woman arrived on a beautiful horse. She was of light complexion, tall handsome—my mother told me that she was her aunt, her fathers full sister, they were chief NKwala's son & daughter, chief of all the Okanagan and Colville. All were dead but her. She was my grand aunt & she came after me to go to school a long way off, & not to cry—I was a big girl, now 7 years old you've got to learn to be nice and don't talk Indian to any body, it will interfere with your English school and hard for you to learn.[19]

Like other descendants of the Syilx Chiefs and their families, it appears Brent spoke many of the trade languages. She writes that Mary Laurence, Theresa Laurence's daughter with whom Brent lived while she was at school, was "I think the most beautiful woman I've ever seen—spoke French, English & Okanagan Indian and Chinook. So did I. I should have studied languages" ("My School Days"). Her choice of William Brent as husband may also have been influenced by her sense of responsibility to her lineage. We know from other sources that her husband William was in fact her cousin. His grandmother, Mary Ann Topakeget Ukatemaish, was also a daughter of old Chief Nkwala from his Colville wife ("Brent's Grist Mill"). He would also have spoken at least *nsyilxcn* as well as English.

Brent's strong stance as someone clearly aware of her responsibility to her people and her Chief's lineage is present in her writing. Her responsibility to record the memory of her lineage, to acknowledge the rights of that lineage, and her anxiety over the loss of rights is clear in her letters. In letters sent from 1956 to 1961 to Ella E. Clark, an English lecturer at Washington State University, and in letters to Hester White, daughter of settler J.C. Haynes in Osoyoos, Brent expressed her deep concern over the loss of her lineal order as she saw it. To Hester White she writes:

[T]he dear old man [Old Chief Nkwala] died pleading for the welfare of his children, their descendants and that of his peoples. . . . [H]e made his younger son chief on his death bed, young Nicola, my mother's father, to take his place when the old man died.

. . .

> [Chief Nkwala] was buried with some of his medals, given by King George III. . . . [H]e had some more medals but everybody of his died, his nephews took possessions of them, Chilihitchas, Nk'wala's own only Sister's children of Nicola Valley, Salista, and his brother Alexander Chilihitcha, took them and said they were made heirs to the Okanagan too. No such thing I reported them to Ottawa, they did not get [the] Okanagan [chieftainship] but I did not say who I was. (April 30, 1958) [20]

Obvious in her memoirs as well is Brent's understanding of her role and her responsibility to her heritage as a Syilx woman of royal descent to transmit family history, which she diligently outlines in "Indian Lore" printed in the *OHS Report*, in 1966.

Brent is deliberate through her writing in her intent to change "relations" between the two groups during her long life. Her views expressed in her articles make apparent the stance she maintained as occupying a space between two realities. In "The Indians of the Okanagan Valley" she makes abundantly clear her responsibility to set straight the misconceptions about Indigenous people in the Okanagan and in Canada in her assertion that "this country is not doing its duty by the Indians" (130).

By signing the article "Mrs. William Brent," she suggests her wish to influence from an informed but not an obviously "Indian" position. Yet she makes clear her standing in both societies, in particular in her passionate statement that "[t]he invasion of their country by the whites not only disrupted [the Syilx's] usual mode of living and crumpled up and destroyed their old-established customs and usages which had endured for centuries, but it deprived them of their country as well" (130).

Brent maintained close ties through her letter writing to prominent non-Syilx women of the times. In the legacy of letters of friendship to Hester White, which contain her clear wishes to assist in informing the settler view of history, she writes, "I am glad you take enough interest in our country to take up some bits of history left and both Mr. Brent and I would gladly assist you if we could" (Sept. 8, 1936). It is clear in her ensuing letters to White how deeply she was concerned about her people and that she communicated to inform and to share her perspective from where she stood between the two cultures. Their letters spanning over three decades provide an insight into Brent's long life and her concerns, and open a window for us into those times.

Nearing the end of her life when she lived in Republic, Washington, Brent also corresponded with Ella Clark, who was well known for her interest in the settler history of Washington State and in Indigenous legends of North America. Clark was gathering material for her book *Indian Legends of Canada* when she contacted Brent in the mid-1950s. Brent also corresponded about Indigenous storytelling with Ella Clark. Letters to Clark written mostly in 1956-7 provide narrative and oral stories, at least two of which appear in Clark's published volume of stories in 1960. In her letters Brent reveals the attitude of the times, but most importantly, her desire to be a bridge between the two cultures that she negotiated and lived within all her life. She writes to Clark,

> I am charmed with the sweat house story [that Clark sent Brent]. Yes, they have it [the same story] here, thank you a thousand times. Do you wish me to save it for you, if so tell me. I have a Legend of Coyote's entertainment of a big banquet of salmon to his friends, the bear, owl, deer and beaver. . . . At that time they were people. This beautifully coincides with the story you sent me, [my story is] a pretty and interesting story of the legend of Shuswap Falls North of Vernon British Columbia. I translated it so it could be read at the opening of the [electrical] Power house built there [in 1929] . . . I can give you a copy. . . . all of Coyote's cooking pot, where he cooked the salmon, a stone kettle he hung in the Falls, his seat, where he sat, & caught the salmon & put into the pot, all there 20 years ago to this day [the opening of the power house]. When the birch and fir trees are in bud, you can still hear Coyote's voice far and near calling "Salmon is running" to come to his feast for his friends. The people were charmed. (June 10, 1957)[21]

Brent ended the letter with a short beautiful prayer poem, sharing in writing a part of her Syilx self, an expression of deep emotion for her people at the silencing of the falls, probably referring to the dam that was built there in 1929, along with the power plant (Candy). She does not say she read it as a part of her speech at the power plant opening; however, it seems most probable that she did. It is simply titled: "Shuswap Falls-Okanagan Falls-Kettle Falls-Spokane Falls":

> To-day we say good-bye to your Sweet Song of the long ago, thro' all the ages past alas tis ever so, when such as you are called to serve a bigger world. Your Sweet Song, to your children forever hushed like a dying prayer. This [underlined] by Marie Brent Great, Great grand daughter of Chief Pelkamulox, Great grand daughter of Chief Nicola (N'Kwala) of all Okanogan & Colville.

Through her writing, Brent points to her stance as a Syilx woman of royal descent who was in the position of standing between. She was a remarkable woman whose voice will continue to be heard in the Okanagan as was her intent.

Mourning Dove

Christine Quintasket, better known as *h?misms* or Mourning Dove (c.1886-1936), lived an extraordinary life given the few rights granted most women, let alone an Indigenous woman during those times. Most remarkable is that in spite of her patchy education in English, she published a collection of Okanagan oral stories and a novel during her lifetime. A manuscript of her autobiography was posthumously published in 1990. Her many letters to her friend and editor Lucullus Virgil McWhorter clearly reveal that she was aware of her role and responsibility to provide the settler with an Okanagan viewpoint. She comments in the preface to a 1976 collection of her stories *Tales of the Okanagan*, edited by Donald Hines,[22] that her primary interest was "in writing novels showing the Indian viewpoint" (*Tales* 14). An examination of her novel *Cogewea, The Half-Blood: A Depiction of the Great Montana Cattle Range*, published in 1927, is one way to consider her "Indian viewpoint" as it provides insight into her desire to bridge the divide between the two cultures.

In the novel, Mourning Dove draws in a masterful way on Okanagan storytelling traditions. Throughout she allows access to an interesting layering of meaning through which she draws out the tensions and impacts of colonization on the Syilx Okanagan people during her times. Set in what was, for her, a contemporary time frame, the novel reflects life during those early settlement times. As Dexter Fisher (viii) and others have noted, the novel represents the choices of those times for Indigenous people and intercedes in the prevailing views of Indian identity. At the same time it validates Okanagan literature in a way that makes it accessible to an outside reader. As well, as others have recognized, Mourning Dove wrote to create "a space for Indian consciousness in the midst of a suffocating dominant cultural obtuseness" (Brown, "Legacy" 55).

Mourning Dove's knowledge of how *captikʷł*, the Syilx oral story method, works is more than evident in the novel. Mourning Dove indicates in the preface to *Tales of the Okanogan* that she had been reluctant to collect and then write Okanagan stories in English. However, she adds that in the work of writing them, she had found "a rich field that had hardly been touched by the hand of the white man" and adds that the "white man cannot understand what an Indian will see, and he cannot know that which comes from the heart and not only from the voice" (14). She writes that the stories are of great importance to the younger generations of Indians and says with conviction, "I will feel well rewarded if I have preserved for the future generations the folklore of my ancestors" (14).

Mourning Dove's understanding of the Okanagan oral story and her use of it in the novel *Cogewea* is one way she stood "between" two cultures, not only by combining two forms, but also by using a *captikʷł* lens as a method of reflecting upon and speaking to societal issues. The novel conveys her view of those times through the way she chose to explore tensions confronting the new generation of Syilx in cultural transition after settlement and the divergent choices before them. Cogewea is framed by the template of a well-known *captikʷł*, the story of qʷəqʷcwiya?, chipmunk and *snina?*, owl monster. The novel's storyline is centered on the conflicts faced by a half-breed Indian girl, Cogewea. Her name is a transliteration of qʷəqʷcwiya? (kots se we ah) or chipmunk, and would bring to mind for anyone who knows of Okanagan *captikʷł* the story of Chipmunk and Owl-woman. A treacherous American easterner, who wants her for money, and a sympathetic half-breed cowboy compete for her attentions. In associating the naive character of Chipmunk, who appears in many Okanagan stories, with the central character of her novel,

21

Mourning Dove relies on *captik*ʷ*ł* to provide a framework to speak about and characterize the dynamics of frontier "relationships" between non-Indigenous and Indigenous. The parentless little girl chipmunk embodied in the character of Cogewea is a vehicle for expressing not only the heroine's pressures and choices, but also a greater pressure faced by the tiny population of Indigenous people remaining after the smallpox epidemics. Mourning Dove referred to her people as "[w]ell into the cycle of history involving their readjustment in living conditions. They were in a pathetic state of turmoil caused by trying to learn how to till the soil for a living" (*Mourning Dove* 3). Mourning Dove provides a historical window into that "pathetic state" in the novel, describing how the character of the easterner, Alfred Densmore, upon his arrival in Montana ranchland, "had expected to see the painted and blanketed aborigine of history and romance; but instead he had only encountered this miniature group of half-bloods and one ancient squaw" (*Cogewea* 43-44).

In the novel, Mourning Dove describes the devastating changes already taking place at that time. She speaks of the scarcity of game, as well as the devastation to forests and the land which, the grandmother Stemteema says, is "'now all turned to the production of the whiteman's food'" (*Cogewea* 128). She also provides a view of Syilx Okanogan life before contact, as Stemteema speaks of her own grandfather's times "when he was a young chief of . . . the *Okanogans*" (122). Through the grandmother's voice, Mourning Dove provides a view of a time of great abundance when the Okanagans observed the "Great Spirit" and "danced in worship" (123). She would have heard of the times her own elders had experienced both before and after the arrival of the fur traders. In the grandmother's voice, she speaks of the time before the white man when they danced so "that the trees, the grass and herbs be perpetual; that the deer and all the game be plentiful . . . and that the red salmon again swim up the Swanitkqah [Columbia River]" (123). Stemteema goes on to say that with the arrival of the "'white man,'" the people "'have died from the pestilences'" brought by them (123), and were gone just like the huge herds of buffalo that had disappeared from the land. Grandmother adds that she was only waiting her time to follow them to "where the pale face cannot dispossess us, for he will not be there. He will no longer lure our children from us with his smooth tongue" (123). Without doubt this reveals Mourning Dove's view regarding her people's situation. She was very much aware of the connection that she establishes between her novel and the *captik^{w}ł* about chipmunk and the monster owl woman that eats the hearts of children, as symbolic of the settler culture consuming the heart of the Syilx people and their lands.

With another *captik^{w}ł* Mourning Dove more obliquely comments on the deceitful attempts to assimilate the younger generations in order to steal their land and cultural heritage from them. The story amplifies the tension between the unyielding Stemteema and Densmore. The *captik^{w}ł* Mourning Dove references is indicated through the title of Chapter Eighteen, "Swa-lah-kin: The Frog Woman."[23] Stemteema ignores the attempts of Densmore, the Shoyapee,[24] to win her over as a way to secure his position with Cogewea. Offensive forwardness, taking liberties without invitation, places Densmore in the role of the ugly Frog Woman creature in the *captik^{w}ł* and, more than that, represents the offensive greed and aggression of the settlers' land seizures. The grandmother, representing the ancestral culture, the source of respectful sharing principles sustaining life, is not willing to be part of this new culture. In the *captik^{w}ł*, the moon is claimed and encumbered forever by the unwanted ugly suitor, the Frog Woman, who splays herself, clinging, upon his face. We can establish that the unlucky beauty of night sun is a metaphor for the colonizers' desire for the land of the Okanagan, and that its people will be forever marked by the Shoyapee. I do not see this novel as a racialized projection of Indian hatred upon the Shoyapee by Mourning Dove, as she casts Cogewea's older sister in a contented and accepted marriage with a settler. Rather, Mourning Dove's use of the Frog Woman story points to the revulsion toward the malevolent greed and arrogance which characterizes the colonial process. In a way that layers and deepens the resolution at the end of the novel. Mourning Dove closes Cogewea's story with these words: "The moon, sailing over the embattled Rockies, appeared to smile down on the dusky lovers, despite the ugly Swah-lah-kin clinging to his face" (284).

Mourning Dove's use of *captik^{w}ł* amplifies in the sub-text the choices between the world of the Indigenous people and the world of the settler as cast through the characters of Cogewea and her two suitors. The main character, Cogewea, serves as metaphor for the cultural transformation her people are undergoing. She is a "half-blood," a deft cultural defining of living one part white, one part Indigenous. She is caught between the grandmother's world and "being lured to a shadowy trail of sorrow by the deceiving Shoyahpee" (*Cogewea* 244). Cogewea's trusting heart is ripped apart by the treacherous Easterner who did not want her but instead was motivated by greed to pretend so. He represents the monster ripping the heart out of the remnants of the vulnerable Syilx people after smallpox has taken its toll on their parents' generation, and the "soulless creatures who have ever preyed upon us" (283). The metaphor in the novel's resolution in the "return" of Cogewea to the half-breed suitor points to living in the ways of grandmother, although as half-bloods in the "corral built round us" (283), a brilliant characterization of living halfway between white and Indigenous culture on the reservations. Mourning Dove makes the novel more meaningful to an Indigenous Okanagan and even some non-Indigenous readers by using the *captikʷł* to Indigenize a settler form of storytelling as her way of standing between the two cultures.

In a letter written in 1915 to McWhorter, Mourning Dove expresses her heart's choice. Perhaps the longing she voices in this letter is also a comment acknowledging that she stood in that space between:

> Let me live among my people a little bit longer. I love nature. I love my hills and mountains who's [whose] voice I seem to understand. Every moan of the wind and the ripple of the brook, has his own music that my nature can answer, which no human hand dare to imitate. . . .
>
> I heard the voice, which seemed but a whisper at first till it sounded so loud to me till it reached the mountaintops. Then, I could not resist. And I threw all civilized life, to the four winds, and I roamed back to my own kind, to live among the golden Race, who I would lay my life for. . . . A Life that no real Indian dare lead and leave his dear life of nature which God gave him, as his own. (February 9, 1915)

The lives and circumstance and the legacy of the personal writing of these extraordinary women reveal a strong connection to their Syilx heritage in their striving to bridge the gap between the settler and Okanagan through writing. They all focus on the dynamic of the divide between cultures established during the period of their lives in which things changed rapidly in the years of exploitative "reservation" imperatives and the ensuing period of racial discord into the early decades of the twentieth century. Although the racialization and colonial discord which then arose persist to the present, their writing speaks with longing for a deeper undercurrent of respectful interrelationship, as a result of blood ties, between local ranching and farming pioneer families and families on local reserves.

I have come to discern that they may have assisted in a much more reciprocal social and economic interaction between the Syilx and the settler than is commonly portrayed. Resistance in many forms of the Syilx to settler colonization increased through the ensuing periods of colonization. What becomes clear is that the writing of these women reflects instead resistance to the divide between the cultures. I cannot escape the view that their writing represents Syilx infiltrations into racially restricted areas of colonial cultural production without compromise to their Syilx perspective. Similar to the invisible nature of the strategic political and cultural infiltrations accomplished by the politically sanctioned intermarriages of their mothers to settler men, their striving to bridge the gap between cultures implies a model of positive resistance intended to neutralize the separating divide of racialization. Each of these works is not only a valuable contribution to the study of Indigenous literatures written in English but also provides insight into the courageous positions these women took to bridge cultural divides through their writing by maintaining a strong stance in their standing between.

Josephine Shuttleworth and her daughter Louise drying salmon, c. 1940.
Courtesy of Okanagan Falls Heritage Museum.

Josephine Shuttleworth

1865 - 1950

Josephine Francois Shuttleworth, while known in the early days of settlement in the Okanagan as a rancher, hunter, and expert basket maker and craftswoman, was also a Syilx storyteller of *captkʷł* and other traditional stories of her people. She maintained the telling of the stories to her family and shared the stories with her friend Isabel Christie MacNaughton.

Shuttleworth was born on December 22, 1865, on what is now the Penticton Indian Reserve. She was the youngest daughter of *k'łpaqcinxn*, known as Chief Francois, and Theresa, the daughter of high Chief Nkwala[1] who appointed Francois sub-chief at *snpinktn* village (now Penticton). Chief Francois was the brother of Chief Sarsapkin of Moses, Columbia, whose ranch was in Loomis, Washington (Raufer 226). Shuttleworth's paternal grandmother was the famous Chieftainess recognized for saving the lives of her people through the power of dream (see Part Three, "How an Ancient Woman Taught Her People Wisdom"). She was a member of Chief Tonasket's band in Okanogan territory in what is now the state of Washington. *ktu?nasq't* (Tonasket or Many Clouds Gathering) was appointed sub-chief in that territory by Nkwala, whose daughter he had first married, according to Marie Brent (see "Indian Lore" in this section). Shuttleworth had three sisters, Mary, Angeline, Ellen, and one brother, Tommy.

The land and the trails from Penticton west to Hope and north to *tk'mlups*, edge of river place or Kamloops, British Columbia were familiar to Shuttleworth. Her father worked as guide and packer for Thomas Ellis, one of the first settlers in Penticton, and Frank Richter of Keremeos (see Part Three) during an era when there was no other way except horseback to move essential goods, packing over Indigenous trails which became Hudson's Bay Company (HBC) routes and wagon roads such as the Dewdney Trail from Hope to Vermilion Forks (now Princeton) and then completed to the Okanagan in 1860-61. As soon as Shuttleworth was old enough, she accompanied the pack train with her father. In 1883, at the age of sixteen, Josephine married Henry (Harry) Shuttleworth at the Pandosy Mission at what is now Kelowna (Sismey, "Shuttleworths" 136).

Harry Shuttleworth was also the direct descendant of another Chief's family, and thus was naturally eligible to marry into Chief Francois's family. He was the son of Henry Digby Shuttleworth, youngest son of Lord Shuttleworth of Lancashire, England. Henry Digby was born in

Bengal, India in 1834 and emigrated to the United States in the 1850s. He worked as an apprentice for the HBC from 1852-1857, stationed from 1853 on at Fort Colville, Washington, in Okanogan territory ("Shuttleworth, Henry"). He married the daughter of a Colville Chief, a "blooded Indian Chief" according to his son George Shuttleworth ("100-Year-Old Rancher" 26). Mourning Dove identifies this Colville Chief as *six^wilxkn* (See-whehl-ken), her maternal great grandfather, located in Syilx territory at Kettle Falls, and asserts that one of his daughters married Henry Digby Shuttleworth (*Mourning Dove* 8). In 1859, he took over the HBC at the Thompson River post for a year, then moved on to raising stock and running pack trains in the southern Okanagan (Sismey, "Shuttleworths" 136). Census records indicate his son, Henry (Harry) was born in 1858.

When Chief Francois retired, Harry Shuttleworth took over his pack train. Josephine travelled with him and took on the job of cook for the outfit. Harry Shuttleworth was also "a guide of some fame" who led hunting trips from Hope (Shuttleworth, "Chief" 3). In 1895, they moved, with their children Charley, William, and Tommy, to the 160 acres Harry Shuttleworth had pre-empted and homesteaded in Okanagan Falls ten years earlier. Two more children, Louise and Henry, were born on the ranch. Harry Shuttleworth died in 1900, leaving his wife with five children, the oldest, Charley, being only twelve years old. They successfully managed the range, raising cattle, sheep, and horses, and maintaining an irrigated garden, hay meadows, and orchard (Sismey, "Shuttleworths" 136-37). At the age of twelve, Charley shot his first cougar and became a noted hunter, spending twenty-nine years working for the British Columbia Game Department (Sismey, "Shuttleworths" 137-38). At the time of his death in 1945, "his fame had spread far beyond Provincial boundaries" (Sismey, "Shuttleworths" 138). There is a record of Josephine Shuttleworth marrying "Eduoard" Houghton in Kamloops in 1903, probably the brother of Marie Houghton Brent and grandchild of Young Chief Nkwala, but this marriage is not mentioned in Shuttleworth's obituary nor on her death certificate, so it may have been a short-lived relationship. In February, 1950, the big Shuttleworth ranch house burned down, and with it went what Hester White called a "wonderful collection" of "Josephine's bead work, buckskin and baskets" ("Shuttleworth"); upon Josephine's death in November of that year, she was noted in the *Penticton Herald* as "famous for her fishing and hunting ability as well as for her handicraft work" ("Okanagan Landmark Burns" 1).

Josephine Shuttleworth (right) and daughter Louise, c. 1950.
Courtesy of MacNaughton Family Collection.

When the Christie family from Nova Scotia bought land next door to the Shuttleworths in 1917, Josephine Shuttleworth befriended the oldest daughter Isabel Christie (later Isabel Christie MacNaughton). Shuttleworth's daughter Louise helped out at the Christie Meadow Vale ranch, as did Josephine's youngest son Tommy, who maintained a close relationship with James R. Christie as well as Isabel and her siblings. From 1937-9, MacNaughton wrote down over twenty-five of Shuttleworth's stories and histories, told in *nsyilxcn* and translated into English by Shuttleworth's daughter Louise, and published them in the *Penticton Herald* (see "Crossing Lines" in Part Three). The combination of Shuttleworth's telling voice and story gestures and MacNaughton's writing created lively renditions of many of the *captikʷł* featuring Coyote and other animal-humans. Below, "How Chipmunk Got Markings" has been excerpted from a longer story cycle told by Shuttleworth called "How Chipmunk Got Markings and Why the Loon Laughs," and her story "The Cranes Herald Spring" was taken from a column by Isabel Christie MacNaughton with the same name. Some of Shuttleworth's memories and histories of her family were also published by MacNaughton, as in "Chief Francois, Who Died at 105, Was Notable Old Figure" below, which describes the oral history of Shuttleworth's stories going back to Chief Francois and even further. Shuttleworth also conveyed to MacNaughton a type of story called *smipnumt* which deals with stories found by divine means (Armstrong "Constructing" 105). Two examples are the stories "This Man Died When the Ice Moved off the Lake in Spring," and "He Dreamed—and Died—With the Falling of the Leaves," printed below. That Shuttleworth shared these stories with MacNaughton suggests the trust between them, as generally they were not shared outside of the Syilx community.

With the encouragement of the white schoolteacher Anthony Walsh at the Inkameep Day School on the Osoyoos Indian Reserve, MacNaughton dramatized some stories to be performed by the children at Inkameep. Through Walsh's promotion, they eventually reached a wide audience between 1939 and 1942 in venues such as the Banff School of Fine Arts, Hart House Theatre at the University of Toronto, The Carolina Playmakers at the University of North Carolina, Thunderbird Park in Victoria, and on CBC radio. Two of the plays were also published in 1942 in MacNaughton's book of poems *Wood Fires* (see Part Three). Shuttleworth was acknowledged by Isabel Christie MacNaughton, but not always by others, as her stories in the form of dramas travelled and achieved acclaim. Nevertheless, her voice and particular tellings were essential to conveying the living culture of the Syilx people in the southern Okanagan to settlers of her time as well as to a larger North American audience then and today.

Folk Lore of the Days
When Animal People Dwelt Here

Long, long ago, longer ago than even the oldest story-teller can remember, before there were any Indian people in the land, there lived a race of Animal People.

There were wolf-men and deer-men and mouse-men, bird-men, snake-men and insect-men—men of every kind of animal just as we see them today, only then they were people. The greatest of these people was the coyote. He had a power above all the others and he could make any wish come true. He had many adventures and might have been killed many times, but he always came back to life again.

The songs that were sung by the animal people, the stories they told, and the happenings of their lives were all signs and portents of what was to be in days after, when real people came to live in the land.

At one time in his wandering life, perhaps when he was getting to be an old man, the coyote had settled down. He owned two homes. One was the odd little sand-knoll that stands out by itself on the brown slope, at the foot of Kruger's hill, at the north end of Skaha Lake. The other was a small knoll back of Parham's at Vasseaux [Vaseux] Lake.

The coyote had four sons and a daughter. His daughter lived with the goat-men in a teepee far up on the face of McIntyre Bluff. They had two grizzly bears as watchmen outside their teepee and for their doorway they had a curtain woven of rattlesnakes. When anyone lifted the curtain all the snakes rattled, and the goat and the coyote's daughter inside knew someone was trying to enter.

The coyote wanted very much to visit his daughter and to see his grandchild. Knowing what a very nervous person he was, his daughter was afraid he could never climb the perilous trail to her teepee on the cliff, so she tried to persuade him to stay home. Finally, however, she consented to take him up, and hand-in-hand they started to climb. "You must never take your eyes from the trail above you, father," she directed, "be sure you don't look downwards or sideways."

Before they had climbed very far the coyote began to get nervous. He looked downwards and he looked sideways. He told his daughter he could climb no farther and then he began to scream. She tried to soothe him, at the same time leading him upwards, till at last with much screaming and shaking they arrived at the ledge where the teepee stood. When she took him down the trail she warned him never to attempt the climb again without her aid.

Feeling strong and proud with his feet once more on solid ground, he decided one day to make her a visit. Step by step, creeping and squirming and wriggling from foot hold to foot hold, he came in sight of the teepee. When he was almost on the ledge he heard the grizzly watchman and in his fright lost his balance. He was hurled far out into the air, turning over and over, and he fell with a crash on the rocks below.

The fox, who was his closest friend, found him there. He

picked him up and took away his hurts, and they went on their way together.

To this day, so that none may doubt the tale, you can see on the face of McIntyre Bluff, just opposite the irrigation dam in the river below, a jagged crack which is the trail leading up to the picture-teepee of the goat-man and the coyote's daughter, who lived in the long ago.

And farther over—on the cliff face above the Twin Lagoons, you can see a rider mounted on a black horse. Many tales are told of this horse and his rider, who is really the coyote's son, put up on the rock by his father after he had caught and broken the outlaw horse for him. This was done so that people might know in days after that horses were to be gentled and ridden, and made the friend of man.

[1937]

When the Coyote
Changed the Lives of the Valley Indians
(As told by Josephine Shuttleworth)

In the days of long ago when the coyote was a young man, when he settled down, he brought the salmon from the great blue waters of the Pacific up the Columbia River.

He came as far as Omak, where he fed all the people with a great salmon feast. There he met a lovely maiden whose hand he requested in marriage. He was refused, so the next day he gathered his salmon together and continued on his journey.

At Osoyoos he saw another band encamped. With a gift of fine salmon he asked that one of their maidens be given him, but the people scoffed at his offer. Once more he gathered his salmon together and went on up the river.

At Okanagan Falls the river swept over great rocks with a voice of thunder and a spray as white as the wild cherry blossoms. The waterfall was far too high for the fish to leap.

The coyote made camp with the people there, and again he tried to barter his salmon for an attractive maiden.

Angry at being met with a third refusal, he decided to go farther north. One morning when all the men were out hunting and all the women were picking berries he started to make the falls lower so that his salmon might swim on to the lake. Working as hard as he could, he tore down the rocks till the great waterfall was hardly more than a rapid, as it has remained to this day.

The coyote was a queer chap in those times, even as he is in these. He could never bear to have anyone see him working. When one of the returning berry-pickers caught sight of him he stopped digging.

"I go back from whence I came," he said, "with my salmon." As he took them down the river, other fish darted from every pool.

"I leave you only the poor fish for ever after," he called back to them. And to this day, though you fish from sunrise till sunset in the river below the falls, you are unlikely to get even a nibble from any fish but carp or sucker.

The coyote left his spear leaning against a rocky cliff near the northern end of Vasseaux Lake, on the western side, where you may see it, if you care to look.

At Keller [Washington, within the Colville Indian Reservation], the coyote again made unsuccessful proposals of marriage. He told the people that, because they had refused him, they would never be able to cure their fish.

"Each year when the salmon run," he informed them, "you may hold a great feast, but none will keep for the months of winter." And every year at Keller during the last week in May and the first week in June they still keep the Feast of the Salmon, and to this day they cannot cure them.

The coyote took the salmon on below the falls at Colville,[2] where you can yet go down in the proper season to catch all the fish you desire. There he married a cheerful maiden and was happy among her people. Working together, they caught and dried salmon enough for a long winter.

Before many moons, however, the coyote began to watch the travellers passing through the valley, and to look with longing on the far blue mountains. He told his bride that he was going to leave her. She wished to go with him, and her father came and told the coyote he must take her.

"It is not so," the coyote replied. "I shall desert her, and what I do now shall be done in days after."

So saying, he went on his way.

[1937]

How Chipmunk Got Markings [3]
(*As told by Josephine Shuttleworth*)

Once, in the time long gone, when all the birds and animals were people, there were two sisters. One was the Crow and the other the Meadowlark. The Meadowlark had a small daughter.

The Crow was a hard worker. The Meadowlark, instead of gathering berries, would do nothing but sing from morning till night. She depended on her sister the Crow to get her food and every day she sent the little girl to her home for berries.

Even when the fresh crop of berries was almost ripe the Meadowlark's daughter still went to her aunt, the Crow.

Then the Crow said, "There are no more berries here. Tell your mother that the berries are almost ripe, and that she should pick them, and not be singing from morning till night. It will be a sign that in days after some people will always work and some will only sing. Go home and tell her that."

The little girl ran home. She told her mother what the Crow had said. The Meadowlark, with a little sigh, threw back her head and fell dead on the ground.

"It is a sign," declared the Crow, "That people will die from shock in after days."

There also lived, in the long ago, a little chipmunk and her grandmother. The little chipmunk had a certain place to which she went for berries. No one else knew of it. She called it her own, and she visited it often to pick berries for her grandmother and herself. When she went she carried with her a little basket.

The old owl watched her running along to the berry patch. He watched her working, counting each red berry as she put it into her basket.

He swooped down to a nearby tree. "Whoo, whoo, whoo," he called, "my berries."

"They're not your berries. They're mine," chirped the little chipmunk. Then she ran home with the owl right after her. Just as she was almost inside her tepee door he clutched at her with his outstretched claws, ripping three big marks down her back.

When grandmother came in the chipmunk had run and hidden herself under the pillow. The grandmother looked for a long time before she found her.

A frightened, sobbing "snu, snu, snu,"[4] was the only answer the little chipmunk could give to all her questions.

"Did the owl scare you?" asked the grandmother.

"He scratched me," sobbed the chipmunk, and turning around she showed her grandmother the three great marks which every chipmunk has carried from that time to this.

[1938]

More Indian Tales

During a recent story-telling hour at the home of Mrs. Josephine Shuttleworth many interesting facts about the life of the Indians of long ago, in the days before the white traders had crossed the mountains, were told.

The traditional digging of the spitlum or rock rose roots,[5] still followed in the present day, was one of the customs described. These roots, dried, were of considerable medicinal as well as food value. Other roots, and many berries were picked and dried. The Indian women made a very palatable dish of crimson foaming berries beaten to a froth, with olallas to sweeten them.

Little willow drying racks, with coals glowing in the sand beneath, were put together for the drying of salmon and venison for the winter's supply.

Blankets were made from hides tanned on the inside, and with the hair or fur left on. Winter moccasins were made in the same way, with the furry sides worn next the feet. The woolly fur of the mountain goat was also used in the making of blankets. It was twisted into yarn, dyed with root and bark colors and then woven, sometimes in intricate designs.

Babies were carried in buckskin-bound pack-boards on their mother's backs until they were three years old. In cold weather the pack boards were lined with the downy fluff of the tule "cat-tails" to keep the babies warm.

Boys and girls underwent a rigorous year's training in separate tepees before they were considered to be grown up. Here they were trained to be strong and healthy in body and mind, in a routine which included the taking of sweat baths, long hours of work, fasting, abstinence from water, and thorough training in the care of their persons. The course was almost spartan-like in its severity.

In those days unless a man was a good hunter, he would very likely have no wife. A good hunter might have two or three wives, and some men had as many as twenty.

The tribal tepees were set in rows of eight, each one joined to the other one ahead of it, as in the manner of a string of sausages, so that a person could pass from one to another without stepping outside.

A fire-hole was made in the center of each teepee, with a smoke-hole in the peak of the "roof" above it. Beds were placed along the sides of the dwelling.

This row of tepees had a door on each end and, inside it, if the tepees were built large enough, the whole tribe lived there. Inner doors were woven of tule matting.

The tepees themselves were built of birch and willow poles, covered with tule matting or skins. Some of the tepees, especially in winter, were dug with a large part underground, or made more weatherproof with earth piled around them.

Besides resting and eating and sleeping, the winter's entertainment was made up in a large part of stick games and tribal dances. If the hunters wanted snow they would sing and dance their weird dances to the "Power" that the snow might come.

While the men did the hunting, the women worked in the tepees with skins and leather work. They boiled their meat in birch bark and cottonwood buckets, putting hot stones in the water to bring it to a boil.

Flat rocks rubbed against one another supplied sparks for lighting the fires. The sparks were coaxed to a flame in spunky wood or bark.

When a tribe moved camp it would move everything, so it was convenient to do rather light house-keeping, and save bother in moving.

Some of the hunters rode small shaggy ponies, wild little horses with tails and manes sweeping the ground.

Many of the tribes spoke a different language in those days than is spoken today, and therefore many of the stories which have been handed down are not exactly clear in the translation, especially of place names.

Death in the olden days was more often due to old age than to disease.

When a man died his body was bent double and bound in deerskin.

Then borne aloft by a few silent mourners, the body was carried away and laid in a shallow grave, with some beads and jewels, a hatchet and perhaps a favorite bow and arrow to accompany the spirit of the departed to his Happy Hunting Grounds.
[1938]

Chief Francois, Who Died at 105, Was Notable Old Figure
(as told by Josephine Shuttleworth)

As a stern but well-loved chief, hunter-extraordinary and teller of tales, the late Chief Francois of the Penticton Indian Reserve[6] will be remembered around many a story-telling fire when we who hear about him now are long forgotten.

Chief Francois' father was an Okanagan Indian and his mother the daughter of the wise Hunting Chieftainess of the Tonasket tribe. It was from her that he inherited his wisdom and skill as a huntsman.

When Francois was a young man he and his brother Michel were renowned amongst their people as fearless and mighty hunters. They had a pack of seven little dogs they used for hunting grizzly bear. The dogs were well trained and well treated, and they were close comrades with their masters.

At one time they captured a magnificent grizzly, almost pure white in color, in a stirring battle at Shingle Creek. The little dogs would worry the great animal and drive it almost distracted with their darting onslaught, while the men loaded their flintlock muskets. In one instance, when the wounded bear charged him after a shot, Francois hit it over the head with the butt end of his gun, knocking it backwards.

While the men were reloading they depended on the dogs to keep fighting with the bear. At last, tired and wounded, it fell down in the shallow waters of the creek, but only after eight telling shots from the hunters' guns did the great beast finally die.

Francois was married at Mission, where he had been for some time working with the priest. He later moved with his family to the site of the present Penticton, where they made camp on a spot just across the river from the Red Bridge [today's Green Mountain Road and Fairview Road bridge].

Of his seven children only two are alive today, Mrs. Mary McLean and Mrs. Josephine Shuttleworth, the eldest and the youngest of his family. Both live at Okanagan Falls. The other children died in their 'teens.

Francois was made chief when the Penticton Indian Reserve was first organized. An official party from England initiated him as Chief of the Indians of the Penticton Reserve in a colourful and impressive ceremony. The officials travelled in fine style, with folding tables, chairs and beds, silverware and china of quality. They entertained Francois and Father Pendozy [Pandosy] at a sumptuous banquet before the ceremony.

The Indians, chanting a song the priest had taught them to the tune of "Auld-Lang Syne," marched around in single file to shake hands with the officials and their newly appointed chief. Francois had been presented with his papers and the flag, and was standing in his ceremonial suit beside the officials.

He was a fine figure of a man, tall and very powerful, with a chief-like bearing and a strong, kindly face. A picture of Chief Francois taken in old age, occupies a place of honour in the home of his daughter Mrs. Shuttleworth. The face, though that of an old man, is one of decided character and strength, with particularly expressive dark eyes.

The chief organized a police force which was a successful factor in keeping order on the Reserve. The chief, himself, could "handle" any man on the Reserve in case one proved too much for the policemen, and to this day stories are told of his prowess on such occasions.

More than three-score years ago there was an earthquake in Penticton, so that all the Indians were sure some mysterious displeasure had fallen upon them. Running wildly from their homes and from their work in the fields they gathered at the Francois house. The cabin was packed with persons, and still they came, huddling close to the wall when they could no longer gain entrance.

Some of them came crawling, led by one old man, walking erect and singing hymns. The people seemed to think they would be safe with Francois, and that his home would stand when others would fall.

Both before and after he was made chief, Francois packe
over the Hope trail for Tom Ellis. His wife did the cooking for
the outfit and while they were alive, his sons worked with the
packing gang. Mrs. Shuttleworth followed the pack-train as soon
as she was big enough to ride behind her father's saddle. Later
she had her own horse, and after a time she took over the cooking.
When her mother died and Chief Francois retired from the work,
Mrs. Shuttleworth and her husband ran the packing outfit for
some years.

Her husband, the late Harry Shuttleworth, was a guide of
some fame. He took out many hunting parties from Hope, in the
old days.

A campfire glowing among the pines somewhere on the long
trail taken by Chief Francois on a pack journey, hunting trip, or a
few days fishing was always a story telling fire too.

There were stories of the Coyote, who used the fog-mists to
protect himself, or to throw over his enemies while he sat and
sang songs of derision to them from above it.

There were stories of the days when the Coyote held great
meetings, attended by all the animal people. Every one of them
contributed a song or story to the program, even down to the
littlest mouse, whose song was as dainty, lilting a little tune as
you would want to whistle on a sunny morning.

Tales there were too, of the merry crickets, who when asked
by the ants the reason they never worked said they would rather
sing in happiness all summer and sleep in the long, cold winter
than be so hurried with living that they couldn't sing a happy
song in either season.

There was a fable of the nervous little ant-woman. While she
tried to persuade the heart-broken partridge mother to bury her
child, she fidgeted and tugged on her belt until it became so tight
that ants' waists have remained small to this day.

Many and many another tale was told around Chief Francois'
campfire – some of them make-believe, some of them hero-stories
and some of them happenings of other days.

Chief Francois reached the end of his trail on June 10, 1909,
at the age of 105 years. With his going there departed from the
Okanagan a great man.

[1938]

The Cranes Herald Spring

In March, when the brown earth patches are dark on the snow, the cranes come flying and calling on the wind.

"It is the sound of the cranes," mutter the Bear people from their beds in the winter caves.

"It is the sound of the cranes," they say again, as they turn over and tumble into the pale spring sunshine.

And the world is no longer asleep, for the sound of the cranes is a sign of the coming of spring.

When the small talk had drifted around to sandhill cranes, and the wondering if they had ever been "story-birds," Mrs. Shuttleworth told the above little folk-tale which she remembered hearing her father tell when the sandhill cranes flew over in the olden days.
[1938]

This Man Died When the Ice Moved
off the Lake in Spring
(Indian folk-tale as told by Mrs. Josephine Shuttleworth)

Many long years ago, when the lake lay ice-covered between the thawing hills, a man sat on the shore and listened. He heard the ice groaning. He heard rumbles like thunder, and sharp cracks.

"Why does the lake groan and rumble so," he wondered to himself. "I must sleep beside the shore, and dream of it."

In those days, as in days after, people often found their "power" in dreams. While their minds lay open in the darkness, things would appear before them, and speak to them.

"The lake may give me its power" thought the man, as he scraped a little hollow in the sand.

But the night wore on, and the man dreamed no dreams. The next night he lay down on the sand again, and while the water murmured under the ice he waited for his dream. Out of the darkness a voice said to him: "I feel sorry for you that you wonder so. I am sad that you try to find the reason for this moaning. But still I must tell you. The ice is a person, and he is dying. When the mountain snow has melted, and the hills are bare, the man of the ice will fade away and die. Whoever asks to share this secret of the lake dies too."

Then the voice was silent, and the darkness was heavy over the shore. In the morning the man went home to the teepee where his old mother lived. She watched him as he went about.

"My son," she said, "What is it? You have songs no longer and glad ways for no one."

"Old Mother," he said, "It is nothing. But see, the ice breaks on the water."

She looked at him slowly and she followed as he went about. Then she said again, "My son, what is it? The ice breaks on the water—but your meat goes uneaten and your days are grey and sorry."

"Old Mother," he answered, "I dreamed a dream." And he told her of the voice on the shore.

"When the ice is gone," he said sadly, "I die." Then he lay down to sleep in the teepee.

Many mornings the old mother called to him, and many mornings he answered her. "My son," she would say, "morning breaks," and he would answer.

But one morning when she called "My son," no answer came. The teepee was silent.

Throwing aside the door curtain, the old mother gazed down at the lake. It lay clear and blue between the hills, and the wind rippled softly over it.

"The ice is gone," she said, and she wept for her son.
[1939]

He Dreamed—and Died—with the Falling of the Leaves
(From the Okanagan Indian folk-tale, as told by Mrs. Josephine Shuttleworth)

Once in the long ago, in the days when the land was greening under the winds of spring and the rain, a man stood thinking beneath a birch tree.

He looked at the green birch leaves; and the long red shoots of the willow, with the little green leaves upon them.

"Why do the leaves come so fresh and green in the springtime," he wondered, "when they must turn yellow and die in the fall."

"If only I knew why the leaves are so, perhaps I would have a power," he said. "I must dream and find me a power."

So he lay down beneath the birch tree, and looked up into its branches. In his dream a voice came to him.

"It is warm in the spring, and the leaves come out," said the voice, "and the world is glad. All summer it is green. With the first gold days the little leaves fall to the ground, and yet they dance in the wind. But when the fall has really come, they are sick and yellow and cold. They drop to the ground and they lie damp and grey together. They are dead then, and are empty of gladness. But the snows are a sleep upon them, and with another spring they wake again."

Then the voice fell lightly away, but it came once more.

"Who dreams this dream of leaves, falls with their falling," it said, and then it was gone.

Slowly the man went home, and the months were passing. He watched while the flowers came, the buttercups and the star-flowers, and he watched them fade and die.

He watched while the grass turned dry and brown on the hillsides, and he saw the paint-brush crimson on the mountain trail.

Then with the first gold days he went again to the birch tree.

"The little leaves fall to the ground," he said "and yet they dance in the wind. When the fall has really come they will be sick and yellow and cold. They will drop to the ground around me and lie damp and grey together. They will be dead then, and empty of gladness," he added slowly. Then he lay down to sleep.

"Who dreams this dream of leaves, falls with their falling," a voice said.

"But the snows are like a sleep upon them," he whispered softly, "and with another spring they wake again."
[1939]

Eliza Jane Swalwell, c.1920.
Courtesy of Peter Simpson.

Eliza Jane Swalwell

1868 - 1944

In this memoir of early days in the Okanagan on horseback, Eliza Jane Swalwell establishes she was as skillful a writer as she was a rider. Her reminiscence provides an interesting companion to Mourning Dove's novel *Cogewea* as Swalwell looks back on being a girl amidst cowboy culture and riding the range on which she was born and grew up. In her only published writing, "Girlhood Days in the Okanagan" (1939), included below, many voices mingle, such as those of a Syilx historical storyteller, a memoirist, an environmental essayist, and also a spokesperson for the rights of Syilx people in the Okanagan.

Swalwell's father, G.W. Simpson (c.1817-1902), was the son of Presbyterian minister John Simpson who emigrated from Scotland to Philadelphia. Following the gold rush, G.W. Simpson moved further west to California, then north to the Fraser bars and in 1859 worked for the Harper brothers who moved cattle from Oregon to the Chilcotin, British Columbia, bringing him into the Okanagan. Credited by Okanagan historian F.M. Buckland with being the first settler to introduce cattle into the Okanagan valley from Oregon, Simpson managed the ranch of Captain Charles Houghton in the Coldstream area in the late 1860s and is reported to have partnered in the cattle business with Judge Haynes at Osoyoos. In 1870 he bought the Frederick Brent ranch at Duck Lake in what is now the Winfield area of the Okanagan, between Kelowna and Vernon. After selling it to the Postills in 1872, he moved south to the Simpson Ranch along Mill Creek in what is now north Kelowna where he lived until 1892, when he sold the ranch to Price Ellison. He died in 1902, at the home of his daughter Eliza Jane and her husband, William Swalwell, and was buried on their family ranch (now Dickson ranch) alongside his wife, who died in 1901.

George Simpson married Sara Stepetsa, the sister of Chief Pantherhead of the village at *stqʷatkʷłniwt*, now Westbank. She was born in about 1851 in *snpinktn*, now Penticton, a few years before Fathers Pandosy and Richard arrived in the Okanagan in 1859 to establish a settlement in the Okanagan Mission. Eliza Jane, born in 1868, had three brothers, George, Thomas and Charlie, and one sister, Sarah. In 1884, at age sixteen, Eliza Jane Simpson married Thomas Jones, who died four years later. They had a son, Thomas William Jones, born in 1887. Eliza Jane Simpson married William Pelissier Swalwell, an immigrant from Yorkshire, England, in 1895. William Swalwell was a cousin of the Postill brothers, notable early ranchers in the central Okanagan. He died in Kamloops in 1926, and Eliza Jane died in Okanagan Mission in 1944.

Swalwell credits her "mother's side" with giving her a particular reverence for the natural world; in her essay, she goes on to analyze why she thinks the culture she inherits from her mother permits that. Her writing shows an education that makes her at ease with references to various geological, scientific and historical texts, and she engages not only in experiencing but also in investigating the scientific causes of the "warm . . . soft and searching" night wind she feels on summer nights sleeping outdoors in the Okanagan.

From the perspectives of her diverse cultural background, she also critically examines the settler culture, which was part of her environment. Her criticism is often indirect, making statements through well-recognized authorities, and surrounding the issue of injustice concerning Indigenous land in British Columbia with observations about other aspects of Okanagan life. She does state directly, however, that "The Indians here have been treated with less consideration than in any other part of Canada, and it is a sore subject with them to-day." Her essay demonstrates her understanding of the British Columbia government's long record of ignoring Indigenous title to the land. This policy resulted in unilateral allocation of small reserves on the part of the provincial government, rather than a treaty process carried out by Indigenous people and the crown or its representative, the federal government, as had taken place in the rest of Canada. The British Columbia government also permitted unbridled pre-emption of Syilx land that was not reserved, sudden cut-offs of reserves in the interests of settlers, the withholding of water rights and interference with hunting, fishing and gathering. Swalwell refers to the 1874 Consolidated Land Act, which refused to recognize Syilx ownership of the land. Its enaction was followed by the Okanagan-Shuswap Alliance in 1874 and threats of war in 1877 (Armstrong et al, 51).

Two federal-provincial commissions followed to attempt to resolve contention over the land, the Joint Reserve Commission (1876-78, followed by another Reserve Commission from 1878-80) and the Royal Commission known as the McKenna-McBride Commission (1913-16) with the result that reserves in British Columbia were allocated with sporadic, unofficial consultation but without final agreement from Indigenous people. Indigenous title was never recognized and thus true negotiation did not take place. Reserve size in the north Okanagan was increased from the Haynes' reductions in 1865 (see "Crossing Lines" in Part Three) by the Joint Reserve Commission, but the McKenna-McBride Commission reduced reserve land in the Penticton

46

area by nearly 19,000 acres. Neither of these commissions succeeded in redressing the land issues for the Indigenous peoples of British Columbia, and the early decades of the 1900s saw numerous alliances and delegations in northern British Columbia, the west coast, and the southern interior bringing their concerns to the federal government and to the British crown through attempts to reach the British courts—the Judicial Committee of the Privy Council or even the Privy Council itself.

In 1924, however, the federal government ratified the McKenna-McBride Commission's allocation of reserves. In 1938, the title of Indigenous reserves in British Columbia, amounting to only a little more than one-third of one percent of all land in British Columbia (Harris, *Making* 261), was conveyed to the Dominion, even though there had been no ratification from Indigenous people and the title was never recognized as belonging to Indigenous people. Swalwell's article, written a year later, shows her awareness of the illegal basis of the British Columbia government's appropriation of Syilx land and the Indigenous initiatives to bring that awareness to the general public. Her voice in her article published in the *OHS Report* of 1939 is another voice added to the protests of the preceding decades.

Eliza Jane Swalwell at right, her son Thomas Jones, and neighbours c.1920s.
Courtesy of Peter Simpson.

Girlhood Days in the Okanagan

I remember this valley when everything was in a wild state, before there was any wagon road and everything had to be brought in by pack-train,[7] and all our dishes were of tin, and we baked bread and pies and roasted meat in a Dutch oven. There was great rejoicing when the road was completed to the Mission. I was grown up and married before the first buggy arrived. It caused quite an excitement among us girls who had been born here and had never been out of the valley. It seemed to us to be the last word in luxury and a pleasant method of travelling, and we were all eager for our first ride in it.

Before the arrival of the wagon road every one had to learn to ride, as it was the only means of getting anywhere, and we girls were all proficient horsewomen. We could round up a band of horses, drive them into a corral, rope the one we wanted and saddle him up as expertly as a man could do it.

And here let me give any one who is contemplating buying a saddle horse a straight tip, although it is rather late in the day to mention it. If you want to know how big your horse is, throw a saddle on to him and see if it takes a long girth to go around him behind the shoulders. If it does and he is big there, he is a big horse, but if he is small behind the shoulders he is a small horse no matter how big he may look. If he is big behind the shoulders and his legs are sound, the rest of him does not matter much. The Okanagan range horses were noted for their large girth and their stamina and their powers of endurance.

The first real industry of this country was cattle raising. Wherever you looked over the hills and ranges you saw cattle, and the sight of them coming out of the timber where they had been resting in the shade of the trees and scattering all over the ranges in droves to feed, with the little calves jumping and skipping wherever you looked, was a sight never to be forgotten. The two great events of the year were the coming of the cattle buyers in May and September. They usually sent word ahead to let us know they were coming, and then we all got busy, and everyone, girls as well as the men, assisted at the round-up.

On these occasions we girls felt that we were coming into our own.

We could handle a horse about as well as the men, and we

could show them that we amounted to something more than a mere nuisance about the place, as they sometimes seemed to think we were.

The conversation sometimes around the supper table would sound rather strange today. Occasionally you would hear such remarks as: "That pinto of mine can turn on a four-point blanket." (This would be said boastfully) or "I saw a steer to-day with a wattle on the left jaw and a swallow-fork on the right ear, but the brand was blurred. I wonder who owns it." Now a four-point was the largest blanket sold by the Hudson's Bay Company, and when a steer was being chased he sometimes bolted as quick as a flash to the right or left to get away from the horse, and if the horse could turn as quickly as the steer without losing time he was said to be able to turn on a four-point blanket. Some of the horses were very quick, and if the rider did not watch out he would find himself on the ground while the riderless horse still pursued the steer.

Sometimes in marking the calves in the spring, they made a half-moon shaped incision in the skin on the jaw, which caused the skin to sag, and when the wound healed over it left a lump which in after years was easily discernible. This was called a wattle on the jaw, but usually the wattle was made by nicking the dewlap and letting it hang down in front, a very good mark. Again, in marking the ear instead of slitting it, they sometimes cut out a V-shaped piece which left the two points wide apart and easy to see. This was a swallow-fork.

Everyone in those days had a brand, and everyone seemed to know everyone else's brand. In the selection of brands all sorts of combinations of the letters of the alphabet and the numerals were used. But a brand could not always be seen in winter when the hair was long, and sometimes the animal had to be thrown and the skin shaved before they were sure of the brand, hence the use of wattles and ear-marks.

Somehow it seems to me the men were better satisfied with the work they had to do when they were engaged in cattle and grain raising, before they became involved in this endless fussing over insect pests, corky core, etc., and the proper functioning of the single disk.[8] They must get tired of it sometimes. In early days they were at least less vocal over their troubles, they did not shout so loudly when things went wrong.

49

It sometimes amuses me at the picture show to see how the cowboys disport themselves on the screen. They usually leave the yard or corral at the full gallop, and more than once I saw a cowboy mount his horse from the off side. If a cattle man saw a cowboy gallop his horse out of the corral or mount his horse from the off side, he would fire him on the spot. He would take it for granted that the cowboy was locoed.

It was a matter of professional pride with a cowboy to take his horse from the corral to the range, where the serious work of the day began, as quietly as possible. A cowboy will always spare his horse whenever he can. If he can induce his horse on the way to work to jog along quietly, he will do so, and if he hears his horse softly champing his teeth as he jogs along, and hears the soft purr, purr of the horse rolling the wheel on the Mexican bit with his tongue, it is music to his ears. He knows then his horse is happy and contented and ready for anything.

When the people of Kelowna finish building the road to Naramata, and build a museum, an effort should be made to secure a complete cowboy's outfit and place it in the museum— long-legged boots with high heels, chaps, Mexican spurs, quirt, Mexican bit and pleated raw-hide bridle.[9] The accoutrements of a cowboy will soon be rarities. How many living here have ever seen a genuine Bowie knife? Yet a few years ago they were not rare.

In the picture shows the cowboys are represented as loquacious men. This is not correct. The genuine cowboy had little to say for himself, and when he had anything to say he hinted it rather than made a direct statement which, I suppose, was his way of being polite. He softened down the bluntness and asperity of a positive and direct statement by indirect speech. A funny story is told of a clergyman who, in marrying a cowboy, had the greatest difficulty in getting him to say, "I do." "I ain't a-kickin." "Didn't say I wouldn't." "This goes for me," were some of the answers he gave. "Yes" and "No" seemed to them quite unnecessarily positive and direct, and therefore impolite, and when they used these terms in a discussion the altercation was getting pretty close to a fight.

Some of them were as vain as a schoolgirl, and when they were rigged out in full cowboy regalia with a silk handkerchief around their neck they rather fancied themselves. They thought they were "some spuds" all right. Most of them that I knew were rascals.

It was nice to ride over the range in the morning and see the bunch grass, sunflowers and lupins, springing up so abundantly and to feel your horse springing under you at every step as if he, too, were enjoying the promenade, as no doubt he was.

There were no fences in those days, and the bunch grass grew so high it waved in the wind like a field of wheat.

The Lewisia Rediviva is a peculiar flower. It was named after Meriwether Lewis of the Lewis and Clark expedition across the Rocky Mountains in 1804-1806. It grows in the Okanagan on sandy and arid ridges where the moisture in the soil is not sufficient to support an ordinary growth of bunch grass. The blossoms, which vary in colour from pale pink to rose in different plants, are about the size of a tulip and appear on a stalk about an inch and a half long without leaves, the leaves coming later so that this beautiful flower growing so close to the ground without leaves has the appearance of a flower recently picked and thrown on the ground. The leaves when they come later are very short and narrow. The plant is very noticeable when it is in bloom, but when the bloom fades the plant apparently vanishes, only to revive again the following year, hence its second name. It is sometimes called the "Sand Rose," and sometimes the "Ground Rose" [or rock rose]. The Indians call it spetlam, and they use the roots for food.

To me it was an exquisite pleasure as a girl to ride over this green and gracious pasture land in the mornings, and to see it stretching before me for miles with the Sand Rose lying scattered on the ground as if a fairy princess had passed that way at dawn and children had strewn flowers in her path, and to see the sun light on the hills. On such occasions I have sometimes seen things, or rather sensed something, so serene and beautiful that it left me weak and weeping as I sat in the saddle.

I do not know whether this responsiveness to certain beautiful aspects of nature comes to me from my Indian mother or from my father's side of the house, but it probably comes from my mother's side. It seems to me the whites are too much bound and limited, too much enslaved by their written creeds and confessions of faith. The Indians are free of that, and consequently they are closer to nature and reality, and to the Creator, than the whites. You cannot argue about such things, you cannot clothe what is eternal and infinite in finite words. Any attempt to do so only leads to an impasse, and too often to a certain hardness of heart that has no reverence for anything and remains unmoved by mystical experiences.

I was taught by my mother to pray to the Great Spirit, my father told me to pray to God, and the priest at the Mission told us we should pray to the holy Virgin Mary, the Mother of God,[10] and I still think the advice of all three was good. One can do more for himself, more in straightening out his mental kinks and twists and putting his inner or subconscious self in harmony with his surroundings by following the advice of any one of those three excellent persons than the most skilful and expensive psychiatrist can do for him, and that door is always open.

In this connection, let me here quote from Sir William Dawson's *Fossil Men*.[11] On page 280 he says: "I by no means desire to unduly exalt prehistoric religions, but I wish distinctly to affirm that they[,] and what we call the heathenism or animism of untaught tribes[,]were nearer to God and truth than are either the ritualisms and idolatries or the materialistic skepticisms of more cultivated times," and again on page 337: "Paul perceived that the Athenians were 'very religious,' because they had an altar to the unknown God;[12] and so in every human heart there is an altar to God as known or unknown, as a father and friend, or as an equitable ruler."

Elsewhere, after giving his reasons for so saying, he couches his conclusion in the following words: "How much happier than either are those on whose last days shines the brighter hope of the light and immortality revealed by the Gospel." Perhaps he is right; I don't know. You can only live such things. The highest and best things in life cannot be clothed in words.

Standing as I do between two races I could never see that intellectually the Indians are not the equals of the whites. The Indians are sadly lacking in culture; that is seen at a glance, but social grace and refinement are things which can be acquired. In Pope's well-known lines:

> *"Lo, the poor Indian with untutored mind*
> *Sees God in clouds or hears him in the wind."* [13]

The non sequitur is as obvious as the false rhyme. Why should any man, whether Indian or white, be commiserated because he sees in the workings of nature manifestations of the Creator? He would be a dolt if he did not.

James Coleman, the Indian Agent at Vernon, an intelligent man who has had a long and varied experience with the Okanagan Indians, had this to say of them in his letter to the local paper of the 4th November, 1937:

> While the Indian Department might achieve much in this direction (in the direction of educating the Indians), despite public indifference, the shortest road to the best results will be via a return to the old-timer attitude on the part of the public, looking on the Indian as good timber in our Empire building activities, and surely there never was a time in the history of the Empire when the full co-operation of a good and loyal people was more urgently needed than at present.

> The Indian on the Reserve is a dignified and shrewd debater as a rule, and his seat in the Council of his white brother would not be a disadvantage to the white brother. May the days of mutual understanding and appreciation soon arrive.

The whites say, you should love your neighbour as yourself, and in one place the rule is laid down thus: "And if any man will sue thee at the law and take away thy coat, let him have thy cloak also. And whosoever shall compel thee to go a mile with him go twain." Yet, in dealing with each other, they are hard. In a horse trade they would skin their neighbour out of his eye-teeth if they could.

I loved and respected my father, and I loved and respected my mother. Both were strict and conscientious in the discharge of their duty, each as they understood it.

My father was George William Simpson. He was born in Philadelphia, the son of a Scotch Presbyterian minister. He died on the 22nd February, 1902, aged eighty-five years.

He was a studious man, and all his life his Bible was his

constant companion. He always took it with him when off on prospecting trips. The one he had when he died was printed in Oxford by the University Press in 1870. It contains the well known dedication to King James beginning with the words: "Great and manifold were the blessings, most dread Sovereign," etc. Dirty, ragged and thumb worn, it is today my most precious possession. As it was so well known throughout the valley at one time (Simpson's Bible), it is now of some historic import and value. Someday I may bequeath it to a museum.

As illustrating the failure of the whites to understand the Indians, something which happened in the County Court in Vernon may be mentioned. An Indian at the head of the lake[14] had married a girl under fifteen. The parents of the boy and the parents of the girl had given their consent, and everything was quite correct and proper, according to Indian customs and usages. The boy, however, had committed an offence under the criminal code in marrying a girl of that age without first obtaining an order of the court permitting him to do so, something of which the boy probably knew nothing. The judge in sentencing him reminded him that the Government had been generous in the allotment of Indian Reserves, and that the least the Indians could do in return was to refrain from breaking the law and give no trouble. By similar reasoning all free miners should be careful to give no trouble and obey the law, because the Mining Act is just and equitable. If it is fair and reasonable in one case it is fair and reasonable in the other.

When the Consolidated Land Act of 1874 was passed, it was disallowed at Ottawa for the reason that the title of the Province of British Columbia to the public lands within the Province was clouded, the territorial title of the Indians had not been extinguished. In his letter of the 15th January, 1875, disallowing the Act, the [federal] Deputy Minister of Justice says, among other things: "There is not a shadow of doubt that from the earliest times, England has always felt it imperative to treat with the Indians in council and to obtain surrenders of tracts of Canada, as from time to time such were required for the purposes of settlement."

And he concludes his letter in the following terms:

Considering, then, these several features of the case, that no surrender or session of their territorial rights, whether the same be of a legal or equitable nature, has ever been executed by the Indian tribes of the Province—that they allege that the reservations of land made by the government for their use have been arbitrarily so made, and are totally inadequate to their support and requirements, and without their assent—that they are not adverse to hostilities in order to enforce rights which it is impossible to deny them, and that the Act under consideration not only ignores those rights, but expressly prohibits the Indians from enjoying the rights of recording or pre-empting land, except by consent of the Lieutenant-Governor—the undersigned feels that he cannot do otherwise than advise that the Act in question is objectionable, as tending to deal with lands which are assumed to be the absolute property of the Province, an assumption which completely ignores, as applicable to the Indians of British Columbia, the honour and good faith with which the crown has, in all other cases, since its sovereignty of the territories of North America, dealt with their various Indian tribes.[15]

The Dominion Government was always willing to recognize the territorial rights of the Indians, but the province consistently refused recognition. At one time the Indians tried to get their case before the Privy Council, but failed.[16]

Sir Wilfred Laurier remarked to a deputation which waited on him at Ottawa on the 26th April, 1911:

The matter for us to immediately consider is whether we can bring the Government of British Columbia into Court with us. We think it is our duty to have the matter inquired into. The Government of British Columbia may be right or wrong in their assertion that the Indians have no claims whatever. Courts of Law are just for that purpose—where a man asserts a claim and it is denied by another—but we do not know if we can force a Government into Court. If we can find a way I may say we shall surely do so, because everybody will agree it is a matter of good government to have no one resting under a grievance. The Indians will continue to believe they have a grievance until it has been settled by the

Court that they have a claim or that they have no claim.[17]

The Indians here have been treated with less consideration than in any other part of Canada, and it is a sore subject with them to-day. If the Judge [in the Vernon County Court] did not know this, the Indian did. The incident in the County Court was thus reported in the local paper of the 5th April, 1934: "Judge Swanson was pointed in his remarks, reminding him that he and all other Indians were well treated by the Department, and given good reserves. The least they could do in return, he added, would be to try and live decently and give no trouble."

When for any reason we were sleeping out in the open in summer the night wind always interested me. It would start up every morning about two o'clock. Everything would be perfectly calm and quiet, and all at once in the distance you would hear it rustling the dried grass and sunflower leaves, apparently quite a breeze, and this would go on for about ten minutes or so and then it would die away, and everything would again be quiet and calm for awhile. And again it would start up in a totally different direction, never twice in the same place, with the same persistent rustling of dried grass and leaves. It never occurred on a side hill, only in the bottom of a valley. I could understand a wind blowing for a considerable time in one direction, but this wind seemed to rise from the ground in spots and blow with considerable force for a short time, and then die away without going anywhere. And when it did reach you it stole across your cheek and around your neck and through your hair, oh, so gently. It was so warm and soft and searching. I did not understand it. And now the modern aviators seem to have found the explanation of the occurrence of this mysterious wind which puzzled me so much when I was a girl.

Frederick G. Vosburgh, in the Geographical Magazine for July of this year (1938) in dealing with air conditions confronting those who ride in gliders and sailplanes, among other things, says:

> The result was confirmation of the theory that the warm air rises in a succession of enormous bubble-like masses. Most astounding to me is this further fact; that

apparently it is possible for mere man to shake one of these bubbles loose.

A modern sailplane flight, in competition, is never over until the ship is actually on the ground, and stubborn pilots, fighting to the last for a breath of breeze that would keep them in the air, discovered something. They found that if a man dived his ship at high speed, seventy or so, above a promising source of thermal currents such as a cornfield, banked sharply when only one or two hundred feet from the ground, and spiralled upward in tight, climbing turns, a surprising thing sometimes happened. A sudden thermal current caught the ship and carried it up, up, up to the neighbourhood of the clouds again. The swirling sweep of the fifty-foot wing-spread, travelling at seventy miles an hour and suddenly twisting upward in a corkscrew fashion, had apparently dislodged a thermal bubble which had been trembling on the verge of rising.

When the first report of this came from a pilot in Germany, most American soarers were sceptical. But they tried it, and found it often worked. Richard du Pont told me he had successfully used this manoeuvre several times. Meteorologists say it is entirely credible. One might use the analogy of a drop of water trembling on the tip of a faucet. If the drop is almost ready to fall, a surprisingly light tap on the faucet will dislodge it.

This seems to afford a reasonable explanation of this eerie and mysterious night wind which so aroused my curiosity when I was a girl. One can easily understand how it would work out. After the sun went down the air in the valley would cool off while the air close to the ground would remain at a higher temperature from the heat of the warm, dry earth. And as the night advanced the difference in temperature would become more marked until the lighter air broke through, and then the ascending column would be fed from all sides by the light warm air near the surface of the earth until the supply became exhausted and the movement ceased. This explosion of the light, warm air would account for the night wind.

In our last Report [of the Okanagan Historical Society, 1937] George W. Johnson explained why the Okanagan is a dry belt, and so from year to year we are learning more about the Okanagan Valley.[18]

At one time there were two Indian Chiefs, one was Enoch who lived at Duck Lake, and the other Chief Pantherhead who lived at Westbank. Chief Pantherhead had two sisters, one was my mother who married G.W. Simpson, and died in 1901, one year before my father. The other sister married a Frenchman, named Boriot, who had a cattle ranch near Kamloops. He went on a visit to France, and while there was conscripted and killed in the Franco-Prussian war. His son, Victor Boriot, and his wife [Eliza Jane's sister, Sarah] are now living on the Duck Lake Reserve [in the Winfield area, north of Kelowna]. After her husband's death, my aunt came to live with her brother, Chief Pantherhead, and later she married Chief Enoch. These two Chiefs, Pantherhead and Enoch, were highly respected by both Indians and whites.

I was born on the 14th December, 1868, and married Thomas Jones on the 6th April, 1884. He died on the 30th July, 1888. On the 10th May, 1892, I married again, my second husband being William Pelissier Swalwell. He got his second name by being named after the French Marshal who commanded the French Army at the time of the Crimean war in 1854. This name was very popular about the time he was born. My husband was a cousin of the Postill brothers.[19] He died on the 14th March, 1926. [1939]

Marie Houghton Brent and William Brent, informal portrait, c. 1910.
Courtesy of Greater Vernon Museum and Archives.

Marie Houghton Brent

1870 - 1968

When the first annual report of the Okanagan Historical and Natural History Society appeared in 1926, "Mrs. Maria Brent" is listed as a "Charter Member." She published several articles for that society, as well as in newspapers in Canada and the United States. One of the few writers in the region to present a Syilx perspective, she also left behind a fascinating unpublished memoir. Throughout her adult life she pursued Okanagan history with vigour, and she celebrated and wrote about both sides of her ancestry—Syilx and Euro-Canadian.

Marie Houghton Brent[20] was born on December 5, 1870, to Sophie or Kr-Se'skrilt (*kʷr'siskʷrilt*, yellow dress) Nkwala and Captain Charles Frederick Houghton (1839-1898). Sophie was the daughter of young Chief Nkwala and the granddaughter of *xʷistsmx̌ayqn*, Walking Grizzly, or Mighty Walks the Earth as Brent calls him in "Indian Lore," the most powerful chief during the fur trade in the Okanagan. He was known to the traders as Nicola or Nkwala (for more on both young and old Chief Nkwala, see Brent's "Indian Lore" in this section). Brent was baptized in 1871 at Okanagan Mission. Her brother Edward was born in 1872.

Brent lost both her father and mother when she was very young. Charles Houghton, one of the first settlers in the northern area of the Okanagan valley, had originally come to British Columbia from County Kilkenny, Ireland, in 1863, with his friends Lieutenants Forbes George Vernon and Charles Albert Vernon. All three claimed land grants available to the British military, though Houghton, the youngest commissioned officer in the entire British Army at the time of his retirement (Candy), had been a Captain for only three years rather than the fifteen required for a grant. He had served in the Crimean War, though he never actually reached Crimea. Finally, by 1872, his persistence won him a crown grant of 1,450 acres at the head of Okanagan Lake. He also pre-empted land on Coldstream Creek that later became part of Lord Aberdeen's Coldstream ranch (Ormsby, "Some Irish Figures" 76). Houghton set out to become a cattle rancher like many of his Irish settler contemporaries and friends such as J.C. Haynes (see "Hester Emily White" in this volume), but he left the Okanagan in 1872, after ten years in the region, selling his Coldstream property to the Vernons. In December of 1871, after British Columbia entered Confederation, Houghton was elected as a representative to parliament for the Yale-Kootenay district, and served for two sessions. While in Ottawa, he made contacts that enabled him to continue a military career in Canada (Ormsby, "Houghton"). According to oral history, he left after his wife, Sophie Nkwala, died in 1872 when Marie was two. In her essay "Indian Lore," Marie Brent attributes her mother's death to a broken heart after Sophie's sister and two brothers had died of tuberculosis.

Brent often refers to her father's military career in her writing. In 1873, after training in Quebec, Houghton was appointed lieutenant-colonel and deputy adjutant-general of the militia for District No. 11 (British Columbia) and posted in Victoria, and then in Manitoba and the North-West Territories in 1881 in Military District No. 10. From 1888 until 1896, he held his last command at the Quebec militia in Montreal (Parliament of Canada, "Houghton"). After his second wife, Marion Dunsmuir, died in 1892 (they had no children), Houghton called upon his daughter Marie to join him in Quebec, which she did. By 1908, Marie Houghton Brent had returned to the Okanagan and married William Brent.

Her father's achievements in the military are usually the subject of Brent's uncritical praise. Historian Margaret Ormsby presents a slightly different picture when she refers to the vetting that took place prior to Houghton's service during the Riel Rebellion in Manitoba in 1885. When asked by his father Prime Minister John A. Macdonald how Houghton would do as a militia officer during that conflict, Hugh John Macdonald, who lived in Winnipeg where Houghton was stationed, reported that Houghton had "'not much head and less judgement' and that 'day in and day out he drinks more than is good for him'" (Ormsby, qtd. in *Coldstream*: 7). Prime Minister Macdonald then chose General Middleton to lead the campaign, which was a disappointment to Houghton (7). In her unpublished memoir "My School Days," Brent also gives a glimpse of a vulnerable person rather than the military hero when she describes him as a "lonely looking old man" with tears "roll[ing] down his cheeks."

Leonard Norris, a founder and president of the Okanagan Historical Society, wrote to Brent in June, 1930, saying "Sometime I hope you will give us your recollections, all about what you remember about the Okanagan valley and the people in it and the people you met when you were in the east and up to the time you returned here." Brent had already published in the second of the annual Reports of the Okanagan Historical Society in 1927. In 1935, she published a ground-breaking analytical article, "Indians of the Okanagan Valley," unique among *OHS Report* essays in its strong stance on the superiority of Indigenous culture and on Syilx rights. (Shorter versions had appeared in 1930 and 1931). It was not until 1957 or 1958, however, judging from Brent's reference in her manuscript to Kelowna having a population of ten thousand, that Brent wrote down her personal reminiscences in "My School Days." The uneven handwriting and expression of the unedited draft, published below for the first time, also suggests it was written when Brent was in her late eighties, suffering from late-in-life infirmities. The informal, more intimate register of "My School Days" contrasts with the formal diction and tone of the early "Indians of the Okanagan," the latter perhaps edited by Norris. "My School Days" offers a lively reminiscence of Brent's girlhood and early adulthood and fills in many of the blanks in her life story as told in "Indian Lore," published in 1966.

In "My School Days," Brent describes herself as a timid "little mountain girl" in 1893, taking the train from the Okanagan to Montreal at the age of twenty-three to join her father. Her reminiscences show, however, that she had coped with many upheavals and transformations by then. At two years old, having lost both her mother and her father, she lived with her mother's relatives at Head of the Lake. According to her essay "Indian Lore," her great aunt Theresa Laurence, old Chief Nkwala's daughter (see the essay "Standing Between"), gave her the role as a young child of being the one to remember traditions. When she was around seven years old, she began schooling according to Euro-Canadian traditions, and moved from the Head of the Lake, nk'mapǝlqs, on the northern end of Lake Okanagan to the Mission (now Kelowna) to live with Theresa Laurence (Lawrence, Laurent) and then with her daughter Mary shortly after the Okanagan Mission Valley School opened in 1876. In 1880, Mary Laurence married settler Donald (Dan) Nicholson, whom Brent refers to as "an adorable old scotchman." (Nicholson, born in Ontario, had come to the Okanagan in 1876 and reports his age as twenty-five on their marriage record; Mary Laurence was nineteen). Brent's article "The Priest's Valley School," which she published in the OHS Report in 1927, tells us she also attended that school in Vernon in 1884 and 1885. In the fall of 1886, Brent was sent to the Convent of the Sisters of St. Ann in Kamloops where she boarded through 1887 and possibly until the spring of 1888, as payment was received for her up until that time. Convent records and "My School Days" show she had a love of music and received instruction in it, probably in piano. Returning to the Okanagan, she continued to attend school either in the Mission or in Priest's Valley until she made her way to Montreal around 1893.

In Montreal, Brent acted as her father's companion and hostess for several years, despite a yearning to continue her education. Her father returned to Victoria in 1897 and died a year later. Although details are few, Brent was now able to pursue a path of study, and according to "My School Days," entered into nursing at Mount Sinai Hospital in New York. There are no records of her there, but records were not kept then of students who did not graduate. Evidence of her attendance is supported by a letter from her husband William Brent (1873-1939) to the Veteran's Administration in Washington in which he refers (with gratitude, due to chronic ill health from his experiences as a soldier) to his wife's training at Mount Sinai hospital. "My School Days" tells us that Marie Brent's own "failing health" caused her return to the Okanagan. She is recorded in the 1901 Canadian census as living in the Okanagan Mission with Daniel Nicholson and his wife "Marie" (Mary Laurence).

After her marriage in 1908, Marie Brent settled into a farming life in the Okanagan Valley with William Brent, whom she had known since childhood when both attended the Mission School. Her husband's father, Frederick Brent, had been a founding trustee. Frederick Brent (1827-1919) was born in Germany and, after emigrating to the United States in 1854, became a soldier in the United States Army, discharged at Fort Colville, Washington territory, in 1859. In 1862, he married William's mother, Mary Ann Topakegut Ukatemaish (1838/9-1890), who also used the names Mary Anne Topake (not *nsyilxcn*), Marianne Titarstsa (*ti?tar̓sc̓a?*), Marianne Titinetsa (*ti?tnic̓a?*), Marianne Litinerestsende (not *nsyilxcn*), and Chulh-mitsa (*cu?ɬmic̓a?*) (Collins 28). Mary Ann was another daughter of Old Chief Nkwala, in Fort Colville, and they came to the Okanagan in 1865. Marie Brent's husband William, like Brent herself, had also left the valley and seen something of the world. He enlisted in February 1900 with the Strathcona Horse and fought in the Boer War in South Africa. He and his cohort returned to London in 1901 as heroes, receiving the keys to the city and the Queen's Medal. He then enlisted in Spokane for the Spanish American War and served as a drill sergeant at the Presidio in San Francisco until discharged for disability from a fall there later that year. He maintained close ties to those with whom he served until his death. William Brent also became one of the first city constables in Kelowna in 1906 and served as a provincial constable at Camp McKinney, a mining town northeast of Osyoos, in 1907.

In 1919, Brent and her husband developed a large market garden on land near the Head of the Lake where "my mother's only near relative, her uncle's daughter" lived (Brent, Letter to Ella Clark, August 23, 1957). This was Madeline Komasket, born Madeline Tonasket (1851-1937), the daughter of a son of Chief Nkwala, married to August Andrew or Komasket (1848-1930), and the place is now Komasket Park at Nkamapulks (Louis 59, 63). The Brents made an effort to work the land which Marie Brent says the government had "condemned because not worked" under the War Measures Act during World War I (Letter to Ella Clark, August 23, 1957). William Brent was awarded first prize for his agricultural efforts from eleven government agencies, according to his wife (Letter to Ella Clark, August 23, 1957). While Marie Brent connected to her Syilx relatives living off of the land in their own ways, she also had conflicts with some who saw the couples' enterprise as interference. Marie and William Brent left the area part way through 1925 (Letter to Ella Clark, August 23, 1957).

It was during this time that Marie Houghton Brent may have gathered stories such as "Coyote and Reindeer" and "The Legend of Shuswap Falls." The latter was published by the Okanagan Historical Society in 1948, and that version is printed here. "Coyote and Reindeer" comes from her personal papers at the museum and archives in Vernon, British Columbia, and is published here for the first time. Her husband also may have written some of his history of settlement in the Okanagan valley at that time, a reminiscence which remains unpublished. Brent suggests that her husband's local history had been completed in the late 1930s and given to the *Vernon News* (Letter to Hester White, n.d., 1938).

In 1936, Brent began a correspondence with Hester White, daughter of J.C. Haynes who had been one of the first settlers in the Okanagan and a friend of C.F. Houghton (see "Crossing Lines" in Part Three). We learn from this correspondence that she and William Brent were living in Lavington, British Columbia near Vernon, where they were farming and mining. After William Brent died in 1939 at the Shaughnessy Veteran's Hospital in Vancouver, Marie Brent went to live near her brother Edward Houghton and Milly Tonasket (Tomasket), Madeline Tonasket's daughter, in Omak, Washington, probably in 1940 or 1941. In 1952 or 1953, in her early eighties, she moved to Mrs. Ernestine Ames' nursing home just south of nearby Republic, Washington, where she lived until her death in 1968.

Brent's correspondence with White lasted from 1936 until 1962, a year before Hester White's death (see Part Three for the correspondence). It sheds light on numerous aspects of her writing, including her interest in local history and pleasure in writing; the tenacity and will which kept her writing through old age and various illnesses; and her determination to disseminate knowledge and understanding of Syilx history and particularly of Chief Nkwala and his line. She had written or supplied information for articles on her father, Colonel C.F. Houghton, in The *Vernon News* in 1927 and 1958, and her writing on the state of the Syilx of the Okanagan valley, as well as historical writing and legends, had appeared in *OHS Reports* in the 1930s, 1948, and 1953. Not until 1966, however, does the story of her own Syilx heritage and the history of Old Chief Nkwala appear in its pages.

Marie Houghton Brent in Republic, WA, c. 1961.
Courtesy of Greater Vernon Museum and Archives.

This material, Brent's story situated within her Syilx ancestors' history, had been in the forefront of Marie Brent's mind for at least a decade, if not for most of her life (see the essay "Standing Between"). Brent writes about Syilx history in letters to Ella E. Clark from 1956-1958; Clark, born in Tennessee in 1896, became a member of the English faculty in 1927 at Pullman State University in Washington and a professor from 1957 until her retirement in 1961. While in contact with Brent, she was working on her book *Indian Legends of Canada*, published in 1960, to which Brent contributed "The Legend of Shuswap Falls" and a speech by her ancestor *pəlk̓mulax^w* or Chief Pelkamulox (later incorporated into "Indian Lore"). Some accounts of Syilx history as told by Brent had appeared in a local Washington state newspaper *The Republic News-Miner* in 1958, reported by Goldie Putnam, a friend of Clark's. As well, Brent wrote about old Chief Nkwala and his ancestry in letters to Hester White, and a draft history of Chief Pelkamulox appears in Hester White's personal papers with the note "as told by Maria Brent to Hester White." An undated draft of Brent's memoirs had been put together in Republic, Washington, as told by Brent to Dorothea Sophia Sprengel, and an amplified version entitled "Indian

Lore" was published by the *OHS Report* of 1966, compiled by Mrs. Harold Cochrane, wife of the editor of the *OHS Reports* and active in the Vernon chapter. This most complete version is reprinted below.

Through her writing, Marie Houghton Brent offers so much to readers today. She passes on stories of the powerful and incorrigible Coyote in whom as a Syilx woman, she very much believed. She writes informed, persuasive pieces for the non-Indigenous people of Canada concerning the strength of her people's culture. She writes as a friend to Hester White. Her memories of her childhood and development provide insights on growing up Syilx of mixed heritage in the Okanagan and in Canada. Towards the end of her life she makes every effort to piece together the valuable history of her Syilx ancestors and pass that history on to the future. Throughout her writing, her intelligence, humour, commitment, and resilience are evident.

Coyote and Reindeer[21]

Long ago lived an Indian (Coyote) and with him, lived a Reindeer [Caribou] and his wife and two children.

Coyote told his friend the Reindeer to be very careful [saying] "my enemy may come and kill you," whereupon Coyote made a bow and arrows, and knowing where his friend the Reindeer went to eat some alkali, he went ahead of his friend and waited for him, and hid himself.

The reindeer, suspecting nothing, he went as usual to the lick, whereupon the coyote shot him through the [indecipherable] chest, then away coyote goes home.

After a while the deer comes home wounded, taking the arrow home and showing it to them, when coyote said show me.

"Yes I know the arrow" [said Coyote]. "It belongs to someone far away, now go make a sweat house & I will make my medicine and cure you there."

In the sweat house, the deer goes, also coyote, so in the heat of the place the fat of the deer melts, and so coyote sucks it all out.

Then the big deer dies.

In they go to tell the wife of the Reindeer that her husband died, so the wife was crying. Then coyote says to her "Now good lady, don't cry," and puts his hand on her forehead and then passes a knife under her chin, cutting her throat.

So now coyote has two carcasses to skin and eat, he sends his own wife away, not wishing to feed her from any of this. His wife was a gopher and had four children, all boys.

Coyote ate all the deer, then moves his house away to other quarters. He camps on the way. He is hungry and roasts one of his boys and eats him. The next day he goes on and camps, where he eats another kid. The next day again another one.

Then he comes along again next day and sees a woman and he asks her to tell him some news. So she says, well, coyote ate all his kids. Makes him mad, he runs at her with a dagger and stabs. She blows red paint on the blade. He looks at it & thinks it's blood so away he goes, not far away comes at a bluff, looks over and sees some people, way on next hill below.

They were mountain sheep. So he turns himself into a stump and takes his boy & lifts him up in one hand & turns him into a limb for the stump. And these other people are looking for eggs, got a lot of egg & buried them in a trench they had dug & piled on a lot of wood limbs of all sorts & cooked the eggs. Coyote being a great medicine man, he blows toward these people & brings a deep sleep to come upon them, so he and his boy go to the camp and he tells his boy to go to the other side and eat and he the other side. He told his boy, "Now don't eat the big eggs, you'll get sick. Give them to me to eat."

Then he takes all the egg shells and places them on the hips of all the sleeping people. This is why the mountain sheep are white on the hip.

He goes on from there, not far away he sees a lot of geese and lets a hoop [whoop] out to them, whereupon four tumbled down. Then he takes the bark off a tree and makes a kettle for boiling the geese in. His boy says to him "I think these birds are coming to—" but he says "No, they are dead," but the geese [start] flapping around. He breaks their arms but it was his boy's arm he breaks and the geese flew.

Went on a ways and came to a River where they saw a grizzly floating down stream.

He tells his boy to wade in, and bring out the bear. The boy was scared but he does go and barely gets it out. Coyote drags the carcass away and makes a hole in the ground and prepares to make a kiln to cook the animal—and to sleep they go, thinking in the morning they would have a feast.

As soon as they fell asleep, the fox comes and eats up all

their meat. Then the fox plays [a joke] with the [indecipherable] sleeper, takes some of the fat and makes putty and greases the coyote's mouth and whiskers up to his eyes and that of his boy's and both their hands. Coyote wakes up and sees his boy's mouth and face and hands. He gives his boy a good licking. The boy looks at him and tells him look at your own face & hands. So Coyote says, then I guess we both ate him, ...
[*circa 1919-1925?*]

The Legend of Shuswap Falls [22]

"A long, long time ago, when the world was young and fresh, before hatred, greed and strife entered, and all was peace and happiness, and all the animals lived harmoniously together, the Bear, Elk, Fox, Coyote and all animals and birds were ancestors of human beings.

"Coyote lived in a lovely but very lonely place far away from everyone, where he had no one with whom to speak or play or feast. At last he became very lonesome and made up his mind ever afterwards to break the monotony and invite all his friends once a year to a great feast and jollification.

"So he set himself to work and built a great rapid and gave it the name of Shuswap Falls. Then he made a big kettle out of stone with legs under it and hung it over the Falls. Over this he constructed a fish trap, also out of stone, where he could catch many salmon and boil them in the Big Kettle. Then Coyote made a seat for himself out of stone beside the Falls where he could watch the fish being caught and being cooked, and also where he could talk with his old cronies and at the same time see the sports and watch the feasting.

"When he got all this finished to his satisfaction, the buds on the fir trees were just bursting out. By this sign he knew the salmon run was due. So he called aloud for his friends to come and feast. His voice could be heard afar and near as it can even to this day; so it sounded in the long, long ago on every hill, in every vale and all Coyote's friends said, 'Hark! There is Coyote calling. Let us go.'"

"Coyote could distinguish who was coming as his friends called out to him on their way, accepting his invitation. He was over-joyed, running round and round to catch his tail, as he heard the bawl of the Grizzly, the howl of the Timber Wolf, the snort of the Elk, the hoot of the Horned Owl, the chatter of the King-fisher and all the other voices he knew.

"Soon they were all assembled and great was the astonishment and rejoicing when they beheld the wonder Coyote had wrought and the provisions he had made for their entertainment. It was a busy time, what with the feasting and the sports which lasted a fortnight with camp-fires burning brightly by day and by night, until all were dead tired, and the time came to depart. Then all shook old Coyote by the hand with grateful hearts for his hospitality. They all promised to come again when next the fir trees were bursting out into bud. So all went home happy.

Now all this happened a very long, long time ago. Now to this day when the firs are in bud each Spring, the hills around Shuswap Falls still re-echo the invitation call of Coyote and the answering call of Coyote's friends, and the camp-fire lights re-appear.

Wise people say this is only fancy, but we know better.

Such is the Legend of Shuswap Falls as narrated by the old folk of the Okanagan tribe, and translated from the Okanagan dialect by Mrs. William Brent.
[1929, 1948]

The Indians of the Okanagan Valley
Mrs. William Brent

When the Indians of the Okanagan Valley were discovered by the white men in 1811 they were not debased savages nor sunk in superstition and there is much to be said in favour of the view held by many that they were a people who at one time had probably attained to a higher degree of civilization than they enjoyed at the beginning of the last century.

They were not idolaters; they did not worship idols. Their religious tenets were simple; they believed in good and bad spirits and believed it was necessary to propitiate both. Their principal religious ceremony consisted of the chief calling his people around him in solemn conclave and then, taking the peace pipe, he blew three whiffs of smoke towards the four points of the compass, and three towards the heavens, in salutation of the invisible and invincible powers beyond. While this ceremony and their religious tenets may have been crude and elementary, there was nothing in either revolting to the finer feelings and instincts of the human heart.

These Indians did not burn witches at the stake as did the Puritans of New England, and such horrors as the auto de fe of the early Christian church and the modern abomination of birth control were alike unknown to them.

It is true that when a marriage was contracted the property consideration passed from the bridegroom to the father of the bride; but women were not bought and sold as chattels as in many eastern countries. Nor was the property consideration the only preliminary; the consent of the two families had to be obtained. A marriage was looked on as an important matter which might affect the honour and standing in the tribe, of the family. And here as elsewhere the story of true love did not always run smoothly; sometimes one of the families would withdraw the consent it had given or the young people might change their minds, and the bad blood thus engendered might involve the whole tribe and fierce fighting take place over the alleged insult or injury or for the possession of some dusky Helen of Troy.

In 1811 these people did not live in fortified villages and raise grain as did the ancient Hochelagans [Iroquois people who lived on the site of what is now Montréal.] It was not necessary for them to plant corn because they had an abundant supply of food in the fish and game and the edible roots and berries of the country, and their mobility—the ease with which they could move from place to place—probably served them better in case of attack than a fortification.

Alexander Ross in his book "Adventures on the Oregon or Columbia River" has this to say of the Okanagan Indians:

> The men lead an active life—between hunting, fishing and making canoes, they are always employed. Nor are the women less busy—curing fish, drying meat and collecting roots and firewood— with their family and domestic affairs their whole time is occupied and indeed they may be said to serve in the double capacity of wife and slave. They

have in general an engaging sweetness, are good housewives, modest in their demeanor, affectionate and chaste, and strongly attached to their husbands and family. Each family is ruled by the joint authority of the husband and wife, but more particularly the latter.

When this was written in 1849 Ross had been married for a considerable time to an Okanagan Indian woman and for that reason we may naturally suppose he would write favourably of them, but what he says is, in the main, probably true.[23]

Their social organization was loose, so loose as to border on anarchy. Each family was a law unto itself; and, while a kind of nominal authority was given to the chiefs by these self-governing families, the authority and privileges of the chief were strictly limited. They tolerated no dominant caste, and they refused to be priest-ridden. The outstanding trait in the character of these men was their independence and love of personal freedom. They would not submit to authority.

With the white man, what his neighbor thinks is a matter of first concern to him, because he knows that what is only public opinion today, tomorrow may crystalize and become a law which he will be forced to obey. No such consideration weighed with the Indian; always he knew he was free to do as he liked, and what his neighbor thought or did not think was a matter of complete indifference to him. The white man, ruled by the majority and therefore more or less always under the thumb of authority of some sort, may, as compared with the Indian, be more prone to take his opinions ready-made and follow the crowd, instead of standing on his own feet and thinking for himself.

The rigors of the life they followed tended in a marked manner to weed out from among them the weak, the vicious, and the incapable, so that today the average Indian, in mental endowment and acumen, is quite the equal of the average white man; it would be strange if this were not so. The want of anything like an adequate education is, however, a tremendous drawback to the Indians. The coming of the white man was not an unmixed blessing to him; but the white man has to the credit side of his account with the Indians two things at least—the schools and the inestimable boon of Christianity.

In Canada, roughly one man in a hundred is an Indian. So that the number of men of mixed Indian and white blood in this country must be small as compared with the total population. Yet when we consider the number of these men who have become prominent as legislators, teachers, members of the learned profession, and in the civil service, the number is astonishingly great. They seem to possess a certain mental aloofness, a freedom and independence of judgment which makes them different from the whites, pure blood; and these qualities make for leadership among men. The half breed will either live entirely to himself, or, if he takes part in community life at all, he is apt to forge to the front. These men are in a sense "well-born." They, on one side of the house at least, have descended from a race of men who for many generations never knew what it was to receive a command from another and feel that they were under compulsion and bound to obey that command. Always they were free men and, they say, blood will tell.

This is an aspect of Canadian history which seems to have been strangely overlooked, viz., the natural aptitude of men of mixed Indian and white blood, for public office and for leadership, as demonstrated in the history of Canada during the past hundred years.

When we see an Indian and notice his casual style of clothing himself, and his want of personal cleanliness, we are apt to grin; but, a few generations back, and the difference in manners and customs between the whites and the Indians was not perhaps so very marked as it is today. R. L. Stevenson, in his essay on John Knox, in comparing the manners and customs of that date with the manners and customs of the age in which Knox lived, says: "We could not let those great folks of old into our drawing rooms. Queen Elizabeth would positively not be eligible for a house maid."

Perhaps nothing illustrates more clearly the extent to which the whites have admitted the North American Indian to an equal footing with themselves, while refusing a similar recognition of the negro and the oriental, than what took place in Washington some time after the inauguration of President Hoover in 1929. The President's wife, Mrs. Hoover, gave a tea and sent an invitation to Mrs. DePriest, who was the wife of a member of the United States Congress, the representative from Chicago. The DePriests were negroes, and at once a storm of dissent and protest swept over the United States and much discussion followed in the press and on the platform. This simple act of official courtesy was looked on in some quarters as striking at the very foundations of society, and in some of the state legislatures in the south it was the subject of resolutions, and many speeches were made denouncing the action of Mrs. Hoover as fraught with evil and dangerous to the future welfare of the nation. In fact, the discussion was so widespread and warm that a new term was invented, "depriestism," meaning, the social recognition of the negro, and it was so much used that for a time it seemed likely we would have a new word added to the English language.

And all the while this unholy row was going on over the invitation to an afternoon tea, extended by Mrs. Hoover to the chocolate-colored lady from Chicago, who "came early, stayed late, and seemed to enjoy herself." Charles Curtis, the vice-president, was reported in the newspapers as being proud of his Indian blood, and proud of the fact that as a boy he was brought up with the tribe of Indians to which his grandmother, who was a half-breed Kaw Indian [Kanza, Kansa, a Native American tribe in Oklahoma and Kansas], belonged.

Yet this fact elicited no unfavorable comment whatever.

One trait which the Salish Indian has in common with all other Indians is his hatred of domination, of anything which interferes with his personal freedom. When the whites first invaded North America along the Atlantic Coast they tried to make slaves of the Indians but they found it was not profitable; the Indians never made satisfactory slaves. In captivity they soon died, and this fact was pleaded as a reason for importing negroes from Africa. The negroes while held in slavery increased and multiplied rapidly while the Indians became extinct. You can, by force, make a slave of an Indian, but you can't make him like it.

In watching the play on the stage, "Uncle Tom's Cabin," in the scene in which the villain, Legree, is abusing and maltreating his slaves, one feels instinctively that if they were Indians instead of negroes, Legree would soon have a knife driven into his back, and the perpetrator of the deed, if unable to escape, would await with stoic composure, death or whatever punishment might be meted out to him and no other denouement of the situation would seem natural. The meek submissiveness implied in the worlds of the old hymn "God bless the squire and his relations / And make us contented with our stations," has no place in the Indian character.

The Jew and the Indian have much in common. Both are individualistic, and both have a tenacious hold on life. It is hard to exterminate or hold either in subjection.

It was given to few white men to know the Salish Indians when they were at their best; when they were living their own life in their own way before they came into contact with, and were contaminated by the whites. But the few men of understanding who did, men like Father De Smet,[24] Father Morice,[25] Alexander Ross and Simon Fraser,[26] speak highly of them.

None of the Indians, however, received much consideration at the hands of the whites. There is a world of meaning in [John Greenleaf] Whittier's well-known lines:

> Beside the scared squaw's birch canoe
> The steamer smokes and raves,
> And village lots are staked for sale
> Above old Indian graves.

And perhaps this gentle [American] Quaker poet himself, delighting as he did in the rapid development of the West, would have seen little to object to in squaring off a townsite by encroaching upon an Indian graveyard.

These people are not at their best. When a revolution occurs the worst traits in the character of a people are soon manifest, and this was clearly shown at the time of the French Revolution. But who could be so unjust as to judge the French people by what took place then? When the revolution had burnt itself out, however, the people and the country still remained. The social, commercial and intellectual life of the nation, which had been disrupted, soon readjusted itself, and the lives of the people soon resumed their normal course. As Carlyle has told us, after the people of Paris had cut their king's head off they were rather surprised on the morrow to find that France was still France.[27] But the Indians never had a chance to come back. The invasion of their country by the whites not only disrupted their usual mode of living and crumpled up and destroyed their old-established customs and usages which had endured for centuries, but it deprived them of

75

their country as well. They were soon exiled to the reservations. The Salish Indian of the Okanagan Valley today is an expatriate, a man without a country, although still dwelling in the land of his forefathers. It will be many years yet before these people fully recover from the shock of this double catastrophe.

The immediate hope for them lies in the education of the children. President Garfield once said he never saw a boy but he felt like taking off his hat to him, for, he said, he never knew what possibilities might lie buttoned up beneath the boy's ragged jacket. Nor should we be too supercilious when we notice those chubby-cheeked, black-eyed little imps of children to be seen playing about on the reservations; we do not know what splendid men and women some of them might make if they were properly trained, if they were educated and their mental faculties drawn out and developed, and they were given a chance in life. Without education they are doomed irrevocably to the narrow and unprofitable life their parents now lead.

Captain Long Lance, chief of the Blackfoot Indians, a full-blood Indian whose Indian name is Buffalo Child, is perhaps the ablest and most reliable exponent of the mode of life followed by the Indians before they came in contact with the whites, we have. He lived with his tribe until he was about eighteen years of age when he came in contact with the missionaries who saw to it that he got some education. He joined the Canadian Expeditionary Force [of World War I] as a private and came back from overseas with the rank of captain.

Later he published a book also called "Long Lance" from which the following passages are copied, as illustrating some aspects of life as seen from the viewpoint of a young Indian:[28]

> Page 8. During the long winters in the far northern zones when the days were just a few short hours, our mothers spent a good deal of their time each day teaching and training us youngsters into the ways of an Indian. Like the white boy we had to take our schooling during the winter. Our mothers spent about two hours every day teaching us how to speak our tribal language correctly. That is a very important point with the Indian— his language—as his social status in later years depends on his ability to handle his grammar properly. Any Indian allowed to grow up without being able to speak his

language with absolute correctness is relegated to the rank of an outcast of the tribe, and he is never allowed to speak in public, lest his linguistic defects should be passed on to others—and especially the children—and thus defile the tribal tongue. Therefore, since we had no books or written language, our mothers had to spend many hours drilling into us the ancient grammar of our ancient speech which is very elaborate, having nine conjugations, four genders and eight forms.

Page 11 Our moral training was entirely in the hands of our mothers. They would tell us about our Great Spirit, and they told us when we grew older the Great Spirit would appoint some other good spirit in the spirit world to be our guide and look after us. This spirit would give us our *medicine*—lucky charm—our medicine song and our death song; the former to be sung at all times and the latter when we were passed on to die. We had no Bible as the white boys have, so our mothers trained us to live right by telling us legends of how all of the good things started to be good. We had a legend for everything— from the care of our feet to the *great shame* befalling those who told lies. Many long winter afternoons we would sit around our mother as she made skins into clothing and listen to the magic stories of righteousness which she was passing on to us from the dark, unknown depths of our history.

Page 34. We never allowed our old people to want for anything and whenever any one of them would stop as he made his silent dignified way through the camp and put his arm across our shoulders and utter a little prayer for us to the Great Spirit we would feel highly honoured. We would stand quietly and when he was through we would remain in our tracks, respectful and silent, until he had disappeared. We looked on our old people as demi-gods of a kind and we loved them deeply; they all were our fathers. This respect for our aged is so deeply bred into us that today I have not the courage to dispute the word of an old person. To me all old people are demi-gods to be heeded and revered at all times.

Page 38. In all our games, in all our playing, I would say that honour was the outstanding characteristic. None of us ever disputed the other fellow's record or the other fellow's word. Our parents taught us that lying was the *great shame*, that it was the *battle shield behind which the coward hid his shame.* We believed them and seldom did we have occasion to assert our truthfulness to our playmates.

This is the prayer they offered up at the annual Sun Dance, their Thanksgiving:

> Page 151. Great Spirit, our Father, help us and teach us in the way of the truth, and keep me and my family and my tribe so that we may be in good condition in our minds and bodies. Teach all of the little ones in your way. Make peace in all the world. We thank You for the sun and the good summer weather again; and we hope they will bring us good crops of grass for the animals, and things to eat for all the people.

In *French Pathfinders in North America* the author, William Henry,[29] makes this observation on the Indian mode of carrying on a debate:

> The discussion was conducted in a manner that would seem to us exceedingly tedious. Each speaker, before advancing his views, would carefully rehearse all the points made by his predecessor. This method had the advantage of making even the dullest minds familiar with the various aspects of the subject and it resulted in a so thorough sifting of it that when a conclusion was reached it was felt to be the general sense of the meeting.
>
> From this it will be evident that public speaking played a large part in the Indian life. This fact will help to account for the remarkable degree of eloquence sometimes displayed. If we should think of the Indian as an untutored savage burning at times with impassioned oratory under the influence of powerful emotions, we should miss the truth very widely. The fact is there is a class of professional speakers who have trained themselves by carefully listening to the ablest debaters among them and have stored their memories with a large number of stock images taken from nature. These metaphors which give to Indian oratory its peculiar character were not therefore spontaneous productions of their imagination, but formed a common stock used by all speakers as freely as orators in civilized society are wont to quote great authors

and poets. Among a people who devoted so much time to public discussion a forceable speaker wielded great influence.

And this author makes this further observation:

> Indian government like Indian society was just such as had grown up naturally out of the conditions. It was not at all like government among civilized people. In the first place there were no written laws to be administered. The place of these was taken by public opinion and tradition, that is, by the ideas handed down from one generation to another and constantly discussed around the camp fire and the council fire. Every decent Indian was singularly obedient to this unwritten code. He always wanted to do what he was told his fathers had been accustomed to do, and what was expected of him. Thus there was a certain standard of conduct.

Judge Begbie had this to say of the Indians of British Columbia after he got acquainted with them:

> My impression of the Indian population is that they have far more natural intelligence, honesty and good manners than the lowest class—say the agricultural and mining population—of any European country I ever visited, England included.[30]

The census returns of 1931 show that Canada with a total population of 10,376,786 has 122,911 Indians, and the Government returns show that during the fiscal year 1933-34 $4,232,506 was spent by the Indian Department, which is about the average sum, and one wonders what the Indians get out of it.

The thorough grounding in the grammar of his native tongue which he received from his mother, and the moral precepts taught him in his youth coupled with the frequent opportunities he had of listening to the men debating matters relating to the welfare of the tribe, must have been a splendid training for a young lad destined to follow the Indian mode of life. It was an education in the truest sense of the word. But this education, elementary as it was, has fallen into decay without anything being substituted for it.

This country is not doing its duty by the Indians. They are degenerating, and yet they are a people capable of accomplishing much if they were given the opportunity. They should be enfranchised at once and given the vote. An adequate number of schools should be built and the attendance of their children made compulsory. Also some sort of municipal government should be established on the reserves and the Indians given the power to tax themselves.

Canada needs her Indians. When all the different races that now dwell within the confines of Canada are finally fused into one—the future Canadian race—it will be all the better for the infusion of the blood of this virile and individualistic race. We have wasted our Indian tribes as we have wasted our forests and fisheries and much else.

[1935]

My School Days [31]

One day I remember an elderly woman arrived on a beautiful horse. She was of light complexion, tall handsome—my mother told me that "she was her aunt, her father's full sister, they were chief N Kwala's son & daughter, chief of all the Okanagan and Colville. All were dead but her. She was my grand aunt & she came after me to go to school a long way off, & not to cry—I was a big girl, now 7 years old[32] you've got to learn to be nice and don't talk Indian to any body, it will interfere with your English school and hard for you to learn. You will be with a little girl, this woman's little daughter, this woman was married to a Boston man—& clever he coached us & got us to a good start—[33]

Next day we had to ride 35 miles or more behind her. This woman put me behind her the last I remember— I learned to ride tied on to a pack horse before that—going a long way off somewhere, but don't know where—from the Okanagan,[34] that's all.

It turned out I was going to Okanagan Mission Valley Public School,[35] with good teachers & [the] only school between Kamloops & way down below Boundary Line South. My first teacher was a young woman from the city of old Quebec, a grand girl who afterwards became a nun in the cloistered nunnery The Ursiline Convent at Quebec—with the world closed out behind her forever; shook hands with mother, father, with 2 fingers through a barred wicket near front door—her name was Sister Mary _____ (forget).[36] I went to see her, with my father after some years' time,[37] the sweetest music was playing way back in there--a nun came to speak to me, I asked for my teacher, she said, Sorry, she died a few years ago. I wept what with that sweet, sad music many things came to my memory. My father had to take me away from there, I guess he thought of my convent days not too long before.

Now that school house she taught us in [Okanagan Mission School] was a big log house built by all the neighbours, from far and near.[38] There were children growing up too fast, took ten to open the school but they had to borrow one boy from below the Boundary Line. No school there either. One man, farmer, just beginning had to come to school to make the ten[39]—these big boys had all gone home farming before I came & I never got to know them, till now.

This was the most disciplined school that ever was, we walked on tip toes in school & [did] not let our pen scratch on paper. Keep Mum, sit up straight, or there was a hazel ruler—

I plodded along & caught up with a dum[b] girl that was already a year in school. We caught up to a big class then the big kids got mad at me & told me that I got to read fast now. Not very long till I passed one of them on a little spelling, Bird, and then I was in the dog house. I guess, & left my partner some where behind [added note, "I don't know"]—then I had to scramble. Lessons were difficult to me but I worked very hard and never once fell down—but I talked to a girl next to me asking a word & all about it, then I was called up to stand way out where I saw others stand ahead of the girls' desks with a long strip of red flannel on white string tied around my head. I tell you there were pearly tears on the scarlet strip—

Another day I was taken up to the Tribunal, teacher's desk, for singing a song. Oh dear, nipped my singing career in the bud by the same girl. Teacher asked me to sing, I did, it went this way—

> Poor old doctor don't you cry, don't you cry
> Your sweetheart will be here by m by
> When she's dressed in blue
> That's the sign she'll marry you

Teacher turned her face away, thought she was going to lick me, but [she] turned & said, little girl don't sing that again, I suppose you heard somebody sing that—I said yes, a French man.

Another time I was nipped in the bud, I sure would have been a born sculptress—I looked back at my clay works, when I was pulled away & saw a little tiny stream of water running to [the] left & against a small bank behind the water, leaning, there was a small horse a little cow & colt & [I] remember I was bawling, brush [bush or shrubs] all around I know not where—never saw it or clay again. Suppose I was white clay up to my knees—don't even know who got me—don't remember being punished, not a thing—but I saw clay no more since.

But now to my school days again. It seems my old grand aunt died.[40] I found myself with another relative still going to the same school. She, a beautiful young woman ½ French ½ Indian, I think the most beautiful woman I've ever seen—spoke French, English & Okanagan Indian and Chinook. So did I. Should have studied languages. She was too big to go to school when school opened. Her name was Mary Lawrence (Laurent) & her father died there[41] & her foster mother made her marry an adorable old Scotchman, Donald Nicolson,[42] who bought that old place which my grand father bought, then he got killed,[43] then William Peon got it his [Brent's grandfather's] brother in law, then sold it to Donald Nicolson our old man.[44]

He sold it years after to Mr. Singer of Singer Sewing Machine Co. in England—bought & now is the show place of Kelowna with city below it. You see the tall trees from East Side, East from Okanagan Lake, overlooking Kelowna from East side, rows of Carolina popplars face you, on brow of Hill as you approach West Side Ferry [terminal] on Okanagan Lake going East, now Cariboo Alaskan Highway 97, now right thro' town—now 10,000 people in City of Kelowna with boat houses along the beach, for this is where the yacht races are run now. Where poplars are is the place from which I went to school, Mission School House & seemed so long a time. Walked 3 miles to school & 3 miles back rain or shine or 30 below zero,—snow—same. Roses [wild rose bushes] on road were my companions summer time.

There were 2 old Frenchmen, August Gillard & Blondeau,[45] latter died they said don't know what year. Mr. Gillard called me "My gal Marad." "Huh, cor-ron, de, dieu." One day he came in a hurry & said to my cousin, Mary, Mary, where Don, where boy, I want my horses, mares, quick—He brought a little nephew out & his mother, 2 brothers & a sister from Paris after Civil War there. He got him to go to school with me to learn English & we borrowed another boy, too, by this time, to go to school. I was glad to have company, I had been alone for a long time. One day I nearly froze to death. A man on horse back happened to come along, saw me standing in middle of the road, that lonely road, and everything he asked me, I answered Nothing, nothing or don't know. I had come half way. He said I nearly froze. It was a lonely road. He reached down & grabbed me by the collar of coat, lifted me up & tucked me under his coat. I only remember getting to the house & him calling Mary, Mary if I ever catch you sending this little girl to school again 30 below zero I'll see about it.

My poor mother had died of consumption before [her] time before this. I knew they said they got all my horses & beautiful milk cow big heifer both pure bred short horn [and] work horses & saddle horses. I never lost time at school but rode [a bit ?] up at 4 o'clock a.m. When the rest got up—helped with the dishes then off to school. Little french boy, with flaming red hair, no English only I understood him, that helped—one day he came running to me at school crying & showed me, he said Suezienne (Susanne) say bud wars in my han - oh (said bad words in his hand—hurt it, I guess). I patted it & said all right, he says aw wight—he forgot. He grew up & joined up in army, 1st World War, fought for France but came back to Kelowna—married a french girl too & they had red headed little daughters, grandmothers by now I suppose.

Then I went to the convent [in] Kamloops & left my little boy pals to go to school on [the] stage[coach]—1st day 35 miles, then 36 miles, then 75 miles. I had friends all the way. They knew who I was, I knew the old stage driver too. I was lucky all the way—he changed horses that were ready for him all the way. Barnerd's [Barnard's] stage between Kamloops & Okanagan Mission Valley—only a few miles to city of Kelowna now—Mr. Barnerd of Kamloops District raised a lot of fast driving horses for the Stages to the Okanagan Valley, Aschcroft, coast way, Nicola Valley, Merritt way—before the trains came in. I suppose I saw one train coming back, at Kamloops. C.P.R. going East to Winnipeg I believe—built thro' the Selkirks and the Rockies, where Banff was built for the C.P.R. Trade (Canadian Pacific Railway). Now Sea to Sea as part of all Railway & boats which encircle the world long since. Empress boats on one ocean, Princesses on the other — from Victoria British Columbia to Yokahama in connection with this R.R., from Quebec to Liverpool, England. Ocean Liners — I saw them all later, each a glorious dream. I saw all the Naval ships from Britain, Scotland, Italy, Empress of Ireland too—into port at Quebec & smaller ships steam into port [of] Montreal in summer—now to be a great water way for all—USA ships as well as Canadian & all clear to Midway & continent.

This poor lonely little girl arrived at Convent School,[46] where I was supposed to be—when I saw the horses drive off that took me there & knew I was not to see horses again for a long time. The old man said good by to me. He asked me if I was all right—I thanked him & said yes I was fine. He turned away. My heart sank, that night I cried.

I liked the sisters [they] were sweet to me and always were. They said I was not a stranger, they knew all about me, I must not be lonesome there were nice little girls coming tomorrow & everything was fixed up for me, just go ahead & enjoy every thing, they would take care of me—

But I thought of my beautiful horse I left behind. I was sad at heart, my horse & I were great pals. He might do things to others but he was always good when I rode him. I had a California Cowgirl saddle. Once I rode him for 35 miles, I was all alone tho he was not too gentle, he never did a thing. I had to go alone that time he got sick & my cousin & her husband had a fast, strong driver, they never worried about me, I was always allright—with a horse. I never met a soul, no body on the road until I was 5 miles from Vernon. Now, a young man came off the hills. I knew him well, he was on a survey job. Asked me why I was alone, tho' he was not surprised, he thought I was going to compete but I told him Barney got sick with colic 10 miles out of Kelowna— he says good job he did not roll with you on him, how could you ever get on him again, he would not stand. Next day are races in Vernon—I was booked to ride around the race track with another girl ½ french ½ Indian a lovely girl, wonderful rider, but my horse could not take it & she was not in trim. Anyway only chance I ever had to ride on the race track—with my beautiful, dark, chestnut blooded horse. I rode him back to Kelowna day after races, 35 miles easy—had company tho. That was my last ride on him—fast walker, ordinary horse trotted to keep up to him—I never saw my Barney again.

While I was in Convent in Kamloops British Columbia with the Rev. Sisters of St. Ann. This order teach & have big schools.[47] We got a visit from their headquarters, from Montreal, on a Tour of Inspection. This head Nun, Teacher & Superintendent, is called the Rev. Mother of all Canada—all were under her jurisdiction & under McGill University.[48] She had a rest for 3 days there, then on to Victoria, Vancouver was only Port Moody yet then. I won the gold medal—can't take it with you but I was on Honor Roll, that burned when Convent burned. This Rev. Mother of all Canada— with big dark eyes, was handsome, jolly, medium height, looked commanding. You never know who they are, until something happens.

She gave us all strict examinations—quite a number in my class, one by one they had to leave the floor. I found myself standing alone. I stood up firmly then, but hoped I would not go down. I answered on & on till it came to one question. I studied & reasoned to myself, then answered from one angle thisaway & that way what could be, trying hard all the time to get an answer. At last, she said to me "dear child, there is no such thing. You did well." Tears rolled down. I felt, She made a fool of me. Maybe my nerves were about gone, I cried & could not stop. She came from her seat & put an arm around me & led me to my seat. She said, I am sorry my dear, I did not mean to make you feel bad. Cheer up, I am going to give you all a ½ holiday, I will ask the Superior. It was a wicked gruelling but I think it meant a lot for me—

The next year, I got a chance to go to Nome on way to the Northern Coast, north of the Cariboo country. From Victoria straight up coast.[49] A big school was being built up there by our Sisters of St. Ann and my own little teacher in our convent was going to be made Superior up there—mines were booming it seems and she asked for me to be with her, help teach and study on my music especially.[50] I was crazy to go—I wanted music. Summer holidays came on & my foster mother wanted me to come back to Okanagan. When Fall came again, I could not go back to Kamloops school.[51] I never did get over this disappointment & leaving my horse. I lost what I had won in Convent, it was better than any scholarship now. My way was paved dear sisters.

Many things happened, sicknesses & deaths, seemed I was born to be a nurse, even so young—then I got able to look after myself. Then my father sent for me. Of course I went there in a few months time when things all settled down again with my folks. I remember then it was 1893.

<u>Little Mountain girl travels alone:</u> I remember somebody said it was July, 1893 — & said Maria you should go now to Montreal. Your father will worry about your travelling alone. Canadian Pacific Railroad now ran from coast to coast—I was put on Train by dear friends with full instructions as to my destination. Conductor said is this the little girl? Thank you Mam, every conductor on our whole Line already are instructed by Col. Houghton. We'll all take good [care] of her.

It was still July after I arrived in Montreal, my father had been to the depot early morning, but [the] train was hours late it seems. Then he instructed his house keeper to meet the next train & be there before time. Conductors put me with a Scotsman & little family & a very sick mother. I was standing with them, he was going to take me to my father's house, when I heard a woman's voice call to the conductor, heard her say, a girl from Vancouver help me find her, she's got off the train. I told my friends, must be my father's housekeeper Mrs. Martin—he walked up to her and the conductor & asked who she was, it was Mrs. Martin and [she] took me home. Father was [in] his office in Drill Hall.

I could have gone to college in Montreal then. On thinking over it all, father asked me if I still wanted to go to college: "he would rather I stayed home under his tuition, he would teach me many things I should know to carry me through life, things I knew nothing about. I can't be at school all my life, I knew enough now as far as this is concerned to go through the world. University boys, even, are walking around uselessly—" He left me to decide, he had a housekeeper—

I looked at him. He was a lonely looking old man & looked so sad, tears rolled down his cheeks. I said I'll stay home, just what you say. What a mercy I learned of human nature from my childhood up. Instinct—I suppose. It seemed all a dream, all heart aches. In fact I had no childhood, seemed a duty all the way—& all our folks, dead.[52] I wept & still weep—big world was too big & going too fast for me, & still is going too fast—I did not know the outside world—father's friends were all so lovely to me, men, & women, they said it was nice to meet a real western girl, no pretence. Even Vancouver, as Port Moody then, barely known in the East. Victoria, older & [the] capital, was better known—of course we knew them all from the Boundary Line to Victoria, for instance, before leaving. . . . [an indecipherable line].

. . . lights, evening & morning in Wintertime [in the Okanagan], they are blue, indigo blue, like the blue, blue sky—and you drive along side these lakes for 35 miles with this landscape before you—we had our narrow, twistie little roads nearly straight up and straight down. You could fall off them at any time if you did not know them, 300 ft. straight down, especially in one place, we had a team of firie colts hitched on to our democrats had a narrow escape from going overboard. Nobody spoke—horses got scared too—all these kind of things Victoria people used to like, we had a lot of these visiting us, at the old Kelowna place, never knew when they were arriving, never knew when they were coming. Our dear old highland Scotchman loved to have them, always plenty for everybody. There was a kind of hotel about 6 miles away at old Mission before I left for Montreal, they did not want that —

One summer evening I was back from school in the Okanagan, & had peeled a panful of potatoes & carrots & stuff. This time I did not walk up to the fence where animals got all that [peelings] in a trough, I got on the kitchen stoop & fired the whole works far as I could & on their way they caught one of the big swells [important persons] of Victoria, from his chin all down the front of his beautiful suit. He yelled, so did I, when I threw [the] pan, water & all, on him. He was hitting [heading?] for a nice place he knew there in days gone by, he just got off the stage[coach], he never saw me until I threw stuff, nor I him. When he saw me, he chased me all over the place, never caught me, I was like a deer. They yelled to him "you can't catch her"—he was sure puffing—all got a kick out of it—never saw him again.

A few days before I left for Montreal, I had to take an old Insurance Man all around the Valley in single rig, he could not drive & all were in hayfield so I asked for Fleeta—I did not wish to be all day on the road. I think he did not forget that ride in a hurry—got all over & back pretty quick. Met one farmer that [indecipherable] while she was inside I had to tie Fleeta up to the post. She would not stand—she was on the bit.

[fragment indecipherable, written partly off the page] . . . country near & joining these 3 cities [possibly Vernon, Kelowna, and Penticton] where there [are] only a few residents in the whole country—in 1919—to 1925—school busses from miles. No kid walks now. This was where I got my big English feet from—walked so far. Some of these little places looks down on you from way up on what look like cliffs but beautiful & all look onto gorgeous scenery. All this my father dreamed long years before, on account of [the] grand soil [in the Okanagan], and for this old dream he pined all the rest of his days, God bless him and all like him, too fine to live—I weep sometimes when I think of all this, till I could die—and when I hear a military band play bag pipes & all that stirring music—I can see him at the head of his men, his officers close to him—

You could pick him out among a thousand men—what a bearing—and what a smile and he wanted his Okanagan home & hills all these years. He would not go to parliament until he had to, left 3 times & back again before he made it away.[53] Returned from the army in old country, then put him on the Reserved List & [he] must go when called.[54] This Army Life, when they're done with you, put you on the shelf—

Little Canada, God bless her, stood up under all kinds of Official Burdens and heart breaks—

Again, I was alone in the big world after being sheltered from every thing[55] & it made my heart feel numb. This, all this, was why I got sick & failed 8 lbs. every 10 days till I had to give up my nurse's career in New York—Mount Sinai Hospital.[56] I had money troubles, loneliness, knew all the Estates [inheritance from C.F. Houghton?] were slipping away from me, no body I could talk to—then I pined away for the blue hills & Lakes of the Valley in the Okanagan—I so loved. I had nervous prostration, & one so young—never told a soul even my fathers Life Insurance for me failed & only 50% given to me refunded—
[circa 1957-58]

Indian Lore

EDITOR'S NOTE: The following series of stories on Indian life in North Central Washington, the Okanagan and surrounding area by Marie Houghton Brent were compiled by Mrs. Harold Cochrane of Vernon and checked by references in The Bureau of American Ethnology, The American Museum of Natural History, Anthropology in British Columbia and the American Anthropological Association.[57]

My Life . . . Marie Houghton Brent (Indian Mother's Tradition)

Father[58] fell in love and married a young Indian princess, grand-daughter to the great N'Kwala. It was Chief N'Kwala in person that married his granddaughter, Sophie N'Kwala to my father. It must have been 1868 or 1869.[59] It was the custom at that time to have the chief marry couples as there were no priests there. A chief could marry any two people. It was the only law there. N'Kwala was the chief of all the Okanogans[60] (Book of Ethnology, Smithsonian Institution, Washington, D.C.). I am proud to state "I am his great grandchild." I was born on December 5th, 1870, and father was on his second 700 head of cattle. I was baptized at the Okanagan Mission in the diocese of Kamloops, June 1, 1871.

When I was two years old, father finally accepted and became the first Member of Parliament at Ottawa for Yale-Kootenay District of British Columbia. He was active in late 1872 and 1873 in Sir John A. Macdonald's cabinet. My brother Edward was born in 1872. We were left with our grandmother.

In an Indian tribe they pick one sober child with a good memory and train them to remember the story of their family and their ancestors. I was chosen for this. It was my great grandfather's daughter that taught me (my grand aunt, old N'Kwala's daughter, young N'Kwala's sister). I now lived with my grandfather's sister. My great aunt was from Colville. She was married to a Frenchman direct from France. Her name was Teresa N'Kwala and his name (in English was Laurence) in French was Cyprienne Laurent. My great aunt spoke French too.

My great aunt taught me as a child the following tradition, which she in turn learned from her father, the old Chief N'Kwala.

Historical Events in the Lives of the Chiefs
As I Remember them — By Marie Houghton Brent

My historical narrations open with Chief Pelka-mu-lox (3-4 Number in the book of Ethnology).[61] Chief Pelga-mu-lox came from a long line of Chieftains who were natural born rulers. Chief Pelka-mu-lox was born a chief in the North Spokane, somewhere around 1675 or 1680 of an Okanogan mother, daughter of an Okanogan Chief from the head of Okanogan Lake. He married first an Okanogan woman (3-4a) from N'kamaplex [nk'mapɑlqs, north end of Lake Okanagan]. She was the mother of his little son N'kwala (49) afterwards called by the Hudson Bay headman (Nicolas) Hwis-tass-em-tre'gen pronounced Whis-tass-um-'ken. This is the title he inherited and means "Mighty Walks the Earth." This name is said to be of Spokane Indian origin, according to the book of ethnology. This son N'Kwala later became known as the Old Chief N'Kwala, and the Great Chief N'Kwala. He was born 1780 or 1785, and died about 1871 [1859]. He is also referred to as Nicoli and Nicolas. Chief Nicoli and Chief Nicolas.

Events in the Life of Chief Pelka-Mu-Lox

Chief Pelka-mu-lox, other spelling Pila-ka-mu-lah-uh.[62] Chief Pelka-mu-lox was chief in North Spokane, connected to the Okanogans through his mother who was the daughter of an Okanogan Chief from the head of Okanogan Lake. Chief Pelka-mu-lox, my great-great-grandfather travelled far in his time. He ruled the different bands of his own people, had business relationships with neighboring tribes and was acquainted with the Flatheads, Coer [Coeur] d'Alenes, Shoshoni, and Blackfeet [or Blackfoot, in Canada] tribes. It was the habit of his tribe together with the Kulspelm [Kalispell], Kootenias [Kootenays], and sometimes the Nes Perces [Nez Perce] and the Coer d'Alenes to band together against the Blackfoot people and cross the mountains to hunt buffalo.

It was on one of these hunting expeditions that Chief Pelka-mu-lox met a party of Canadian trappers of Courier des bois at the eastern end of Hells Gate Pass, near the site of the present town of Helena, Montana. Pelka-mu-lox and his people made friends with the trappers and in the fall when they set out on the return trip, two of the trappers accompanied them (Legace, a Frenchman and Finan MacDonald, a Scotchman). These two men were made guests of the Colville Chief, who took them to their winter quarters at Kettle Falls, on the Columbia, at the north end of the Colville Valley. They in turn, (Legace and MacDonald) married the two daughters of the Chief and afterwards had children by them.

It was here that Chief Pelka-mu-lox made his great speech to the white men, and his people. Chief Pelka-mu-lox thought the white men were spirits come to look after him and his people. When the Indians heard this they all wanted to hear about the wonderful people.

After exacting a promise from the white men to stay with the Colville Chief and a promise from the Colville Chief to take care of the white men, he (Pelka-mu-lox) made this speech to the white men in the presence of the Colville Chief and his followers.

The Chief's Address to the White Men (He First Saw)

> You are my white children, and I do not want to lose you. I want you to live in my territory. I have a big country, big enough for all of us. I have plenty of everything— enough for all of us, for our children and for our children's children.
>
> Our mountains are green and full of fruits. We have many roots for food. We will show you which ones to eat and which ones not to eat, so that you will not be poisoned. We have grouse and many other birds for the hunt. We have plenty of deer for meat and hides. We have all kinds of fur, large and small for use, and salmon to eat.
>
> As long as the waters run and until yonder hill is no more, you and I stay here, your children and my children. From my waters, I drink, you drink. From my fruits I eat, you eat. From my game, I eat, you eat. You are my white children stay with me.[63]

Chief Pila-ka-mu-la-uh (Pelka-mu-lox) went into winter quarters with his Okanagan wife near Penticton. Chief Pelka-mu-lox was a descriptive and forceful speaker. He spent the winter and spring telling his wonderful stories of the white men. At one of the feasts given in his honor, when he had almost finished, a chief from Seton Lake [freshwater fjord at Lillooet, British Columbia], afraid he might lose his chieftainship arose and declared all these stories false. That there were no people with white skins, or eyes blue like the skies, or light short curly hair like wood shaving, who wore clothes made of woven stuff, which kept them warm without making it hard to move. There were no weapons that could kill birds in flight. There were no moccasins one could walk over cacti and not get stuck. No weapon that could kill animals as far as across the Fraser River. That nothing could be thrown so fast you couldn't see it. There was no weapon that made a noise like thunder and smoke like a fire at the same time. There was no animal that one could ride that ran faster than a buffalo. He said Pelka-mu-lox was a liar and shouldn't be listened to by men and warriors. It can't be true a stick could make thunder, make smoke and fire and kill all the same time. He must be a liar. No animal beat buffalo.[64]

This was a challenge for Chief Pelka-mu-lox to get bow and arrow. The little Chief shot him with two arrows before he could get his bow and arrows. Chief Pelka-mu-lox's own people took him to their camp.

Chief Pelka-mu-lox called his little son to him. "Hear me. I make this little boy a Chief in my place. I leave my boy in my brother's care." The brother and son saw Chief Pelka-mu-lox die. Chief Pelka-mu-lox means "Revolving Earth."

Chief Pelka-mu-lox was buried at his winter quarters at Na-kam-a-plex. Na-kem-a-plex means at head of Okanogan Lake.

This son that Pelka-mu-lox made chief on his death bed was Chief N'Kwala. Chief N'Kwala when grown to manhood did avenge his father's untimely death, and did show this tribe that what his father said was true.

Chief Pelka-mu-lox was the first chief to bring white men into this country and the country of the Okanogans, Okanogan Basin in Washington and extended into the Similkameen and the great Okanogan Lake in British Columbia. The Okanogans were a powerful tribe when the fur traders first came among them.

Events in the Life of Chief N'Kwala As I Remember Them

My great grandfather, Chief N'Kwala was chief of all the Okanogans and Colvilles. He was born about 1780 or 1785. There are many ways to spell his name depending on the references. N'Kwala, Nicola, Niqualeas, Niqualla, N'Kuala, and Ni-kua-la

[N'Kwala and other spellings are all variants of Nicola]. He was the son of Chief Pelka-mu-lox. He was made chief when only a lad on the death of his father, Chief Pelka-mu-lox.

Chief N'Kwala (Nicola) was considered a very wealthy man, he had numbers of fine fur robes and other wealth, large bands of horses and before 1858 had a good many head of cattle. The first of these cattle he obtained from some Indians and whites and half Indians from Colville and Spokane. He also cultivated some patches of corn and a little tobacco, before 1860. He obtained the seeds from traders from the south and from Kamloops. The Hudson Bay Company directed his cultivation and gave him seeds of different things. This he raised at his home by the lake, eight miles down from the head of Okanogan Lake.

N'Kwala (Nicola) looked after trading goods during the summer for the Hudson Bay Co. He also looked after and wintered a bunch of cattle for French traders who thought the world of him, and paid him well for his honesty, faithfulness and kindness. The white traders gave him ten guns and lots of ammunition, the first that came into the country. Chief N'Kwala gave them a lot of valuable furs he had collected. N'Kwala had a horse given him by traders from Walla Walla.

During the winter Chief N'Kwala trained the best of his tribe on how to use these guns. When the Lillooets were salmon fishing in the Fraser River, Chief N'Kwala (Nicola) met the Thompsons, Shuswaps, and Similkameen in council and asked them to join him in an attack on the Lillooets for his father, Chief Pelka-mu-lox's untimely death. They fell upon the Lillooets about the middle of the fishing season as they were salmon fishing. Taken unawares the Lillooets were completely upset by the noise and the deadly effects of the guns, and the appearance of N'Kwala on horseback directing the attack. After a short resistance they fled. Three hundred were killed and many women and children were taken prisoners. Thus Pelka-mu-lox's death was avenged. Chief N'Kwala had kept his word with his father, Pelka-mu-lox, to prove his word as being true.

In return from his victory, Chief N'Kwala gave a feast for his allies in the Nicola above the lake. (The fur traders named this area of the country "the Nicola" meaning Nicola's country.)[65] The meat for this feast was obtained by driving a large heard of wapiti (elk) into an enclosure and killing them with spears. The antlers from the kill at this time could still be seen in two well built heaps as late as 1863. Also they drove a herd of big horn mountain sheep over a cliff near Stump Lake. You can find record of this by J.W. MacKay [McKay] ([pronounced] Kie), Indian Agent at Kamloops. MacKay gave Dawson this story pieced together from several sources of information. I knew Mr. MacKay when I was a little girl.[66]

Old Chief N'Kwala (Nicola) was a kind humane man. He was the chief who came down to the Nicola Valley and buried the Thompson and Stuwix victims of the Shuswap raid at Guichan. (See Smith *Archaeology of the Thompson Region*, page 432).[67] This was about 1846. Fur traders recognized Chief Nicola as the most powerful and influential chief in the interior of British Columbia. He was noted for his sagacity, prudence, and fair dealings. He was honest and more of a peacemaker than a fighting man. He was greatly respected by the Indians. His word was law among his own people and even among the neighboring tribes. There was no other law. He overshadowed all other chiefs of his time in power and influence.[68]

Like all head chiefs, Nicola usually had a body guard of young warriors who did his bidding and accompanied him on all important trips and visits to neighboring chiefs. During his lifetime, the Okanogans were his friends. The first white men were the fur traders in the very early part of the century from 1803 to 1811. About fifty years later, from 1856 to 1864 the first gold miners came. On the advent of the latter, Chief Nicola used his great influence for their protection, and in preventing the Indians from making war on them. During the Fraser River trouble between the Thompsons and the whites in 1858 and 1859,[69] he advocated peace, although preparing for war had the affair not been settled. The Thompsons were against the miners and the settlers. Although he was begged by the Spokanes and Thompsons to join them in war against the whites, he refused to allow his people to join them. He said that he was an ally of the whites, fur traders, King George and the Queen and that they were all good to him and his people. When the boundary line was being surveyed, he asked for a reserve where he and his children and his people could live quietly unmolested. All of his life and until his death, he worked for the welfare of his descendants and one and all of his people. Queen Victoria recognized his urgent request for his children and promised him it would be so, for it was his father, Chief Pelka-mu-lox who welcomed the first white people with open arms. The reserve given him is now called the Okanogan Reserve at the head of Okanogan Lake. Reserve number one.

In 1840, Chief Factor Samuel Black was assassinated by a foolish misinformed Indian boy.[70] Mrs. Black sent for Chief Nicola to help her family. Chief Nicola went at once to Mrs. Black and the children. He ordered the assassin be brought and punished. They got the assassin and while bringing him back by canoe, he upset the canoe and jumped into the whirl pool at Tranquille Lake where Kamloops River enters the lake. When once and a half around, his screams imitated a loon and he was swallowed up by the whirl pool. It makes a big black hole in the water. The noise is terrifying, like a big waterfall. All the Indians were good swimmers and got home safely as they were trained for this kind of swimming. Some were Chief N'Kwala's own boys.

Chief N'Kwala died about 1875 or 1880. He died in Grand Prairie[71] on his way to Kamloops for a conference with the Hudson Bay men. His body was taken to Kamloops by a great cortege of Indians and temporarily buried near the Hudson Bay people. During the winter a large number of Indians remained with the body and either the Indians or Hudson Bay men kept a guard of honor over it in military style. In the spring the body was exhumed and carried on horses to Nkemaplex (head of Okanogan Lake), where he was finally buried with his medals. Chief Nicola generally wintered there at Nkemaplex as his father, Pelka-mu-lox had done.[72] He was buried with the medals King George of England had given him years before when he made a treaty with him (King George), when Chief Nicola got his reservation for himself, his children and people.

This is now the Okanogan Reservation on the west side of Okanogan Lake. Her Majesty, Queen Victoria, also gave him recognition and medals. Some of these must still be in existence and someone must know where they are.

Upon the death of Chief N'Kwala, his young son also named Nicola was made chief. Upon the death of young Chief Nicola, he was buried in the same grave with his father. A large wooden cross was erected on the grave. It was still there about thirty years ago.

Incidents in the life of Young Chief N'Kwala (Nicola)

Before Old Chief N'Kwala died in Grand Prairie enroute to a council, he called his people to him and made his youngest and favorite son Chief. This son was to rule in his place after his death. There were three sons. One had died, the oldest and youngest were left. He chose the youngest son for Chief. It was his people he was thinking about and for some reason of his own he chose the youngest son. This was my mother's father. He had helped to take care of the Old Chief. Young Chief N'Kwala and wife, G-pee-cha (Suzette, priest's name for her) were grandfather and grandmother of Marie Houghton Brent and Edward Houghton. Young Chief N'Kwala ruled but a short time as Chief. He was killed by his older half brother, jealous because the younger brother was made Chief. Sophie N'Kwala, daughter of young N'Kwala was my mother and wife of Charles Fredrick [sic] Houghton, my father. Sophia's two younger brothers and sister died of tuberculosis about this time. My mother, Sophia N'Kwala died of a broken heart soon afterwards. Young N'Kwala's full sister took Marie Houghton Brent to raise. She put her with her own daughter to go to school. It was she that taught Marie Houghton Brent the traditions and ancestry of her tribe. Edward Houghton was put with a friend of his father's, Mr. Tronson,[73] to go to school with his boys. My father was a Lieutenant Colonel in the Canadian Army at this time.

Incidents in the Life of Joseph Tonasket
Chief N'Kwala (Nicola) Makes Tonasket a Sub-Chief

After one of the Indian Wars, N'Kwala found Tonasket an orphan. Tonasket would not go back to his people. Old N'Kwala saw good stuff in him and had him trained to be a chief. When he was old enough, Chief N'Kwala married him to one of his daughters, as N'Kwala, though he had seventeen wives, had few sons to follow in line.

The Okanogan Indians fought a great battle with the Shuswaps. The Shuswaps had come down here and ordered great grandfather, Chief Nicola, and his people away from here saying "They wanted this land and country for their own." My people said "They were not going. This was their home." The Shuswaps gave them till sunrise to vacate or be wiped out of existence. Our folks knew they were sadly outnumbered, but they also knew they were skilled in warfare and that the enemy was not.

The Shuswap moved back a little way and made camp. Chief Nicola moved behind their own camp and held a conference. The Chief told his folks to stand up to the last man. He thought they might have a chance if they watched every step. He said to let the Shuswaps make the first move and then mow the first line down and keep fighting. They did and killed everyone in sight before the Shuswaps knew where the Okanogans were. The dead were piled up. Many of the Okanogans were killed too. But after a strong assault, the Shuswaps were on the run. The Okanogans mowed them down as they were running. They came to rocks and brush, but the Okanogans went right on. The Shuswaps made another stand, but they were falling right and left. Then they were on the run again. At this time they were almost half way back to their own country. They made another big stand and fought foot by foot. These different spots are all named by the Indians. At last the Shuswaps gave up and the Okanogans chased them until they were back in their own country across the Shuswap River. Only a few of them were left to tell what happened. They were told never to put foot on Okanogan soil again and that they should never marry into the Okanogan tribe. They never did, they were so badly beaten. They never forgot it to this day. A few of the younger ones have intermarried of late years.

The Okanogans came back from the Shuswap River and Chief Nicola held a conference with all his people. He told them they were still in danger of losing their country to other western tribes. He told them he must go back to the head of the Okanogan Lake to hold that land and that some of the people would go with him. He said he would leave young Tonasket here [Washington state, where Brent resided at this time] to help the rest of them. He knew the young man well, being with him a long time and growing up with him. He knew that Tonasket was honest, kind, with good judgement and that he could trust him. Chief Nicola said he would make Tonasket a Sub-Chief to take care of the Indians here, and that he would marry his daughter to Tonasket. Then Chief Nicola would not be alone and would have help when it was needed. This daughter of Chief Nicola who married

Tonasket was my mother's aunt and Millie Tonasket's aunt. This was Batiste Tonasket's mother of Republic, Washington. Chief Tonasket's wife (Batiste's mother) died very young at the head of Okanogan Lake in British Columbia. After a long time, Chief Tonasket married Antonia Somday, a widow with two children.

Then Chief Nicola went north to the head of Okanogan Lake. Later the boundary line was established between the United States and Canada on June 15th 1846, dividing the Okanagans in half. This was a cause of great regret to Chief Nicola that his people should be separated. Only then did the people accept Tonasket as their real chief, though Tonasket was greatly respected by the Indians north and south of the boundary line.[74] They all felt bad, north and south, when the boundary line was made. Then Chief Nicola got his big beautiful lakeside reserve from King George III. It was very rich soil and creeks came down from the mountains every short distance to enter Okanagan Lake. The King gave Chief Nicola medals to seal the treaty that gave the Indians this land for themselves, his children and their descendants. When Chief Nicola died, most of his medals were buried with him. After his death, the ruling was divided into different districts.

Chief Nicola married one of his daughters to a young man by the name of Francoise [Francois]. He was made Chief of Penticton. When Francoise died, my grandmother's brother (my mother's uncle) was next in line. His name was Gabbian and he was Chief of Penticton until his death. Then his brother came and took up the duties. That was my grandmother's brother Edward. He became Chief Edward of Penticton until his death. After that the Chief was decided by election. The first elected Chief was Michel. My grandmother referred to above was my mother's mother. Her name was Susette Pepetsa (Chief Edward's daughter).[75]

During Indian unrest and settling of the Indians on reservations, the Indian Department sent General Miles to get four chiefs, Tonasket included, to come to Washington, D.C. for a conference. The result was the Moses Agreement.[76] In the Moses Agreement, Tonasket's people would be furnished with a grist mill, a saw mill, a boarding school for one hundred pupils and a doctor. The school was located where the town of Tonasket now stands.

Tonasket always worked for the good of his people. His last home was above the town of Curlew, Wash. Close by is his grave. A granite monument was erected June 21, 1958. The inscription on the stone reads as follows:

Chief Joseph Tonasket
1822-1891
He proved himself a strong and able leader, and although his was not an inherited chieftainship, he was officially recognized as Chief of the Okanogan Indians in about the year 1858. His whole life was a series of accomplishments for his people.

This sums up Chief Tonasket as a Chief as fine as any words could say it.
[1966]

Christine Quintasket, Washington State, c. 1901.
Courtesy of Washington State University Libraries,
Manuscripts, Archives and Special Collections (MASC).

Mourning Dove
1886 - 1936

Christine Quintasket, also known as Mourning Dove, *h?misms* or Hum-Ishu-Ma, is today a much-studied writer whose contribution to Indigenous literature has been extraordinary. Dedicated, hardworking, and resourceful, she also became prominent inside and outside her community during her own lifetime. Now thought of as one of the first North American Indigenous women to write a novel, she was hailed in her day by the *Spokane Review* in 1916 as "the first American Indian novelist" (D. Fisher xiv) after she had completed *Cogewea, The Half-Blood: A Depiction of the Great Montana Cattle Range*—though it took another eleven years to appear in print—and was a "regional celebrity" while living on the Colville reserve from 1919 on (Miller, Introduction viii). She also wrote a book-length autobiography which was published posthumously as *Mourning Dove: A Salishan Autobiography* (1990). Especially after the publication of *Coyote Stories* in 1933, she became a knowledgeable spokesperson who travelled and gave public lectures on Indigenous traditions and concerns (D. Fisher ix), speaking at Kiwanis and Rotary clubs, women's meetings and schools (Arnold, *"More"* 36). Mourning Dove lived much of her life on the Colville reservation in the state of Washington, Okanagan Syilx territory that became part of the United States when a border between western Canada and the United States was established in 1846. At the same time, she had not only cultural ties but also family ties to Syilx Okanagan country in what is now Canada.

United States Indian Census Rolls of 1896 list her as eleven years old "at Colville mission school" and her birth date as "about 1885"; however, according to her autobiography, Mourning Dove was born in 1886 in a canoe crossing the Kootenay River while trying to reach camp near Bonner's Ferry, Idaho (*Mourning Dove* 10). Her family was on a pack train between Fort Steele, British Columbia, and Walla Walla, Washington. Mourning Dove writes that her mother's name is Lucy Stuikin (*stu?iqn*), daughter of Chief *stu?iqn* or Beaver head of the Trout Lake Band and that her grandmother is Soma-how-atghu (*sumaxatkʷ*) known as Maria, whose father See-whelh-ken (*sixʷilxkn*), was head Chief of the tribe and who was succeeded by his nephew, Kinkanawah (*knkanaxʷa*), as Chief at Kettle Falls (on the Columbia River in what is now northeastern Washington state). Mourning Dove also informs us in her autobiography that she is the daughter of Joseph Quintasket, (T-quin-task-et, *tqʷntasq̓t*) or Dark Cloud, born in 1864 at "En-hwx-kwas-tanun" (*nx̌ʷaqʷastn*) or Arrow Scraper Village (4). Arrow Scraper Village, in what is now the City of Kelowna at Mission Creek, was one of the largest fishery villages for kikinnee or landlocked sockeye salmon. Like the great Syilx salmon fishery at Kettle Falls, it was a shared Okanagan fishery and central crossroads of village groups traveling from the Upper Okanagan, the Similkameen, the Upper Nicola, the Kettle Valley, and the Upper Arrow Lakes. James Teit lists *nx̌ʷaqʷastn*, "Nxoko'sten–arrow smoother," as one of the eighteen main camps of the Okanagan (207). It was probably selected for that very reason as a site for establishing a Catholic mission in 1859, now known as the Father Pandosy Mission in Kelowna. Joseph Quintasket, Mourning Dove's father, was listed as being a "Lakes" (Arrow Lakes or *snʕackist* people, *nsyilxcn* speaking people) in the same United States Indian Census Rolls of 1896.

In establishing the ancestry of her father, Mourning Dove writes in her autobiography that Joseph's paternal grandmother was Pah-tah-heet-sa, (*pʕatəhic̓aʔ*) from the Nicola, but was only part En-Koh-tu-me-whoh (*nukʷtmixʷ*, Thompson-Nicola). Pah-ta-heet-sa had two daughters, one of whom was Joseph's mother. She also writes in a letter to settler Hester White, included in Part Three of this volume, that her grandmother was "part Nicola Indian," that is Okanagan from the Upper Nicola people at Douglas Lake. Mourning Dove's letter indicates, as well, that the other daughter of *pʕatəhic̓aʔ* was the mother of Matilda and Mary Kruger, and thus they were first cousins to her father. Hester White had known Matilda and Mary well as daughters of trader Theodore Kruger, a neighbour of the Haynes family at Osoyoos. Looking at her grandfather's side, Mourning Dove has claimed that Joseph's father was "Haynes or Haines" of Irish descent (Letter to McWhorter, Nov. 10, 1925), suggesting perhaps he was Hester White's father, J.C. Haynes of Osoyoos (see Part Three of this volume), but in her autobiography she states Joseph's father was "a Scot named Andrew" (4). However, it is asserted by her family and generally agreed today that her father Joseph Quintasket was not of mixed heritage. Joseph Quintasket was a member of the Colville group and is listed as a "full blood" on the tribal rolls (Miller, Introduction ix).

Historical records reveal that Mourning Dove received three years of formal schooling at Sacred Heart Convent at Ward, Washington, from 1896-99, and that she briefly attended government Indian Schools. Her mother died in 1902, and, after caring for her siblings until her father remarried in 1904, she attended Fort Shaw Indian School near Great Falls, Montana where she was also employed as a teacher's aide (Arnold, *"More"* 33) and where she could visit her grandmother, Maria, who was living at Tobacco Plains (Miller, Introduction vii). At Fort Shaw she met Hector McLeod, a Flathead, whom she married in 1909, though they often lived apart (Miller vii). Mourning Dove lost a child during this marriage (Brown, "Mourning Dove's Canadian Recovery" 115). In 1912, living alone in Portland, Montana, Mourning Dove drafted the novel *Cogewea, The Half-Blood: A Depiction of the Great Montana Cattle Range* and assumed the name Morning Dove, which she changed to Mourning Dove in 1921 (Brown, "Legacy" 53). Her novel incorporates the people, the setting and the history of the Montana region she had lived in, as well as that of her Okanagan culture. In 1913 she enrolled in a business school in Calgary, Alberta, to learn typing and to improve her English.

Mourning Dove was also familiar with the Okanagan region of Canada. She states that when she was a child, her family travelled annually from Kettle Falls winter village to "S'oo-yoos Lake" in British Columbia (*Mourning Dove* 3). She frequently visited her sister Margaret (Brown, "Mourning Dove's Canadian Recovery" 114) who was married to Narcisse Bone of the Osoyoos Indian Band, and who lived on Nk'Mip land near Fairview, British Columbia, now a ghost town (Musgrave). It is here that she could have heard of J.C. Haynes, though he would have died around the time she was born. In October 1913, she helped translate for Chief Baptiste George at meetings with the Royal Commission on Indian Affairs for the Province of British Columbia (McKenna-McBride Commission[77]) on the Nk'Mip reserve (Musgrave). She was urged by Chief Baptiste to teach at the Inkameep Day School, which she did from 1917-1919 (Musgrave). At the same time, she helped with her sister Margaret's family. Being with them was both a place for her to recover her roots and her health, but it also meant struggling with measles and the flu epidemic that afflicted the family (Brown, "Mourning Dove's Canadian Recovery" 115-16).

By the time she came to teach at Inkameep, Mourning Dove had met Lucullus Virgil McWhorter (1860-1944), a Yakima Valley businessman who, despite his "minimal frontier education" (Brown, "Evolution" 176), had a deep interest in Indigenous history as well as concern about the exploitation of Indigenous people. He had been an ally to the Yakima, working with them to protect their access to irrigation and writing a pamphlet in 1913 entitled *The Crime Against the Yakimas* (D. Fisher vi). They adopted him into their tribe, naming him "Old Wolf" and nicknaming him "Big Foot," which Mourning Dove used affectionately in correspondence. After meeting her in 1914 at a Frontier Days celebration in Walla Walla, he helped her edit and finalize *Cogewea* in the winter of 1915-16, inviting her to stay with him and his wife in their home in Yakima (Brown, "Mourning Dove's Canadian Recovery" 117). McWhorter also urged her to write down traditional stories, stories she had heard throughout her life and had already begun to collect. On Nk'Mip land, she gathered "valuable material" to add to her own knowledge for her second book *Coyote Stories* (see letter to Hester White in Part Three). Listening to and recording stories, helping with her nieces and nephews, and at the same time teaching at Inkameep Day School was a typical pattern of strenuous effort that Mourning Dove continued throughout her life. She also worked seasonally picking hops and fruit, particularly apples, and continued to do so after her marriage to Fred Galler in 1919. The couple based themselves near Omak, Washington, on the Colville reserve.

Mourning Dove and McWhorter worked together through 1921-22 to edit the many stories Mourning Dove collected, enough material to fill two volumes (Brown, "Evolution" 165), resulting in a manuscript Mourning Dove originally entitled "Okanogan Sweat House," referring to Coyote's other identity. McWhorter had been working to find a publisher for *Cogewea*—difficult while World War I was in progress and then afterward when "there was a mania for war stories" (Brown, "Legacy" 53). He and Mourning Dove also tried to raise money, since many publishers insisted that the authors defray the costs (D. Fisher xiv). When Mourning Dove decided to go to Nk'Mip to teach and live with her sister Margaret, they had already suffered repeated disappointments (Brown, "Evolution" 166). Before it was finally published in 1927 by The Four Seas in Boston, McWhorter, hoping to make it more saleable, had made substantial interventions and additions such as ethnographic descriptions, denunciations of federal policies, and poetic epigraphs at the beginning of each chapter which had earlier been removed (Brown, "Legacy" 53-54).

Similarly, it took years to find a publisher for "Okanogan Sweat House." In 1928, McWhorter hired an editor, Heister Dean Guie, who called for changes that resulted in publication. He reduced the number of stories, changed the title to *Coyote Stories*, suggested illustrations[78] for the volume and directed that the stories be suitable for children, which meant Mourning Dove removing some parts of the stories considered inappropriate (Brown, "Evolution" 175). Neither McWhorter nor Mourning Dove had envisioned a book for children, and over the years Mourning Dove had worked hard to convey some of the subtleties of Syilx language and of Coyote's particular powers to McWhorter (Brown, "Evolution" 171-72). Nevertheless, Guie was "thorough" on "technical issues involving translation" and brought energy to the project (175). *Coyote Stories* was published in 1933 by Caxton Printers with much success and almost immediately reprinted. After Mourning Dove's death, a second collection of stories from the original "Okanogan Sweat House," entitled *Tales of the Okanogans: Collected by Mourning Dove*, was edited by Donald M. Hines and published in 1976.

After the publication of *Cogewea*, Mourning Dove did not stop writing, but continued to draft her autobiography (Miller, Introduction vii). *Mourning Dove: A Salishan Autobiography*, published in 1990, was compiled and edited by anthropologist Jay Miller from unsorted boxes of papers Mourning Dove left in the attic of Heister Guie. Her many letters to her editor and friend Virgil McWhorter clearly reveal that she was aware of her role and responsibility to provide the settler with an Okanagan viewpoint. Mourning Dove also comments in the preface to *Tales of the Okanogans* that her primary interest was "in writing novels showing the Indian viewpoint" (14).

Mourning Dove chose the novel form as her first vehicle to reach the public with the "Indian viewpoint." Despite McWhorter's editing which affects its language, tone and content, her genius and particular Okanagan background and knowledge are evident in *Cogewea, The Half-Blood: A Depiction of the Great Montana Cattle Range*. Mourning Dove threaded that popular literary form with traditional knowledge and stories that could also reach Indigenous readers, incorporating names of characters and allusions to plots of *captikʷł* that would be understood by them. The excerpts from *Cogewea* reprinted below show her referencing traditional stories, creating multi-layered meanings for diverse readers in a complex construction (see the essay "Standing Between" in this volume). Two such stories, "Chipmunk and Owl-Woman," and a story of Swa-lah-kin, here entitled "The Gods of the Sun and the Moon," were included in *Coyote Stories* and are reprinted below. Another story entitled "House of Little Men," comes from the Syilx of Nk'Mip where Mourning Dove's sister Margaret lived. Mourning Dove wrote it down and sent it to McWhorter after visiting Margaret in early 1930 (Brown, "House" 49). The version below comes from Mourning Dove's original typescript included with her correspondence to McWhorter, given to Jeannette Armstrong by Alanna Brown.[79]

Particularly while living at Omak after 1919, Mourning Dove also chose to reach out through writing and speaking about the Syilx peoples' rights and needs, whether on the Colville reserve or across the border in southern British Columbia. "The Red Cross and the Okanogans" written in January, 1919 (Brown, "Evolution" n. 180) expresses her deep concern about the conditions affecting the Syilx people in Canada during the flu epidemic, an epidemic that had touched her own sister's family as well as others in that British Columbia community. She was active up until her death in 1936, not only continuing to write her autobiography, but also joining in efforts on the Colville reserve to have the Indian agency staff reduced and to resolve land claims (Miller, Introduction viii). In the 1930s she was a founding member of the Colville Indian Association and supported some of the reforms of the US Bureau of Indian Affairs in its "Fair Deal for Indians" (Musgrave). In 1935, a year before her death, Mourning Dove became the first woman elected to the Colville Tribal Council, becoming its tribal chair (Arnold 43).

Mourning Dove in East Omak, Washington, c. 1919.
Photographer, Ed Valentine.
Courtesy of Okanogan County Historical Society.

From *Cogewea, The Half-Blood*

Under the Whispering Pines

To love the softest hearts are prone,
But such can ne'er be all his own;
Too timid in his woes to share,
Too meek to meet, or brave despair;
And sterner hearts alone may feel
The wound that time can never heal.

—*The Giaour*[80]

Two weeks had passed since the incident of Densmore's riding everything drifting along the usual channel. *[Earlier on Densmore, a "tenderfoot," had been set up to ride on a very difficult and testy mount by the mischievous cowboys. His arm was broken in a fall.]* The hot July days were beginning to heat the great Clay Banks of the Pend d'Oreille, [a tributary of the Columbia River flowing through Montana, Idaho and Washington], but under the dark pines lining its shore, were found spots cooled by the breeze from the stream. It was here that the injured man was spending the morning alone with a book. Cogewea, his nurse, had gone for a ride, an errand to a distant neighbor's. He had exhausted an hour in a vain attempt at becoming interested in the pages that he turned to no purpose.

At last: he would lay aside the volume and study nature. He noted the many colored flowers which perfumed the air; the squirrels and chipmunks frisking among the boughs overhead, or scurrying along the ground. The birds caroling in the thicket, and the fishes swimming lazily in the waters where the shadows fell dark.

But he grew more restless. There was a disturbing element to his meditations. The wild life interested him no more than did the book. That "breed" girl came ever before him. It was vain that he tried to blot her from memory, to banish her from vision. She peeped from every flower; those flashing black eyes reflected from the pebbles glinting in the sunshine. Her tresses streamed on the eddying current, and her voice was in the notes of bird-song and the chipmunk's chatter.

Alfred Densmore, the cold, calculating business man out

from the East for adventure and money, was half in love with this wild, tawny girl of the range, the romantic "Chipmunk of the Okanogans."

The idea struck him as absurd. He shook himself as if to throw off the shackles of irresolution. It was impossible! Such weakness! He was only fascinated, he argued. Those liquid, mesmeric eyes had cast a spell over him—a dangerous spell. With a gesture of impatience he flung his half-smoked cigarette into the water and spoke so the squirrels could hear him:

"What a fool! I am not really falling in love with that squaw! Ridiculous! What of my club associates? My sisters would never tolerate it, and it would break my mother's heart. My father would never dare call me his son again. He would disinherit me! It is impossible that I so far forget myself, my birth and my social standing. Besides, there is another who—"

He bit his lip, extracted a fresh cigarette from its case, lit it and drew at it furiously.

"*Never! Never!* I don't dare! Pshaw! She only takes my fancy. What if she has been good to me?" he muttered. "I have known others of her 'stripe' just as kind. It is the way of all such women! They are alright as objects of amusement and pleasure, but there it must halt. Fairly educated, she can show refinement when the mood strikes her, but she makes easy to fall into the rough, uncouth ways of her associates—the ill mannered rowdies of the cow-trail. None of such for you, Alfred Densmore! A be-pistoled woman who can swear a little on occasions may be picturesque, but she is no mate for a gentleman of the upper society. Had she strings to a good mine there would be an inducement, but a squaw without compensation—a sacrifice without adequate requital—bah!"

With this soliloquy, he dismissed the "dream," and casting himself upon the ground, was soon buried in his book.

Cogewea returned from riding at an unusually early hour. She seemed interested in the welfare of her patient, for she went immediately to him under the pines. Densmore heard the jingle of spurs and glanced up to see the girl advancing, swinging a quirt [a small whip] in idle abandonment. A neat riding habit set off her splendid figure to advantage and the Easterner felt his heart bound a trifle faster as he surveyed this "exquisite living picture." Perhaps he had been too harsh in his deductions. Could there be guile in a face of such open frankness? What could be expected of the best with such environments? Her forward ways were but those of innocence. A wild flower unscathed by sun, blight, or frost—a ruby unflawed—a jewel worthy of any setting. But after all, she was a *squaw*, while he was of an altogether higher cast. Densmore brushed aside all feelings kindred to love, but he gazed at her with a fascination ill becoming one of his superior breeding. Cogewea, ever observant, grew slightly confused as she exclaimed:

"Well! Have you nothing to say? Am I such a curiosity that—"

"O! pardon me. I was just thinking."

"Of what?"

"Of—of how nifty you look in your new suit."

"John bought it for me, a summer present. [John Carter of "Scotch descent" and husband of her sister Julia. He owns the ranch where Cogewea lives.]. I guess he savied it was time that I possessed some glad rags! Maybe he tumbled that I had about earned them, cooking for the broncho busters and playing nurse at the same time."

"You certainly have been a royal little nurse, and I am afraid that I can never thank you sufficiently for your kindness. But I hope to compensate you for it all some day."

"Aw! Come off! I am not asking pay! Guess I owe my services for the part I had in getting you busted up. How is your arm?"

"Seems to be getting along finely; but there is a dull pain in my head most of the time. I trust that it is nothing serious."

"Doubtless a mere 'aching void' and no occasion for alarm," came the solemn reply. "If the malady is deep seated, an abatement must not be expected in so short a time. An absorption remedy of any nature is usually slow of results and a persistent and potent application is ofttimes necessary."

Cogewea had seated herself at Densmore's side and was listlessly flecking the grass with her riding lash. Her patient hardly knew how to take this diagnosis of his head trouble and its remedial prescript. He gazed at her steadily, boldly, as an enigma to fathom; but the mask was impenetrable.

"Yes! I know," he at length acquiesced, "but I feel so lonely at times. No one to speak to; every body busy but me. Only the birds and squirrels for company. Can you blame me for growing impatient?"

109

"Birds and squirrels are good company. The wild creatures are primitive and are closer [to] the creative Spirit than we imagine. I love them! But if they do not interest you, why don't you talk to Stemteemä? Both of you have time to throw away. Go visit in her tepee."

"I am afraid that she would chase me away with her cane as she does Bringo and Shep at times," he rejoined with a short laugh.

"That only attests that you no more understand her than you do your little companions here of the grove; for they are similar in character. I'll tell you what we will do some of these days. We'll call on her together. Do not expect your afternoon tea of fashion's boredom, but you will be regaled on jerked venison, dried roots and berries. I will have her tell some stories that may hold interest for you—stories of the past—of the time that was. She will speak in Okanogan and I will interpret for you. I love my Stemteemä for her very golden worth. She has been a parent to all of us children. When mother died, she was the only relative we had—after daddy left us for the glitter of gold in the Yukon; and which—"

Cogewea caught herself as though she had betrayed a secret; for seldom was the father's name ever mentioned. The girl tried, in charity, to believe that he had long since followed her mother, but there was an ever haunting uncertainty—a dreaming of that which is more fearful than death—gnawing at her soul. With her, the present only is to concern us, is to be lived sacredly; and that somewhere out on the trail awaiting us, is the best friend that mortal [has] ever known. *Desolution!*, who liberates us from the perishable. Nor does he watch for our coming with sinister designs and foreshadowing the gloom of an invisible night; for the door which he swings back opens into the dawn of a morn redolent with renewed life; where avenues of progression wind along shimmering streams—tree-lined and where birds are singing—coming down from wondrous mountain heights. To this girl of "heretical" philosophies, Death was but the unfolding of a long bud-bound flower; the bursting forth of a rock-hampered fountain. Imbued with such lofty ideals, it is not surprising that she preferred thinking of her parent as dead—in the general acceptance of the term—for that most dreadful of all denouncatories: *Thou art weighed in the balances, and art found wanting"[81]*; loomed terrifically against the back-ground of her conception of a life of profligacy.

The touch of sadness in Cogewea's voice as she spoke of her parents, was lost on the Easterner. But the mention of "gold in the Yukon" had aroused to new life his latent passion for wealth. It was the one god of his ambition to go back home a rich man. For this, he had left the city and society. He must make good; he was not so particular how, but in some way. He had struck a rough, strange people and was gaining an exuberant experience with which to regale his associates upon his return to his old haunts. There must be wealth somewhere in this new country—mines of it among the Indians—requiring only brains and strategy to possess. He had discovered that this romantic girl was a nature's religionist. He would court her ideals, but it would be for a purpose. He would amass this fortune—transfer it to his own pocket—and then—his reverie was broken by Cogewea:

"I must go now! Sister will need help with the dinner. You better be there within an hour or you might miss your fodder."

"Wait! Just one moment," remonstrated Densmore as she hurried away. "I want to ask a favor."

"Spit'er out!" she called, half turning back.

"Will you write a letter for me this afternoon?"

"Is that all? Surething! I thought you were going to strike me for a round thousand, from the way you hesitated. Come to your trough at sitkum sun. S'long!" with the wave of a hand.

"*Trough! system sun!* What do you mean?"

"Grub at noon. *Sitkum sun* is midday. *Chinook.* I learned it on the Columbia. It is hardly spoken here."

After dinner, and the kitchen work disposed of, Cogewea joined her patient under the pines. She sat near him on the river bank, writing material in her lap. With his left hand Densmore was awkwardly tossing pebbles into the water.

"What do you want me to write?" she asked cheerily.

"A letter to mother," and by way of emphasis, he pitched a larger stone farther into the stream.

"All right! You rangle and I'll use the brandin' iron."

Densmore settled in an easy position and dictated as follows:

111

"Polson, Flathead Indian Reservation, Montana.
July 21, 19—

 "Dearest Mother:
 "A friend is writing this for me. I recently met with an accident to my arm which precludes the use of a pen. However, it is not serious and with the good nursing that I am receiving, I will soon be fully recovered. My nurse, while not a professional, is one of the very best; kind and affectionate. It is refreshing to meet with true friends in a strange place, and my nurse is certainly devoted to—"

Densmore paused. Cogewea looked up, a deep blush suffusing her dark face. Her startled eye caught his steady gaze, and her head dropped lower over the tablet as he finished the sentence:

 "—her trust. She is writing this for me in the open and under the river pines. I think that I will remain here for an indeterminate time, since I have formed a strong attachment; and even love for my—"

Cogewea was not trapped a second time. She did not lift her eyes as she inquired in frigid tones:
 "Is that all?"
Densmore concluded without seeming to notice her question:

 "—environments. The people here are all in marked contrast to our home society. Of this I will tell you when I am able to write you myself. There are both thrills and romance out here.
  "Address me as above. Tell sisters to write me.
  "With love to all,
   "Your son,
    "Alfred Densmore."

 "Shall I add a post-script and say that your nurse wrote this and that she is an Injun squaw?" asked Cogewea severely, looking her companion level in the face.
 "N—no! I—I hardly think it necessary at this time," he stammered confusedly. "Mother might not understand."
 "Very well. You can look the letter over while I address the envelope and if it suits you—if it is true to your dictation—it can be posted this evening. Rodeo will drive to town and return with supplies in the morning."
 Densmore took the proffered sheet and glancing through

it, returned it with an ill suppressed smile, expressing his satisfaction. Cogewea folded and sealed the missive without comment and tossed it into his inverted hat at his side. There was an embarrassing silence for one short moment, when she rose and said simply:

"I must go and help sister with the children and the house work."

"Why such hurry? I thought you had the afternoon off, and that perhaps we could visit your grandmother and hear those wonderful stories you promised me."

"Not today!" she called back without stopping. "I think that Stemteemä is sleeping."

"Touchy as powder!" he chuckled as he lay back on the grass in evident delight. "I thought so! She tumbled—gave herself dead away. Now Mr. Alfred of the 'circle,' go your length in untrammeled pleasure with this brown beauty of the range. But no matrimonial tangle! Bah! What a match! A scion of the ancient house of Densmore, wedding a breed girl of the Okanogans. What a figure for the ball room and social functions of city life. Ye gods! My family must never know. But that possible gold of the Yukon! Who can tell what fish may be swimming my way. Surely, the catch would be worth the bait!"
[1927]

Swa-lah-kin: The Frog Woman

With her moods of shade and sunshine
Eyes that smiled and frowned alternate,
Feet as rapid as the river,
Tresses flowing like the water,
And as musical as laughter;

—*Hiawatha*[82]

A week had passed since the roundup outfit left the ranch. The lengthening days brought with them the indubitable evidence of an early and short lived autumn. The deep green leaves were transforming to mellow golden and the blaze of crimson glory. The grass was sere, with no indications of the usually short, velvety after-crop so peculiar to the arid range. The song birds no longer trilled among the pines of the Pend d'Oreille. Flown to the South land, their notes were supplanted by the discordant honk and scream of the migratory water-fowl, echoing along the winding shore.

Densmore often went shooting on the big flats where numerous small lakes were in evidence. To the surprise of all, he proved a successful hunter and bagged a goodly number of both ducks and prairie chickens along with an occasional goose. Badger, a noted wolf-hound and Bringo, were his constant companions on these excursions, ofttimes chasing down the wily coyote and the fleet footed jack rabbit. Densmore had also become handy with the rod, bringing home fine strings of fish. Stemteemä was kept bountifully supplied with these delicacies, nor did the sportsman forego an opportunity of ingratiating himself in her favor. But the ancient woman received the gifts with stoic indifference and with doubtful gratitude. Perhaps it was more to please Cogewea, that she accepted the offerings, regarding them as part of her daily food supply. The girl sometimes accompanied the donor in these presentation visits, acting as interpreter. The keen witted grandmother discerned that her grand child was growing more fond of the hated Shoyahpee;[83] and that she was also endeavouring to win her to regard him with greater favour. These symptoms she noticed with increased perturbation and had spoken to Julia on the subject. But the older sister, who had given the situation but scant or no thought during the process of summer work, was inclined to regard the possible alliance in a different light. She, herself, had married a white man who was good and kind to her, and consequently her racial prejudices were not so strongly pronounced.

Cogewea, in walking habit, stood gazing pensively from the window. She saw Julia, leading little Denny, enter the low doorway of the smoke-browned tepee just as the well proportioned form of Densmore emerged from the bunk house. He carried two fishing rods and had a trap slung over his shoulder. Coming up the path, he stopped at the gate, turning towards the house. Mary, the shy girl, sitting on the blanketed floor of the veranda beading a pair of moccasins, paused in her work to glance at her sister as she passed down the steps to join him. Mary could not like this Shoyahpee with his smooth tongue and beguiling smile. She and the Stemteemä had many times counselled concerning him and Cogewea, but she had never revealed to the old grandmother how much the two were together. Resuming her task, the girl frowned with evident vexation as the couple strolled towards the river.

Densmore was discoursing on the charms of city life as they passed the tepee door. Inside, Stemteemä was crooning an Indian lullaby, which intoned musically with the sleepy baby prattle of Denny. The song was hushed suddenly. No bird carols greeted them as they approached the stream, and the squirrels and chipmunks appeared too busy storing their winter hoards to notice the intrusion. Following the bank for a mile or so, they came upon a promising pool, deep and clear, at the base of an overhanging cliff. Here they prepared to cast.

"The kale [money prize] that I land the first one," challenged Cogewea as the two flies struck the water simultaneously.

"Taken!" was the quick acceptance. Scarcely had Densmore spoken when his line cut the water in a straight drive, the reel spinning yard after yard of singing cord. Far out in the stream a silvery form leaped, scintillating in a radiant curve, sending up a shower of sparkling spray as the fish clove the water. The played out line slacked and the fisherman reeled in, minus hook and fly.

"King of the Pend d'Oreille!" exclaimed Cogewea. "How gamy! You. . . ."

Her own line spun with a musical purr, and deftly handling the reel, she slowly brought the stampeding salmonoid to, in a wide, sweeping circle. The battle was on, but with a skill attained only through experience she finally landed a shimmering beauty of rare size.

"Lost! Shoyahpee!" she taunted. "Lost two ways; your trout and your wager."

"I will lay an even five thousand against your hand that the next is mine," bantered the Easterner as he adjusted a new fly.

"I fade you!" was the prompt acceptance.

Again they cast and again she won.

"Please ante!" laughed the girl, as with dextrous movement of thumb and fingers, the catch was rendered unconscious before removed from the hook.

"Would you have been as prompt in delivering, had I won?"

"An *honest* gambler is supposed to meet all obligations unequivocally," was the evasive answer.

"Nor will the true sport deny to an unfortunate loser the

opportunity of retrieving," came the ready counter.

"Certainly! My digits and winnings against an even ten thousand."

"You are mine!" was the confident response as the fly was twirled over the water for "luck." "Now listen for the wedding chimes."

The game was growing wild and fascinating. This time the Easterner lost only by the fraction of a minute.

"Betting is off!" declared Cogewea when Densmore proposed a still higher wager. "Those chimes are remote, for I don't believe that you could redeem even now."

"There is where your reckoning is faulty," a crafty light in his eyes. "I am nothing near my limit. I can make good several such doubles."

"Well, I make no more wagers today," in a tone of finality. "My *tahmahnawis* tells me that the signs are bad. Besides, we have enough fish already. There are still a few left of your yesterday's catch and it is wrong and wasteful to hook them just for misconceived sport. Indians take only enough for food and no more."

"Wait a moment! I think there is a big shiner by that rock and I want him."

"Aw! come on and don't be selfish. Leave a few for the next fellow who may really need them. Let's rest on this mossy log and watch the river as it glides on its way to the ocean. You can tell me something of interest."

No further urging was required, and Densmore, reeling his line, joined her on the fallen forest giant. Spying a small land-toad, with the end of his pole he mischievously turned it over and over towards her. Noting the action, the girl exclaimed in agitation:

"Oh! Alfred! Don't do that to the poor little helpless thing. Besides, it will bring a storm sure. Indians claim that if you place a frog on its back, it will cause a storm without a doubt. There is an old legend which tells the story of Swa-lah-kin the 'frog woman.'[84] It is in connection with the sun; that if you turn the frog thus, she will look up at the sun and flirt with him as in the beginning. He hates her so badly that he will wrinkle his brow and a tempest gathers which wets the earth. This forces her odious flippancy to find shelter out of sight."

Densmore picked up a fragment of bark and getting the Batrachian [frog or toad] on it, threw both into the stream with the observation: "I guess with that cold bath the little miss will do no more flirting for a while. Anyhow it is too clear for rain today."

Cogewea glanced upward. The sky was blue and limpid with the exception of a single diminutive cloud which appeared to draw nearer to the hot, blazing orb of day. Pointing to it, she admonished: "I told you that she would bring rain. See that little cloud? It will unfold and spread until the heavens are covered in no time. It is her! The Swah-la-kin of the myth. She has flirted with the Sun and soon we will get soaked. There will be a downpour swift and without warning. You have done the mischief and spoiled our afternoon."

"I supposed that you were enough educated to know better than to believe all those ridiculous signs of your people," chided the Easterner.

"What if I am slightly educated!" came the retort with a tinge of resentment. "The true American courses my veins and *never* will I cast aside my ancestral traditions. I was born to them!"

"And the Pend d'Oreille has its birth far up in the mountains, but it does not remain there; slumbering within the gorges and fastnesses of wooded slopes. Bursting from its gloomy confines, it grows into a thing of magnificent grandeur, averting stagnation by constant action."

"But it is no less water than when it issues from its rocky defiles, only less pure. And is it really so enigmatic that fluid should run down hill? You white people will never understand us. I think it is quite easy for us to turn to the Shoyahpee's ways, compared to his qualifications to become Injun—honest Injun. I refer especially to his word of promise. He seldom keeps an agreement, while the word of a tribesman is law—or was until he became contaminated with the touch of your civilization."

Densmore made no reply. He drew a handkerchief from his pocket when a loosely folded letter fluttered to the ground. He picked it up, glanced at the heading, then tore it into fragments, scattering them to the wind.

"From your sweetheart?" queried Cogewea, with a mischievous smile.

"My mother," he answered carelessly, but with a degree of

embarrassment.[85]

"Tell me of your mother. You have spoken but little about your family."

"Why!—I —I thought that I had told you."

"No, you never have. But you have learned all about my people, from Stemteemä to my very cousins. I have never realized what it is to have a mother's love. I was too young when she died."

"I have one of the best mothers in the world! You would like her! Cogewea!" he exclaimed with sudden impulse, as he placed his arms about her. "I love you and some day I want to take you to her. Will you go?"

She did not resist his advances, but asked pleadingly: "*Do you think that your mother would like me? Would* she really be glad; do you think?"

"Sure! little one! Why do you doubt?"

The plotter felt the girl tremble as he drew her closer. Was realization within his grasp? He had lied broadly, but what of that. There was pathos in her voice as she made her reply: "Because I am a breed!—only part white. But few recognize my kind socially. We are often made to suffer from the ungenerous remarks and actions of those who feel themselves above us."

"To the truly high minded there are no racial barriers. Why should you care to remain exclusively Indian? What is the incentive?"

"I have my Stemteemä and my sisters, besides other kindred ties. Then, there are the traditions of my ancient race."

"But you can not exist on sentiment alone. With no vested or property interests to demand your continued presence, you should feel at freedom to see something of the world. I take it that there are no such bonds."

"Sure! Not only my allotment of eighty acres of the finest land, but I have—Why do you ask?" She broke off suddenly, lifting inquiring eyes.

He stood the scrutiny with calculating coolness. She had very unexpectedly increased in value. Taking her shapely hand in his, he answered with apparent sincerity: "I meant nothing. I am only anxious to make you happy. Listen! my little Injun sweetheart! I have plenty, all that you could wish for. I want to share my wealth with you. You won the wagers at fishing. Suppose we form a partnership and call it settled by me doubling your winnings!"

"I would not sell myself!" was the scornful reply. "Money cannot bring happiness. Too often its heritage is one of unfathomed misery."

Densmore, realizing his mistake, retrenched hastily.

"You misunderstand me. I am but endeavoring to show you that I care deeply and am anxious to be all that a husband should. If I could only hear you say that you care for me—that you love me ever so little."

He was straining her to his breast and he felt her responsive form quiver. He attempted to lift her warm lips to his own, but she held aloof.

"Cogewea!" he whispered, smoothing her raven tresses. "I love you to distraction! I am willing to meet you in every way you desire. I will be Indian. Tell me more about your tribal customs. That marriage ceremony—"

The girl, struggling free, started up in sudden fright. With arm outflung, she exclaimed in terror: "Look! See how the frown of the Sun-god darkens the earth! He bends his shaggy brow over the portals of the West-wind and hurls his anger along the sky! He breathes! and the air is thick with anguish! It is the *Swa-lah-kin*! *You* did this!" she cried angrily. "You should not have turned the frog! Come! Let us hurry home! We will be fortunate if we escape with only a drenching."

Densmore's eyes followed her outstretched arm and he leaped to his feet in amazement. The western heavens were overcast with a mighty canopy of black, billowing clouds, hurtling upwards towards the zenith with appalling rapidity. The onslaught was swift and terrible in its silence. Only the faintest hum, like the smothered chords of an Aeolian harp[86] struck by the softest zephyr, was audible. Never had the Easterner witnessed an elemental conflict of such awe-inspiring grandeur. Seizing their effects, they departed hurriedly for home.

Gathering momentum, the storm came sweeping onward with a lowering front; the chaotic cloud-rack, a sable wall blotting out the universe. The low, indistinct murmur increased in volume until the cadence became a mournful dirge in the pine tops. This was but a prelude. Murky with misty shadows, the wind, in one fell swoop enveloped the fugitives, nearly carrying them off their feet. Clasping hands, they struggled in the face of the gale now shrieking like a thousand Harpies[87] about their bursting ears. Densmore's hat went sailing out over the river, while Cogewea's broad-brim fluttering, was held secure by feminine anchorage. Bracing hard, they made but slow progress and were still a considerable distance from home when the first spattering raindrops, like the skirmish shot from a hostile army, struck them. When within a hundred paces of Stemteemä's lodge, the anguished heavens were rent by a lurid tongue of lightning, followed by a crash which seemed to rock the earth's very foundations. The dreaded *Thunder-bird*[88] was abroad on the storm and at the gleaming flash of his eye and the booming crash of his ponderous wing, the rain descended in torrents.

"*The tepee! The tepee!*" screamed Cogewea above the roar of the tempest.

Densmore tore back the door-flap and completely soaked they stumbled through the opening. The interposition of the canvas walls against the sudden gale was most grateful. It was a solace to hear the deluge beating against the swaying roof. The wings of the smoke-flue had been closed and the seemingly frail structure made entirely proof against the onslaughts of Thor.[89] Not only Julia, but Mary was there and, what with the two children sleeping among the blankets, the wigwam was well crowded.

Stemteemä spoke to Cogewea, her tone sharp and emphatic. The girl answered at length in Okanagan and without her accustomed blithesomeness. The little audience gave rapt attention as she narrated the frog incident on the river bank. The grandmother and Mary cast looks of displeasure at the Shoyahpee, but Julia appeared less impressed. The conversation was necessarily loud, because of the howling of the warring elements without, which seemed to increase in momentary violence. However, the storm ceased as suddenly as it began and the sun shone upon a drenched world.

After a futile attempt at gayety, Densmore departed for the bunk house; and the aged woman requested Cogewea to go change her clothing and then return to the tepee. She had a story of the past which she desired to tell her three grandchildren. [1927]

From *Coyote Stories*

Chipmunk and Owl-Woman

Kots-se-we-ah—Chipmunk—was a little girl. She lived with her grand-mother in the woods. Chipmunk liked to walk through the woods and pick berries. Some of the berries she ate, and some she put in a little basket that hung at her side. The basket was made from a deer's hoof.

There was one berry bush that the little girl visited every day. She called it her very own. It was a *see'-ah* (service berry) bush.[90] She would climb into it and eat all the berries she could hold. As she ate them she would count: "One berry ripe! Two berries ripe! Three berries ripe!"

One sun, while in the bush counting and eating berries, Chipmunk heard steps on the ground below. She looked. Standing under the bush was *Snee'-nah*—Owl-woman. On Owl-woman's back was a big basket, and in the basket were many little children that Owl-woman had stolen. Owl-woman travelled from camp to camp, stealing children. Whenever she got hungry, she ate one or two of them.

Chipmunk was not frightened very much, for she knew that Owl-woman could not reach her up in the *see'-ah* bush, and Owl-woman knew that too. But Owl-woman was cunning. In her best voice, she said: "*Kots-se-we-ah*, your father wants you."

"I have no father," Chipmunk answered. "He died long ago."

Owl-woman thought for a moment. Then she said: "Your mother wants you. She wants you to come home."

"My mother died many snows ago," Chipmunk replied.

"Your aunt wants you to come home."

"I never had an aunt," and Chipmunk laughed.

"Your uncle is looking for you," lied Owl-woman.

"That is funny," said Chipmunk, laughing some more. "I never had an uncle."

"Well," Owl-woman sighed, "your grandfather wants you."

"That is strange, for my grandfather died before I was born."

Then Owl-woman said: "Your grandmother wants you at home right away!"

Chipmunk could believe that. She was silent for a little, then she said: "I will not come down unless you hide your eyes."

"All right, I will hide my eyes. See! I have them covered," and Owl-woman pretended that she had. She placed her claw-hands over them.

"I can see your big eyes blinking behind your fingers," cried Chipmunk. "I shall not come down until you have hidden them entirely."

Owl-woman pretended to hide her eyes entirely, but she left a small space between her fingers—just a little crack to look through.

Chipmunk really thought that the eyes were covered, but she wasn't taking any chance of being fooled. Instead of dropping from branch to branch to the ground, she jumped from the top of the bush. She jumped over Owl-woman's head, and, as she went sailing over, Owl-woman reached for her. Owl-woman's fingers clawed down Chipmunk's back, ripping off long strips of the soft fur, but the little girl got away. Ever since that time the chipmunks have carried the marks of Owl-woman's claws—the marks are the stripes you see on the chipmunks' backs.

Chipmunk ran and ran, and Owl-woman followed as fast as she could.

When Chipmunk reached home, she was trembling and out of breath. She hardly could speak. All she could say was: "*Sing-naw! Sing-naw!*" ("Owl! Owl!").

The deaf old grandmother misunderstood. "Did you step on a thorn?" she asked.

"*Sing-naw! Sing-naw!*" Chipmunk kept repeating. She was so frightened, it was all she could say.

Only after Chipmunk had said that many times did the grandmother understand. Then she tried to hide the little girl in her bed, but Chipmunk would not keep still there. She ran around under the robes. Anyone could see she was there. So the grandmother took her out of the bed and dropped her into a berry basket. But that wouldn't do, for Chipmunk rattled around in the basket and made a lot of noise. Then the grandmother tried to hide her in a basket of soup,[91] and poor Chipmunk nearly drowned. She and her grandmother were in despair. They did not know what to do. Then they heard a voice—it came from a tree near the tepee. It was the voice of *Wy-wetz'-kula*, the Tattler— Meadow Lark, who was singing:

122

"Two little oyster shells
Hide her in!"

Quickly the grandmother put Chipmunk between two little oyster shells. And, knowing Meadow Lark was a gossip and a tattler, she took off her necklace and threw it to the singer. She hoped that the present would please Meadow Lark and keep her from telling where Chipmunk was hidden. Meadow Lark put on the necklace and flew away.

Soon Owl-woman came along.

"Where is the child I am hunting?" she said.

The grandmother pretended that she had not seen her grandchild, so Owl-woman began to look around. She looked in the bed, in the berry basket and in the soup. She looked everywhere she could think might be a hiding place. At last she turned to leave, and just then Meadow Lark flew back to the tree near the tepee. Meadow Lark sang:

"I will tell you, if you pay me.
I will tell you, if you pay me.
Where she is! Where she is!"

Owl-woman hurried outside and threw a bright yellow vest to the Tattler, who put it on, and sang:

"Two little oyster shells,
Take her out!
Two little oyster shells,
Take her out!"

Then Meadow Lark flew away. The necklace she was given for helping Chipmunk and the yellow vest she earned for tattling she wears to this day.

Owl-woman pushed the grandmother aside and snatched Chipmunk out of the oyster shells. With her sharp fingers she cut Chipmunk open and took out her heart and swallowed it.

"*Eh!* Yom-yom! It is good. Little girls' hearts are the best," said Owl-woman, smacking her lips.

Owl-woman went her way, carrying her big basket of children.

In a little while the weeping grandmother heard a familiar voice. Meadow Lark was singing again from the tree. Her song was:

> *"Put a berry in her heart!*
> *Put a berry in her heart!"*

Drying her tears, the grandmother put a half-ripe *see'-ah* berry in Chipmunk's breast and sewed up the hole. Then she stepped over Chipmunk three times, and Chipmunk jumped up as alive and well as ever. . . .[92]
[1933]

The Gods of the Sun and the Moon

Mole was lonely. Coyote was away on one of his long trips. Mole would not have felt so lonesome if all her children had been with her. But there were only two left with her at home. The others had grown up and gone separate ways, as families do. The two that were left were boys. They were little.

Every sun Mole became more lonely. One day she saw a rock of odd shape. She liked it. She pretended it was Coyote; she made love to it. After it she named the older of her two small boys. She named him *Stee-qu'-lot*—Heated Rock Child. The rock was warmed by the sun. On another day, while digging roots she found a root that was white. It pleased her. As her smallest son's skin was light in color, she named him after the root. She named him *Swee'-elt*—White Root.

The moons passed and Coyote did not return. The boys grew. *Swee-elt* told his mother that he could hear whispers coming up from the ground, and he asked her the reason.

"You are named after the roots," Mole explained. "The roots are your relatives. They call to you."

Stee-qu'-lot said that he could hear the rocks whispering to him, whisper-ing sounds of friendship, and his mother told him that the rocks were his relatives.

Coyote finally came home. He found his sons grown to fine big boys, and he was glad. He was sorry that he had stayed away so long. He took the boys to himself to train. Every morning he got them up and made them swim in the cold river; he taught

124

them to pray for strong medicine-powers. He was preparing them to meet hardships, to become good warriors. They became strong in body and spirit, and Mole was proud of them. *Swee'-elt* was handsome and white of skin, while *Stee-qu'-lot* was red of skin and strong and long of limb. He was a good hunter.

Coyote heard there was to be a big council in another country to decide on who should be the gods of *Kya'-len-whu*—the Sun— and *Skuk'-ach Kya'-len-whu*, the Night Sun—Moon. Coyote told his sons about the council. They wanted to go. They killed game, enough to last their parents while they were at the council. As they were leaving, Coyote suddenly decided to go with them. That left poor Mole all alone.

When Coyote and his sons reached the council they found the people worried. The people said they had not found anyone suited to take charge of either Sun or Moon. Many of the people had sought those honors, traveling in the Sun-lodge or the Moon-lodge across the sky, but all had failed. Either they were too hot or too cold or too bright or too dim.

"I will be the Sun-god," declared Coyote, and the people allowed him to try. He took the Sun-lodge across the sky. But he watched everything the people did. Seeing people in secret love, he yelled down to them, much to their embarrassment. He told on those who were hiding. The people were glad when that day was over. They lost no time in taking Coyote from the Sun-lodge. Then they asked Coyote's sons to try, but the sons refused. They wanted to remain on earth.

Now, among those at the council was *Swa-lah'-kin*—Frog Woman. She was old and ugly, but she was in love with *Swee'-elt*, the white-skinned. Her special medicine was rain. She caused a big rain to fall, and everything got sopping wet; the people were soaked to the skin and could not get dry, as all their fires were put out. All the fires but Frog-woman's were killed. Everybody shivered with cold—everybody but Frog-Woman.

Swee'-elt did not know that Frog-woman's heart was soft toward him. He suggested to his brother that they go to her lodge and get dry by her bright fire. *Stee-qu'-lot* did not want to go. Knowing that Frog-Woman loved his brother, he warned *Swee'-elt*; he told him to keep away—told him she was bad and powerful. But *Swee'-elt* became so cold that he went to her lodge by himself. Frog-woman was dressing a deer-skin by the fire. Her

125

lodge was warm and dry. *Swee'-elt* was glad he had come.

Looking up at him, Frog-woman said: "My husband! Take your place on the honored robe of your lodge."

Startled, *Swee'-elt* did not cross to the robe. Instead, he sat down near the entrance. He knew he should leave, but he did want to get warm. Frog-woman coaxed him to move to the husband-robe, but he shook his head and stayed by the doorway.[93] Seeing that her coaxing was of no use, Frog-woman became angry. Suddenly, she changed herself into a real frog and jumped—smack!—at the young man's smooth white face. She struck his cheek and clung there. "Now," said Frog-woman, "you cannot leave me. Not if you go to the edge of the world will you ever get another wife!"

Swee'-elt tried to take Frog-woman off his face. He tugged and scraped in vain. All the people came and tried to take her off. Nothing could budge Frog-woman. The people even tried to cut her off and to burn her loose from his cheek, but she did not move. At last *Swee'-elt* gave up hope. Ashamed of his appearance, he decided what to do. He said to the people: "I will take charge of the Moon-lodge. I will go with it across the sky."

Stee-qu'-lot wished to be near his unhappy brother, so he said: "I will take charge of the Sun-lodge. I will take it across the sky."

In his Moon-lodge, *Swee'-elt* travels by night. That is because he is ashamed of his ugly wife. He hates her. She still clings to his cheek. Sometimes you can see her when the nights are clear. And if a frog is killed and laid on its back or held belly toward the sky, you will see a cloud-blanket spread over the Sun or the Moon. The brother-gods always hide their faces from frogs that are placed in that way. Perhaps they think that the frogs are trying to make love to them.

Because he is of the heated rock, *Stee-qu'-lot* is well suited to sit in the Sun-lodge. *Swee'-elt*, being related to the white roots in the cool ground, is suited to stay in the Moon-lodge. His white face gives the Moon its light. That dark spot on his face is the hated Frog-woman. Moonlight is cool, because *Swee'elt* was of the root growing earth. His descendants are the white-skinned people. The descendants of *Stee-qu'-lot* are the red-skinned people.

When Swee'elt left the council-camp to sit in the Moon-lodge he said: "In the future handsome warriors will marry homely women, and pretty women sometimes will marry homely men. "

What *Swee'-elt* said is true to this day. He made it so from the Beginning.

[1933]

House of Little Men

The boney crooked fingers of Old Stem-tee-ma (grandma) commonly known among the Okanagons by old and young, shook and her beady one eye half shut, sparkled as she pointed to me the house of the little men. We stood over the weed sage-covered huge holes where deep under were tunnels partly caved in of the clay of the Okanagon hills. Still the memory of the sage brush smelly odor comes to my mind, the odor loved by the cowboy on the range and the frontiersman. They love it as well as the Indians, a mere handful of whom are left behind. They too will follow to the happy hunting grounds of the ancestoral race once strong in wars with neighbouring tribes of the land of the setting sun. Stemteema spoke in a hushed voice, and cautioned me not to tumble any dirt down the sacred home of the little men, for fear that the wind might rise against us in revenge on the bigger people, to blow their tepees down and raise the dust to the skies, and bring the water from the heavens, and anger the Thunder Raven Bird that spits fire in rage on any who makes light of the Cotszee (dug out dwelling) of the little people. Stemteema paused a moment to wipe the tear which stole [down] her wrinkled cheek, and told the story as follows, in her simple way:

This is the home where once lived for a time one of my forefathers, who later became famous through the powers that the little men gave him. His name was Left Hand, and all the people still speak of him among the Okanagons as a powerful warrior and medcineman. There has been no one who has been born since that could compete with him in knowledge and wisdom. I am the last of his descendants, and I have passed more snows (years) than any one living among our tribe.

When my grandfather was a little boy, he was very lazy, and he failed to hunt the Shoomesh (powers of a medicineman) no matter how much his parents urged him to hunt it in the darkest of the night, he would go only a short distance and lay down and sleep the rest of the night. When he was sent to the sweat to hunt powers, (the sweathouse is a cone shaped structure used for cleansing. They sweated in them and washed in water afterwards) he would fall asleep rather than watch and sing his prayers for the animal powers to come to him, to make him a warrior of bravery.

Each morning his parents would be obliged to hunt him up and waken him for his daily cold baths that would strengthen his sinews so that he might be strong in later years. He was not like other children, he was very greedy and lazy. No matter how much his elder talked and advised him he turned a deaf ear to the good word.

At last the father of Left Hand gave up hope for his only son, because he was ashamed of him. Rather than keep a child that would be worthless, he decided that Left Hand should die, rather than see him grow a cowardly warrior. In spite of all the begging of his mother, the father of Left Hand took him one dark night close to this [house] of little men, and he tied a strong buckskin string around his waist, he dropped him down in the deep unknown fathoms of the cotszee, there dwell the fearless little people. No one ever returned to tell of their death among them when once condemned to die, such was the customs many snows past. When a warrior is found stealing a man's food or furskins, or stealing the love of another one's wife, such is the price he has to pay when convicted by the members of his tribe. It was supposed that the little men ate them. A person can never get close to the little people without being chilled to the marrow, and cannot make the moccasioned feet move, nor the hand lift up. This made the Indians very afraid of the little men, and they held their haunts very sacred. Their hunting grounds were never touched by the feet of the braves, only in the dead of night would they dare come close to their home to punish the evil doers.

When Left Hand was dropped easily down the bottom of the cotszee half asleep he woke up surprised to see so many little people under-ground, almost as small in body as he was, but as they came closer to view him in surprise, his body chilled, it was without feeling in numbness. He tried to cry out in fear, but his speech failed to come, his tongue was dead, so was his body. The little men came to pick him up, and he lost the use of his mind.

Next that Left Hand knew, they had him in one of the deep under ground tunnels beside a sparkling dancing fire, and a sweet herb was smoking at his side to bring him back to life. The little people spoke an unknown language, and no smile ever passed their lips as he came to know. He saw that among them were women and little babes that were much smaller than any papoose he ever saw, wrinkled up little old men and women, that looked like they were nothing but little children of the bigger people that Left Hand had come from.

It was not many sundowns (days) after when child like, Left Hand forgot his own parents and began to take interest in the ways of this strange and new people, whom he came to love as his own tribe. He found that mysterious long and deep tunnels were dug everywhere under the hill sides of this mountain, and fountains of spring water dripped in wonderful hues, where the bathing places of the people were made. Soon he found that he could find the outlets either at the bottom of the mountain, or else at the sides and top. He unconsciously forgot his own people in exploring this hidden play ground underneath the hill, and when any of the big people would pass close to the mouths of the tunnels, he could smell them as the human odor which he learnt to dislike like the little men.

He learned to eat all the birds, and animals that the little men brought in from the hunt from the outside world. Reptiles were brought in and made pets of, while others were fattened to eat, and the skins of them were made into gowns for the little women and papooses. Moss, and tree hair were brought in for the bedding of the infants.

Left Hand played with his pets, the frogs and snakes, till one sun-down his favorite pet frog gave him the vision of the Shoomesh song, and before many moons passed Left Hand came to know all the powers of the underground animals. The bow and arrows he made from the ribs of the mountain goat which the little men killed on the outside hunt. But no arrows ever touched his pets, for he loved them. He would shape the clay into imaginary animals and practice shooting at them, pebbles were also his "wounded victims" with the little arrows. Soon he was capable of shooting an arrow straight at the aimed mark. The little men taught him the shoomesh powers of all the animals. Each sundown (day) he took his daily bath in the underground springs, so that his body would be strong of sinew for the future warrior that he was to be. The oldest men and women gave him the good word for the future in cunning, and in tracking the hunt.

Whenever a pebble or clay came down the smoke outlet of the cotszee it angered the little people and they would start their strange Shoomesh songs and soon the whizzing songs of the wind would be heard above in accompaniment to their music, and the thunder-bird would travel over the skies in anger, because of the powers of the little people. It is their revenge for being made light of by the bigger people of the outside world.

Thus Left Hand lived with those little men for many moons (months) till he grew larger than the wrinkled up old men and women. He found that the underground tunnels of the little people were too small for him to travel through. This cramped feeling caused him much worry. Thoughts of his early life came back to him of how bright the outside world had looked to him, when the sky was clear and wonderful blue in color, and how white the snow lay in winter. He remembered how with the coming of the spring the birds sang so joyously. Such thoughts caused him to lose interest in his pets, even the beautiful colored rattler lost its hue as he sat in thought brooding of his own people.

Left Hand approached the Chief of the little men with a sad heart, because he had grown to love them better than his own tribe. He laid out the troubles of his heart before them. The Chief called all the male members of the tribe of the wise little people and held a council to decide what was to be done with Left Hand, because he was outgrowing his adopted people. Soon it was decided that he should return back to his own tribe. Because he had found the ways deep into the hearts of the little men, he was given powers of the Shoomesh from them, equal to their strength, as a token to their friendship.

The little men climbed the steep walls of the smoke flue of the cotszee where Left Hand had been let down when a little boy by his father to die. It was the only big enough hole to let him out of the under-ground home. Soon they had hewed steps, so that Left Hand was able to climb out to the open world. But he had a sad heart for the people that he had left behind him. In his belt he carried the sweet-herb of life in preparation for the meeting with his own people.

As Left Hand drew near the first encampment of Indians he

fell down because of the strength of their scent. He was found and picked up, and after failing to have him come back to life, they found the herb in his belt. With the wisdom of the old, they burned it and smoked the nostrils of Left Hand, and life came into his limbs, but his tribal speech was only a fragment of a memory. He had almost forgotten his mother tongue. He soon learned it again, and found that other children had come into the home of his parents. They were a beautiful boy and little sister. He was welcomed back to the tepee fireside of his father, because he was soon to be found a wonderful hunter, and powerful warrior. Also they learned that he was capable of changing himself into an animal when needed.

One day after his parents were dead, Left Hand lived in the *Inwa-petk-qua* country (Kettle River) with his younger brother and beautiful virgin sister. Warriors came far and wide to ask her in marriage, but on token of refusal she would not prepare food for the braves who came to her tepee.

One time Left Hand and his brother were on a fall hunt, and were with a large Indian encampment. As was Left Hand's habit, he hunted only with his brother, while the rest of the hunters usually went in groups for fear of meeting the enemy. They had many wars with the surrounding tribes, especially with the hated Shu-swaps. Of this Left Hand had no fear, and he hunted alone.

Soon Left Hand tired of the chase. After killing all the game that he and his brother could carry, he decided that he would build a sweat-house and enjoy a plunge into the mountain stream. He gathered fire-wood and taking his flint arrows he struck them together over the rubbed dried bark of the cotton-wood, which soon started a blaze of fire and a cloud of smoke curled up skyward. Through the smoke a vision came to him. He jumped up suddenly with a growl like a grizzly bear and said to his brother:

"Brother, the Shu-swaps have killed all our people and have stolen our sister. Follow me." He quickly took up his arrows and went in pursuit after the enemy, after putting out the blazing fire smoke, which gathered and made itself look like a rising fog against the sky. This the quick eye of the enemy soon saw, and they said to one another:

"That is the smoke of Left Hand, he is close to us." But while others said it was only a fog rising. They ended the argument by taking the virgin sister of Left Hand as prisoner of war, with quick mocassioned feet they flew back toward their country. The Shu-swaps left in a large number, after killing the whole encampment, women and children.

Left Hand and his brother followed till they came close to *Nee-eh-hoot* (site, near Rock Creek British Columbia). Just as they crossed the creek, they saw the possession [sic] of the enemy where walked in their midst their sister. The quick eye of the Shuswaps saw them. But Left Hand immediately changed himself into an Ol-la-la bush swinging its branches from side to side with loaded berries, while his brother stood behind him hidden in the bush. The enemy argued that people were on their trail, while others said that it was only an ol-la-la bush. But the sister knew it was her brother, for she knew his ways, and was comforted.

The Shu-swaps continued their journey much faster, but had not gone far, when Left Hand again came in sight, and he was again spied by the enemy. This time he was too far ahead to hide himself and he turned into a fox, while his brother followed in his wake also a fox. They climbed the hill over-looking the enemy. This brought out another argument among the Shu-swaps. Some said they were positive that it was two men, while others now there pointed [signalled] that it was only two foxes, and their eyes were deceived. But the girl had courage for she knew it was her brother. The enemy went till darkness over-took them, and to be sure that Left Hand was not to find them, they went off the trail into the depths of the brush close to the river and camped after surrounding the bed of the girl so that her escape would be impossible.

Left Hand soon lost the tracks of the Shu-swaps and failed to follow by the help of the light that was left. His brother was discouraged. Left Hand soon found a way. He took the bear pelt stripped from nose to tail from his belt, and putting it over his nose he crawled over the ground and scented the tracks of the enemy, like the bear does. About the time that his brother thought Left Hand was deceiving him, Left Hand told his brother to stab the first enemy he came to, and keep killing till overpowered. He was to escape by the way of the river by fording it across and they would all meet on the other side.

Left Hand started killing the Shu-swaps, but his Shoo-mesh [was] getting the best of him, and instead of quietly doing the stabbing he soon gave a war-whoop which awakened the remaining warriors. They were too many for him and his brother. So he cut the strings that tied his sister, and the younger brother took her across the ford, while Left Hand stayed in the glory of murdering the enemy, but soon they over-powered him and he made his escape by jumping into the river. Left Hand wore a skin cape, and a sharp snag in the river caught his fur blanket. He was almost drowned when the frog that he played with, as a child in the house of little men spoke to him under the waters, saying, "Have you forgotten me in your haste? I told you that waters would never kill you; because it is my home. Why not sing my song and loosen your blan-ket and swim to shore?" Then Left Hand thought of his shoo-mesh song, and as he sang it, he was loosened and he swam like the frog to safety to his waiting sister and brother.

Left Hand, satisfied with his hunt with his sister and brother moved back to his home close to the house of little men.

Many snows had past and Left Hand was the only person of the big people that ever could visit and talk with the little men in their unknown language. One day far from the rising sun (east) came word that men of the pale-face were coming in hordes to hunting-grounds of Left Hand and his people. This caused the Indians many thoughts and worry of the heart. Soon Left Hand heard that the men with the pale faces were drawing nearer and nearer to his home. In the darkness of the night, he went to his adopted little people and consulted them on these men with the white skin. Then the hearts of the little men sank with chill of fear, because they foresaw that their under-ground home was soon to be wrecked by this strange people. Left Hand told them of a wonderful rocky hunting [ground] toward the setting sun (west) where he would take his adopted little people; where the moccasioned feet of the palefaces will not intrude, where new homes can be built away from all the big people, red and white faces.

One dark night, Left Hand led his little men away to the rocky tops of the big mountains of the setting sun. He took them all—men, women and papooses. That is why the little people moved their camp forever to the sinking of the sun, where they still live and enjoy the wilds of the woods and the animals to their command, where hunting-grounds are not turned into the whiteman's herbs of food, nor their berry trees chopped down, and [re]placed with the pale face berry bush.

Heaving a little sigh, Stemteema turned away. Picking up her pee-cha (root digging stick) she started to digging more spit-lum (bitter roots), she stripped the dirt which left the herb white and tender. She soon filled her basket and started homeward. Before following her, to satisfy myself I threw rocks down the sage covered holes of the old home of the Little men. The wind came soon accompanied by thunder and lightning just as Stemteema warned me, and this made me believe her story to be true.

Stemteema turned her wrinkled face towards me and asked: "Did you throw stones into the House of Little Men?"

I shook my head in denial. Pointing her accusing crooked finger at me, she said, "You lie."

Note: Location of the House of Little Men is situated near Oroville, Washington, some 18 miles north in B.C. Scientists have made researches, but no one is found small enough to investigate the tunnels of this legend.[94]
[1930]

The Red Cross and the Okanogans

The Red Cross today has a far more significant meaning to the Indians of the Northwest than ever before. It is no longer a mere "money making scheme of the white man," but in reality an institution of charity. The soldier of the trenches and prisoners of war have long known its worth, the Belgians, young and old have blessed it, but not until now, since the coming of the white man among us with his new ideals, have we from our hearts felt gratitude of his coming. The charitable efforts of the Red Cross has put us in touch with the unselfish side, with the true nature of the foreign brother who lives in our midst. It is an historic fact that the Indian in general entertains no love for the "higher civilization," and that he is ready to grasp at the most forlorn hope held out for the recovery of his halcyon tribal days. Perhaps this Government will never know the full extent of the German propaganda that was spread among the different tribes, how the old and ignorant were excited by the promises made them by the mercenaries of the "Baby Killers," how their vast hunting domains would be returned to them if only the arms of the Kaiser prevailed. To this end the Red man should join cause with his overseas friend. Many disputes arose among the tribes. The old and uneducated sympathised with the Hun, while the younger and more enlightened counseled peace and continued allegiance to our own country. It is to these half-educated tribesmen the nation owes a debt of gratitude for fidelity maintained. The splendid patriotism of the thousands of our best young men who joined in the world fight for democracy, attests the true steel of the Red race, hampered though it is by undue Governmental restrictions. And now the Red Cross has effected a change of heart among many of our fathers and mothers, and we younger Indians feel a joy in the closer union of the two races, the brotherly love which "peace on earth" should bring to all peoples.

Marcus, a little town on the Columbia River,[95] was the first to come to the rescue of its Indian population suffering with the dreaded Flu. Assisted by the Deputy Sheriff, John Lane, the Red Cross reopened the old hospital which was proffered free by its owner, a physician residing at Newport. Liberal donations poured in and commodious quarters were provided for the stricken Indians, who were wholy unable to cope with the strange malady. Mr. Lane found several homes with corpses lying in the same room where the remaining living members were too weak and emaciated to bury their dead or care for themselves. Using persuasive methods, with that generosity of heart for which he is noted, he carried these poor invalids in his own car to the "Sick House" [hospital] of the white man. In some cases the aged and superstitious could not be induced to leave their squallid homes, but remained to fight fate with that stoic indifference to death for which our race is renowned. To these, such aid and comfort was rendered as possible under the conditions.

The Indian population of Kelly Hill[96] and adjacent valleys would no doubt have been wiped out by the epidemic had it not been for the Red Cross. The lady members of this humane body devoted themselves to the dusky patients who filled the wards of the hospital. Day and night they relaxed not their vigils, but cared for the sick with all the tender patience of the true mother and sister. The simple minded recipients at length understood and appreciated this care and attention. Dr. Parker donated his services and his wife and others kept close watch over the afflicted. One boy in particular, an only lad, the sole comfort and aid of his aged parents, came down to death's door, but was saved by the experienced nursing of the Mother Superior of Ward Mission, who came daily until the danger point was passed. Father Schyler of the same Mission visited the hospital whenever called, sometimes on foot and untiring. The Catholic Indians wanted to be right with the white mans' God before leaving for the Happy Hunting Grounds with its visions of wild freedom which finds place in the mind of every tribesman, however Christianized.

Mr. Lane, in company with Dr. Parker, went down to the South half of the Colville Reservation, visiting all the sick and arrousing the Red Cross spirit of Enchelium.[97] Aided by the Indian Agent, they partitioned the dance hall into two wards, where many lives were saved to the tribes. The Indians were well cared for, either by the Red Cross or the Indian Agency, as far North as the international boundary line; and we feel that we are fortunate in having a place in this great republic. In the upper part of the reserve, about Oroville, there were no deaths from the Flu; but just across the boundary, where lies Smilkameen, Penticton and Inkameep reserves, the grim reaper harvested unstaid [unstayed]. Canada, renowned for her generosity and wisdom in her management of Indian affairs, rendered no aid. War-torn and exausted, with her thousands of maimed and health-ruined soldier boys to care for, the Government seemed powerless or inert to the condition of the tribesmen, and the suffering and mortality has been appalling. Many pathetic incidents could be narrated. Chief Antoin Nachumchin[98] lay ill in the same room where his younger brother was dying with that dread scourge, tuberculosis. It devolved on a young sister to care for the two brothers in addition to the nessesary work both inside and outdoors. One day the girl spoke of feeling unwell and Antoine warned her not to leave the warmth of the house. But fuel must be had. She went out, gathered wood and began chopping it. Soon the sound of the axe ceased. Antoine arose from his fevered couch and went out to find her lying unconscious by the little armfull of wood which she had succeeded in cutting. The brother carried her into the house, and a half hour later, her spirit fled. Her teeth had burst in the awful agony of death. Despite such suffering, this devoted sister had not, to the last atom of her strength desisted from ministering to the wants and comfort of her stricken brothers. The patience of the Indian woman endures without murmur or complaint even unto death. Can greater love and fidelity be found in any race?

An old blind Indian lost his four children on whom he leaned for support. His aged wife was nearly as helpless as he. He rallied from the Flu, went out willingly to try doing the work which would never again be done by his children, took relaps and sank rapidly. While dying, he said: "God has surely forgiven me my sins, for the blindness and afflictions which I have suffered. The sunshine I have missed in this life, will be all the more resplendent in the next world. With sight restored, I will there see my children again. I am willing to let go."

In Penticton, there were many deaths. The custom of indiscriminate visiting of the sick among the Indians is prolific of fatalities. The Indian police forbade this, and by enforcing the edict, many lives were saved. At Inkameep, notwithstanding no medical aid could be had, there were no deaths. The Indians began sweat-housing as a "sure cure" for the Flu. I warned them of the danger of such course and they desisted. It was soon learned that keeping warm was a better system of dealing with the scourge.

137

We also found that mentholated Okanogan sage brush was an infalable remedy for the Flu. Make into a strong tea and drinking it hot, effects a cure within three or four days with no after attack of [p]neumonia. It is a vile smelling, nauseating liquid.

The Flu put fear into the Indians as much as did the dreaded smallpox which swept them off by the hundreds in past years. So long as the Indian can understand what he is combating, he has but little or no fear, but it is the subtel, incomprehensible which mystifies and terrorizes him. When the scourge first struck the Okanogan country, many of the Indians said: "It is the white mans' sore throat disease which is killing him off. The white man dies too easily. It will never hurt us." It is different now. Many of our people have died. Some resisted it from the first with good results, while others made light of it until too late.

The casting aside of the tepee and adoption of modern houses has had an evil effect on our race beyond calculation. Fresh air is lacking. Owing to his former mode of life—in the open and well ventilated tepee—the Indian does not understand how the air can become poluted and deadly, does not understand the value of clean air. In his ignorant and primitive state the Government and misguided reformists thrust upon him a condition unfitted to his needs and bodily comfort. Windows are "for the admission of light," the tepee had none. Oftimes a large family will occupy a single room, day and night with the windows hermetically sealed. Diet is also neglected. Many die from overeating. They believe that food is strength and why resist an inclination to take it when wanted?

But while we are proud of America's part in the Red Cross, thankful for what it has done for the Okanogans, there is something lacking in its true efficiency, in all that it is supposed to stand for. No aid has been offered the stricken Indians across the Canadian border. Relief is sent to foreign lands, not even denighed the baby murdering, women mutilating Hun, but none has been forthcoming for the dying, simple minded natives at our very door on the North. Perhaps this is because of the lack of publicity. Whole families have been, and are afflicted, in many cases not one is left to provide firewood for warming the fevered sufferers. Oftimes corpses have rotted in the room where the sick lay moaning in delerium—dying with the piteous cry for water

scarce articulated by baked and parched lips. I would that there were more white men and white women like those of Marcus, the little hamlet on the banks of deep rolling Swanetka.
[*1919*]

PART TWO

EARLY SETTLEMENT AND RELATIONS

Something Very Real

Janet MacArthur

Susan Louisa Moir Allison (1845-1937) is an intriguing figure in British Columbia settlement history. Long seen as an exemplary "pioneer gentlewoman,"[1] she is also someone who stood between cultures as did the women of Syilx descent discussed by Jeannette C. Armstrong. Like Mourning Dove, she left an extensive body of writing, much of it devoted to Syilx ethnography and story, and accounts of her interactions with many Indigenous people of the interior. Similarly, she developed respect for the Syilx way of life and conveyed this in her work; and she had relatives on both sides of what became a deep divide between peoples. And like many of the other white writers whose record appears here, Susan Allison had her Indigenous informants who enabled her to leave a rich legacy of writing about the Syilx, the only trace, in some cases, of many of the *sməlqamix* or Similkameen people of the settlement period. In addition, she was motivated, as were Marie Brent and Hester White, by a desire to leave an account of early settler experience. She and her husband John Fall Allison (1825-1897) are numbered among the "first wave" of interior settlers as are Brent's and White's fathers. As the eldest by a generation or so of all the women whose work is collected here, she is the only first-person voice in this volume of someone who was of age in the earliest days of settlement. Allison's work also stands as an invaluable detailed account of the interdependence of Syilx and settler women in the domestic contact zone in early British Columbia. It is therefore fitting that the Historic Sites and Monuments Board of Canada unveiled a stone monument to her in Veterans' Square in the city of Princeton, British Columbia, in 2010. At that time, she was honoured as a person of "national historic significance. . . . who worked very hard to promote friendships with the Aboriginal people in the area. Susan Louisa Moir Allison wrote about her experiences, including those concerning Aboriginal people and their contributions to the community" ("Government").

Susan Allison arrived in the *snməlqytkʷ* or Similkameen River area in the 1860s with conventional views of the inferiority of the

Indigenous people. The selections of her writing in this volume indicate a shift over time away from this perspective because of an experience of transculturation, which occurs when "peoples geographically and historically separated come into contact with each other and establish ongoing relations, usually involving conditions of coercion, radical inequality, and intractable conflict" (Pratt 6). While such relations do indeed characterize settler and Syilx contact, and while it is important not to lose sight of Allison's privilege as a white person, her early decades in the interior were nevertheless positively transculturational, leading to the development of "copresence, interaction, interlocking understandings and practices" (Pratt 7) between herself and the Syilx. Her accumulated knowledge of and respect for the Syilx way of life and ways of seeing emerge in a chronological reading of her work.

Susan Allison first came to the interior as a new bride in 1868 over the Hope Trail to her husband's ranch near what is now Princeton. The British Columbia interior was sparsely settled at this time, yet, in spite of living largely in the absence of white community there, an exuberant one-sentence paragraph in her "Recollections" introduces her account of her new life: "Then began my camping days and the wild, free life I ever loved until age and infirmity put an end to it" (Ormsby, *Pioneer* 21). For most settler women, this move would have constituted an enormous rupture in identity—loss of family and community ties, particularly the company of other white women, and a confrontation with that most challenging aspect of displacement, the inability to speak the language of the majority. To be sure, she was not the only white woman who lived in the Similkameen and Okanagan at this time, but others did not leave her extensive written record. She was also an engaged listener, open to observing and trying to understand another culture. Thus, she came to occupy a liminal or in between space. On the one hand, she was a well-connected early settler, both on the coast and in the interior; on the other, she had respect for, understanding of, and close community and kinship ties to the Similkameen people. Hers became an ambivalent position which was often very difficult to negotiate as increasing racialization[2] of settler and Syilx communities in later settlement periods created enduring hardship for the Syilx. Haunted by this, she became critical of settler attitudes though it was difficult for her to state this publicly. We have therefore included excerpts not only from her published writing but also from her personal papers, letters, and other unpublished material. In the latter, she is more frank and direct in her criticism of settlers.

Critical Framework

My use of the terms "contact zone" and "transculturation" signals the influences on my analysis of postcolonial theory and studies of race that put in question some of the assumptions upon which the mainstream histories of this region were built. These tended to foreground and celebrate settler experience, establishing a pioneer heroic myth largely focused on male settler experience, and they made little mention of the Syilx and what settlement meant for them. Instead, a "genteel frontier" (Reimer 1) that honoured the ethos established by middle-class British settlers was constructed by important twentieth century historians such as Margaret A. Ormsby and Leonard Norris. British law and codes of civility were seen to positively inflect British Columbia settlement, particularly when compared to what occurred in the United States. Quite recently, studies of settler colonialism, a branch of postcolonial studies, have interrogated this interpretation of history producing an analysis of settler attitudes and psychology foregrounding some of the darker legacies of the Canadian civilizing project. I draw on this work too. I also take gender into account in settler and Syilx experience, drawing attention to Allison's awareness of the radically different subject positions[3] instituted for Indigenous versus non-Indigenous men and women. While this essay is not concerned with unseating the figure of the pioneer gentlewoman, it disrupts the stereotype of the middle-class British settler woman as the beacon of propriety and consolidator of white sovereignty so confidently depicted in nineteenth-century British Columbia as the remedy for the "wild, free" life in the new areas and among new peoples seen as a threat to civility.

I begin the ensuing discussion by recounting the development of Allison's friendships and kinship ties to the Similkameen people, as this was the context that produced transculturation. Then I compare her early writing about the Syilx, where conventional settler views shaped by what have been termed the European "Racial Contract" and "Settler Contract" are very much in evidence, to later writing which records her loss of faith in these. Even so, she shared the settler view common in the late nineteenth and early twentieth century that Indigenous people were being diminished, even to the point of extinction.[4] I then argue that her writing therefore increasingly becomes an attempt to "re-member"[5] or commemorate, as she says in her introduction to her long poems, the Similkameen people and their way of life observed during her early days in the interior. This commemorative objective—with its concomitant goal of depicting injustice—emerges as a central motive for extended projects such as her long poems about the Similkameen chiefs, Quin-is-coe and In-cow-mas-ket.[6] It also explains her interest in depicting many Indigenous women, particularly in a writing project she called "Some Native Daughters I Have Known." These character sketches reveal the dynamics produced by the intersections of attitudes toward gender and race in the settlement period. I then examine evidence of Allison's knowledge of Syilx spiritual practice. Finally, I address her very unsettled[7] feelings late in life, largely represented in personal letters, as she discloses her views of injustices endured by the Syilx people and her anxieties over the precarity of her Similkameen friends and relations in the 1930s.

Friends and Relations

In her "Recollections" (circa 1930-32), Susan Allison's depictions of specific "camping days" that "she ever loved" always contain accounts of native orature heard on the trail. Interestingly, she also asserts that "they [Indigenous people] told me more than they told other white people" (Ormsby, *Pioneer* 41). She appears to have learned a great deal from the many Indigenous people who traded at the Allison store or lived near or worked on the Allison ranches, particularly members of the Chuchuwayha[8] band —they were the mainstay of her community for many years. Accounts of the lineage, accomplishments, movements, and relationships among the Syilx, and her contact with them, are fulsomely represented throughout her writing. Ledger books which she kept at the Allisons' store and trading post contain accounts of Syilx customs (Ormsby, Introduction xxx). She frequently refers to Tatlehasket, brother of Chief Quiniscoe, as "my good friend" (Ormsby, *Pioneer* 56), and to Ashnola John, a notable Syilx Chief from traditional lands in the *Asynulox* (Ashnola River)[9] area, as a friend to the couple. Suzanne Cole, sister of Quiniscoe who assisted at the birth of Susan Allison's first children, is remembered as "a perfect treasure and so was her boy, Hosachtem, and I always feel grateful for the kindness I received from them" (Ormsby, *Pioneer* 28). She also uses honorific titles for the Similkameen medicine men and healers, "Dr. Cosotasket" and "Dr. Scuse." Among her friends was Shlawhalakan (Ormsby, *Pioneer* 35) whose elderly father Tamtusalist told her stories that she transcribed and titled "Tales of Tamtusalist;" Charlie Yacumtecum (Tuctac),[10] employed throughout his life by the Allisons; Johnny Suzanne, a packer; Cockshist, "the well-known Indian guide who had served [Edgar] Dewdney and [Peter] O'Reilly" (Ormsby, Introduction xxviii-xxix);[11] Métis Johnny McDougall[12] in the Okanagan; and Chief Incowmasket, the source of many of her stories (Phillips-Wolley 158). Moreover, many of the names of Syilx people she knew are used for characters in her long poems and sketches, suggesting her desire to commemorate them.

Susan Allison was also related to the Syilx. During the early 1860s, John Fall Allison had been married to Nora Yacumtecum (1847-1926). She was a niece of Quiniscoe, the sister of Charlie Yacumtecum, and likely the daughter of the medicine man and knowledge keeper Dr. Scuse.[13] Nora Yacumtecum and John Fall Allison had three children--Elizabeth Lily (Lily) (1863-1943), Albert (Bertie) (1865-1933), and Charles (Charlie) (1868-1913). Lily is mentioned many times in the recollections though she is not identified as John's daughter.[14] Tip Anderson, an Indigenous descendant of Nora and John Fall, asserts that "[a]ll the white [Allison] kids knew that Lily was a half-sister and they were all great friends...There was no animosity" (qtd. in DeMeer). In addition, Susan and John Fall's first child Edgar Moir Allison (1869-1943) was in a first marriage with Emily Sicamen, a woman from the Lower Nicola Indian Reserve. He had two daughters from this marriage: Nellie and Christine (L. Thomas 205). The Allisons' second child, Robert Wilfred or "Will" (1872-1926), was married to Rachel Pierre,[15] the daughter of Chief Quiniscoe. They had ten children by the time of his death in 1926. On the evidence of 1930s letters written from Vancouver—where she lived from 1928-1937—the struggles and poverty of Will and Rachel's children were a source of considerable anxiety for her.

Settler Ways of Seeing

I have found the concepts of the "contracts"—the Racial Contract and the Settler Contract—that guided colonial and settler activity in British Columbia useful in my analysis of Allison's life and writing. These created not only the settlers' sense of entitlement, but also the enduring, difficult social position of the Syilx. Charles W. Mills identifies the Racial Contract, widespread among settlers in Canada, as having its roots in "biological racism" which was constructed by Euro-western science during the Enlightenment of the eighteenth century. At that time, classificatory studies of species of animals and human beings were vastly expanded. Biological racism is a key component of Euro-western cultural thinking about physical difference, particularly skin colour. It is based on the belief that one's race is inherited genetically, that is, passed through the bloodline, and that this biological inheritance (or "blood quantum")[16] determines much more than physical differences. It is said to form essential aspects of our capacity, character, and morality. Mills asserts that the Euro-western Racial Contract instituted during the early modern period (circa 1400-1600) designated certain people as "white" and others as "non-white," the latter bequeathed "a different and inferior moral status" which justified the exploitation of the "bodies, lands, and resources" and denied them "equal socioeconomic opportunities" (11).

Incorporating Mills' work on the Racial Contract and extending her own earlier work on sexuality and gender,[17] Carole Pateman has traced the foundations of what she calls the Settler Contract based on the Euro-western concept of *terra nullius*. "New World" lands were perceived as empty—as wilderness or wasteland in the "state of nature," not put to use, not owned, "unhusbanded" (Pateman, "The Settler" 36), and therefore not civilized. This view was inherited from Roman law which defined that which is not put to use or owned as *res nullius*, "an empty thing, or a thing that belongs to no one" (36). She elaborates:

> Defenders of colonization in North America, including political theorists, frequently invoked two senses of *terra nullius*: first, they claimed that the lands were uncultivated wilderness, and thus were open to appropriation by virtue of what I shall call the *right of*

husbandry; second, they argued that the inhabitants had no recognizable form of sovereign government. In short, North America was a state of nature. (36)

Both the Racial and Settler Contracts pivot on the perception of Indigenous people as animalized creatures without full human status, and of their social organization and relation to the land as inadequate for any claim to sovereignty over it (or themselves); in other words, they are not en*titled* to (civil) subject status, that is, citizenship, or land. Pateman has also called attention to the intersections of the Racial and Settler Contracts with patriarchal conceptions of gender ("Race" 154). Until recent decades, the role of gender and sexuality seldom formed part of mainstream accounts of settlement history in Canada and elsewhere. Allison's written record, however, subtly reveals her growing awareness of how European notions of gender difference that are part of the Racial and Settler Contracts have had a traumatic impact on the lives of Indigenous men and women whom she knew. The perspectives of many non-Indigenous Canadians on land and sovereignty were (and to some extent still are) shaped at the convergences of Euro-western ideologies that have produced racial hierarchies, patriarchal concepts of gender difference, and the assumption that "wild" or unhusbanded land is an unencumbered commodity.

Her Shifting Perspective

In "Sketches of Indian Life" written in the 1870s, Susan Allison identifies Indigenous people as "by nature" uncivil and congenitally inferior, thus lacking intellectual, ethical, and affective capacity in comparison to white people. Written much earlier than many of the other pieces collected here, it bears all the hallmarks of colonial thinking about Indigenous people. Upholding the civil/savage, legitimate/illegitimate, human/sub- or non-human oppositions grounding the Racial Contract, it contains a series of confident pronouncements on the humane treatment of Indigenous people in British Columbia, their gratitude for white luxuries, and on cordial relations between settlers and them. She is, moreover, hard on their polygynous marital customs and the practice of exhumation. Finally, she implies that without the white man's sovereignty over them, the "old savage in their nature" makes a quick return.

She gradually moves away from this kind of discourse and its implicit support for racial and settler entitlements. Indictments of settler treatment of the Syilx penned by Allison appear in later (mostly unpublished) writing. In her academic journal article (1892), she notes the physical and mental decline of the Similkameen people ("Account" 305): "civilization has nearly finished the work begun by small pox, viz., the extinction of the tribe" (305). Instead of the satire of the "savage" attempts at civil dress and culture among Indigenous people evident in the "Sketches," civility and civilization become increasingly ambivalent, even negative, terms. "Civilized" is often used in earnest to describe the behaviour of Indigenous people (Ormsby, *Pioneer* 52) in the "Recollections" (circa 1930-32), and the term "savage" is very hard to find in later writing. Her long poems about the Similkameen chiefs also indicate her support of Syilx people. In her unpublished "Introduction to Incowmasket: A Poem of Indian Life, Part One" (circa 1890s), she states, "This [her sequence of long poems] ... is an account of the lives, manners and customs of the Similkameen Indians as I knew them in the sixties, seventies and eighties, while they were still a 'free' people—I may say a passing[18] people" with "beautiful religious ideas and their own manners and customs." Declaring that alcohol, among other things, has diminished them, she concludes: "the white man has much to be ashamed of in his treatment of the rightful owners of the land."

Based on the dating of some of the "Tales of Tamtusalist" focussed on Chiefs Quiniscoe and Incowmasket, it appears that Susan Allison was working on narrative poems about them as early as the 1870s. She met them in the spring of 1869 when the Chuchuwayha community passed her house on its way from winter quarters. Her sequence of long poems about them consists of four parts: an "Introduction," "In-Cow-Mas-Ket, Part One," "In-Cow-Mas-Ket, Part Two," and "Quin-is-coe." Quiniscoe died and was succeeded by his brother Incowmasket sometime in the late 1800s. The sequence of poems recounts Similkameen life before and during the early settler period, ultimately subverting many of the mainstays of white settler thematics shaped by the Racial and Settler Contracts. When published in 1900 by Scroll Publishing in Chicago under the pseudonym "Stratton Moir,"[19] the "Introduction" and "In-Cow-Mas-Ket, Part Two" were left out, likely because of their direct or strongly implied criticism of settlers, which would perhaps have alienated a largely white readership. Settlers as characters are not present in "In-Cow-Mas-Ket, Part One" and "Quin-is-coe," which attempt to capture idyllic pre-contact life.

"In-Cow-Mas-Ket, Part One" depicts this chief's traditional way of life with his wise "grandsire," his two wives, and his children. Allison inserts much *captikʷɬ* (Syilx narrative) she had been told into the grandsire's stories. The main plot relates the attenuated illness and tragic death of the chief's only son Hosachtem. "In-Cow-Mas-Ket, Part Two" begins with a priest coming to the village to comfort the grief-stricken Incowmasket. Particularly exercised about the Syilx practice of polygamy, the priest recommends conversion as the best remedy for all that has gone wrong. Incowmasket's anxiety worsens after an earthquake, which he has been encouraged to interpret as a sign of the Christian God's wrath. After a period of agonizing indecision on this issue, exacerbated by the Chief's dotage on his young and flighty second wife Chin-Chin (whom he may have to renounce), Incowmasket considers conversion. He calls a council and various voices speak for and against conversion. The strongest rhetoricians are the councilors (the grandsire, Cosotasket, and Tatlehasket)[20] who stand against this assimilative pressure; nobler descriptors are applied to them than to the supporters of conversion. These latter are either sheepish, ravished by illness and barely able to stand, dressed in the trickster garb of the coyote (*sənk'l'ip*), or possessed by the myopic fire-and-brimstone bombast of the newly converted. "In-Cow-Mas-Ket, Part Two" ends in widespread alienation of many of the leaders and the breakdown of the Chief's own family. (His older wife Semminatcoe, whom the Chief forsakes in favour of Chin-chin, seeks out a spell which is cast upon and fatal to the latter.) Cosotasket, a privileged voice in the piece, vows to leave the community. Rather than the conventional settler faith in Indigenous survival and spiritual evolution via assimilation, conversion brings cultural dissolution. And whatever theme we can extract from the deadly deployment of occult forces by a scorned wife, the story does not seem to demonize traditional polygynous gender relations among the Similkameen.

"Quin-is-coe" is a discrete narrative about the last days of this

151

great Chief whose encounter with Souie Appoo, the evil spirit of Mount Chippaco (*c'q^waq^w* or Mount Chopaka in northern Washington State), results in his decline and death. The Souie Appoo first appears in "In-Cow-Mas-Ket, Part One" in the grandsire's brief account of the story of the evil spirit of Mount Chippaco who kidnaps women (lines 72-75). Susan Allison writes at length about the Similkameen conception of the Souie Appoo as a complex figure in an essay in the *Similkameen Star* in 1912. Here she repeats the story of Quiniscoe's encounter with the Souie Appoo on Mount Chippaco that she includes in her poem "Quin-is-coe." In the article, she notes that these spirits are not "altogether as bad as their name indicates (devils), most of them seem to be neutral" and that other manifestations of the Souie Appoo discussed with her by Similkameen people are partly human and partly animal with the body and face of a man but with antlers, deer hair, eyes, and limbs ("Origin" 3 Apr. 1912).

In "Quin-is-coe," the Chief encounters a Souie Appoo, here a "spirit of evil," when alone on Chippaco, "the bearer of clouds." Chippaco is repeatedly figured as an overpowering site of fog and darkness. When Quiniscoe returns, beaten and dazed, the men decide to go back to vanquish the Souie Appoo, against the forewarning of the grandsire. Beaten back again, Quiniscoe and the men return, and Quiniscoe falls gravely ill. A wise doctor, Scuse,[21] attempts but fails to wrest the "evil foul one" from Quiniscoe and he dies. Allison's "Souie Appoo" could be a rendering of the Syilx term "Sho-yah'-pee" widely used—in variant forms among the Syilx and other groups—to denote the white man. Paul D. Kroeber identifies as shared vocabulary "Okanagan *suyapix*, Kalispell *suyapi*, Coeur d'Alene *suyepems*, Nez Perce *so-ya-po*, Sahaptin *snyapu*" (426) all with this meaning.[22] Whether or not Susan Allison was aware of this connotation, interesting interpretive possibilities are left open either way for this story and its transmission.

Three years after his death, the "disquieted spirit" of Quiniscoe, half grizzly and half man, returns and commands that his body be disinterred, his bones reassembled in new skins, his spirit feted at a funeral feast, and all reburied since his people have forgotten him and what he represents. In its attention to Syilx funeral, burial, and exhumation rites, the poem seems to assert the importance of preserving and maintaining links with the pre-contact past. The thundering prose Allison uses to depict the revenant Quiniscoe suggests that Similkameen traditions, though under threat and increasingly forsaken, have a profound and enduring reality. This work marks a significant departure from her depiction of the Syilx in "Sketches."

Re-membering Indigenous Women

In my view, much of Allison's writing can be read as her attempt to "re-member" her friends, acquaintances, and kin among the interior Indigenous people, to honour the ancestors of her mixed heritage grandchildren, and to leave an account of a vanishing people and their lifeways, a motive shared with many other white people of her time who subscribed to the "dominant ethnographic myth of [the] cultural demise of indigenous people" (Wickwire, "They" 299). Many passages from Susan Allison's "Recollections" are yet another record of her ambivalence, and her uneasiness about the Racial and Settler Contracts. When passages from them are juxtaposed with some unpublished material in this anthology, it becomes clear that Allison was chary at times of her largely white public readership.

Allison's "Recollections" often take the side of Indigenous people, for example, in her version of the story of the "wild" mixed heritage McLean brothers: Allan, Charles, and Archibald. In the late 1870s, the "wild McLean boys,"[23] who were all hanged, were portrayed as alcohol-inflamed "breeds," a common epithet for mixed heritage people, on a rampage who got what they deserved for terrorizing the settlers.[24] She links their crime spree in 1879 to their fury over the dishonouring of their sister Annie McLean by a prominent official and wealthy white businessman in Kamloops though she does not name him. In the "Recollections," he is described as "a man of high standing" (Ormsby, *Pioneer* 46) with whom Annie McLean became too "intimate" (46) before marriage, resulting in a pregnancy. He spurned Annie, then married a white wife. Recent accounts of the McLean episode link it to the widespread and easily triggered dissent of all kinds among interior Indigenous people being displaced by settlement, as well as to the McLeans' anger over their sister's predicament. Allison departs from the mainstream view of her time, expressing sympathy for the injustices that led to the McLeans' crime spree. In the account in the "Recollections" of her own frightening encounter in the Okanagan in the 1870s with one of the McLean brothers—who was passing by her house with his sister Annie— she states: "His sister, a fair girl wearing a sunbonnet, passed riding a side saddle and carrying an infant. Poor girl, she was going to her mother's people! The Indians are good to those of kin to them" (Ormsby, *Pioneer* 47). This depiction registers her awareness of the struggles and vulnerability of a mixed heritage woman like Annie McLean (though "brought up in a convent and most accomplished . . . [and] in Kamloops society" [Ormsby, *Pioneer* 46]) on the margins of the white civil order. An implied comparison of the Indigenous community's acceptance of Annie McLean and her child versus their abjection as "illegitimate" under the provisions of the Racial and Settler Contracts seems to be present here. Adele Perry discusses the many ways in which Indigenous and mixed heritage women were often excluded from "legitimate" and "respectable" subject positions (48-56). Allison does identify and excoriate the businessman and politician John Andrew Mara (1840-1920) as the man who seduced and betrayed Annie McLean in a letter written to her daughter Louisa Johnston on November 28, 1930, where she confides some troubling things still haunting her from the past: "And the poor McLean boys hunted to death, because their mixed blood (wild highland and Indian) could not brook to see [John] Mara sitting in high places and their poor sister [Annie McLean] driven out an outcast from all but her Mother's people. I have of course not mentioned Mara's name—I knew and liked the little girl he married." Her state of being in between is writ large here in the difference between public and private accounts.

The "Recollections" also provide another glimpse into the gendered contact zone in a long description of an unnamed woman who, according to Allison descendants, has been identified as Nora Yacumtecum, John Fall Allison's first wife. Shortly after her arrival in the Similkameen in 1868, Susan Allison received a call from "a niece of Quiniscoe, the 'Bear Hunter'" (Ormsby, *Pioneer* 23) who was dressed up "for the occasion" (23). Discomfited by the unnamed woman who spoke little and "fix[ed] her eyes on the opposite wall" (23), Allison confesses that she was "not used to Indians then and knew very little Chinook" (23). Remembering her relief when the woman left, Allison tells us, "I know now that I should have offered her a cigar and a cup of tea" (24). Given the severe penalities for disclosing the existence of a union between Syilx and settler, or white paternity for their offspring,[25] Allison's decision to depict Nora Yacumtecum at all invites speculation given that the Indigenous wife was widely inveighed against in early British Columbia as an affront to white ideals of sacramental, monogamous marriage as the foundation of a wholesome civil society. Perhaps Allison's negotiation of various audiences, two in particular—white Vancouverites at their Sunday papers versus an "insider" white and/or Indigenous readership who knew the contact history of the Syilx with the Allisons—provides a clue. For her (white) newspaper audience, Allison provides an account of Nora's indecorous hybrid dress and of the culture shock of a "gentlewoman" in first contact with Indigenous people represented as a threat to the implementation of "white civility" (Coleman *passim*). On the other hand, insiders would likely find the passage a particularly amusing account of unsettlement in a new domestic contact zone, but perhaps not view Nora as the interloper. The failure to offer the cigar and the tea hints at her ignorance in the early days of some contact zone (or perhaps Syilx) protocol. The description of Nora comprises one discrete paragraph with no further commentary.

Allison may have wanted to commemorate Nora for the descendants of both women—this latter group likely one subset of the insider readers; she may also have been leaving a trace of what Jean Barman has termed the "lost history" of the "first families" (post-contact) of the southern interior ("Lost" *passim*) who were created by the union of white men and Indigenous women. Long occluded,[26] this history has only recently become part of some popular and academic histories. In a slide presentation at an Allison family reunion in 1999 attended for the first time by white and Indigenous descendants, the presenter noted that John Fall Allison "left Hope on July 9th, 1860 a journey that would have consequences for all of us. On this trip he probably met Nora Baptiste [Yacumtecum] who was the leader of the trail. It is believed Nora was responsible for showing [him] the Hope-Skagit-Snass route" (Meldrum 2), which became part of the Dewdney Trail. Nora was likely an important guide on routes into the Similkameen that became parts of both the Hope and the Dewdney Trails. Susan Allison also notes that John Fall Allison was following "Indian trails" in the early 1860s (Allison,

"Early" 5 Jan. 1923, p. 3), describing what is now the Allison Pass on Highway 3. Perhaps Nora Yacumtecum's foundational role in establishing John Fall Allison's reputation as a "trailblazer" motivated Susan Allison's depiction of her. To this day, John Fall's fame (and Susan's for that matter) for being among the first to arrive in the Similkameen and the Okanagan is based on the Euro-western concept of *terra nullius*.

Nora Yacumtecum's descendants affirm that she was from "a royal blood line," had a "pack train venture" with many horses and employees with which she "hauled groceries and mining supplies from Hope to Greenwood," and that she "likely . . . made John Fall aware of the Allison Pass route" (Martens). As Jeannette Armstrong suggests, marriages or unions such as theirs were not perceived as "illegitimate" in the fur trade era and early settlement days. They established a solid network of kinship that worked well for both partners. An Indigenous wife was important for a myriad of things: basic survival needs, companionship, security of passage through Indigenous lands, business dealings, translation, and safety as one began to "prove up" an isolated pre-emption. It is not that the Racial or Settler Contracts did not exist during the time that Nora Yacumtecum was with John Fall Allison, or did not inform the behaviour of white people in the early period; more likely, it was expedient to suspend specific aspects of the Contracts for a time. As the Contracts were implemented with increased white settlement in the late nineteenth century, the majority of early settler men of the interior separated from their Indigenous or "country" wives and sought out non-Indigenous ones. Under the terms of the Contracts, non-Indigenous men with Indigenous wives would risk "deracination" (Perry 70), losing their place within the "civilized race" (Perry 70), and being identified as "squaw men," a common settlement-era slur.

Indigenous and non-Indigenous descendants of John Fall and Nora Yacumtecum, however, have asserted that she went back to her people before he married Susan Moir. Nora Yacumtecum's successful business could have been the reason. By the mid-1860s, John Fall had a big stock operation and was often away. Running the store likely would never have appealed to Nora as she could maintain a good living with her pack train. (Susan herself states that she "hated storekeeping" [Ormsby, *Pioneer* 60]). Whatever the nature of her relationship with John Fall, Nora Yacumtecum most likely continued to capitalize on her skills as a horsewoman— the Similkameen people were (and still are) renowned for their riding skills and played an important part in life on the trail.[27] A nostalgic glimpse of the early days at the Allison store and ranch by Susan and John Fall's grandson Alfred Thomas calls attention to the presence and importance of Indigenous women like Nora in the southern interior's early transportation industry. Based on his mother Caroline Allison Thomas's (Carrie's) recollections, he suggests that by the time of John Fall Allison's death in 1897, the trail life and camping days were coming to an end:

> The pack horse and the pack train as a means of transportation were beginning to pass. No more would the cry go up from the younger [Allison] children, "The pack train's coming." No more would they run up the path on the long flat to meet it. No more would the Indian women who accompanied the men on the trail, reach down and grasp a child by the hand and pull it up onto a horse for the ride the rest of the way to the store.
>
> (30)

This particular way of life would soon disappear as would the livelihood it brought to men and women like Nora. What happened to her livelihood is likely related to many developments that confined and impoverished the Syilx: increased settlement, the Indian Act of 1876, the reduction of reserve lands, increasing segregation and restrictions on mobility and employment opportunity, destruction of wildlife and fisheries, and programs of forced assimilation, most infamously, the residential schools. It is therefore not surprising that Susan Allison often draws a distinction between early settlers as hardier and ethically superior particularly in their treatment of the Syilx to those who came later, however shaky that distinction.[28] Though interior Indigenous people were organizing against encroachment in the early settlement period that Allison re-members with nostalgia, the negative impact of contact seems not to have been as profoundly evident to her until later.

Another Similkameen woman is depicted in Susan Allison's piece "G-he-nac, Sister of Quin-is-coe," also included in this anthology, confirming Allison's interest in leaving some kind of evidence of the ill treatment of the Syilx. "G-he-nac" is one of the essays in Allison's unpublished sketches entitled "Some Native Daughters I Have Known." "G-he-nac" points up the ways in which the Contracts—enshrined in civil and criminal law, and practice in the penal system—could emasculate, animalize, and "disappear" Indigenous men at this time. Allison makes clear that in her first meeting with Ghenac, Ghenac held her in contempt and would only speak to her through an interpreter. Allison also adds, "she hated all white men," without giving any back story. Gradually, as trust builds, Ghenac calls upon Allison to write letters for her, one of which is a request to authorities on the coast for permission to retrieve Ghenac's deceased nephew's body from New Westminster for burial in the Similkameen. The body is that of George Jim (also known as Ashnola George) who had died in New Westminster Penitentiary while serving a sentence for killing another man.[29] Permission is granted, the body retrieved at Ghenac's expense, but it is not that of George Jim. More inquiries are made, a second body retrieved, but it is that of a "Chinaman," suggesting another venue in which the Racial Contract was fully operational in the 1880s. According to Allison, yet another body is sent, but the people "would not open the coffin;" they just buried it and "refused to cross the mountains anymore."

In the archives of the Department of Indian Affairs are a series of letters written during the year 1889.[30] They begin with a letter written for Ghenac from the Similkameen Valley on April 8, 1889, which bears "her mark" (G-he-nac, Letter) to Arthur H. McBride, warden of the New Westminster Penitentiary. Whoever did the writing on her behalf is not indicated. Ghenac asserts that the body she paid to have sent to her in the Similkameen is that of "a Chinaman," and not her nephew, and asks, "Will you please kindly tell me the truth? I know you will not lie to an old woman like me." In a reply of April 18, 1889, McBride admits that the wrong body was sent and offers to pay for another coffin and to cover the expenses of sending the right body but only to Hope (McBride, Letter to G-he-nac). Another letter written for Ghenac in the Similkameen by Father LeJeune, OMI, dated May 13, 1889, gives McBride notice that George's body cannot be retrieved at Hope until July 6, "on account of high water in the creek," then itemizes and asks for recompense for the expenses she incurred for the retrieval of the first body and the funeral (LeJeune). In a reply, McBride (Letter to G-he-nac, 28 May 1889) refuses to cover any additional costs. In other letters in this file, Joseph W. McKay,[31] Indian Agent for the Okanagan, appears to have then taken over advocacy for Ghenac (Letter to McBride, 13 June 1889). In this terse letter, McKay demands that McBride cover full expenses for the coffin and the transfer of the body all the way to Chuchuwayha, but in a reply dated June 21, 1889 (Letter to Joseph W. McKay), McBride stands firm on his offer of transport to Hope only. McKay then becomes pro-active, writing to his superiors in Indian Affairs who contact federal authorities (Letter to Hamilton Moffatt, 4 July 1889). The case appears to have been resolved after much back and forth among McKay, McBride, and McKay's superiors in the Department Indian Affairs who refer the case to the federal Department of Justice. It rules in Ghenac's favour and McBride complies with an order to send the body to the Similkameen.

Confirming many details of this archival record, Susan Allison's account in "G-he-nac, Sister of Quiniscoe" also discusses the aftermath of various unsuccessful attempts to have the body of George Jim delivered. Allison also recounts how Aunt Ghenac is told some time after these episodes that George Jim had been spotted in Buffalo Bill Cody's Wild West Show. Allison claims that she wrote to Cody on Ghenac's behalf, but his "nice polite answer" was that no one among the Indigenous employees knows or knows of him.

Allison's narrative "G-he-nac" is also similar to one told by Okanagan storyteller Harry Robinson to anthropologist Wendy C. Wickwire in the 1970s titled "Captive in an English Circus" (Robinson, *Write It* 244-66) about a Sylix man allegedly pressed into service in an English circus. Robinson's story is much more detailed than Allison's, including specific dates, and recounts the story George Jim told someone else about his plight after he disappeared from the jail. Again, Robinson tells of the bodies— of people other than George Jim—that were packed into the Similkameen Valley at the behest of an aunt and uncle.[32] Rather than his being in the Wild West Show, however, Robinson claims that George Jim was encountered in England by a "half-breed" named Charlie Harvie from Enderby who had been stationed in the Canadian military in England, possibly during the Second Boer War (1899-1902). Robinson's account (based on what George Jim told Harvie) cites 1886 as the year that Jim was sent to the penitentiary to do a seven-year term. Robinson states that "he was in there three years" after which he was taken—without explanation—by the policemen and guards to the train in Vancouver, then sent across Canada and to England. Overseas years later, Harvie, who spoke the Okanagan language (*nsyilxcən*), is told of Jim's presence in England and taken to see him. George Jim tells him about how he is forced to work for one or two months at a time as some kind of spectacle in a travelling show (Robinson, *Write It* 261). He appeals to Harvie to contact his "well off" aunt and uncle in Ashnola and ask them for help in getting him back to Canada. Harvie delivers the message when he returns to Canada a year later, but through miscommunication and lack of understanding of how they can obtain money from Indian Affairs to cover travel costs, they "never get him" (263).

Canadian soldiers were in England from 1899-1902[33] making Robinson's timeline plausible. George Jim could have arrived in England in the late 1880s or early 1890s and been performing for around ten years before Canadian troops were in England. The letters in the Department of Indian Affairs assert that George Jim died in April, 1888. Jim could also have been with the Wild West Show when it toured England and Europe in 1887, 1891, and 1902-04. There were, of course, many other circuses, human zoos, travelling shows, and installations that exhibited non-white people in Europe at this time, a particularly contemptible outcome of European notions of sub-human species and race. That Susan Allison was motivated to bear witness to the tragedy of George Jim and that this story continues to circulate among the Syilx people is a testament to a poisoned history of which she decided to leave a trace.

We have also included three other essays written as part of "Some Native Daughters I Have Known." These provide more evidence of Allison's connection to and respect for the Indigenous women who were part of her life in the Similkameen. "Our Louisa" provides a detailed account of Susan Allison's household under the strain of taking care of extended family during a measles epidemic around 1904-05. Susan Allison and her youngest daughters Alice and Angela ("Angie") are helping nurse their older brother Edgar, his wife Marguerite, and his young son Percy. Grandson Wilfred, Jr., better known as Buck

Allison later in life, and son of Susan's son Wilfred (Will) Allison and his Syilx wife Rachel, is also there, as is Babs (Constance Thomas), the infant daughter of Susan and John Fall's daughter Grace. It is to this ailing household that "Louisa" (Susan Allison's middle name and the name of her mother) gives invaluable help. A fragmentary essay on a woman named Emma Hutchy gives us an entertaining glimpse into the Cariboo frontier in its heyday and of Indigenous women making their way in marriages and partnerships with white men, adapting and contributing to the new way of life that had transformed the interior so quickly after 1858. "Kind Penquinac or the Princess Julia" is an elegiac piece written to honour Penquinac (1874-1901), beautiful daughter of Chief Incowmasket and the namesake of a character in both "In-cow-mas-ket, Part One" and "In-cow-mas-ket, Part Two." She died a tragic death at an early age. Allison depicts her idyllic childhood and adolescence, compared to her later struggles, another record of the effects of settlement on the Syilx over time.

tmxʷ ulaxʷ: Loving/Ancestor/Land/Spirit

Allison's writing also reveals her understanding of Syilx sacred figures and religious practices. In the early 1870s, she witnessed such practices "from a log at the fence" (Ormsby, *Pioneer* 39) and of them, she states,

> Well, I watched the doctors and came to the conclusion that they used a force or power that we know little of. You may call it animal magnetism, telepathy, or give it any name, but it was something very real.
>
> I am afraid I have been mooning over my memories. I put in a good time one way and another in the early 70's.
>
> (Ormsby, *Pioneer* 40)

After this, she does not elaborate on these practices but moves to another unrelated topic. This passage is typical of the "Recollections" where there are abrupt transitions and truncations of anecdotes which seem to encode a repression of the urge to bear public witness to her feelings and what she knows about the Syilx, that is, to give us the whole story. Accounts of Susan Allison by descendants and some unpublished personal papers cast light on what "mooning" might entail and on this confidence in "something very real" in Indigenous religious practices. She was interested in eastern religions, psychical research, spiritualism, theosophy, and a lifelong devotee of meditation: "sunrise, high noon and sunset would find Grandma and my mother [Alice Perkins Wright] observing this practice," writes granddaughter Evadne Perkins MacKenzie (81). Allison also met with theosophist Krishnamurti[34] in Vancouver on one of his tours. He came to visit Susan Allison, having read and been impressed with her essays on spirituality (MacKenzie 81-82).

Susan Allison also gives careful treatment in the "Recollections" to what she knows about $n\check{x}a\textipa{P}\check{x}\textipa{P}itk^w$ [35] or what the Vernon Rotary and the Vernon Board of Trade dubbed "Ogopogo" in 1926 (Ormsby, *Pioneer* 109, n22:2) in their appropriation of this mythical figure for tourism in the Lake Okanagan Valley. She gives a more detailed account of the creature in a handwritten piece in the BC Archives titled "What I Know of Ogopogo," published in this anthology. Comparing the accounts is revealing. In the "Recollections," she states that her Indigenous friend, the packer Yacumtecum (or Tuctac), told her "yarns" about it when she first travelled to the interior:

> The Indians did not call him that [Ogopogo] but spoke as if it were some supernatural entity and pointed out where it lived on an island in Okanagan Lake as we passed the spot. My husband always laughed at the Indian yarns but I did not, for I thought that there must be foundation for what they said. They told me more than they told most white people.
>
> (Ormsby, *Pioneer* 41).

In "What I Know of Ogopogo," she shares more, affirming that she "listened to the stories of the Indians with an open mind" and "being Highland Scottish on my father's side . . . partially believed in the monster." Here she also admits to having seen the creature and affirms that the stories are not "yarns." Fear of ridicule or of sexist accusations of "hysteria" or perhaps circumspection about providing another Ogopogo story for white cultural appropriation may explain her decision to leave this sighting out of her published "Recollections." A summary of Susan Allison's sighting based on "What I Know of Ogopogo" did appear in the *Similkameen Star* in 1926. It was written by the editor as a preface to Susan Allison's poem "Okanagan Lake," which was published beneath it. This poem tells the story of the lake creature devouring some white canoers, while the Indians, who know the signs and go ashore, listen to their screams (Sterne 57-60). Allison's circumspection about sharing her sighting in her "Recollections" may convey her awareness of its spiritual significance in Syilx life.[36]

Her discussion of the lake creature in "What I Know of Ogopogo" contains references to the differences among white, Chinook, and Syilx nomenclatures for it, and to Indigenous reverence for the creature. She states that the Syilx used the Chinook names for it, referring to it as "'*Ook-ook mis-achie coupa lake*' (the wicked one in the lake) or as the '*hyas-hyas gust scaca cupa lake*' meaning the 'huge animal in the lake.' This creature they seemed to dread and spoke of it with lowered voices." She states that she never knew the Syilx name for it. In contrast to the widespread binary thinking in western culture that underwrites the notion of the human/non-human, the Okanagan language does not signify binary and hierarchical distinctions among land, people, animals, and so on. But the term "Ogopogo," bereft of Syilx meaning, appropriates, fragments, and degrades—put in western terms, it would be a kind of iconoclasm. Some sense of the sanctity of this creature that belongs only to those with an understanding of the radical difference between Syilx and settler ways of seeing seems present in the subtext of Allison's various discussions of it. Perhaps this constitutes another nod to the "insider readers" such as Syilx and mixed heritage descendants and friends.

Some of what she may have learned is best explained by Jeannette C. Armstrong's discussion of Syilx story and how it conveys Syilx thinking about the relations among people, land, animals, and language, which is in contrast to European hierarchical organization of created things and rigid distinctions between subject and object, spirit and matter, the human and the non-human, the animate and the inanimate:

> Syilx Okanagan *captik^{w}ł* device and structure articulates and mimics the Syilx Okanagan *tmx^w ulax^w*

or land animated by *tmixʷ* - the land's life forms, referred to as "relatives," embodying the dynamics of the interrelationship between the flora and fauna of the Okanagan land. *captikʷɬ* expresses and demonstrates a concept of *tmixʷ* which translates better as life-force. The concept extends to the Syilx Okanagan understanding of the land as the *tmxʷulaxʷ*, which translates better as a life-force-place, rather than of land as location or ecology type. The *tmixʷ* are understood to be many strands which are continuously being bound with each other to form one strong thread coiling year after year always creating a living future.

(Constructing 2-3)

Allison's characters the old grandsire and Cosotasket, both important voices in the poem "In-Cow-Mas-Ket, [Part Two]," express this conception of the relationality and interdependence of a whole living system (lines 48-72, lines 427-480 respectively) in their rejection of the arguments of other councillors for conversion to Christianity. Indeed, the vexed council depicted in this poem that comes to an impasse over conversion also reveals Allison's understanding of collaborative decision-making known as *Enowkinwixw* that grounds Syilx political process. The poem reveals how this has been violated by those urging conversion.

"Looking back on my past life with all its pleasure and pains"

A set of Susan Allison's letters, from a private collection, written from Vancouver in the 1930s confirms some of the conjectures in this essay about her in between position. Struggling financially as many people did during the Depression, Allison expresses concern for the financial challenges of many of her descendants. She looks to her writing for the *Province* newspaper primarily as a source of income, telling her daughter Louisa Johnston (living in Princeton) that "It is only need that has made me write and I have left untold more than I have written" (November 28, 1930). Moreover Allison's concerns for the particularly acute poverty of her Indigenous grandchildren and widowed daughter-in-law Rachel in the Chuchuwayha community frequently surface in these letters, as does her knowledge of the fates of so many Indigenous people she had known for much of her life. Most importantly, the writing records her difficult position in its account of her frustration about what she knows, how she views it, and the anxiety she feels about disclosing it.

A letter dated February 18, 1930, makes clear that the contemporary Racial Contract is creating ruptures in the family—here she expresses her appreciation to daughter Louisa for her "goodness to Will's children." These would have been the children of her eldest son Robert Wilfred, who had passed away in 1926, and his Syilx wife Rachel:

> . . . . their [white] cousins who have had so much better chances and have done nothing with them, have the gall to look down on <u>breeds</u> [Allison's underlining] as they call them who have made the most of nothing. Will's children are like himself always dear to me— even if I can't help them as I wish to—I promised both Will [her son or his son Will, Jr., aka Buck] and Henry[37] [Will, Sr.'s eldest son] to do whatever I could for Mary [Will, Sr.'s, daughter] and that seems to be nothing. I will write to her—I can do that anyway . . . . I think I can understand my elder children better than the younger—Ed and Will, BJ [Beatrice], Rose, and You— seem to belong to another generation . . . .

Will, Sr.'s, daughter Mary,[38] who turned 17 in 1930, appears to have been confronting difficulties of some kind. In many letters, Susan Allison asks Louisa about Will's children, particularly Mary and Mary's ailing little sister Maggie (Margaret). In one, she suggests a Roman Catholic school for Mary either in Vancouver or Kamloops, and a letter written later in the year confirms that Allison herself had contacted Sacred Heart School in Vancouver on Mary's behalf. Will Allison, Jr.,[39] or Buck, appears to have been her principal contact with this family at this time, a regular correspondent, and an occasional visitor. Will, Jr., is also a source of information that Susan Allison shares with Louisa about Maggie who is enduring a prolonged illness—Maggie died at Hedley on March 3, 1932, at the age of 14. Susan Allison's reference to her elder children in the letter cited above—coming on the heels of her condemnation of the use of the term "breeds" by some white grandchildren—seems to imply that some of her descendants do not hold the same views as some others in her extended family.

In her letter to Louisa, written on November 28, 1930, at the time her "Recollections" were appearing in the *Province*, Allison appears to be considering writing a more substantial book-length memoir to generate some more income. But the tone of the letter suggests that she knew that an even longer life writing project[40] would have meant further confrontation with the ghosts of the past, and her white status and the cultural capital it had accrued, compared to the sad legacies bequeathed to her Indigenous friends and relations. The following haunted passage from the same letter to Louisa conveys her anxiety—in its uncanny juxtapositions— along with the writer's block that this has created:

> If Mr. Scott [editor of the Vancouver *Province* newspaper] would help with a Book it would I humbly think sell looking back on my past life with all its pleasures and pains. I seem like a spectator of the events instead of an actor—and when I think of my first trip out to the Similkameen with Tucktack [Tuc Tac or Charlie Yacumtecum] as bell boy, I grieve over poor old Yacumtecum—blind and helpless being mushed up by an Auto!! Dear old Joe McKay I love to think of but I have not told all I know of anything. And the poor McLean boys hunted to death. . . .

This passage conveys great tension induced by the narratives she knows and the narratives she can tell. She must choose between the story of a settlement process that is destructive to the Similkameen or the highly marketable story of pioneer success. There seems evidence here of her awareness of the injustice of a white cultural apparatus that was having a negative impact on her grandchildren and others. These unsettling images return to disrupt any plans to write a triumphalist pioneer memoir. Near life's end, many things remain unreconciled.

But to conclude that her life's work and writing were a futile exercise would be mistaken. Susan Allison clearly belongs among the group of non-Indigenous Canadians in settlement-era British Columbia who were uneasy with the implementation of the contracts that underwrote settlement.[41] During their time, they struggled with limited venues and opportunities for action and dialogue. But their record is not unrelated to contemporary decolonization movements. For example, the *Truth and Reconciliation Commission of Canada: Calls to Action* can be used as a means of speaking to the many spectres that unsettled Susan Allison and that she left an account of, such as the inattention to Indigenous child welfare and health care rights (*Truth* 1-2), the presence of racialized victims of injustice in the legal system (*Truth* 5-6), and the lack of respect for "Indigenous spirituality" (*Truth* 7). Her recognition, however conflicted, of Indigenous people as the "rightful owners of the land" invites us to "repudiate concepts used to justify European sovereignty over Indigenous lands and peoples such as the Doctrine of Discovery and terra nullius" (*Truth* 5). As part of the process of breaking the old Contracts today, restoring the role of Syilx people in settlement history, perhaps by "including First Nations, Inuit, and Metis representation" in Historic Sites and Monuments (*Truth* 9) in regional centres in the Similkameen and acknowledging them as persons of national historic significance, would go some way to re-membering the stories she "left untold."

Susan Moir Allison (circa late 1850s). Location unknown.
Courtesy of the Princeton and District Museum and Archives.

Susan Louisa Moir Allison
1845-1937

In British Columbia settlement history, Susan Allison (1845-1937) is renowned, in no small part because she left an extensive body of writing, much of it focused on the Syilx people of the Similkameen and Okanagan Valleys where she lived for many decades in the late nineteenth century and early twentieth. Most famous are her "Recollections" written in the early 1930s for the Vancouver *Sunday Province* newspaper.[1] The "Recollections" convey deep nostalgia for her life after her marriage in 1868 and subsequent move to the interior which marked the beginning, she states, of her "camping days and the wild, free life I ever loved till age and infirmity put an end to it" (Ormsby, *Pioneer* 21). Besides the "Recollections," she left a large body of written work, both published and unpublished, a significant accomplishment given her demanding life as a stock raiser, storekeeper, and parent of fourteen children, born between 1869 and 1892. It was the conditions of the early decades of settlement—she identifies them as the 1860s, 70s, and 80s (Allison, "Introduction to Incowmasket")—which provided her with the opportunity to learn a great deal from her Indigenous friends and associates about their lifeways. Her extensive record of the Syilx and of her contact with them make a very useful contribution to the study of British Columbia history.

In 1860, at the age of fifteen, Susan Moir came to the Colony of British Columbia, residing at Hope, New Westminster, and Victoria over a period of eight years. In 1868, she married Similkameen prospector and rancher John Fall Allison (1825-1897), moving to his ranch and trading post called "Allison's" in what is now present-day Princeton when the area was sparsely settled. From 1873-1880, the Allisons also ranched on the west side of Lake Okanagan (West Kelowna area) where she led what she describes as a "perfectly ideal life" (Ormsby, *Pioneer* 47) at the home she called Sunny Side. The Allisons and their children returned to the Similkameen in 1880 after a bad winter and loss of stock. As the area grew in population, Allison's became one of the biggest ranches in the area. John Fall Allison died in 1897 though his wife maintained their ranch for some time after this. In the early twentieth century, she sold off property and moved into Princeton. By this time, she had many descendants and had become a revered early settler. By tradition, the Thursday in August of each year closest to her birthday became celebrated locally as "Similkameen Day" which culminated in an Old Timers' banquet at which she often spoke ("Similkameen Day"). In

1928, she retired to Vancouver to live with her youngest daughter Alice where she continued to write well into the 1930s before her death in 1937.

At first blush, this educated daughter of the British middle class may not have seemed predisposed to embracing the rigors and isolation of settlement life, much less to developing an interest in the culture of the Syilx. Born Susan Louisa Moir in Colombo, Ceylon (now Sri Lanka), on August 18, 1845, she was the youngest of three children—Stratton, Jr., Jane, and Susan—of a Scot from Aberdeen named Stratton Moir and his English wife Louisa Mildern. Allison's references to the Moir family's long record in the colonial service often emphasize their colonial sense of adventure, which may account for her own adaptability as a settler. Stratton Moir, Sr., was the third generation of Moirs to live and work in Ceylon. Like many educated British people of the time, the Moirs and other relatives found opportunity in the military or colonial civil service and also acquired land in Ceylon. Moreover, Susan Allison's lifelong practice of meditation and her interest in non-western spiritual traditions are arguably linked to the family's residence in south Asia. Stratton Moir, Sr., died there when Susan was only four which necessitated Louisa Moir's return with her young family to England to live with relatives. There Susan received what appears to have been a very solid education for a young woman at that time in London schools. Evidence of this education and of wide reading appears in her sophisticated diction, and many references to Greek mythology, the Bible, history, and literature in her writing. Likely seeking the only escape from dependency on relatives available to a middle-class Victorian widow whose independent income was shrinking, Mrs. Moir married Thomas Glennie, also Scottish, in the late 1850s. Glennie, who had had considerable inheritances, was keen to live as a "country squire in a virgin country" (Ormsby, Introduction xii) on cheap land in the recently established Colony of British Columbia. Thus the family, except for Stratton, Jr., embarked from Southampton, England, to the Colony via the Panama Isthmus in 1860 when Susan was fifteen.

In the first wave of the British middle-class settlers in the coastal colonies, the family formed close ties with many who became renowned businesspeople and politicians. In the "Recollections," she states that she lived among those "whose names are commemorated in the Vancouver streets and have passed into provincial history" (Ormsby, *Pioneer* 19). In 1864, her sister Jane Shaw Moir (1843-1906), two years older, married Edgar Dewdney (1839-1916) of the Royal Engineers and moved with him to the capital of the Colony at New Westminster. Dewdney became an important political figure in early Canada, serving as an MLA, a federal cabinet minister, and Lieutenant Governor of the Northwest

Territories and eventually of the province of British Columbia. Shortly after the wedding, Glennie, with legal proceedings pending for debt, disappeared. However, little mention of this desertion is made in "Recollections" of the 1860s; instead, Allison focusses on the routine of dances, dinners, horse races, leisure trips, visits, and so on, in short, on the "jolly good time" (Ormsby, *Pioneer* 13) typical of life in British colonial enclaves.

Susan Moir and her mother went to live with Jane and Edgar Dewdney shortly after Glennie left and began to make adjustments, Susan working as a governess in Victoria for awhile, returning to New Westminster in 1866 after getting an inheritance with which she bought a small house, which she shared with her mother. After this, she and Mrs. Glennie, then in late middle age, opened a school in Hope in 1867 (Ormsby, Introduction xxii). Their connections notwithstanding, the challenges confronting these two single women attempting to make an independent living in colonial British Columbia cannot be overstated. Another misfortune came in 1866 at the news that brother Stratton, Jr., had perished of yellow fever in the West Indies on his way to the Colony to support his family (Ormsby, Introduction xxii). Some time after, Susan and John Fall Allison began a courtship which culminated in their marriage on September 3, 1868.

John Fall Allison (1825-1897) was originally from Leeds, Yorkshire, his family immigrating to the state of New York in 1837 where they settled in Oriskaney. John Fall departed as a young man for the California gold fields. He arrived in the Colony of British Columbia in 1858 then worked claims on the Fraser River bars the following year. He was commissioned by Governor James Douglas in the spring of 1860 to prospect the area around the forks of the Similkameen and Tulameen Rivers (akɬtulmn, meaning "has red paint"), known early on as Vermillion Forks, for the red ochre cliffs in the vicinity. Susan Allison writes that Douglas directed him to "go and inquire into the facts about some rich placer ground reported to have been struck by some Hudson Bay employees on the north fork of the Similkameen river, or the Tu'a-meen as it was called by the Indians" (Allison, "Early History," 5 Jan. 1923, p. 3). Going by way of the Similkameen River, though thinking he was on the Tulameen, he came to the forks where he eventually settled, via the long southerly route that would come to be known as Allison Pass. The first person he encountered in the area was Johnny McDougall, "a Hudson's Bay half-breed, with his Indian wife and family" ("Early History," p. 3), mining on the river. Chinese and white miners were also in the area. John Fall pre-empted land in the Princeton area in 1861 where he began to raise cattle for the coastal and other markets.

Nora Yacumtecum (left) with granddaughter
Maggie Terbasket (née Allison), 1925.
Courtesy of En'owkin Centre.

During the early 1860s, John Fall had an Indigenous wife—
Nora Yacumtecum (1847-1926)—a member of the Syilx people of the
Similkameen River area who owned a pack train and is acknowledged
by many today as his guide on a number of the trails he explored and
reported on as good routes for railroads or wagon roads, most likely
including the Allison Pass and other routes. In her recollections, Allison
recounts her first journey to the Similkameen over the "Hope Pass"
which became the principal route for settlers moving between Hope
and the Similkameen, the Okanagan, and the Kootenays. He and Nora
had three children: Elizabeth Lily or Lily (1863-1943), Albert or Bertie
(1865-1933), and Charles or Charlie (1867-1913). Whatever the nature of
their life as partners was, Indigenous and white descendants claim that
Nora went back to her people before he married Susan. Lily was often
with John Fall and Susan Allison's family over the years assisting with
the store and the household, a common position for mixed heritage
daughters in the settler period. Moreover, Susan and John Fall Allison
had fourteen children between 1869 and 1892: Edgar Moir (1869-1943),

Robert Wilfred (1871-1926), Beatrice Jane (1872-1956), Susan Louisa (1874-1955), Rose Isabella (1875-1902), John Stratton (1877-1908), Caroline Elizabeth (1878-1975), George Mortimer (1879-1948), Elfreda Flora (1881-1961), Alfred Edward (1883-1954), Valeria Grace Helen (1884-1969), Harold Archibald (1886-1951), Angela Aurelia (1889-1982), and Alice Olivia Ashwick (1892-1971). The elder two sons, Edgar (Ed) and Wilfred (Will) were married with children to Indigenous women, so Susan Allison had friendship and kinship ties to the Syilx.

Throughout their marriage, John Fall Allison was often absent on cattle drives, maintaining herds and doing business on the coast and in many areas of the interior. Susan Allison was therefore frequently on her own running the store and ranch, long known to people in the interior as a stopping point and supply centre. When she first arrived, she was under pressure to learn Chinook quickly to cope with her role. In the early decades, there were few non-Indigenous people in the vicinity of their ranches in the Similkameen and the Okanagan. Miners and a few pre-emptors were in the area, and government officials, researchers, hunters, visitors, and other settlers occasionally stopped by. However, her "Recollections" suggest that the fabric of day to day life consisted of the presence of Indigenous and mixed heritage people coming and going at the store, assisting with family emergencies, giving advice, and doing paid labour for the family. The situation was similar in the Okanagan where her closest neighbours were the Syilx in what she termed the "Indian camp" below her house. She relied on them for protection, she tells us, when "there was a strong undercurrent of unrest" (Ormsby, *Pioneer* 48) in the late 1870s. In the bad winter of 1879-80, the Allisons' losses set them back considerably. Sunny Side, as she called their ranch, was therefore sold and they returned with their young family to their land at the forks, so they could avail themselves of the livelihood that the store provided while they rebuilt their herd.

Here, the Allisons continued to expand their holdings. In 1897, in her early '50s, she lost her husband, but she was able to maintain the ranch into the early century. By the turn of the century, many of her older children had families of their own although she still had children at home. She gradually sold off parts of the ranch and moved to a small house in Princeton. She was often called upon to give accounts of the "early days" and she obliged, speaking and writing numerous pieces for the local newspaper. In 1928, she permanently retired to Vancouver to live with her youngest daughter Alice Allison Perkins (later Wright) and her family where she continued to write. Here she became a member of the Order of the Star of the East, an international theosophical association, and it was here that she penned her "Recollections" published in the newspaper beginning in 1931, six years before her death in 1937.

Her written work is wide ranging and some of it difficult to date. Our selections are mostly taken from her writing about the Syilx, but she also wrote historical long poems about European and American history, essays on her travels and spiritual interests, and many other occasional pieces. Evidence of a life-long inclination for writing seems to exist in a piece dated 1867 and entitled "A Day in the Life of a British Columbian Storekeeper" whom she calls Ulysses, characterizing him after Homer's hero as a "much afflicted, much enduring man." If the date on the manuscript is correct, it was likely based on anecdotes that John Fall Allison told her during their courtship at Hope. Notebooks and ledgers from the Allison store also contain her writing on many things.

That she was interested in disseminating her knowledge of the Syilx to a wide readership is clear. "Some Sketches of Indian Life," written in the 1870s and the first selection of her work for this book, implies a non-Indigenous reader interested in the peculiarities of native people of North America. Its sometimes condescending and sardonic tone is characteristic of much of the journalistic travel writing of the time. This piece is included because of its tonal contrast to later writing on the Syilx after she had become better acquainted with them. A later work employing formal diction appeared as a scholarly article entitled "Account of the Similkameen Indians of British Columbia" in *The Journal of the Anthropological Institute of Great Britain and Ireland* in 1892. It reveals her keen powers of observation and her ethnographical inclinations.

While tending the Allison store, she spent time with a disabled elder and knowledge keeper named Tamtusalist. His son Shlawhalakan ran a ferry at the forks nearby and seems to have relied on Allison's as a place where his father could sojourn while the son worked. Tamtusalist is acknowledged as the source of a number of works of prose and poetry on the Syilx that she identifies as "Tales of Tamtusalist." These "Tales" consist of a preface, "The Blue Lake," "The Little White Dog," "Incowmasket, second part," "A Strange Story Told to Tamtusalist by the Indian, 'Pony'," "The Mysterious Hound," "The Glittering Hair," "The Big Man's Horses," "The Rain Stone," "Quinisco's Adventure on Mount Chopaka," "The Burial of Quinisco," "The Big Men of the Mountains," and "Ne-Hi-La-Kin." The last two of these appeared in the 1926 *OHS Report* with a note indicating that they had been written in the 1870s. All of the "Tales" have the following subtitle, "translated by S.L. ," and in her preface to them, she states, "In giving these tales to the public, I have called them translations, but, who can translate accurately a language that is in part voiceless, for Indians convey their meaning by gesture and facial expression as much as by word spoken. The mind of the listener must be en-rapport with the mind of the narrator to give their full meaning" (Preface). Some of the material from these tales is incorporated into other writing, for example, her long poems which we include in this book.

Allison also wrote some other essays, not directly or clearly attributed, based on Indigenous stories such as "The Ghost of the Canyon," "Kill-is-tim-me-nack-quilly," "The Mother of Kille-ketza," and "The Story of Narsishist, Told by a Mission Indian." On her honeymoon trip to Similkameen, she heard stories about the Okanagan lake creature *nx̌a?x̌?itkʷ*, eventually referred to by settlers as Ogopogo, from Charlie Yacumtecum (Tuctac who was Nora Yacumtecum's brother), Cockshist, and later from Johnny McDougall.[2] Lucy Lambley (nee Postill), an Okanagan neighbour in the 1870s, recounts that Allison was writing a poem about the lake creature at that time (Lambley 116). This poem is likely one found in Allison's personal papers entitled "The Monster's Island" dated 1872. It was published in the *Similkameen Star* in 1926, and reprinted by Diane Sterne (2010). Allison also left a handwritten, undated essay which includes a report of her own sighting of it entitled "What I Know of Ogopogo." We have included this essay.

Shortly after John Fall Allison's death, she signed a contract with Scroll Publishing of Chicago who brought out *In-cow-mas-ket* in 1900. The book contains some of the long poems she had written on two important Similkameen chiefs, Quiniscoe and his successor Incowmasket, brothers whom she had known since 1869. Archival papers indicate that she was writing verses in the 1870s on Quiniscoe, some of which were later published in *In-cow-mas-ket*. In the fair hand manuscript of her long poems in the BC Archives, there is an "Introduction" to the long poems critical of settler treatment of the Syilx, and three separate poems, "In-cow-mas-ket, Part One," "In-cow-mas-ket, Part Two," and "Quin-is-coe." However, the published book *In-cow-mas-ket* contains only "In-cow-mas-ket, Part One" and "Quin-is-coe." *In-cow-mas-ket* was published under a male pseudonym—Stratton Moir—a practice not uncommon among Euro-western women writers in the nineteenth century used to improve the chances of their work appearing in print. We have included the introduction and all three long poems (somewhat abridged) here.

That Allison was interested in the comparative study of religion and a believer in intrapsychic realities, karma, and revelatory knowledges throughout her life is evident in some of the following surviving essays: "The Eternal Now," "Christianity," "The Caterpillar, A Story for Old and Young," "The Child of the Mighty Ocean," "The Order of the Star in the East," "On the Study of Ancient Wisdom," "National Karma," and "A Paraphrase on the 37th Chapter of Ezekiel," the Old Testament prophet.

Susan Allison and a pet coyote (Senklips) in the Similkameen (c. late 1920s).
Courtesy of the Princeton and District Museum and Archives.

She also left four essays that were to have been part of a work she titled "Some Native Daughters I Have Known." As they are a detailed account of the interactions of Syilx and settler women, we have included all of them: "G-he-nac," "Our Louisa," "Notes for 'Some Native Daughters,' Emma Hutch or Hutchy," and "Kind Penquinac." Internal evidence suggests that they were written in the twentieth century. That she intended to include more portraits of Indigenous women is indicated by a note in the manuscript written by her daughter Alice

Perkins Wright. It states that "I remember her writing these and heard her mention that 'I must write of Salley and Bohah'" (Wright, Note). After Allison's death in 1937, Wright had possession of most of her manuscripts and corresponded with publishers and archivists about them.

In the early 1930s, Susan Allison came to an agreement with the editor of the Vancouver *Sunday Province* to write her "Recollections" for serial publication in the paper's weekly magazine section. Long read as an exemplary account of the pluck and stamina of the British Columbia pioneer, the "Recollections" are also an important record of a close contact between Syilx and settler in the domestic sphere. Nineteenth century Indigenous people, their practices, and their contributions— whose traces are very faint today—are fleshed out in their pages. The "Recollections" appear to have been as much an attempt to leave some record of the Syilx people as of the spirit of the first settlers. Excerpts from the "Recollections," taken from the manuscripts in the Vancouver City Archives, are also published here.

In the introduction to her long poems on the Similkameen chiefs, she makes a strong (but unpublished) declaration, asserting that the Syilx people she knew in the early decades were "a free people" and "in the majority," not yet subjected to the white man's "religion and civilization" ("Introduction"). Her struggles with what to say or not to say to a non-Indigenous audience about the British Columbia settler colonial project seem to be implied by the decision not to publish this "Introduction" as part of her book *In-cow-mas-ket*. Reconciling her desire to leave a trace of the Syilx and their challenges often conflicted with the demands of a non-Indigenous audience not only for tales about intrepid and virtuous pioneers, but also for romantic stories of pre-contact people living in a "state of nature."[3] The challenges confronting her in writing about the history she was part of is forthrightly represented in personal letters written to her daughter Louisa Allison Johnston in the 1930s, some of which are published here. These challenges are not unlike those facing non-Indigenous Canadians today who have begun to acknowledge the truth of the past and to seek to reconcile themselves with it.

Sketches of Indian Life [4]

The Indians of British Columbia unlike their confreres in Oregon and interior Washington Territory and like [their] brethren the [F]lat [H]eads of the coast are as a rule peaceful and law abiding, and the reason is they have ever been justly and humanely treated both by the settlers and the various Governments that have existed in the country since the first great immigration of white men in -58- [1858]. Another reason [is that] they have learned to respect laws that are impartially administered, alike to the red and the white Man. The settlers and natives, (thanks to this) never having been brought into conflict by deeds of violence, entertain no bitter hostile feelings towards one another. Indeed, their relations are characterized by amity and good fellowship—they are mutually dependent on one another—the settlers want laborers and the Indians want labor.

The Indians are now, whatever may be said to the contrary, more comfortable and quite independent as formerly when they ranged the country "Sole." Monarchs of all they surveyed, they have learned an appreciation for the luxuries of civilization, and they are enabled to earn a fair share of them by their industry.

The Indians possess a singular degree of acuteness and penetration, but at the same time they are also very childish, confiding, and sensitive; they have a great idea of their own dignity, and are as proud and jealous as the Highlanders of Scotland were two centuries ago.

The Roman Catholic clergy with their usual self-denying philanthropy have mixed freely with the natives, and have with unfailing sympathy and kindness won their confidence and respect. The priests possess great influence with the natives and it has been said that they are inclined to exert it in a rather arbitrary manner, but it must be acknowledged that they always show their influence on the side of decency and order. The Indians have many peculiar habits and customs that must be very disgusting and shocking to their instructors whether Catholic or Protestant; viz swapping their wives and selling their daughters, to say nothing of the loathsome practice of exhuming their dead every now and then, and dressing the smouldering remains in new garments and holding a feast or potlatch in their honour. The Indians' religion is purely emotional, and they will join in religious services with great fervour, but they cannot carry it into their daily life. They will refuse to eat meat on Friday, or to work on Sunday but think nothing of lying, or petty stealing. Under the influence of the priests, polygamy is dying out, and few of the men have more than one wife at a time, but their domestic relations are decidedly complicated owing to their propensity for trading their wives—sometimes for new ones, sometimes for horses. There seems to be no real love or affection amongst them, save in some rare instances between father and son or mother and daughter, though they always mourn and lament over their dead relatives, and pay their debts in a most exemplary manner; superstition no doubt has a great deal to do with this, as they are horribly afraid of the Spirits of the Dead. The Indians are inveterate gamblers and will often gamble away every rag of clothing they possess, even the garments they are wearing, and leave themselves in a state of utter destitution.

Their civilization is very much retarded by their passion for strong drink for in spite of the stringent Canadian Laws, the Indians in the interior of BC can get all the whiskey they want— and they do get it, the settlers are all too indolent and apathetic to try to put an end to practices that may eventually bring ruin on themselves as well as demoralizing the unfortunate savages.

Let us glance at one of their encampments. On the bank of a clear shining river, under a shade of a clump of cotton and alder trees, stands a small Indian encampment—Some of the lodges are made of rush mats thrown over a circular frame of poles, an aperture is left at the top for the escape of the smoke from the fire which smoulders in the centre of the lodge. The door is made by simply throwing back an end of one of the rush mats, and opening a space sufficient for the ingress and egress of the occupants. In this encampment civilization has made some progress, and you may see a number of well-made tents. These are mostly used by the younger members of the community, who like to imitate the whites in all things, good and bad. The elders prefer their old manners and customs possibly because their habits were fixed before the whites settled in the country, and it is impossible for them to change now; though nothing seems to delight them more than to see their sons and daughters growing up in the ways of civilization. The occupants of the tents are all well dressed and their surroundings comfortable if not luxurious—just look at yonder tent. Inside you will find two comfortable beds made upon the soft silky bear skins, the blankets are fine, the sheets white and clean, the quilt is neatly made of pretty bright coloured calico—to the ridge pole is hung a good sized looking glass. Outside the tent a canvass is spread about a foot from the door and china cups and saucers are set on it for four—a tin of coffee stands close to the fire which blazes about two yards off and a sputtering frying pan full of beans and bacon is set on some coals raked out of the fire, and there in front of the fire is a plate full of pancakes guarded by a boy dressed in a striped shirt and blue jeans trousers, while the owners of the tent have gone down to the river to make their morning toilet; leaning against the side of the tent,[5] strapped to a stick about two feet long and ten inches wide, is a small brown baby, with a very low forehead and very black eyes, and enormous cheeks. It watches the sputtering frying pan, and as its eyes and mouth are the only parts not immovably bound up, it sticks out its lips making hideous grimaces, and rolls its large black eyes in an appalling manner. Near the baby lies a large white dog, and a cock and two hens are pecking just outside. Sometimes they come dangerously near the pancakes, and the boy throws up his arms at the "cish cishing" and yelling at the very top of his voice. But while he pursues the hens, the old cock doubles on him, and running round the tent manages to dab his beak into a pancake. The boy starts after him, then the hens return to the charge, and the unfortunate youngster gathering up all the sticks and chips within reach begins to throw them at the troublesome fowls. The dog now thinks it high time for him to join in the fray, and rushes out barking furiously upsetting the poor little mummy on the stick in his haste. The yells of the boy, the cackling of the hens, the barking of the dog, and the screams of the baby bring the mother up from the river.

Fresh and clean from her morning bath in the river, she looks as if she had brought back some of the bright sparkle of the water with her. Her black shiny hair is smoothed carefully and hangs down her back in two thick glossy braids. Her neatly made calico dress fits tightly on the figure whose only fault is square shoulders, and is fastened at the neck by a gaudy broach, earrings to match hang in her ears, and if her ears are not all that could be desired, the hands and arms that dandle the little mummy are faultless. Her face if not pretty is pleasing. She looks so young no one would believe that the man just sauntering up from the river is her seventh husband but it is true. The man is somewhat older than the woman, and is dressed in black broadcloth, and is in sports [?] with a white shirt with studs, across his vest is a showy chain connection with a large silver watch he carries in his vest pocket. He is very proud of his watch and as he comes up, he takes it out and looks at it. An elderly woman in a loose jacket and short petticoat joins the group and they sit down to their breakfast.

But they are the exquisites of the tribe. Look under that pine tree—four men are squatting together playing cards. One is a half gaunt fellow with long hair hanging over his shoulders and a most repulsive countenance. He has no clothing except a pair of buckskin trousers. The man opposite him is a short thick-set ruffian, very comfortably clothed. He is playing with an air of indifference with a contrast to the two eager boys from whom he is winning their week's wages—they have been playing all night and will not stop till they have nothing left to play for. But see there, lying on a deer skin outside the entrance of one of the mat houses, is an old Indian "in puris naturalibus" [unclothed]. His thick shaggy hair is of an iron gray, his skin is so dark and wrinkled, his broad chest, excessively long, powerful arms, and short legs reminding one of W. Du Challon's [Paul Du Chaillu] description of the gorilla. He is resting on one elbow; in his hand, he holds a pipe made of a peculiar kind of stone much used by his tribe for making pipes and knives and many other articles; he seems to be enjoying his smoke to the very utmost for every time he puts the pipe to his lips, he inhales a long breath of the smoke then slowly exhales it through his nostrils, and his cunning old eyes follow the white smoke as it ascends into the clear morning air and is dispersed by the gentle summer breeze. Near him at play with some old dead bones is a dirty untidy young savage. Her thick unkempt hair is plentifully sprinkled with dust and ashes, though she does not seem to be mourning for her youthful sins. Indeed, she seems rather to be enjoying throwing the ashes up in handfuls and pouring them on her ugly little head. Her cunning little kiougolian [Mongolian?] eyes bear a strong resemblance to the old man's, and they light up and glisten with love and delight every time he calls her to his side to take a whiff at his pipe.

A little way off are two women dressing a deer skin which is stretched over a stool. They scrape and pound at the skin which is done with pieces of sloop iron set in rough wooden handles. These two women are quite as savage looking as the old man and the child. The elder woman wears a short buckskin dress ornamented by sundry fringes, and her short rushy black hair hangs loose on her shoulders, her feet are bare. The other woman wears a jacket and petticoat of some kind but dirt and rags are the more prominent features of her attire—we have looked at them long enough. Let us truly turn to the large white tent—it belongs to one of the head men of the tribe. In the absence of a regular priest, this worthy also officiates, and now he sits waiting for the sun to pop up from behind the mountains to ring the prayer bell. This Indian is a very respectable looking fellow, but his face is thin and emaciated. He is decently dressed in blue serge and like the old man appears to be enjoying his morning smoke. Near him (also smoking) is his wife mixing bread on a canvas cloth. A naked youngster stands at her elbow looking on, and another a little older with some clothing is trying to quiet a small baby. The woman mixes the bread and puts it to rise in a camp kettle; then seizing the small child forces him into a pair of pants.

The sun ris[es] over the distant mountains sending a flood of light and glory over the whole scene. The man throws aside his pipe, takes up a hand bell, and rings for the natives. Soon the whole of the little encampment is astir, gathering at the call to prayers. The old savage gathers his blanket round him, and giving his grandchild his hand walks slowly to the white tent. The two women leave their buckskin and follow and here comes the exquisite and his family and about a dozen others in all stages of civilization, and all sorts of costumes. Now the deep guttural tones of the acting priest giving the opening prayer can be distinctly heard and a loud hum of voices join in responsive and a lull—and then sweet and clear rises a hymn of praise to the Great "Father of All." It may be that such music would not satisfy a fastidious ear, but to anyone looking on and listening at a little distance, it seems to rise through the clear air and bright blue dome above right up to the throne of God. The music is in keeping with the scene. The grand old mountains, the clear shining river, the tall pine trees swaying in the light breeze—the green grass and the cloudless blue sky, they too "Though with no real voice or sound" seem to join in the Indian's hymn of the thanksgiving to the divine Being that formed all and is all in all.

No one can accuse the Indians of hypocrisy for while they are praying and singing, they enter heartily into the spirit of it all, but when it is over they forget and are as ready to lie and steal as ever.

When the old savage in their nature breaks after, the fault nearly always lies with whiskey and unprincipled traders. If left alone to the priests, without temptations few white men can resist, they would soon form a useful and orderly class of people. [187?]

From the Long Poems
"In-cow-mas-ket" and "Quin-is-coe"

Introduction

This must be taken as a part of my recollections, for it is an account of the lives, manners and customs of the Similkameen Indians as I knew them in the sixties, seventies and eighties, while they were still a people—I may say a passing people. Now they are nearly gone—just a downtrodden remnant whose land is coveted and whose end is eagerly waited for by most of their white neighbours.

The first part shows them a free people—then they were in the majority; the second part, when they were coming under the influence of religion and civilization. They [originally] had their own beautiful religious ideas and their own manners and customs, which perhaps were not so beautiful from the white man's point of view, but they had no bestial sots [habitual drunkards], no maddening spirits. The white man has much to be ashamed of in his treatment of the rightful owners of the land.

The form in which I have told the story of the Indians as I first knew them has been severely criticized by some of my friends, bad poetry, neither rhyme nor blank verse. I own up to that, but it is written just as the thoughts came. I have told the story as I felt like telling it. The folklore and similes are Indian, the faults are my own.
[1890s]

In-cow-mas-ket

A POEM OF INDIAN LIFE [Part One]
By a rapid flowing river
In-cow-mas-ket built his dwelling[6]
Called it by the name Chu-chu-e-waa [*cuʔcuʔwixaʔ*];
There his kinsmen dwelt beside him,
In their circular mat houses,   5
Made from bark of fragrant cedar.
With him dwelt his aged grandsire,[7]
Now sightless, helpless and infirm;
But his mental eyes were opened,
Things he saw which others see not,—   10
And men loved him for his wisdom.
In the lodge of In-cow-mas-ket
Lived his first wife Sem-min-at-coe;[8]
She was plain in face and figure,
She had borne him many children,   15
And she was now no longer young;
In-cow-mas-ket's aged grandsire
Tenderly she loved and cherished,
When the men had gone a hunting,—
When the young men left the village,   20
Then she would lay him in the sun,
On a pile of soft warm bearskin.
She would sit and work beside him,
While he told her wondrous stories
Of the men and of the creatures   25
That lived in days long past and gone;
Stories told him by his father,
Old even then, when he was young;
How the rapid flowing river
Once but a tiny brook had been;   30
How the earth once shook and trembled
When the Father in stern anger
Reft the solid rock in twain,—then
The deep lake pent in the mountains,
Down—downward dashed to join the stream,   35
Tore its way on through the valley

And formed the great Similk-ameen.
Madly dashing, like a wild horse,
That hath broke its curbing rein, it
Rushes swiftly, tearing downward,   40
Swells Columbia, joins the main.

*[Lines 42-63—He also tells her a story about his own experience in a sudden
high altitude snow storm in the summer, which buried all the men and horses.
Only he and a dark gray stallion survived. He also sings of Chippaco,[9] a
mountain in northern Washington State.]*

"Once upon the Mount Chippaco
    There lived a monster grim and dread,[10]   65
Awful as that dreadful mountain
    When thunder clouds enveil its head.
Awful was his devilish laughter
    And fierce and scornful was his ire,
When he found men on his mountain   70
    Where he hides 'midst clouds and fire.
Women had he taken captive
    And kept them on that mountain lone;
Men he mocked with fiendish laughter
    Who sought to take the women home."   75

*[Lines 76-85—Chin-chin,[11] Incowmasket's beautiful young second wife, also
lives in the lodge, but she lacks Semminatcoe's virtues, leaving all the hard
work for Semminatcoe and not honouring Incowmasket's aged grandfather.]*

But she loved not In-cow-mas-ket,
She cherished not his old grandsire,
Thought of nothing but her beauty,
Cared for nothing but her pleasure.   90
Mounted on her fiery broncho
See, see her dashing o'er the hills
Driving in her herds of cattle,
And laughing—jesting with the boys.
Snatching at a long 'reata [lariat]   95
She swings it lightly o'er her head,
Lassoes, catches, overthrows one,
Laughing she gives her horse his head;

185

Shouts as on he swiftly gallops,
She makes him yet more madly run;

. . . .

Little Chin-chin braids her tresses,
Bedecks herself in gay attire,
Smokes her dainty cigarettos,   110
And lounges idle in the sun;
In-cow-mas-ket dares remonstrate,
Then little Chin-chin pouts and frowns.

[Lines 114-155—A great hunter, Incowmasket often gives his trophies—
grizzly bear paws and beaver tails—to Chin-Chin. After a hunt, he returns
and greets his virtuous and beautiful daughter Penquenac. Incowmasket
holds Penquenac[12] "dearer than all the world beside."]

Like her mother Sem-min-at-coe
She was gentle; she was kind; thus
All who knew her ever loved her   155
For her goodness and her beauty.

[Lines 157-220—Incowmasket and his community leave the valley in the late
summer for hard work at their mountain camp. Hosachtem, Incowmasket and
Semminatcoe's son, enters the narrative. Into autumn, infectious mists arise from
the swamps.]

From the noxious exhalations
Of the foul marshy mountain fen,   225
All unseen there rose a spirit,
That slowly draws the life from men,
While unconsciously they sleep. This
Spirit foul and awful fasten'd
Upon young Hosachtem, and preyed   230
Upon his life unseen. Larger,
Brighter grew his dark eyes, glowing
With consuming fires, kindled by
That baneful spirit; and redder,
Brighter flushed his young cheek with the   235
Hectic hue of fever . . .

186

[Lines 237-292—In his decline, Hosachtem longs to see his Similkameen River Valley home; hence, they return to "Looloo-hooloo" [nlulu?ullaxʷ].[13] Hosachtem asks his father to shoot down an eagle so he can deck his head with feathers. Incowmasket obliges him. The prescient grandsire chastises Incowmasket for not realizing how ill Hosachtem is. A Syilx doctor is sent for from the Columbia River area.]

"Wherefore are thine eyes so blinded,
That thou seest not thy boy is
Wasting as the snow in summer   295
Melts fast before the burning sun,
When the noontide rays refulgent
Shine strong upon the mountain Peaks?
Bid thy young men bring a doctor . . .

[Lines 300-394—Incowmasket orders Toupes and Whylac[14] to ride south for the doctor. At the behest of Hosachtem, the group returns to Chuchuwayha. The doctor arrives.]

Potent was the wise old doctor,   395
And he labored hard and long to
Drive the foul one from Hosachtem;
But the foul one was too strong, he
Threw the doctor when they wrestled,
He threw him far and threw him hard.   400
And he nearly slew the doctor
With his foul fiery baneful breath.
Vainly did the doctor charm him
With powerful herbs and potent spells;
Naught would make him leave Hosachtem.   405
See the wise, the strong old doctor,
Lying on a couch of pine brush,
Fainting, weary and exhausted.
Then he cried to In-cow-mas-ket,
"Thou canst keep thy skins and blankets,   410
Keep thou thy horses—keep thy kine [cattle];
I am strong to fight with spirits
I am subtle, I am wise; but
Now my wisdom is as folly
For now in naught can I prevail   415

187

'Gainst the foul and evil spirit
That doth cling to young Hosachtem."

[Lines 417-433 — Then Incowmasket sends for his "near kinsman" and healer Cosotasket,[15] a mountain Indian who lives an isolated life.]

Glowing eyes had Cos-o-tasket,
Full of strength and full of power;   435
Thin and spare was Cos-o-tasket,
Lithe and limber his slight frame. His
Nights were spent in eerie vigils
In the dark lonely mountain caves;
Well he knew the powers of nature,   440
He knew them in their own abodes;
Well he knew the viewless spirits
That throng the mountains' misty peaks;
And well knew he the flitting ghosts
That at still midnight leave their graves;   445
Yet his heart was stout and fearless
And he spake to In-cow-mas-ket,
His nearest kinsman and his chief.

[Lines 449-501 — Cosotasket grapples with the spirit who shuns the man's gleaming eyes, the source of his power. The spirit vanquishes the man by throwing hot ashes in his eyes.]

Then cried brave Cos-o-tasket:
    "Oh, my kinsman, oh, my chief,
I am beaten, I am vanquished,
    And my heart is sick with grief.   505
I have struggled, I have wrestled,
    I have striven with all my power
To avert from young Hosachtem
    The sad agonizing hour,
That shall free his youthful spirit   510
    From the form that holds it now;
But the great Father hath spoken,
    And to him we all must bow.
He alone can tame this foul one,
    Alone can give the power   515

That can drive him from Hosachtem
 And avert the dreadful hour.
When thou called me from the mountains
 And the caves so dark and dim,
I heard the call, I lingered not,   520
 But I came in hopes to win
The fierce fight against the foul one.
 Yet who living can withstand
The Great Father? for the foul one
 Now but fulfills his great command.   525
Now return I to the mountains,
 I return now to the caves,
To hold commune with the spirits
 That at midnight leave their graves.

*[Lines 530- 572 — Over the ensuing winter, Hosachtem fades. The old grandsire
tries to comfort all of them by singing "stories of his youth." He tells the story
of Immanchute who slew a grizzly in its den by holding a knife against its
body; of the maiden Catlemtennac who was abducted by the "Great Souie-ap-
poo"; of a dreadful river in the mountains that he once followed to its dreaded
source; of his capture and domestication of two bear cubs.]*

Softly sang he of a maiden:
"Fair, fair was Cat-lem-ten-nac,
Who roamed from her father's camp   575
And went in search of berries;
She lingered and she lingered,
Still she lingered all that day;
At evening she returned not,   580
When the sun was in the west.
At morning she returned not,
When the sun was in the east.
Her people vainly sought her:
They sought her in the mountains,   585
They sought her in the prairie,
And they sought her in the woods;
Never, never more they saw her.
For while far she thoughtless roved
Away from the encampment,   590
The Great Souie-ap-poo came,

And took away the maiden,
And they saw her ne'er again!"
[Lines 594- 698—*The grandsire continues to tell stories of an evil river in the
depths of the earth and of his own youth hunting in the "Ashenola" area.*[16]]

The worn spirit of Hosachtem,
Now wearied out with tears and pain,   700
Burst forth from out its cumb'ring [encumbering] clay,
Left its cell of pain and anguish,
And soar'd to realms beyond men's ken.

[Lines 704-724—*Semminatcoe and Penquenac grieve at Hosachtem's tomb.*]

In the day she [Semminatcoe] ever saw him   725
Low lying on his couch of pain;
Ever heard his sad voice calling,
"Oh, save me, mother, I would stay."
Through her midnight dreams he floated,
Now an infant, and now a child;   730
Happy, joyfully he sported
And looking at her sweetly smiled.
[*1890s*, 1900]

In-Cow-Mas-Ket [Part Two]

From across the Big Salt Water
From the fair sunny south of France,[17]
To the "Sea of Rugged Mountains"
There came a good, a holy Priest,
Came to help his heathen brethren   5
With his love and loving kindness,
With his fine and patient spirit,
By his faithfulness and courage
By his simple saintly life
Setting them a bright example.   10

[Lines 11-20—*The kind priest works hard on behalf of the people, coming in all
kinds of weather to soothe the sick and dying, and to win converts.*]

Oft repulsed, he never waver'd,
He never wearied doing good.

[Lines 23-37 — The priest comes to Chuchuwayha "bearing balm and healing kindness" which are well-received by Incowmasket who "owned the truth of all he [the priest] said." Semminatcoe, Chin-chin, and the old Grandsire reject the priest's religious point of view.]

Sternly the old Grandsire listened,
Sternly shook his Reverend head;
He would serve The Father only,   40
White Men's Gods were nought to him.
Loudly laughed he at the devil
Forever luring men to sin,
For The Father was all powerful,
His will no spirit dared withstand;   45
How then could the priestly devil
Cause men to break His great commands?
How could White Men make him know God?
He had known him from his youth,
With his eyes had seen him daily   50
And daily felt his wondrous truth.
When the Priest said, "Hear him calling,
Aye, calling to you by my voice,"
Then the old man cried out boldly,
"Say, who art thou, oh Stranger Priest?"   55
"The Father speaks forth in thunder
When the swift lightning shivers trees,
His voice sinks in gentle whispers
In the soft balmy summer's breeze.
I hear Him in the river's tone   60
As past it murmurs low and clear,
I hear him in the foaming flood,
Then He fills my soul with fear.
I can see Him in the sunshine,
I can see Him in the shade,   65
His swift glance darts forth in lightning;
The bright track by the meteor made
Is the pathway of His arrows.
Lo now, His many coloured bow

Is drawn far across the mountains   70
Where it reflecteth in the snow
All the heavenly hues it weareth.

. . . .

He is near me, ever near me,   80
I need not the White Man's Gods,
I will live as lived my fathers
And like them I'll gladly die
What time the Good Father calleth,
Without craven fear or tremor."   85

[Lines 86-124—Moved by the priest's teaching, Incowmasket becomes anxious
about his present state, since the priest has "said that as a Christian / He could
only keep one wife." Incowmasket cannot part with little Chin-chin, yet is
troubled at the thought of losing Semminatcoe "his first and ever loving wife,"
which would also mean the loss of his daughter Penquenac, "dear to him as
life." He wavers.]

He could not ask his Grandsire [for counsel],   125
Although men held him wondrous wise,
For he would not be a Christian,
He ever said the Priest told lies.
For the old man felt indignant
That a stranger—a white man and a priest—   130
Should be listened to before him.

[Lines 132-200—As Incowmasket broods alone, the rapidly flowing river
nearby begins to rise. A violent earthquake¹⁸ then shakes the village, churns
the river, and creates a huge rockslide and flood. The people are terrified.
Incowmasket calls a council of the Elders to determine what has "roused The
Father's anger."]

Rising slowly In-cow-mas-ket
Thus the assembled throng addressed:
"Oh, my children! Oh, my people!
My heart is dead with grief and fear;
My tongue can hardly utter words   205
Ye all must hear, lest The Father
In stern anger cause yonder

Rapidly rising stream to wash
Away our Village, or He bids
The Mountains fall and cover all   210
Our dwellings.

*[Lines 212-220—Incowmasket fears that the commotion caused by the
earthquake and the rising river is a sign of the Christian God's anger.]*

Ye are guilty, oh my children!
Lo, The Great Father is in ire,
Ye have sinned, Oh my people,
Ye have sinned against His laws,
For ye heeded not the good Priest   225
But each went on his way, as a
Horse that's broke his bridle or a
Prisoned hawk set free. Bethink ye,
Oh my children, of all the words
The good priest said, bethink ye   230
Oh my people, of the blameless life
He led and how he cheered the sick
And soothed the dying with his words
Of heavenly life and love, and of
The Father's message he brought us   235
From above. We were stubborn,
We would not be baptised, we were
Stubborn, oh my people, we would
Keep many wives. The Great Father
Vainly warned us through the mouth of   240
The good Priest, but ye mocked him with
Your laughter, ye scorned his kindly
Gentle ways; so now The Father
Speaketh forth to you more loudly
By the earthquake's vehement shock.   245
Hearken, oh my people, ere yet
It be too late. List, list to me
My children, ere overwhelm'd by
Fate, we sink into oblivion.
Now I this counsel give: quickly   250
Send and bring again the good Priest,
Confess and purify your lives,

Try to follow his example;
Then will he ask The Great Father
To pardon our many sins."   255
Ceasing, Chief In-cow-mas-ket
Gravely resumed his former seat.
The night was dark and dreary now,
Yet the camp fires blazed bright and clear;
The leaping flames shone brightly   260
On the old Grandsire, who rising
Slow and feebly, propped his tall frame
Erect by the aid of a slim
Sapling, while most eagerly the
Assembled tribesmen listened   265
His voice to hear, for they ever
Loved and fear'd him. When first he spoke
His weak voice waver'd, but as he
Spake his spirit slowly kindled,
Excitement lit his sightless eyes,   270
His shrill voice grew loud and louder.
"Oh, my children! oh, my people!
Ye have heard what In-cow-mas-ket
Said. He blames you, harshly blames you
For the evil lives you have led;   275
And how he would have you hearken
To the stranger Priest,
Lest in anger the Great Father
Condemn ye all to death. I've lived
Many years, my children, I know.   280
Ye hold me wise; I tell you this
My children, I like not the white
Priest's lies. Why should we, my children,
Leave our ancient mode of life?
Think ye the Father's angry   285
Because he shook the earth? 'Tis said
He did so when the river had
Its birth; some say that in anger
He reft in twain the rock that pent
Its snowborn waters in the steep   290
Vermillion[19] Cliffs; but I tell ye
Since that time our valley

194

Has been wondrous fair and fertile.
We are all the Father's children,
In His firm hands he holds our lives;   295
He of his great bounty gives us
Our cattle and our wives. Children,
If His anger be enkindled,
Let us now fall before his face
And humbled in the dust let us   .   300
Beg the Great Father for his grace.
Shall a white man, a stranger,
Stand between us and our God
To shield us from his anger?
Nay, Nay rather let us bear it   305
For the Great Father made us men,
Then like men let us approach him,
Let us receive from Him our doom
And not crawl behind a white man.
Think for yourselves, my people,   310
If ye like not our ancient ways
Ye can now reject my counsel
And do as In-cow-mas-ket says.
I am very old, my children,
I'll not be with you long, I know   315
In-cow-mas-ket loves you, although
His voice and influence is strong
In favour of the white Priest.
I'm tired now, my children,
Let my son Collosasket speak."   320
Then tired out by his exertions
The old man tott'ring, fell back on
In-cow-mas-ket, who caught him and
Gently led him to his seat.
Lightly rose young Collosasket,   325
Throwing aside his buffalo robe,
He stood forth attired in buckskins
Adorned with many tags and fringes,
Across his strong broad shoulders
A brightly coloured strap was   330
Gracefully suspended, from which
A gaily broidered fire-bag

And powder flask depended,
While the skin of a coyotie[20] [sic]
Served him for a hat; the pointed   335
Ears in front he wore, while the tail
Hung down his back. As he rose his
Movements were full of pride and grace,
Then when he spoke his voice was sweet.
A smile was on his face, as thus   340
He addressed the Chiefs and Elders
Sitting round the Council fire:
"Well ye know that In-cow-mas-ket
Is my own brother and my Chief,
Ill would it become me against   345
His voice to speak. I despise not
Our forefathers, I respect their
Ancient ways, but I think with our
In-cow-mas-ket, that we live in
Other days, that the Father hath   350
Sent us a message by His Priest:
It were well we should receive him
And yield to his words belief. Then
For wives, I think it well that we
Should keep but one, that is, I mean   355
I'm sure of it if she hath born
A son to care for us when age
Shall wither the hopes and strength of
Youth. I am not wise in counsel
Nor know I how to speak, but think   360
That I have spoken all the words
Our good Chief In-cow-mas-ket said."
Stepping backward Collosasket
Sat down on his buffalo robe.
Next to speak rose Clackumnasket   365
A convert, whose tall, meagre frame
Was enveloped in a blanket.
The brilliant flame reflected from
The brightly blazing Council fire
Now lit his dark and sunken eyes,   370
His hollow cheeks were glowing
With the hectic hue of fever.

Through the silent midnight his voice
Sounded in accents shrill and clear,
"What wonder Chief In-cow-mas-ket   375
That this great visitation's come,
This evil hath befallen us,
Think of all the ill we've done; think
How we've scorned the Father's message
How we've mocked His holy Priest,   380
Despising all he taught us, clung
To our forefathers' old beliefs
And sought counsel from our Doctors.
They're the children of the Devil,
They teach nought but filthy lies."   385

Then Cosotasket starting up
Indignant stood upon his feet.
His dark eyes flashing forth lightning;
He quiver'd with scorn and anger
And could hardly hold his peace.   390
But stern Clackumnasket heedless
Of his just anger, thus went on.
"Thyself, oh In-cow-mas-ket, art
Very much to blame. Set us
A good example and send forth   395
One of your two wives, send and bring
Again the good priest, that we may be
Baptised, banish our evil Doctors
That hold foul commune with the dead,
Invoking powers we know not bring   400
Evil on our heads, provoking
The Father's anger. I marvel,
Chief In-cow-mas-ket, that this was
Not done before—and I tell you,
In-cow-mas-ket, great sin lies at   405
Your door." Here he gasped—a sudden
Fit of coughing seizing him
Full abruptly stopped his speech.
Springing forward, Cosotasket
Stood fronting the assembled Chiefs.   410

Quivering with excitement, his lithe
Slender frame seemed to increase in
Stature, his eyes blazed with a flame
Of scorn and indignation and
Like a bell his clear voice sounded 415
On the ears of those who heard—sweet
'Twas, yet it filled them with terror;
Well they heeded every word that
He addressed to In-cow-mas-ket.
"Thou art my kinsman, In-cow-mas-ket, 420
Thou art my kinsman and my chief,
And I ever bow before thee.
Thou hast heard, oh In-cow-mas-ket,
The words that Clackumnasket said,
The insulting voice he spoke in 425
When he hurled them at my head.
Well thou knowest, In-cow-mas-ket,
My kinsman and my Chief,
How much I love and venerate
Our forefathers' old belief. 430
Well thou knowest that from The Father
I've received much strength and power.
I can wrestle with the Foul One,
I can make the Foul One cower,
Make him flee away in anguish. 435
Thinkest thou, oh In-cow-mas-ket,
That the Great Father gives his aid
To those that work iniquity?
No! He loveth all he hath made
As a Father loves his children, 440
To guide us through the gloom
That in this dark world surrounds us;
He hath placed a light within us,
Lo, in some of us 'tis brighter,
In some of us 'tis dim, yet still 445
I tell you, the Light within us
Emanates from Him, the great source
Of light and knowledge. The Foul One,
His servant, ever waits on Him.
But Cluckumnasket tells you that 450

By the Foul One's aid I bring these
Evil things upon you, and hold
Commune with the dead. Now the dead
Are in His keeping; when they've left
This earth, no mortal man can raise 455
Them, unless The Father bids them come.
In the dead His light burns brightly
But they too must work His will.
When The Father bids them waken
To revisit this dark earth, 460
He sends them to those that fear not
To behold what he hath sent.
The Foul One is his servant!
By the Great Father's might, he and
His evil spirits cannot bear 465
The blessed light with which our hearts
Are lighted—only when 'tis dim
The Foul One dares to approach us
Unless he's sent by Him. Listen,
In-cow-mas-ket, heed well the words 470
I say. My Chief, I am willing—
Ever ready to obey—and
If it please ye, In-cow-mas-ket,
In the Mountains I'll abide midst
All the wondrous powers of nature 475
And the pale flitting ghosts that ride
Upon the midnight breezes that
O'er the lone mountains sweep, but list,
Chief In-cow-mas-ket, I will not
Be baptized and be a Christian, 480
For I despise the Christians' lives.
They say all men are brethren, but
Us they treat like dogs, and with drink
They are besotted. They do not
Feed the hungry, they drive him from 485
Their door. Better that all of us,
Chief In-cow-mas-ket, should shun the
White man's ways and live as lived our
Fathers. We live in other days,
As your brother Collosasket 490

Has very wisely said, for now
Our warriors are women and I
The Mountain Chief, alone of all
The young men hold our fathers' old
Belief." Raising his head proudly   495
Brave Cosotasket looked around;
Then, with a quick impatient sigh,
He flung him on the ground.
"Cosotasket, say not thou art alone in
Thy belief; while Tatlehasket   500
Liveth ne'er shall the Mountain Chief
Be banished from our Village." As
These words were utter'd a stately
Form arose clad in Hunter's
Garments; his eyes were fixed on those   505
That agreed with In-cow-mas-ket.
Before his stately presence all
Men shrank back in whisp'ring awe,
For they dreaded Tatlehasket
Who knew no other law than the   510
Sharpness of his knife. Now his words
Were few but sharp and biting for
He liked not that his Chief should be
Ruled by a white priest and forsake
His forefathers' old belief, but   515
Many others spake against him and
His great friend, the Mountain Chief.

[Lines 518-528 — Daylight dawns then the Chief speaks.]

In-cow-mas-ket's eyes were lighten'd,
Calmly he rose to speak once more.   530
"Now my children, ye have spoken,
But lo, your voices are not one,
So the burden falls upon me
To decide what shall be done.
I fear no man's anger, I fain [earnestly]   535
Would do what's right, and the will of
The Great Father. Clackumnasket
Sorely blames me for my present

200

Mode of life and he would have me
Banish my kind and gentle wife,   540
Or part with little Chin-chin
Who is the sunshine of my days.
He is right, the truth is spoken,
Full well I know it must be done;
Oh, it wrings my heart with anguish,   545
But I am your Chief and Father
And I must show you what is right.
No longer, my Clackumnasket,
Shall ye reproach with scorn your Chief
For his evil mode of living.   550
Fear not, Cosotasket, my friend
The Mountain Chief must remain
Within my village, for like my
Good brother Collosasket I
Respect our fathers' ancient ways,   555
Though myself I hold not with them.
Now hearken, oh my people,
If ye will really mend your lives,
I will bring again the good Priest
That ye all may be baptized . . .

[Lines 560-567 — Toupes and Whylac are sent to get the Priest.]

. . . seek ye
There the good Priest, tell him how by
The dreadful earthquake's vehement shock   570
The Great Father hath chastised us.
Now like little children cowering
Beneath an angry Father's eye
And dreading further punishment,
We know not where to turn for some sure refuge.   575

[Lines 576-614 — Incowmasket, "full of grief," tells Semminatcoe to leave
his household.²¹ Heartbroken, she mourns at Hosachtem's grave.]

. . . Watching
By her mourning mother, the young   615
Pen-que-nac stood; to her
Excited fancy her brother
Seem'd to stand in the sunbeam
By her mother, pointing with his
Hand up to the dark stormy   620
Heaven, whence through the purple cloud
The ray of Light was darted down.
As she gazed he vanished with that
Bright beam of light; the purple clouds
Grew dark and darker as gather'd   625
The gloom of night.

*[Lines 627- 638 — Heavy rain falls all night long on the two women. At sunrise,
Semminatcoe feels renewed hope.]*

Thus the Father in his mercy
Hath ordained that sorrow and night   640

Alike shall pass away, although
The morn's but clouded and the heart
Of happiness and joy bereft.

Sem-min-at-coe's hope was Kitecoe,
Kitecoe, old and wise, a woman   645
Ever dreaded—one before whose
Inner eyes rose visions, visions
Of the present, visions of what is
Yet to come; well knew she all the
Secrets of life beyond the tomb.   650
There was none so wise as Kitecoe,
To weave a potent spell.
She could sunder loving mortals,
She could make them love too well.
Hideous was old Kitecoe, foul as a   655
Fiend from the nether Hell . . .

*[Lines 657-683—One hundred year old Kitecoe, of "crooked body, crooked
mind," "wither'd lips," and "snaky tongue," lives in a "dismal dreary den"
where she works her spells.]*

Toads and vipers seem to gather   680
Close round her in that darksome den,
Firelight only makes it darker
'Tis here she works her spells on men.

List, the hideous Kitecoe singeth,
List to her voice so cracked and shrill.   685
Kitecoe's Song
"Kitecoe once was young and lovely
Long jetty tresses, flashing eyes,
Straight and slender as a sapling
Kitecoe's smiles were once a prize.
Kitcoe now is old and wrinkled,   690
Feeble, toothless, gummy eyed,
Now men call her 'hideous Kitecoe'
Quite forgetting she is wise.
Curse on pretty sneering Chin-chin,
She too shall wither and decay.   695
Will she laugh at hideous Kitecoe
When her beauty's passed away?

. . . .

Chin-chin now is young and lovely   710
Long jetty tresses, flashing eyes,
Chin-chin soon will lose her beauty
Men will turn their looks aside."

[Lines 714-773—Semminatcoe and Penquenac bring her gifts. Then in "angry
passion / As like a snake," she brews a concoction of herbs and toads on a fire—
while "muttering spells and incantations"—from which a misty vapour begins
to rise in the shape of "a dead man's mouldering form." The air is "mixed with
groans of dying men, / All is weird, unholy, awful."]

Closer clung the young Pen-que-nac
To her half fainting mother's side,   775
Soon the fiendish voice of Kitecoe
Soundeth full shrilly through the gloom:
"Wherefore is Sem-min-at-coe weeping?
Comest thou now to my abode?
Tell, that I may ease thy sorrow."   780
203

[Lines 781-796 — Semminatcoe confides her sorrow at being banished.]

"Wilt thou aid me, Mother Kitecoe,
Wilt thou work a potent spell,
Make my In-cow-mas-ket love me
That I may end my weary days   800
In the village of Chu-chu-e-waa
Near all my little children's graves."

[Lines 803-814 — Kitecoe assures her that those with whom she has a compact, "those who have left their graves," have heard her lament. Kitecoe asks if she would like her to bid Hosachtem's spirit to rise, but Semminatcoe refuses.]

"Fare thee well then, Sem-min-at-coe,   815
For thee I work a wondrous charm,
Fare thee well, now hie thee homeward."

[Lines 818-824 — The next spring, the dying Chin-chin remembers her carefree life as a little girl.]

The swollen river's mournful voice   825
Filled her heart with thoughts of childhood;
It brought before her glazing eyes
Visions of a little maiden
Light of heart and gaily singing,
Wading in the clear cold water,   830
Then springing lightly o'er the stones
With her quivering wand of willow
And her line of twisted horse hair,
Her birch basket full of fishes
Hanging from her sunburnt shoulders   835
By a band across her forehead.
That dream followed by another,
Of a young girl proudly mounted
On a swift fiery foaming steed,
Flying happy o'er the stretches   840
Twixt the river and the mountains,
Riding down the swift coyotie
Or lassoing the gentle fawns,
Hidden by their fearful mothers

Where the grass and brush were thickest.   845
Then she felt the soft sweet breezes
Refreshing pass above her head
As she knelt beside the bushes
Whence the black serviceberries hang,
Gathering in their rich ripe harvest,   850
Gaily jesting with the maidens
Of their lovers who were hunting.
Next she saw a bride unwilling
Led to Chief In-cow-mas-ket's lodge.
Faded all her hopes of childhood   855
Now all her love of life is done.
Then she saw a hideous fury
With withered hands and arms upflung,
Cursing, calling vengeance on her
For the thing by which she suffer'd   860
She sought not In-cow-mas-ket's love.
. . . .

So little Chin-chin faded fast
From off the gladsome face of earth,
E'en as a tender blossom fades
When the sun flings down at noontide
Hot, burning rays that scorch and wither
Then sad In-cow-mas-ket mourned her
For three long, long dreary moons,
He lined his shirt with spruce brush,
He cut off his long, black hair.
In his tent doorway sitting, he
Would sadly call her name, "Chin-chin,
Chin-chin, pretty little Chin-chin."
As a fiery meteor flying
Quick through dull and darksome sky,
Flashes brightly o'er the heavens
Leaving a shining trail behind,
Soon to fade from the sight of man,
Such the life of little Chin-chin,
Fiery, brilliant and quickly done,
Soon, alas, to be forgotten.
[1890s]

Quin-is-coe,[22] Part One

Ah, what aileth our hunter Quin-is-coe,
And wherefore blanched is the cheek of our chief?
Hast thou come from the Mountain Chippaco,
Snow-crowned Chippaco, the bearer of clouds?"
"I have come from the Mountain Chippaco,   5
Snow-crowned Chippaco that beareth the clouds.
I've seen things that are frightful and awesome,
I've seen strange things that I dare not repeat."

[Lines 8-41 — In this call-and-response stanza pattern, the people ask Quiniscoe
why he, a famed lone grizzly hunter, is so uncharacteristically frightened, and
how they might allay his fear. He says that while on Mount Chopaka, he slew a
"callowna" [kilawna? or grizzly bear] at sunset. He slept in the bear's bloody
hide, his horse nearby and the bear's flesh piled between them to guard it from
wolves. He then slept through a "black and weird" night full of wolf howls,
but was awakened by something mysterious. His horse broke tether and fled.]

My first thought was to follow, but near me
There stood a form that was awesome and grim.
Souie Appoo, the spirit of evil,
Was devouring—was tearing my bear's meat,   45
And he laughed as he tore it from limb to limb.
Then close wrapped I the bear's skin around me,
And each quick beat of my heart sounded loud.
A thick mist seemed to gather around me,
And just then methinks, methinks that I died.   50
But soon life again quickened within me,
And trembling once more I arose and looked,
Fearing to see him; but, no! he had gone,
The great Souie Appoo had gone—had gone;
And with him had taken all my bear's meat.   55
Then, half dead, I descended the mountain,
Snow-crowned Chippaco, that beareth the clouds,
The dread home of the great Souie Appoo.
Weary, on foot, I have travelled thus far;
My poor horse, too, is lost on the mountain,   60
Snow-crowned Chippaco, the bearer of clouds.
Say, then, wherefore should men call me coward?

And you, why shame ye with insult your chief?"

[Lines 63-82—Quiniscoe's special weaponry is then catalogued: his spruce bow tipped with the "horns of a wild goat," his bow bound with rattlesnake skin treated with a charm taught him by his grandsire to keep off harm, the string of his bow made of twisted deer sinew, and his flint arrowheads produced under the a crescent moon by the grandsire.]

With his keen arrows hath Quin-is-coe pierced
The heart of the great eagle, as upward
He soared in the sky, to meet the bright sun.   85
With his deadly arrows hath he struck down
The enche-chim [nčičən or wolf], as boldly he leaped forth
From out of the dark woods of pine, on his prey.

The skumahist [skəmixist or black bear] and the fierce cal-low-na
Have both fallen prone before the arrows   90
Of Quin-is-coe; yet now even his bow
Is powerless, for where is the keen arrow
That can pierce the evil Souie Appoo?
Yet strong, strong is the heart of Quin-is-coe,
Strong, strong is the heart of the hunter chief;   95
Brave and strong are the hearts of his kinsmen,
His warriors and friends; and loudly they cry;
"We will go to the mountain Chippaco—
Aye, we will go with Quin-is-coe, our chief,
To search for the great Souie Appoo; we will   100
Bind him with ropes and reatas [lariats]; we will
Drag him along at our feet—yes, at our feet!"
"Oh, list, list to thy grandsire, Quin-is-coe;
List to the words of the man who is wise;
Seek ye not the high snow-crown'd Chippaco,   105
Chippaco, mountain of wonder and dread;
Oh, search not for the great Souie Appoo,
Who maketh on that dread mountain his bed."

[Lines 108-131—They do not heed these words, but set off to capture the Souie Appoo though thunder sounds loudly from the mountain.]

"Why, what aileth our hunter Quin-is-coe?

And why thus blancheth the cheek of our chief?
Hush! hush! there is the great Souie Appoo!
Hush! look yonder, where he lieth asleep,   135
Yes, asleep on the mountain Chippaco.
See, his huge form is stretched on the mountain;
Hark! hark his breathing so laboured and loud;
His black face is upturned to the sunshine."

[Lines 140-145—Finding the sleeping Souie Appoo, they bind him.]

Souie Appoo awakens, he sneezeth;
Slowly he stretcheth his long, hairy limbs.
See, they take up their bows and their arrows,
And their sharp darts fly as thick as the hail,
And they strike on the great Souie Appoo;   150
But like hail from a rock, back they rebound.
Ah, vain, vain are their bows and their arrows.
Great Souie Appoo hath opened his eyes.
Then they jump on the great form before them
And they cling to his long, silky, black hair;   155
He yawneth, and half sleeping he riseth;
Ropes and reatas are snapped like a thread.
The men that clung to his long, silky curls—
Ah, ah, he lifted them up with his head.
Losing their hold they roll off him, trembling   160
They fall to the ground, and Souie Appoo
In scorn shaketh his black, silky ringlets;
His mocking laugh peals out scornful and loud.
Then Quin-is-coe would fain [earnestly] have pursued him;
But, lo! he hid in a dark, thunder cloud   165
And mingled with the thunder, his laughter
Broke loudly forth from the dark, threatening cloud.
Quickly fly they the mountain Chippaco,
Snow-crowned Chippaco that beareth the clouds;
Quickly fly they the great Souie Appoo   170
Whose mocking laughter is scornful and loud.
[*1870s*, 1900]

Quin-is-coe, Part Two

A wail is rising from the dark valley,
And as it ariseth and ascendeth
The mountains, it swelleth louder, louder!
The voices of nature wake and echo   175
The lament, and the wooded mountain slopes
Join in the wailing chorus. The chill winds
Of night moan sadly through the straight, dark pines;
The flitting shnee-nas [*snina?* or owl] raise their doleful cry,
"Poom-papoom-poom!" The enche-chim, listening   180
In his deep lair, howls in concert. Harken!
What saith the hooting shnee-na in the dark,
Gloomy wood; what answereth his mate in
The valley, as she resteth on the pole
Of Quin-is-coe's lodge? "Poom-pa-poom-poom!"   185
List, the shnee-na in the wood is saying,
"I come for you, I come for you!" His mate
In the valley repeats, "I come for you!"
The Indians collected round Quin-is-coe's lodge, sing low.
A sad, low, wailing chant are they singing. "He is going,   190
He is going; the brave, the mighty, is going from us.
From amongst us is he going, whither his father went."

[*Lines 193-208 — The mournful chant continues as the people prepare for the departure of Quiniscoe.*]

"What saith thy sister, what saith the wise one, Cumme-tat-coe?"
"Bring hither the Pinto mare,—the Pinto mare of your chief,   210
Bring hither the steed most loved by my brother, Quin-is-coe
Bind on her back a saddle, put a bridle in her mouth,
Put on her the saddle and bridle of our Quin-is-coe;
Take ye good heed the reins hang loose, and tie ye fast her colt,
Tie her colt fast near the lodge of my brother Quin-is-coe!   215
Now lead forth the mare, lead forth the mare and let her go free.
Lo! If she travel up the valley toward the sunrise
Then will our Quin-is-coe live—your much loved chief shall not die.
If she travel down the valley toward the sunset, then
He dieth with the sun, Quin-is-coe dieth with the sun!!   220
Haste! haste! Lead forth the mare, lead the Pinto forth, lead her
forth."

[Lines 222-253—Kiwis, Quiniscoe's son, saddles the horse who gallops west. The people lament. But then the great Dr. Scuse emerges on horseback from the darkness. He has come from "Loo-loo-hoo-loo[23] / Where the red earth soundeth hollow under [his] horse's hoofs" to save Quiniscoe by wrestling with the spirit. He treats Quiniscoe by a huge fire.]

More! More! Make it blaze, make it blaze, and make the darkness light.
What strange thing appeareth? It hath the beak of an eagle,   255
It hath the claws of a bear, round its body is the hide
Of a buffalo, round its neck a necklet of dried toads,
Its waist is girt with a dead rattlesnake.—Ah, what is it?
Who is it? It is Scuse, the mighty doctor, the great Scuse.
With the eagle's beak he will peck—he will peck out the eyes   260
Of the evil Foul One; with the bear's claws will he tear him;
With the toads will he make him groan; with the dead rattlesnake
Will he cause him to writhe in great anguish. Who is so strong
To fight with the Foul One, as Scuse the wise one, the strong one?
Ha! see, see how he danceth! Ha! list, list how he singeth!   265
Oh, harken now to the song he singeth, as he draweth
The Foul One, the evil one, from our hunter Quin-is-coe.

        "Hither, come hither, thou Evil One
          That draweth the life from Quin-is-coe.
          Hither, come hither now, thou Foul One,   270
          And fight with me, even with me, Scuse,
          Lo I, Scuse the doctor, defy thee.
          Come now, come, let us fight and wrestle,
          Our prize is the life of Quin-is-coe."

[Lines 275-332—After a hard battle with the spirit, Scuse is defeated. Quiniscoe's sisters Cummetatcoe and Pilehatcoe wail and lament as the chief fades. Scuse tells the people—Quiniscoe's sisters, Kiwas, Lucca, Owla, and Yahoolo—to send messengers to all parts of the valley to give notice of the impending funeral feast. People bring in quantities of firewood and game. As the sun sinks, they pile many robes over him. As he dies, the women shear their hair; the men pluck their beards and eyebrows; and all blacken their faces. People begin to assemble.]

The Burial

Fast, fast are they coming; fast they come from up the valley,   333
From down the valley, from hither and thither ride they in.

[Lines 335-355 — The huge fire is built and the feast prepared. The dead Quiniscoe is brought out on his couch in his best clothing.]

And thy portion of the feast, mighty chief, the flames devour it,
The fire consumeth it! Bring ye rich gifts, bring offerings
To the mighty chief; cast them into the fierce fire quickly,
Cast them into the bright blaze, let fiery flames consume them.
Lead out the horses of Quin-is-coe, lead them round the corpse;   360
Lead them again, and yet again. Speak, speak, Cumme-tat-coe,
Speak, Pile-hat-coe, ye sisters of the mighty chieftain:
Who shall ride Quin-is-coe's horses? Let Kit-tu-la take ten,
Let Kiwas take ten, let Lucca take ten and Owla ten;
Let the remainder be driven out into the darkness;   365
Let the kinsmen of Quin-is-coe take lassos in their hands,
Let them pursue the horses through the darkness of the night,
That which they capture let them keep; haste, haste ere the day dawn.
Ah, the sun riseth. Wail, children of Quin-is-coe, wail—wail!
What saith Scuse the Wise One,
what saith the mighty doctor Scuse?   370
Let not Syn-ke-lips howl over him and break his rest;
Let not En-che-chim disturb him; nor the Ska-loo-la [*skalula?*][24]
Hoot and hover near the grave where our chief lieth at rest;
In peace let the mighty hunter sleep, while we still sorrow.

[Lines 375-445 — After three years, Owla, Cummetatcoe, and Pilehatcoe feel uneasy. Owla has seen a "tall gaunt thing, a form, a fearful form" rise from Quiniscoe's grave during the night. All notice strange sounds and other presences. Dr. Scuse apprehends the ghost of Quiniscoe, which has the "head and skin of a grizzly" and "feet and arms like a man." Scuse draws out and speaks with the dead chief's spirit.]

"I talk with a spirit departed, with the shade of the
Hunter, our chief; and he answereth in language that [is] voiceless;
This is the answer he giveth, this troubleth our chief."

"In the ground am I laid and forgotten;
    My memory and flesh have departed;   450
Because I am not, none thinketh of me;
Other men ride my horses and saddles;
My dogs follow other men to the chase,
And my sisters have ceased to lament me."

"What wouldst thou, O being departed—gifts and rich offerings?   455
Cumme-tat-coe and Pile-hat-coe, thy sisters, never
Can cease to lament thee. Say thou but a word and 'tis done."

. . . .

"My robes are all musty and mouldy
    With the must and the mould of decay;
No feast hath been held in my honor,   460
    My spirit is vexed by the delay.
See, thou, then, that this wrong is righted:
    A great feast let my sisters prepare;
Bid thither my friends and my kinsmen;
    I in spirit will also be there.   465
Dig open the tomb where ye laid me,
    And my body raise up from its hold;
My sisters, prepare me new garments,
    And a fur robe my body enfold.
Then peace to my spirit returning,   470
    My dry bones restore ye to the earth;
No more shall my phantom affright ye,
    Never more shall my shade mar your mirth."

[Lines 475-491—All Quiniscoe's kinsmen are summoned to come for an
exhumation rite, so his "disquieted spirit may calmly rest in peace." They
come in "hot haste," bringing offerings and gifts.]

"We come from Cumme-tat-coe, from Pile-hat-coe are we come, to bid
Ye to a feast in honor of Quin-is-coe, our dead chief.
Scuse the wise doctor hath said: 'Shall Quin-is-coe, the mighty   495
Hunter, be forgotten? shall his memory and his flesh
Perish together? shall no man think of him because he
Is not?' Come raise him from out the deep, dark house wherein ye

Laid him to rest with many sighs; feast ye with him once more,
And pay him much honor. Come ere the moon waneth;
　　　　come ere　　　　　　　　　　　　　　　　　　　　　　　500
Three suns have died, ye kinsmen of our dead chief Quin-is-coe."

[Lines 501-508—Scuse directs the ceremony.]

"Pluck grass, I say,
Pluck sweet scented grass; stuff it in your ears, and your nostrils,　510
Lest ye sicken when ye smell that that was living, and is
Dead. Pluck sweet scented grass now, ye kinsmen of Quin-is-coe.
Open, open the house, the deep, dark house wherein ye laid
Our chief to rest with tears and many sighs. Raise up the dead,
The mighty dead; bear him to the lodge of Cumme-tat-coe　　515
And Pile-hat-coe, his sisters."

....

　　　　　　　　　　　　　"Now open up the robe,　　　　520
Even the robe whereon lieth that that once was your chief.
Let each kinsman raise a bone, even a bone from out the
Mass of corruption: lay it on the robe, the new, clean robe
Prepared by Cumme-tat-coe and Pile-hat-coe, sisters
Of the chief; search diligently, leave not one bone behind　　525
Raise the skull, place it at the head of the robe; now raise the
Rib bones, place them in the middle; place the footbones at the
Foot. Search, oh search ye diligently amidst that that was
Mortal living flesh, but is not. Search ye for the bones of
Quin-is-coe your chief. Lay his bow and arrows at this feet,　530
Put his sharp knife at his side; lay on the new buckskin shirt,
The shirt rich with beads of many colors. Lay it upon
The bones. Lay a pair of embroidered moccasins at his feet,
Moccasins embroidered with the quills of the porcupine.
List, list to Scuse, the wise one. Wrap the chief in his new robes. 535
Tight, wrap him tightly, lay him in the midst, gaze ye on him.
List, list to Scuse, the doctor. Hither, hither, bring hither
The robe from whence ye took the bones of your chief Quin-is-coe.
Quickly bring it to the fire. Aye, bring it to the bright blaze.
Hither, hither, bring hither that that was mortal living　　　540
Flesh, but is not; bring hither that that was corruptible

And is corrupt. Let the fire devour it and flames consume it.
Bring hither your gifts and your offerings to the mighty
Hunter; let the fire devour and let the flames consume them.
Now bring hither that portion of the feast prepared for the   545
Great chief; let the fire devour and let the flames consume it.
List, list, ye kinsmen of Quin-is-coe, list to Scuse the Wise.
Eat, eat, ye kinsmen of Quin-is-coe, make merry with him
Till sunrise. Dance ye, sing ye, ye kinsmen of Quin-is-coe.
Lo, the sun ariseth. Lift up the mighty hunter,   550
Bear him with many sighs to his place of rest; let him sleep,
Let him sleep the sleep that is dreamless; lay him in the deep,
Dark house that is prepared for him; throw in many warm robes,
Throw on the earth. Wail, wail, ye children of Quin-is-coe, wail;
Wail, wail, ye that are his kinsmen, wail! Never more shall he   555
Slay the cal-low-na; in silence shall he rest forever."

[Author's] NOTES
        Quin-is-coe, an Indian hunter and chief.
        Cumme-tat-coe, his sister.
        Pile-hat-coe, his sister.
[*1870s*, 1900]

What I Know of Ogopogo

I will try to tell all I know of the Amphibian, now known
as Ogopogo. The real Indian name I never knew, I suppose the
Okanagan Indians had a name for it in their own language and
the Similkameen Indians had a name for it in theirs. But to me
they generally spoke in Chinook—and it was spoken of as "Ook-
ook mis-achie coupa Lake" (the wicked one in the lake) or as the
"hyas-hyas gust scaca cupa Lake" meaning the "huge one in the
Lake." This creature they seemed to dread and spoke of it with
lowered voices.

I first heard of it by the camp fires on my first trip to the
Similkameen [1868] and the Indians, I could see, were sincere in
the awe with which they told their stories; I gathered from those
stories that the creature was an amphibian. My husband told me
the Whites spoke of it as "The Monster" but he said that none
of the white men had seen it and though the Indians seemed

terrified, he did not believe in it.

Well I listened to the stories of the Indians with an open mind—(and being Highland Scottish on my father's side)—I partially believed in the monster.

Yacumtecum[25] told of how he had gone to Priest's Valley [Vernon] with his people and crossed the Okanagan Lake in a canoe and taken a chicken with him to drop into the lake as an offering. He said that the creature would seize the chicken and leave them to cross unmolested—the women in the canoe were so afraid that they threw their shawls over their heads lest they should see it.

That was the first time I heard of Ogopogo—the next time, I was on my way to Sunny Side [1873], now Westbank [West Kelowna], and when we were about midway between Penticton and Sunny Side the Indians pointed to a small island in the lake where "Nah-a quansem stop" (where he always lives). Here, they said, when he got hold of a man or a deer, he would drag it and devour it on the rocks, which were stained with blood and on which there were piles of bleached bones. This was its home.

This, I understand was afterwards purchased by Lord Aberdeen—why I don't know, unless for its association with Ogopogo. I don't even know how he ever got there, for the Indians said no boat could possibly land at the island. Every time anyone tried landing on his island, the monster would cause a strong wind to blow and baffle the attempt. From this I got the impression that the monster was something more than an amphibian. It was always in some way connected with high winds. I was told that both Forbes and Charles Vernon had tried to land on his island and were driven off by strong winds—there was a strong wind the night he swamped the fishing boat and carried off the fishermen. This idea was certainly confirmed by the yarns told by Johnny McDougall as we sat round our camp fire on the first night of our arrival at Sunny Side. Perhaps I should not use the word yarns—that implies doubt, and who could doubt the truth of any story of Ogopogo, not I, for I saw the creature long years after.

Johnny told us that once he had occasion to use a team of horses that ran in pasture on the other side of the Lake. He had made up his mind to cross them at the narrows, about a mile or so above The Mission [now part of Kelowna], but when he took them to the edge of the water, they baulked, refusing to take the water. Again and again they were driven to the lake, each time they broke wildly back—then losing patience Johnny told his boys to rope them. Taking the ropes, Johnny stepped into his canoe with one of his boys holding the ropes to tow the team and the other boys surrounding the horses on the bank and driving them into the water. This they accomplished after a struggle, but alas the little pig was forgotten! When they were midway across the lake—there was a tug at the rope, a struggle under the water and the team disappeared. The angry water almost swamping the boat, indeed it would have been dragged under but for the presence of mind of Johnny, who cut the ropes attached to the horses and made hot haste for the opposite shore. When there he realized the mistake he had made in forgetting the little pig and felt sure that that was the cause of the disaster.

The Indians at Sunny Side seemed afraid to speak much about the entity, seemed to dread being overheard by it.

The day I saw it, it was just after a night of terrific storm—the wind blew a hurricane, the tops of the strong pines both on the mountain slopes and the plateau were wrenched off and blown about like straws. Towards morning I went to a cliff overlooking the lake to see if there was any chance of our boat returning. (My husband and son had gone over to the Mission the day before.) The wind had indeed subsided but there was still a strong current on the lake, sweeping down to Penticton, too strong still for our light little boat to cross.

The sun was shining and I stood on the cliff admiring the beautiful lake—when I observed below the harbour, what I at first took for an uprooted pine. I was trying to think where it could have been torn from, then, I observed that instead of floating down the lake with the current that it was coming rapidly up the lake, towards where I stood—it passed the harbour and still came on with a swift undulating motion—just like a huge log in the water going the wrong way. I watched it pass me and disappear round a bend, feeling convinced that it was a living creature—it looked just like the trunk of a huge pine but I saw neither head nor tail—it was not a bit like the serpent—since seen by others—but it might have been a big Saurian—and I am convinced that it was one. However when my husband and boy returned from the Mission, I told them what I had seen, they laughed at me and

216

said that a fellow had come to the Mission and reported seeing the same thing from the other side of the lake—but they thought he had been drinking. The man's name was Smitheran, someone may still remember his story—and I can bear witness to its truth. I think the storm the night before, which was of unusual violence, had driven it from its lair.

Since then I have known men who say they have heard the monster at night in a swampy meadow—and thinking that their pack horses had broken loose, they went to look for them, but saw nothing. Their horses were still tied on the plateau.
[undated]

From Some Native Daughters I Have Known

G-he-nac—Sister of Quin-is-coe

I first saw Ghenac in 1869—Octr [October] I think it was—I was looking out at the door when I saw a magnificent Black Horse coming prancing and curvetting [leaping] up the flat, it was held in check by unseen hands, a little way behind but well off at one side on a fairly good sorrel rode a tall Indian boy. I watched with some curiosity their approach, then I saw as they came nearer that the Black horse had a very high peaked saddle on, behind which I could see what appeared to be a bundle of some kind and a pair of powerful hands which drew the curvetting Black almost to his haunches at the Store [in Princeton] door; the Indian had quickly dismounted and the bundle rolling off the Black horse and throwing the bridle lines to the boy, turned to me, to my surprise I saw it was a woman—such a woman! She stood about four feet high and had a dreadful hump on her back which was exaggerated by the woollen shawl thrown round her, her face was long, very long and wooden, absolutely expressionless. The forehead was high and smooth but the thin lips were tightly compressed—not a smile nor a frown—just wooden. She stepped into the store—she walked painfully and slowly refusing to see the hand I held out to help her—she made several purchases through her attendant nephew, who spoke for her, he had enough to say—told me that her name was Ghenac, that she was the daughter of old Louie and sister of Quiniscoe, the Bear Hunter.

217

All the time the boy chattered on she never raised her eyes nor looked at me, only addressed herself to the boy—gave him the money to pay for what she had bought, then she was ready to go—She turned to me and for the first time she appeared to see me—such eyes—large—black as coal, not brown like most Indian women, her glance swept me from head to foot, a hostile glance—she folded her strong large bony hands—turned and went out without shaking hands, an insult, which the boy tried to make up for by offering his hand—behind her back. I did not see her mount but she was up on her horse's back before I realized she had left the store, her strong hands controlling the impatient animal—the boy tied their purchases (in the ever present flour sack) to the back of his saddle and away they swept full gallop to their camp. That was my first meeting with Ghenac—from the other Indians I learned that she was considered a rich woman, she possessed cattle and horses, she never rode any but the best of her horses and was utterly fearless—but she hated all white men.

It was a long time before I gained her friendship. She would come to the store to trade moccasins or gloves and I never had any bother with her; she just asked what she wanted for her stuff and I said yes or no—we never disagreed, but she never really was friendly till her brother Jim Gahulach died—Jim too had a lot of cattle and horses and was considered well off but he had a son who was a good spender and always getting into trouble with the cowboys. My husband generally managed to straighten it out. Once Jim deposited four hundred dollars with me (I was banker for many of the Indians);[26] he had just sold some cattle—he left the money for more than a year, then I heard that he was very ill and could not get better. He felt very miserable over the misdeeds of his son George against whom a warrant had been issued for murder (though it was not really a murder)[27] and George was in hiding somewhere and his father in great distress. It was the rainy season and I got a great surprise when in the midst of a dreadful downpour I saw Jim ride up to the door—My husband brought him into the dining room where we had a fire in the huge open fireplace, and told me to get him a cup of tea and get his money for him as he wanted it now. Jim's clothing was soaking wet, he looked very thin, and his eyes were very bright. I told him he ought not to be out in such weather—he said it did not matter he was dying—he had come to get his money and say good bye to us all–then he would go home and die—I told him nonsense, he would soon get better—how would a dying man ride forty miles. He smiled, counted his money, drank his tea. He could not eat but shook hands, he said for the last time, bade us be good to George if we could, got on his horse and rode off—he rode for fifteen miles to the Looloohooloo.[28] It rained so hard that he made a little fire and rested under the slope of a big rock—he felt that he might not finish the journey so he picked an old Yeast Powder can some Camper had thrown away—wiped it dry—put his money in it, hid it under a rock and resumed his weary ride—when he reached home he went to Ghenac's house, lay down and died—poor Jim. In a week his brothers came to me for Jim's money. When I said I had already given it to him—they doubted, said that Jim had more than four hundred dollars in my keeping—One man spoke up and said that I spoke the truth—that Ghenac said Jim had only four hundred dollars that he had left with me and I had given it to him and he had hidden it at Looloohooloo—Ghenac said Jim had told her just before he died—they agreed to go and hunt for the hidden money—they said that the money was never found but I always thought that the old lady had been given the money in trust for George and she thought the brothers might use it to bury Jim instead of putting up their money for his funeral expenses—however that was, Ghenac shortly after rode up on her best horse and held out her hand calling me Nooka (sister) and after that we were good friends till her death—Meantime poor foolish George was being hunted like a wolf for the murder of Killeketza—My husband tried to persuade him to give himself up that he would only get a few years if he told all the truth and who it was took whiskey to his camp—but George would not listen to reason so he led a hunted life protected by his Aunt Ghenac. Once when two constables had hailed him down the river, he hid at Looloohooloo in the rocks and let them pass. When he thought they were well on their way, he followed behind them. He hid at Ashnola[29] while they searched the houses and when they struck out for Keremeos, he crossed over to his aunt's house hoping to pass the night in peace. The old lady gave him his dinner and was preparing to make a feast for his supper when a walking Indian darted in to say the constables were coming back—Ghenac signed to George to stand against the wall at the back of the door—which she instantly opened wide but he was over six feet in height and his feet were plainly to be seen under the open door. Ghenac threw a pile of buckskin over his feet then sat down with her back to the door and took up her gloves–when the constables came they dismounted but only saw a poor hump backed old woman sitting sewing in a litter of buckskin. She through a small boy asked what they wanted— then she told them to look for themselves which they did but did not find George—when they had gone back to Princeton, George had his supper and a quiet sleep.

At last to Ghenac's grief George gave himself up and was sentenced to I think ten years. After he had served three or four years in [New] Westminster [Penitentiary], he got sick and died. Ghenac came to me and asked me to write to the Tyee[30] and ask for George's body to bury with his father. Her wish was granted and she dispatched several of George's friends and relations to meet the body at Hope and bring it across the mountains. I can remember that Johnny Collosasket, Dauchenelac, Yacumtecum, Cultus Frank and 'Good Dick' were in the cortege; it took them nearly a week to bring the body from Hope, they were mourning and making lamentation as they came. Ghenac met them at Chuchuwayha. She was grave and silent as usual. She sat down on the ground covering her face, for a long time, then she rose from the ground,—"Why do you lament," she cried, "that is not George." The young man who had brought the body out told her that the Tyee would not lie to them in that way—but she stood her ground—finally she got angry and said, "George was a tall man, taller than Johnny Collosasket–measure the box–you could not put Collosasket in it. This they did and found it was too short for George. They opened it and were convinced—back they came to Princeton with the body and coffin again, I had to write to the Tyee (I think it was MacBride) and he courteously and promptly apologized for this mistake and sent another body back; this time George's friends were not so long on the road crossing the mountains but they said they were sure they had the right man in the coffin this time—not so Ghenac. She was all ready for them at Chuchuwayha as before, she sat by the coffin a shorter time, then she said "Chinaman" and turned away in wrath and disgust. Again the coffin was opened and a Chinaman it was. There was his pigtail to prove it. Another journey across the mountains and another coffin was brought—Ghenac again said that George was

220

not in it, but this time his friends would not open the coffin and refused to cross the mountains anymore. They just buried whoever was in the box and Ghenac still persisted it was not George. She even said that George was not dead. I thought the old lady had let it drop, but—no—in two years' time she came and told me that George was alive and in California with Buffalo Bill in his circus—a Keremeos Indian had seen him there—would I write to him. I was sorry for the old lady—she seemed so sincere in her conviction about George being alive. I wrote to Colonel Cody and got a nice polite answer—he had called over all the Indians in his employ and could find no trace of George—Ghenac went to her grave mourning for him and saving her money for him thinking he would come back but he never came.

[undated]

Our Louisa [31]

It is enough that I will call her our Louisa—she has relatives that might not like me to give her real name. What a jewel she was in time of need—clean, delightfully clean, a good Catholic, and a thorough housekeeper. I did not enquire where she had learned her housekeeping but being but a poor housekeeper myself I admired it.

Louisa came from one of the highest Indian families and was the daughter and sister of a chief. She was not obliged to earn her daily bread as some poor Indian girls do, but her own kind heart and perhaps a little curiosity led her to offer help to her neighbors where she thought help was needed. There was an epidemic of measles at Princeton and one of my daughters who resided at Princeton brought her infant daughter over to stay with me at the ranch to be out of danger. I had quite a house full at the time. I always enjoyed that. There was Ed, his wife, and boy, and Will's little boy Wilfred, Angie, Alice, and myself, so little Babs was a very welcome addition to the family. We heard that after leaving Babs at the ranch my daughter was taken down with measles.[32] Then almost simultaneously Babs took it. We did our best to keep her quiet but she wanted her mother and kept calling for her. In a day or two, Ed's boy and little Wilfred were down; it was too much trouble to be running upstairs every few minutes so I turned the sitting and dining rooms into a hospital. Ed and I being chief nurses—Angie and Alice helping with the cooking—but the day Angie sickened I was in despair—Edgar's wife was ill. We had now six patients and my daughter from town much as she wished to help was not yet able to come to the rescue—Providence sent our Louisa. Then poor Ed sickened so there was only me to nurse and cook. Louisa took the whole situation in at a glance. Without my asking her she volunteered to help. She had no fear of measles or anything else—she was too good a Catholic, she always said her prayers and grace before she ate, she never ate meat on Fridays, why then should she fear. No, she never worked for pay. I was her friend. She would help and she did not mind accepting a dollar a day from a friend, she would not take money from nor work for anyone but a friend—so it was settled. Louisa would help me a few days. This sight of her pleasant smiling face and the sound of her light quick step, alone was a comfort. She went to town and turned her horses out and then came back with a clean flour sack full of her belongings. In early days both Indians and White people learned the value of a flour sack instead of a valise, it would not break nor spoil when lashed on a horse—if one only had one horse—we tied the inevitable flour sack of necessity back of the saddle.

Well Louisa came and brought her [illegible]—Then with her help we made a bed in my room next the living room for Edgar and his boy who clung to him and gave him no peace. Ed's wife we put in a bed near the sitting room window, while Angie and Alice had a bed in the dining room. Little Wilfred and Babs slept with one another at either end and Louisa pulled up a couch for herself under the arch between two rooms—when everything was arranged to her satisfaction and looked fairly comfortable she gave a nod and departed for the kitchen. I could hear her washing herself and then she presented herself for a moment at the hospital door—such a changed Louisa, shining from soap and water her hair shining, neatly braided in two long braids which she wound round her head in a tidy becoming fashion—a clean calico dress and wrapper. "Now," she said. "I cook." She found everything in the pantry by instinct and soon I heard kettles boiling and a frying pan sizzling. In about two hours she had gruel and custards for the sick, and a good substantial meal for the two of us who could eat and when we had seen to all the sick and got them tolerably quiet Louisa and I sat down to the first comfortable meal I had had for some days. I felt thankful. Louisa said grace. Comfortable, comely Louisa seemed to me like a saint—helping first one and then another, and full of bright lively chatter. We got our patients quiet and asleep and then went to bed early—we were up several times in the night, but slept as soon as we went back to bed. Louisa rose with daylight, chopped wood, made fires, scrubbed the house, washed her clothes in the bathtub and then bathed herself and put on clean clothes—then began a smell of cooking—When I got up I found all the house work done up, a chicken killed and cleaned ready to make soup for the invalids. The same went on for nearly a week and those who were first taken sick were getting better and were more exacting at night calling for drinks. One beautiful night after a beautiful day during which I fancied that I detected slight signs of uneasiness in our Louisa, so much so that I had urged her to take a run uptown and gather any news she could. She came back brighter than ever, humming as she worked. She helped me get everything quiet for the night and went to bed with the rest of us as usual. We must have slept two or three hours when Edgar's wife called for a drink—but Louisa did not spring up as usual. It was a beautiful moonlight night and the moon beams flooded Louisa's bed with light. I could see the form of the poor tired girl lying on the bed covered with the blankets. Even her head and face was covered—so I got up and gave the water without disturbing her. I thought she needed her sleep after all her hard work. Ed's wife called for water again and again. I tired of getting up so called Louisa, but she still slept too soundly. I gave the patient her drink and was returning to my bed when little Alice whispered, "She's not there. I went to the bed and shook a stick and a pillow beautifully arranged to look like a sleeper..." I told Alice not to say a word and rearranging the sham went back to bed.

At an early hour Louisa stole quietly into the room, made up her bed—then set about her scrubbing as usual and was her cheery good humored self—this went on night after night, no one but Alice and myself knew anything of Louisa's nocturnal wanderings.

At last Louisa thought that we could manage without her. Then she graciously said that she thought she ought to return to Nicola[33] —she would not have stayed so long with any but her

brothers' friends. So she got up her horses, washed her clothes and when they were dry and ironed departed, as she had come, gaily, leaving a very grateful family behind. I never can forget the simple kindness of "our Louisa."
[undated]

Emma Hutch or Hutchy

I first saw Emma Hutch or Hutchy in 1886 or 7—I had heard of her before I saw her and this is what I heard—that in the early '60s [1860s] there had been a wedding at Cariboo.[34] This was a time when men were foolish enough to put gold shoes on their horse and wash their gold out of the dirt in champagne. Mrs. Hutch or Mrs. Hutchie's wedding was celebrated with lavish splendour and the cost to him was three thousand dollars—among other presents to the bride was a seal skin coat, very costly. There had been a ceremony some years before at the bride's home. That one was in accordance with Indian customs when her father was an Indian Chief. I heard that he was a Fountain Indian,[35] gave his daughter to Hutch.

[second page of notes] I first saw Emma in 1887. One day when I was in our store, a tall handsome woman walked in, smiling in a friendly manner—I was rather taken by surprise for she was dressed in a remarkably handsome seal skin coat—was wearing a pretty hat and nice gloves. She did not look as dark as the Indian women generally did—she said, "I am Mrs. Sanders and would like to buy some sale (cloth) to make a [...] shirt for my old man." That was my first introduction to Emma—I had heard much about her before—this is what I heard.

[third page of notes] Notes on Emma Hutchy. Hatch or Hutchy was married to old Emma in early days at Cariboo, the wedding feast cost 3000 dollars—he amongst other things bought her a seal skin coat. They lived together till his death. Then after due mourning, she lived with a man named Saunders—he was good to her and they were thrifty honest people in—at Kalso [Kaslo?]. Emma left her treasures—nursed the sick miners—In 1885 they tried their luck at Granite [Creek]. In 1886 or 7—Saunders took up a ranch on Whipsaw Creek [southeast of Princeton]. What I have put down before is hearsay but after 1887 I personally knew Emma who was still a handsome woman—After some years

Saunders died left will. Emma sold her ranch for 13,500 dollars—
Emma after the fashion of her kind after the lapse of a few months
giving all he died possessed of [ms ends]
[undated]

Kind Penquinac or the Princess Julia[36]

The early days of this sweet natured girl were spent in the
happy innocent pastimes of the Indian child of seventy-five
years ago.[37]   Barefooted, she would stand in the icy waters of
the Similkameen with a long willow rod, fishing for trout or
grayling—a sport she loved. Sometimes she would take a birch
bark basket and go up the One Mile Creek to a place the Indians
called Stitor and gather wild potatoes (or as they called them
Stitorn). Another time she would gather rock rose roots, and on
the same expedition, she would kill a few prairie chickens with
her slingshot. That was lots of fun; she would return to camp
laden. She was an expert with the bow and arrows and delighted
in outdoing the boys in a contest. Climbing a tree and getting a
young hawk from its snug nest was a joyous event. When her
father Chief Incowmasket (some white men called him Tyee
Moie) went hunting beaver or bear, she would ride by his side
carrying his spare musket and hold his horse while he crept on
his quarry.
Penquinac was her mother's helper too, tanning deer skins,
drying venison and fish, making moccasins and other Indian
household duties, singing joyfully. When I first saw her she was
a bright happy little girl with two long braids of beautiful well
kept hair. This hair was her mother's pride, as it well might be—
as she grew her hair grew till it hung about her like a garment.
Incowmasket was justly proud of his daughter [ms written
over in another hand obscuring what seems to be an account of
something Penquinac and her mother did] [ms ends]

[Another fragment on Penquinac]

When I first saw Penquinac she was a bright happy little
girl, with two long braids of beautiful well kept hair of which
her mother was justly proud. As she grew her hair grew till it

hung about her like a garment. Incowmasket was justly proud of his affectionate sweet dispositioned daughter. When she grew to a maiden, Penquinac had many suitors. Incowmasket made an unfortunate selection for her, and Penquinac obediently accepted his choice. She had one son Enock; I was living in my stable home—our temporary quarters between the loss of our home by flood [June, 1894], and the building of our new log house, when Penquinac brought her little son to visit us, he was a fine child, of whom Incowmasket his grandfather was justly proud. My little girls flocked around Penquinac and little Enock, they released her beautiful tresses—sitting on a chair they swept to the floor like a garment around her. Penquinac laughed and chatted with the children and me. She looked very unhappy when her attention was not on the children—she made no complaint. Soon after I heard that her husband had left her and gone away from her people. Later I heard with great regret, that she had gone to live with a white man. I believe he was kind to her in a way—but she died an early and terrible death. Poor Penquinac! Always kind to the poor, the helpless or the indigent, kind to her mother, her father and her grandfather, to all she met.

"Let kind thoughts be her monument."
[undated]

From Susan Allison's Recollections

From "Some Recollections of a Pioneer of the Sixties" [38]

I was married in September, about the eighteenth or the twentieth [of 1868], I am not sure which. My husband went to [New] Westminster and got a special license from Governor Seymour, and Archdeacon Woods came up to Hope to marry us. My sister and brother-in-law [Jane Moir Dewdney and Edgar Dewdney] were visiting in Hope at that time. Also Mr. and Mrs. O'Reilly, so they and of course Mrs. Landvoight[39] were present at the parsonage when we were married.

Then began my camping days and the wild, free life I ever loved till age and infirmity put an end to it.

On the journey out we rode the two Kates, Cream and Grey.

My husband sent the three packboys on ahead to fix camp. (This was over the Hope-Similkameen Trail.) As the three boys will often appear in these memoirs, I may as well pause and introduce them—Cockshist[40] was cargodore, that is, he looked after the packs and cargo generally, storing it under shelter when removed from the horses and assigning each horse its load. Johnny Suzanne[41] was packer. Cockshist assisted in the actual packing but Johnny had to round up the horses, mend saddles, see that the ropes were dry. Yacumtecum[42] or Tuc-tac as he was then called was bell-boy and cook. He led the leading packhorse with the bell when the train started and cooked meals when in camp. We left town just at dusk and in a little over an hour reached the Lake House where we found the tents up and a blazing log fire and Yacumtecum cooking. In the tent a canvas was spread over the floor and a bed made of "mountain feathers," spruce branches, and a buffalo robe. A wash basin was mounted on the box. Outside, there was the most delicious smelling grouse cooking. I went to the creek and washed and did up my hair in the darkness and when I regained the camp Tuc-tac had spread a canvas in front of the fire with fried trout, grouse, bacon and bannock. That washed down with tin cups of delicious tasting tea. We sat and talked till late, the Indian boys sitting with us and telling us stories of the place. Here, Yacumtecum said, one of the Big Men (giants) lived and had been often seen.[43] Cockshist said they also lived on the Okanagan. This led to talking of the creature now called "Ogopogo." They looked on it as a superhuman entity and seemed to fear it, though none of our boys had seen it nor did they want to. . . .

My husband had just finished a new log house—large and comfortable. There was a store attached and Indians came from miles with skins and furs. . . . Mr. Hayes [John Fall Allison's American business partner until 1880] had a good supper ready for us the day I first saw Princeton, though he did not approve my dressing for dinner, a habit I was drilled in as a child and has always stuck with me to some extent. I did not see why he objected to my habits, but I think he half forgave me when he found I could milk cows and was not afraid to go into a corral full of cattle.

As it was getting near snow-fly when the Hope Mountain was closed and all travel stopped with horses or cattle, my husband could only spend two weeks at home, most of the time seeing to the horses and rounding up the cattle for another trip with beef for the [New] Westminster market, so I was virtually alone. I had a visit from an Indian woman,[44] a niece of Quiniscoe, the "Bear Hunter" and Chief of the Chu-chu-ewa[45] Tribe. She was dressed for the occasion, of course, in mid-Victorian style, a Balmoral petticoat,[46] red and gray, a man's stiff starched white shirt as a blouse, stiff high collar, earrings an inch long, and brass bracelets! I did not know my visitor seemed to think she ought to sit upright in her chair and fix her eyes on the opposite wall. I think "Cla-hi-ya" ["Kla-How-Ya," Chinook for welcome or hello] was the only word she spoke. I was not used to Indians then and knew very little Chinook. I felt very glad when her visit was over. I know now that I should have offered her a cigar and a cup of tea. . . . The winter soon passed. About March [1869] that year the Chinooks began to blow and the snow melted gradually, leaving green grass all over the range. Then the Indians seemed to awaken from their winter's lethargy and the whole of the Chu-chu-ewa tribe started out, some to the mountains, some to hunt, and some to visit friends at Nicola and Coldwater. Now I got my first good look at the Indians, my husband telling me their names as they passed on horseback. First rode the Chief Quiniscoe's two brothers, fine looking men dressed in buckskin shirts and leggings of embroidered cloth. One of these men like Quinisco was a great hunter and utterly fearless. His name was Tatlehasket (the man who stands high), the other Incowmasket—he was supposed to be the peacemaker of the tribe. And then came a lot of young men like Cockshist and Johnny Suzannne, all these were armed with rifles (old style), then two or three more of the Chief's brothers and their sons, last of all the women, children and boys such as Tuc-tac. Very last rode Quinisco himself with To[u]pes and Whylac.[47]

They crossed the ford, then camped across the river.

At the time I am writing of, the tribe living at Chu-chu-ewa were under Quiniscoe, as the Bear Hunter, and numbered nearly two hundred (today I doubt they number ten). Quiniscoe gained his name as a hunter from the courageous way he hunted and attacked grizzly bears—he would go out quite alone, armed only with his knife and follow them up until they stood at bay. Then, without waiting for them to charge, he would rush on them and plunge his knife into them while they were hugging them. That is how his brother, Shla-wha-lak-an,[48] described his method.

The women of the tribe wore a garment something like the ladies wear today, cut like a Victoria chemise,[49] and the foot of the garment which reached below the knee, cut in tags and fringes. This dress gave them a certain dignity and grace that was absent when they tried to dress like white women. The women were not as friendly as the children—the children flocked around and I got lots of help with my housework from them. . . . I was all doubled up with pain [July 1869]—I did not know what to do. I called my husband and he came with the only two medicines we possessed, Castor Oil and pain killer. I swallowed both and then exhausted by the pain fell asleep only to wake again worse than ever. My husband, alarmed, left me and ran to the Indian ranch returning with one of Quiniscoe's sisters, Suzanne (the mother of Johnny), afterwards married to Tom Cole,[50] so we will call her Madame Cole. She smoothed up my bed and suggested "whiskey" which I swallowed. I think I would have swallowed anything to get rid of the pain. About nine o'clock next day my baby was born [Edgar Moir Allison] two months too soon, the first white child born in the Similkameen Valley. . . . Suzanne was very good to me in her way—though I thought her rather unfeeling at the time. She thought that I ought to be as strong as an Indian woman but I was not.[51]

It was about this time I first really became acquainted with the girls. There was Lily,[52] Yacumtecum's niece, Sibyllakim, Cosotasket's[53] girl, Marie, and a host of others. I tried to keep Lily with me to look after the baby, but in a few days she was wearied and so went back to her people. Suzanne was a perfect treasure and so was her boy, Hosachtem, and I always feel grateful when I think of the kindness I received from them—they have passed away long ago. . . . Lily . . . said she would stay the winter. . . . The winter passed much as the former one had except that I kept plenty of medicine on hand, and had more work to do. We had a jolly little Christmas as before. Shortly after Christmas some of Lily's people came and she bawled to go with them, so she went. Then we had a visit from Cosotasket—Medicine Man and Hunter—he and one of his wives were going to hunt and set traps.

[*circa 1930-32*]

From "Some Recollections of a Pioneer of the Seventies"

.... About the middle of the month [March 1870] Cosotasket felt like going to the Hudson's Bay Company in Keremeos. Cosotasket said that that year he only had a few martens as his favourite trapping ground at the Skagit[54] was spoiled by the fire. The martens always climbed up into the trees to escape and perished instead. Cosotasket at that time lived mostly in the mountains and was known among the tribesmen as the Mountain Chief.

.... I was rather put out about help that year as both Johnny Suzanne and Yacumtecum or Tuc-tac thought that they were too old for housework. Then a boy of Tatlehasket's came from Kamloops where he had been at the Rev. Good's Mission.[55] He was warranted to be capable of doing any kind of housework and, indeed, I found him all that could be wished for. I could depend on him for everything. He was kind and gentle—at least I thought so. . . .

One of the Indians camped near the house was very sick and called in a doctor. They promptly made the night hideous with a tomtom and chanting, varied by yells and shouts. I was dying with curiosity to see what was going on, so when it got dark enough to hide me from sight I crawled out and, screened by a log fence, watched the proceedings. In the centre of the camp there was a blazing fire, and a little distance from the fire lay the sick one. With a mat separating her from the patient stood the doctor—a very powerful one, I had been told. She sang and swayed from side to side without changing her place, making gestures with her hands, filling her mouth with water which an assistant passed to her, and spitting. She seemed to get very excited and hot but I got cold and cramped watching and went into the house. I was told that she had removed a snake from the body of the patient and the patient was expected to recover. I saw the woman after in our store—such a nice looking, pretty woman. I could hardly believe it was the frenzied creature I had watched in the night. I told one of the young women that I had watched and she said I ought to have come over and sat with the others.

This year I first made acquaintance with Ashnola John,[56] or, as he was better known in Westminster, Captain John. My husband possessed a treasure. A Henry rifle[57] was then considered the last word about guns, and as a marked favour he lent it to some of his Indian friends. John had borrowed it to hunt and when he came to the store to return it, brought a haunch of venison. I foolishly asked him how much he wanted for it. I did not know gun etiquette demanded a haunch for the use of the gun. John asked a big price and I told him to keep it. Then began an argument that got somewhat heated. He wanted me to take the meat but pay twice its value. Then he roared at me, stamped his foot, pounded with his fists on the counter. I was so astonished that at first I did not know what to do—then I remembered that to give him a dose of his own medicine might help, so I roared at him and stamped my foot and pounded the counter. John was as astonished as I had been—he stood back, looked at me and burst out laughing. "Take the meat," he said, "we are friends. Allison is my friend and you are my friend." Ever after we were the best of friends. I used to write his business letters for him for many years and one still lives in my memory. It was to Mr. Vowell[58] (I think). John said to tell the Governor that there was an insect or bug infecting the trees and if they did not fell the infected ones and burn them now, there would be no trees left. It had happened before, the old Indians said their fathers said. The answer was that the trees were alright and would last our time. What money would have been saved by the appointment of an inspector! Though Governor Douglas, who understood the Indian character, made due allowances for John's behavior, the present government looked on him with suspicion. He on one occasion took a prisoner out of Judge Haynes'[59] Court while in session, not through any cowardice on the part of Mr. Haynes, but be it remembered that the white settlers were in the minority in those days and the Indians, who then could be numbered by the hundreds, could have done in a sparsely settled district the same as those across the Line. All honour to those in authority that they knew to keep the peace.

Another Indian friend I made was Shla-wha-la-kan, a very old man who brought his father, Tam-tu-sa-list, to visit me. This man had been a great chief and warrior, the father of the tribe. Now he walked on all fours just like a child seated, his elbows on the ground—he could just enjoy the sunshine and smoking tobacco. Joe McKay[60] told me that this man was known to be one hundred and twenty-five years old from Hudson's Bay Company records but was really older. . . . That summer I again visited my mother at Hope [1873] but as I had three small children with me [Edgar, Wilfred, and Beatrice] it was no picnic. While in Hope I met the sweetest, most gracious lady that ever lived in the upper country—Mrs. Ellis.[61] She had just come out a bride from Ireland. To me, after seeing no one but Indians, she looked lovely. . . .

When I returned to Similkameen I found little change except that my friend, Dr. Cosotasket, had traded wives with Dr. Scuse[62] and as all parties were agreeable it was alright from their point of view. Cockshist had eloped with a Thompson River woman, very good looking as most Thompson River women were. . . .

I had lots of fun watching Indian debates and doctors from my log at the fence—if I had known what most of the debates were about I might not have been quite so amused. There was great unrest stirring across the Line[63] and some were kinsmen of Quinisco, the late chief, and his brother Incowmasket, the present one. Incowmasket had a loving memory of Governor Douglas[64] and a great respect for the powers that be so kept his people from too open sympathy. And indeed the Indians on our side of the Line had in those days little to complain of for the few whites there were in the country treated them honestly and fairly. Well, I watched the doctors and came to the conclusion that they used a force or power that we know little or nothing of. You may call it animal magnetism, telepathy, or give it any name, but it was something very real.

I am afraid I have been mooning over my memories. I put in a good time one way and another in the early 70's.

In October '73 my husband asked me how I would like to go to the Okanagan and take charge of Red Oak [a steer] and fifty of our best thoroughbreds. He himself would be there all winter and would cut a very short trail over to the Similkameen so he could continue his fortnightly drives to Hope through the summer. He would, he said, build me a good house and make everything comfortable. I loved adventure, so in spite of my growing family, I agreed to his plan and never have I repented my decision. My husband arranged with Johnny McDougal to build a house for us. Johnny always cut our hay in a natural meadow, also oat hay which he planted for us. . . .

We had a jolly time in spite of the bad roads and went rather a roundabout way by Dog Lake [Skaha Lake]. . . . It was round a cliff—such a narrow ledge the horses with the packs could barely make it. My husband told me to trust my horse and not to try to guide him, and this I did. In one place where the cattle had broken down the trail one could see down a dreadful abyss into the lake. I was afraid, but the Indians did not seem to be and the horses took it in their stride. I had learned that even if you are terrified it is best not to show it, then you get the credit for being fearless—I certainly was not.

Our evening camp (at Trout Creek) [near present-day Summerland] made up for all—there were two camp fires, one for Hayes and his outfit and ours. Yacumtecum was cook. Yacumtecum told yarns about the Big Men who live in these mountains and the creature now known as Ogopogo. The Indians did not call him that but spoke as if it were some supernatural entity and pointed out where it lived on an island in the Okanagan Lake as we passed the spot. My husband always laughed at the Indian yarns but I did not, for I thought there must be some foundation for what they said. They told me more than they told most white people. . . .

When I first sighted the beautiful Okanagan Lake it was in a dead calm. The distant mountains were reflected in its mysterious depths—a deep silence prevailed. The Indians, unused to vast water stretches, ceased their merry talk and gazed at the blue waters with awe—there was not a cloud in the sky—no sign of life, save a few late swans. There was frost in the air. We rode silently through wild rye grass that was up to our shoulders on horseback, then we came out on our meadow at the harbor.[65] I believe it was the only natural one on the lake. . . .

[As their house was not completed, they put up tents.]

We had a merry supper and when it was over McDougall joined us, expatiated on the delights of terrapin stew, and gave us the general news, which might have been true or not—it was very amusing. After putting the children to bed I joined the story tellers. Lily played with Cockshist and Yacumtecum. Saul, the Chief, came up for a chat and was properly introduced. . . .

Johnny [McDougall] had some tobacco he had grown from seed the priests [Father Pandosy,[66] Father Richard, and Brother Surel at the Mission on Mission Creek in present-day Kelowna] had given him and he had grown, cured and fixed it up himself. The talk turned to the Monster (Ogopogo). Johnny wanted to bring a team across the lake to assist haying so he drove them to the Narrows [site of the bridge between present-day Kelowna and West Kelowna] where he often crossed the horses he used hunting, but he had always taken a chicken or little pig and dropped it into the lake when they neared the middle. This time he forgot the chicken and was towing the horses by a long rope. Suddenly something, he couldn't see what, dragged the horses down underwater and the canoe he was in would have gone too had he not severed the rope with his sheath knife and hurried across. He never saw any vestige of his teams again. These stories had a strange charm for me. I could have sat up all night and listened to them but the air was getting cold so turned in and slept the sleep of the just, having first been promised a visit from the Chief's wife and Theresa,[67] both ladies of high standing and near of kin to Chapeau Blanc, the Penticton Chief. . . .

In the spring of '74, which was mild and pleasant, the Indians were all sick. They had an epidemic of very bad grippe, and all were ill at once. There were not more than one or two families on our side of the lake besides Saul, who was only a small chief. I used to make large kettles of soup and send down to the ranch with buckets of milk. At one home there was no one fit to cook, but soon some of them were well enough to do so. Some two or three died and their near relatives asked my husband to get me to make shrouds for them which I did. Then poor young Michelle was dreadfully ill—the Indians expected him to die any time, so we beat a few eggs in a bowl and put some whiskey in it and my husband rode down to the ranch, opened Michelle's mouth and poured a spoonful down his throat every ten minutes or so till finally he opened his eyes. After that the others fed him in the same way till he could eat alone. Some of the women fancied the cakes I made them and soon learned the way to do it themselves. When they all recovered they all moved off on a hunting trip except one man who told them to go. He wanted to die he was so sick. So they laid him on skins, piled blankets over him and left [him] to die at sunset. As soon as they were gone my husband went down to see if the Indian needed anything but he was already dead, smothered by the blankets most likely. That was the first case of that kind that I knew of but afterwards I found it was nothing unusual, just a custom.

The Indians did not return for some weeks and then there

seemed to be great unrest among them [1874]. They talked of a Great Chief across the Line named Joseph[68] —such stories of his strength—and how he drank a cup of blood every morning, no matter what or whose blood it was. This was all nonsense, for Joseph was really a good man, fighting as a chief for his people's rights, but it indicated the starting of the unrest among the Indians. No one really knows what we owe to the influence of the priests and Joe McKay. . . .

When the haying was over my husband went to Hope with his steers. That very night there were wild unearthly whoops and yells and drum beating. I knew Saul was not at home. The noise was blood curdling. Next day some of the women told me that Killestim-nix-quilly had arrived from a battle with the Britons[69] —he had come naked, with a strand of bark for a bridle, bare-back, and his horse nearly dead and he wanted help for his people. The war dances were kept up every night till Saul came back and then the Indians either moved off or he stopped them. When my husband returned he said he had met the naked Indian riding bare-back. He would not stop to speak but he thought that Saul would protect us. I suppose he did as far as he could but I got well scared first. I had read of what was going on in Washington and Oregon in the papers. And one day when I saw a dozen armed Indians charging down on the house, shouting and yelling, I grabbed a heavy 44 navy revolver my husband gave me for protection, locked the front door, and putting the children in the back room, stood ready to empty it at them. But for some reason of their own they whirled their horses round, shouted and rode off—leaving me trembling and unnerved when it was over. . . .

I think it was the summer of '75 [1879] that the McLean boys kept the scattered settlers in a state of unrest.[70] People now will wonder how four or five young men could terrorize a large district but when one considers that people were living twenty to thirty and in some case fifty miles apart, and all the men were working in the fields, perhaps for a distant neighbour, and the women kept the home fires burning, believe it or not, it is true the McLean boys, with the exception of Hector, kept us in terror. I had heard about them and Nick Hare[71] but scarcely gave them a thought till they came to the lake. Nicola, Kamloops and the vicinity were out after them.

The McLeans were the sons of a Hudson's Bay Company Factor, their mother a chief's daughter nearly related to Kamloops Louie. They were always considered fine young men. They had a beautiful sister who was brought up in a convent and most accomplished. She was in Kamloops society and met a man of high standing in the Province[72] and became engaged to him. They were very intimate, too much so—then he went down to the lower country and married the daughter of a man of standing there, leaving the poor girl to bear her disgrace the best way she could. The brothers were furious, if they could have got at that man they would have killed him then and there. They took to drinking and running wild, and took whiskey to the Indians. A summons was issued but they tore it up—then a warrant was taken out and the man who brought it driven out of camp. Johnny Ussher who had known and been friendly to the boys for years said he would take another warrant and tell them that it would be much better for them to give themselves up for trial. He hunted them up, and found Nick Hare had joined them, and began talking to them like a friend. One of them upped his gun and shot him. This was a signal to the others. They all in turn shot at him—then leaving their camp, continued a career of murder until finally they were arrested by John Chappalo at Nicola [December 13, 1879].

It was after they had killed Ussher [December 8, 1879] that I was expecting my husband to return from one of his drives. I looked out of my window and saw six Indians passing. Frosty Nose was with them so I ran out to the fence with little Edgar following me to ask if they had seen him coming. They stopped, and one put up his gun pointing at an object behind me. Frosty Nose rode up to him, threw up his arms, and said something to him. I turned to see what he had aimed at—it was my son, little Edgar! When I turned again they had all ridden on except Frosty Nose, who, never at a loss for a lying excuse, said that the man had seen one of our pet deer in the distance and would have shot it had he not intervened.

Times were very risky so I did not argue. I was afterwards told that it was one of the McLean boys on his way to the head of the lake and that he thought I had gone out to take off the attention of those who would arrest him. His sister, a fair girl wearing a sunbonnet, passed riding a side saddle and carrying an infant.

Poor girl, she was going to her mother's people! The Indians are good to those of kin to them.

My husband returned from his drive next day and looking over the cattle found a three year old steer not long killed, with one hind quarter cut off. The Indians said the McLeans had done it. He hurried to the harbour to give information but our boat was gone. Afterwards an Indian brought it back and said that he had found it across the lake.

After a wild career of death and destruction these misguided boys were taken and hanged, the eldest twenty, the youngest fifteen. . . .

That fall [1876][73] when Mr. Hayes brought the cattle to winter quarters he brought a very sick woman with him. Poor Augusta [his Indigenous wife] was fading away[74] —in vain he got patent medicines for her. Then she begged for an Indian doctor so Tamula was brought and he made night hideous with his singing and drumming. One evening my husband and the children were playing—they generally did before they were put to bed—when Hayes came bursting into the house white and trembling. He said he could not stay in his cabin a moment longer as he felt that there was more there than the eye could see. The doctor had begun by chanting a low song and dancing, making gestures as if he were drawing some skin from Augusta who lay on a pile of skins on the floor. Then he hauled with all his strength towards a mat, then clenched with someone or something that alternately threw him and was thrown. Then there was a dreadful climax—a struggle in which the perspiration just poured off the doctor and he breathed hard. Hayes then fled—he had no doubt that the man was wrestling with some unseen enemy. He would not return until the noise and singing ceased. This went on for a week and then the poor woman died. . . .

[*Susan Allison recollects meeting up with Gilbert Malcolm Sproat (1834-1913), A.C. Anderson (1814-1884), and their party near her ranch in 1877. Sproat and Anderson had been appointed commissioners of the Indian Reserve Commission and had come to meet with the Syilx. Sproat was sole commissioner after 1878. Sproat was somewhat sympathetic to the Indigenous people and their land claims; for example, he believed that they should be given enough land to guarantee their self-sufficiency.[75] This made him unpopular with the members of the provincial and federal government, and with many settlers in the southern interior.*]

The Indians were much more quiet and content after the visit of the Commissioners. . . .

Penextitza was one of the head men at the Head of the Lake [near Vernon at the north end of Lake Okanagan], a chief, and like our own Highland Chiefs, always took a tail of young men (gillies)[76] with him, also an interpreter, whenever he went. He was too dignified to understand English. When he did any trading at Eli's [Eli Lequime's store near Father Pandosy's Mission] or the Mission he would stand back in state, surrounded by his satellites while the interpreter did his business for him, only nodding assent or shaking his head to the white men.

I was very much surprised one day when he rode up to my door and the interpreter came forward and asked to see my husband. He said that he had business with him. I told them my husband was out but, if they would come in, lunch was on the table. The interpreter talked with Penextitza, who, with a wave of his hand to his little band, rode to the hitching post, dismounted, and came to the door hat in hand, like a gentleman. His followers rode on.

Penextitza was a perfect gentleman and during lunch kept up a pleasant conversation on the weather, the crops, the cattle, the races at the Head of the Lake, and the children. He said he had known Governor Douglas and was a friend of his, also Mr. Anderson and Mr. McKay. Then when lunch was over he said I must excuse his leaving so soon but he wanted to push on to his home, and bowed himself out. And that man was considered uncivilized by our civilized people!
[*circa 1930-32*]

From "Memoirs of a Pioneer of the Eighties"

[*Allison then recounts the very cold winter of 1879-1880 where they lost many of their cattle necessitating their move back to the Similkameen. She tried to persuade her husband to stay, but his mind was made up. John Fall had also experienced financial loss when he and his partner Mr. Hayes split their assets at this time and went their separate ways.*]

. . . . It was with a sad heart I went around to our old haunts, said goodbye to my little mountain garden that Dumby

[Indigenous ranch hand] and I had ploughed—I drove the team and he held the plow. We visited the little mountain spring which my husband had led down to the house in an underground ditch. We said farewell to the harbor, the ant-hill, and I stole the little humming-bird's nest in the rose bushes of the mountainside. It was a sad cavalcade that left our dear little home where we had been so peaceful and happy. It had been a busy life, too; no day was spent in idleness.

My children were good and obedient. I had taught the four older ones to read and write, and as I had few books fitted for children, I had made stories from English history, and Grecian and Roman history, too. I don't think they ever forgot what they learned at Okanagan, though they learned little enough after. I, myself, had learned patience, to fish and cure the fish, and dry venison. Dumby taught me to gather straw and grass and make hats for the children, even my husband did not scorn the hats I made. I now could mend the little boots, make moccasins, cut rawhide into strands and make a braid for lariats to lasso the horses. . . .

We descended to the meadow and when we were abreast of the meadow out came Bill and Min and Mary, our pet deer.[77] The children were delighted for we thought we would never see them again, but there they were and joined the cavalcade. They continued with us for about five miles. . . .

When the Indians heard we were back [in Similkameen] they soon came riding up from Chu-chu-ewa to see us and we found a few of the usual matrimonial changes. My good friend, Tatlehasket, had sent away his old wife and taken one much younger, and Cosotasket had exchanged his and Sinsenecks was Mrs. Cosotasket. Incowmasket kept both his and Penquinac (Princess Julia) his daughter, was prettier than ever.

Our Okanagan Indians after visiting a few days with the Similkameen left and went home.

[Allison mentions visits from Henry Nicholson and Barrington Price who both had land in the Keremeos[78] area. She states that they "were both college men from Oxford, I think, and very nice gentlemen, but with a strong taste for brandy." The Allisons bought supplies including flour from Price's gristmill. She also discusses the Allisons' acquisition of more acreage for farming, including the Princeton townsite, since they needed to put more crops in as they had few cattle left.]

239

In the fall of '80 there was an earthquake which shook the country for miles,[79] reaching the Okanagan. Our Indians were much disturbed except Cosotasket and Tatlehasket and a few others, hard old nuts. They thought the "Father" was angry and sent for the priests, and many were baptized. They resolved to build a church and to have only one wife and there was a sort of revival among them. . . .

The Indians were still religiously inclined but Incowmasket sent pretty Chin-chin away and kept the mother of his boy and Penquinac. (I saw an article in the "Province" about a month ago describing Penquinac under the name of Princess Julia—she was christened Julia by the Priest and her father Incowmasket called Moses). The good priests came up the river every month always ready to christen, marry or bury anyone, and they got nothing but abuse. The old priests were good men. . . .

The river rose rapidly that year [1881]. Our old scow had gone with the ice and the only means of crossing was in a dugout canoe owned by Shla-wha-la-kan and he usually put his own price on the accommodation which varied from fifty cents to five dollars. This year his daughter, Sally, had got married for the fifth time. She was quite a young girl but there were skins and blankets exchanged every time and it was profitable to the old man, but this time it had not been very satisfactory and he was irritable. So when a party of miners came out over the Hope Trail and signalled for the canoe, the old man took his time about going and when he did we noticed that he did not land but kept his boat some distance out in the water. We had no means of knowing what was going on but after a long time we saw him land. Then he went back to the canoe with a bundle. Two white men stepped in with him and came across. We noticed that they seemed half clad and when my husband went out to speak to them they unfolded a tale of woe. Shla-wha-la-kan had refused to take them in his boat unless one man gave his coat, the other his shirt and pants, so he had to cross in his underwear. He had to buy overalls of course. Selling an outfit to the old man's customers was profitable for our store. Mr. Allison thought he would build a scow and cross anybody for the fixed price of fifty cents. . . .

I longed more than ever to go back to Okanagan in the fall of '81 when the cattle started back. I hated store-keeping. The poor little children,[80] I felt, were neglected but it had to be.

When the cattle left the cowboys left, too; but we had the Chinese men in the cabin[81] as before, and we made the best we could of the winter of '81 and '82. It was a mild winter and in the month of March '82, the hills were green and the grass in fine condition. So, on the twenty-eighth, my husband and Edgar, now a good-sized useful boy, started off to the Okanagan to bring the cattle home. The children joined me in raking up chips and cleaning up the winter disorder. The Chinamen had gone back to their mining so we were all alone, except Lily was with us, and Tatlehasket, who had brought us two fine yearling deer. I made him put them into the milk house till I had time to cut them up, before he rode down the valley. When the first of April came I rose with the sun and took my salt and spice to the milk house to cure the venison, charging Lily to get breakfast and then call me. . . .

[*At this point, a chimney fire breaks out in the house. They evacuate and throw what they can out the windows including saddles, fifteen pounds of flour, a picture of Susan Allison's brother, and a small piece of bacon. Someone remembers that there are one hundred pounds of gun powder upstairs. Lily runs in and throws it out the window. The family loses "many old relics." They move into a cabin on the property and have very little to eat. Squakin, an Indian travelling down the valley to Keremeos, sells them some sugar and agrees to let others know of their plight. After five days, supplies arrive from Barrington Price; Ah Lee, a Chinese miner, makes wooden sandals for the children; clothing and sewing material comes from other settlers. A new house is built.*]

. . . .That year I met for the first time A.E. Howse,[82] who had just been appointed Indian Agent. He was a fine looking young man and a man's looks went a long way with the Indians. I thought he was rather young for the position but I did not appoint him. I was sorry we had nothing on hand when he called for supplies. He had, I knew, a hard task before him settling petty quarrels; no one can satisfy both sides. Mr. Howse has ever shown himself to be a public-spirited man. At the time he came I think we were out of everything but sago [a starch]. . . .

[*In 1883, Susan Allison and her family are visited by U.S. General William Tecumseh Sherman (1820-1891), the famous Union general during the Civil War.*]

241

When the General announced he was coming to call I had nowhere to receive him but the nursery or the kitchen, so I had chairs placed outside the door for him and his staff. He made himself at home, took a chair, turned back in front, and bestrode it like a horse. Resting his chin on its back he surveyed us all. Then he asked abruptly how many children we had. I told him nine. "Where are the rest," he said, "parade them all." I told him the little ones were in bed but he insisted that I should "parade them in their night shirts."

General Sherman was a healthy, intelligent man with shrewd piercing eyes that seemed to take in everything and look into your mind. With him was General Nelson Miles, Captain Chas. King and Lieutenant Mallory, who came to the place and played with the children every chance he got. He was a young Southerner and not quite at home with his brother officers. The General was delighted to see my little boy, Jack, just seven, perched on his big horse riding back and forth with his messages and little Jack was proud to ride the General's horse. They did not stay long for some of the men deserted, so they passed through the country as quickly as they could. [83] . . . .

[*Allison's memoir ends in about 1884. She writes that she "would have liked to tell" of many other things but ill health prevents her.*]

. . . . I am unable to do more at present. I shall leave sundry notes behind me, which may or may not be, of use to my children. My pen is shaking in my hand and I really must stop writing for a time at any rate. . . .

[*circa 1930-32*]

Correspondence with Louisa (Allison) Johnston, 1930s

3984-W21 St. Van[84]
18th Feb 1930

Dear Louisa,[85]
. . . . Do you know that times seem to be as hard and harder than at Princeton? I know so many poor fellows that can't get work

and have families to keep. Louisa I appreciate your goodness to Will's [Robert Wilfred and Rachel's][86] children—their cousins who have had so much better chances and have done nothing with them, have the gall to look down on breeds as they call them who have made the most of nothing. Will's children are like himself always dear to me—even if I can't help them as I wish to—I promised both Will and Henry[87] to do whatever I could for Mary[88] and that seems to be nothing. I will write to her—I can do that anyway—Poor Angie[89] like the rest of us seems to be having a hard struggle—but she has a brave heart. Poor you must feel glad your children are all settled down. Although perhaps it is like me—poor old Ed[90] seems to be no better off—I doubt if he is happier. We don't see him now though I have written to him. I know him so well I can make allowances for him—I think that I can understand my elder children better than the younger— Ed and Will, BJ [Beatrice], Rose, and you[91] —seem to belong to another generation

. . . .

With love to Al[92] and all,
Ma

Aug 3 [1930?]

Dear Louisa,

Sunday comes round so quickly, and finds us plodding on in the same old way, just living our lives in the same old way. Well there was lots of variety when we were younger—and even now if we look round us, we will find strange things, taken as everyday occurrences—a flight of airplanes passes overhead, such as we used to dream of, but never hoped to see. We only say "There goes the Air Squad" but it really is wonderful. I can remember the first train that came into Aberdeen [Scotland]. I think it went fifteen or twenty miles an hour, and we thought that speed.

Aug 4th Albion[93] and Alice are cooking breakfast and the children are anxiously waiting their hotcakes so I will continue [the] letter I began yesterday. . . . You, Louisa possess that blessed quality, you can be cheerful in adversity—it really helps a lot, not only yourself but those around you. I can remember my stepfather Glennie[94] being so enraged the first time we sat down to a makeshift dinner, wild spinach—celery and huckleberries but it was dished up in silver dishes—(Auntie[95] had them after) laughing at our poverty—and really we were—My dear, this tirade is [apropos] . . . of the terrible times [the Depression], not only here in Vancouver, but Mrs. Daly[96] and others tell me worse in the United States. What will it lead to! One meets the direst poverty where one least expects it, so we, you and I, are better off than those who don't know when to laugh. I am sending you a little book, the Star Bulletin. Read it if you have time and get Al to read it—it is unusual at any rate. I have been reading Sir Oliver Lodge's Oxford lectures.[97] We got it from the library or I would send it to you. . . . I am behind with my house payments—as long as we have a roof over us we can manage for food—my clothes and Alice's thanks to the dye pot last well. Have you seen Wilfrid [Buck Allison] or Mary [Allison] lately? . . .

Your affectionate old Ma

Oct 4th, 1930

Don't mention memoirs except to Mrs. Daly, who knows I am writing but not about the *Province* [Vancouver *Province* newspaper] taking them.

Dear Louisa,

. . . . Have been writing my memoirs—in BC they cover seven decades—I have only just finished the [18]60s. I think the 70s will be more thrilling as it deals in war dances and the McLean boys and lots of things. Can you get any dates for me? . . . I sent one installment with a letter to the *Province* and the answer was that they would pay for each installment—one every week, if I could finish by Dec. but I have finished the 60s and it will take a long time for six decades more. I don't think I can and as you may see by my writing my sight gets worse. . . . I am going to write to Hughie[98] and Wilfred re: the girls—they could go to a convent near here. My friend Mr. Johnston has his girl at it or perhaps Asel likes the Kamloops[99] school better. Poor woman I feel for her too. Life is pathetic anyway—and it is best to be brave and meet it with a song—You always do. . . .

Friday [nd]

Dear Louisa,
.... Wilfred [Buck Allison] came up from Hedley to see me—but I was asleep in bed when he came. I shall go down and see him. Grace[100] is out prospecting. I only wish I could have gone too ...

With love, Ma

Nov 28th—1930
My Dear Louisa,
I have just finished the Seventies[101] —which with the sixties makes nine installments for the *Province*. I think that they will take the eighties as well, but am not sure. They wanted me to continue to the nineties but I will stop at the eighties—I would like to get my dates as near as I can. . . . I have been promised fifteen dollars for each installment. The regular price is five so I hope that the editor will stick to his verbal bargain. It is only need that has made me write and I have left untold more than I have written. I will send you the first letters I received from both the [Vancouver] *Sun* and the *Province*. If Mr. Scott [editor at the *Province*] would help me with a book, it would, I humbly think, sell looking back on my past life with all its pleasure and pains. I seem like a spectator of the events instead of an actor—and when I think of my first trip out to the Similkameen with Tuctac[102] as a bell boy, I grieve over poor old Yacumtecum—blind and helpless being mushed up by an auto!! And the poor McLean boys hunted to death, because their mixed blood (wild highland and Indian) could not book to see Mara[103] sitting in high places and their poor sister driven out an outcast from all but her mother's people. I have of course not mentioned Mara's name—I knew and like the little girl he married. Dear old Joe McKay[104] I love to think of, but have not told all I know of anything. Well I have written more than enough about myself so will now proceed to discuss conditions in Vancouver—poverty and wealth cheek by jowl. I am sure that one of the surest cures would be a graded income tax—not to stop a small sum out of the poor man's wage—Oh about Mary I inquired about the Sacred Heart[105] here and was told she could be received here for fifty dollars per month and

extras—make her bank her money—if I can I will come up in the spring and try to figure out something. It is hard to be poor. I am sure that Alf's Gladys[106] would be good to her if she visited her without belongings. Must stop. Tell her I will write soon.

Feb 1932

Dear Louisa,

. . . . This morning I had our one letter, a small cheque for $10.00 for [?]—I have promptly ordered more coal for here. It is cold—freezing. I am now sitting by my radiator. Shivering. People here are growling about the extreme cold. What would they say to a touch of 40 below zero? This ten dollars is the first I have made this winter—darned glad to get it. Hope they will take more [of her recollections for the newspaper]. I was in hopes you could get down for a few weeks. I had a letter from Wilfred [Buck Allison] who told me how cold it was at Ashnola and Hedley.

. . . Wilfred says poor little Maggie[107] is very sick, has been in bed since Christmas—poor little kid—how hard it must be on her.

. . . Do you like the Bulletins I send you? [illegible] is indeed a great teacher—he himself prefers to be called our Elder Brother. Such greatness and simplicity combined—when I get through with the last one I will send it. I just hate to think of you trapping alone. Write or come soon,

Ma

Feb 29th 1932

Dear Louisa,

Cheer boys, Cheer!![108] I am just writing to cheer you up a little—you must learn to look upon these hard times with philosophy—perhaps you think that philosophy and an empty stomach do not agree—but I think that they do—it helps a lot— first I think that we are at a period spoken of in many scriptures as "the distress of Nations"—Philosophy tells us "endure thy lot patiently—doing the best thou canst to better it." Every man, woman, and child should begin reform by reforming himself.

. . . as individual beings reforming ourselves and facing our present . . . with courage and patience—doing our level best to better ourselves we will be better off—not trying to do the impossible—Take a smoothly running stream and put rocks in its

246

way and it begins to bluster—I believe our government is now doing the best it can. The treasury is almost empty—of course the treasury should not have been empty but it is, that is past, it is with the present we are living in—in the eternal now,[109] and now let each one of us do his or her best or we will have famine at our door. Enough of that. I saw in the Province a sketch of old [illegible]—I am sure she deserves a place amongst pioneer women. I am going to give her a place in my book. . . .

May 3, 1932
Dear Louisa,
. . . . It is lovely here just now and there is a swamp close by that I long to go to, but can't—you would almost live there. Here too we are out of the downtown rows [altercations]—one good thing they are pretty well prepared for downtown rows—what with airplane and gun boats—if it should come to that—but here are lots of honest Scots—and Mounties if things get bad without troubling for Mariners. One never knows what will happen.[110] Alice has just gone uptown and will gather some news—A neighbour was just in feeling very blue and we grouched together over hard times till we both burst out laughing and agreed that we might be a lot worse off. She went home to cook her beans and port feeling more cheerful. We can grow quite a lot of things and put away for winter; meantime we must not forget to enjoy summer while it is here. Live in the Eternal Now if we would. How much happier we would be—all of us. I wish you could make a run down.

Ap 27th I got tired and stopped abruptly—but will manage somehow to fill up my paper. . . . Our Beatrice[111] plods along and when hard times come works harder both with her head and hands. She says that at present Terence [Beatrice's son] is the only one in the family earning, but her letters are always cheerful and bright. . . . I am so pleased—a Jewish neighbour has lent me one of the Jewish magazines—I got from it that many of the Jews are in favour of letting in Palestinians. Others don't want to. It is most astonishing how liberal minded the Jews are getting—I just loved to read their magazine—there was a criticism on Shakespeare's The Merchant of Venice—and I really might have written it myself—I have always thought the merchant Antonio a weak-minded extravagant fool, who could not say no to the young [illegible] Bassanio, a rather contemptible young spend-thrift waiting to recoup his fortune by marrying a rich girl. Lorenzo and Jessica—just two thieves—taking the old man's [Shylock's] money bags and what he valued more than money, Rachel's [his deceased wife's] jewels and earrings. I really enjoyed reading the criticism for I always took old Shylock's part[112] —poor old man robbed alike by foes and child—and there is another article on the four greatest Jews. It gave—Moses—Isaiah—Jesus and Spinoza—saying no Jew could overlook the teachings of Jesus—but they could not stand for his being Divine—but really I can't see why when one of their own great ones says, "Ye are Gods, ye are all the children of the most high" [Psalm 82: 6]. . . .

> With love,
> Ma

Sept 20th[113]
Dear Louisa,

As it is Sunday and I have just got a fresh supply of foolscap [lined paper] to write my fool's thoughts on, I will write you a long letter. . . . Oh Louisa you have no idea what a city of possibilities Vancouver is. One morning Mrs. Granger called just about nine or ten o'clock with boxes of vegetables for us and she asked me to go for a short spin in the car with her, so I put on my Mrs. Corbett coat and went. Mrs. G drove to the top of Dunbar Heights where we got such a sweeping view of the city—it has such possibilities by water, air and land. It will be queen city of the coast, that is, if it pulls through its present difficulties which are great. Why won't our millionaires be patriots? They could do so much more at this juncture for their city and their fellow men. I told you I wore my Mrs. Corbett coat—well just think of the kindness of the dear old woman—she had bought herself a handsome winter coat, then her people in England sent her a still better one. She said that was enough for her, would I accept the one she bought for herself—she put it so nicely and kindly that it was impossible to refuse. Here everyone seems built that way—we meet with kindness on every hand. Did you get the few [illegible] Alice sent you? She felt sure you could use them on the ranch and after awhile will send you an old winter coat you can wear round home—I shall take a lesson from Mrs. Corbett and pass my old coat on to Rachel,[114] poor soul. I do wish I could help them a little! . . .

> Love to all,
> Ma

[1930-32]

PART THREE
CONTINUING RELATIONS

Crossing Lines

Lally Grauer

"... [Y]ou are far from a stranger to me. Tho—I have never met you, we are truly kindred spirits. . . . our fathers were old friends who respected each other very much," wrote Marie Houghton Brent to Hester Haynes White in 1936. Though both she and White were daughters of settler fathers, "kindred spirits" might not be the language one would expect Brent, who had identified as a Syilx all her life, to use for relations between them. Settler and Indigenous are so often, for good reason, understood and framed in opposition to each other in contemporary writing, and much of historical settler writing simply leaves out reference to Indigenous people.

Yet, in the archival papers of Hester White and Isabel Christie MacNaughton, two settler women writers whose work we had decided to investigate with an eye to inclusion in this anthology, we began to uncover close relationships with not only Syilx women, but also Syilx women writers or storytellers. The archival papers of Hester White (born in 1877), located in Penticton, British Columbia, show she carried on a long correspondence with Marie Houghton Brent (born in 1870) from the 1930s to the 1960s, a correspondence which reveals mutual and individual concerns as writers and local historians. This correspondence also came to light in Brent's archival files located in Vernon, British Columbia. Evidently it was important to them both, as each had saved the other's letters. Another discovery was a handwritten letter from Matilda Kruger (1864-1935), a woman of Syilx and mostly unacknowledged settler heritage, to Hester White, which was kept at the En'owkin Centre on the Penticton Indian Reserve, and also partially preserved in White's papers in the Penticton Museum and Archives. It sheds light on early Okanagan history as well as the relationship between Kruger and White, whom Kruger had cared for throughout White's childhood. Letters from Hester White also turned up in settler Katie Lacey's files in the Osoyoos and District Museum and Archives (Lacey was a founder of the Osoyoos Museum) in the 1960s, underscoring

Kruger's importance in White's life. Mentions of Kruger in White's writing, both published and unpublished, began to take on more significance for this project.

Meanwhile, we discovered another intriguing archival trace of Syilx and settler interaction which began in the 1920s and 30s. Twenty-two-year-old Isabel Christie MacNaughton (1915-2003), from a settler family in Okanagan Falls, had published in the *Penticton Herald* in 1937 the first of many Syilx stories naming seventy-two-year-old Josephine Shuttleworth of Syilx heritage as her source. MacNaughton began to transform some of Shuttleworth's stories into dramas that were then performed by the children of the Inkameep Day School in the South Okanagan in 1938. Now a connection with Syilx writer Mourning Dove began to appear—Mourning Dove had taught at that same day school and gathered stories there twenty years earlier, some of which were published in her book *Coyote Stories* (1933). Pursued further, references to Mourning Dove also began to surface in Hester White's writing. The longer I worked with these papers as part of my contribution to the project, the more I could see a network emerge between Indigenous and non-Indigenous women in the early settler period and beyond—women who developed relationships with each other, who shared and often wrote stories, who were interested in the recording or preserving of Okanagan history. I hope to illuminate at least some of these crossing lines in this essay.

Correspondences

In the early 1930s, Hester White, a doctor's wife living in *snpinktn* or Penticton, British Columbia, sent out letters to friends and acquaintances—including Marie Houghton Brent—asking for information about her father John Carmichael Haynes as she was working on an article about him for the British Columbia Historical Society's *Quarterly*. Her father had died suddenly in 1888, and she wished to commemorate his life and work. Haynes, who had arrived in British Columbia from Ireland in 1858, became one of the first settlers in the southern Okanagan, beside a narrows in what is now Lake Osoyoos near the United States border. In 1862, as customs collector, he established a post at Sooyoos after the Syilx word *s?wiws*, meaning [lake] shallows in the middle, where he later pre-empted land, and which became the settlement of Osoyoos. Assuming the roles of gold commissioner, member of the colonial Legislative Council of British Columbia and County Court Judge, Haynes became the government representative in the Okanagan region. Brent's father also emigrated from Ireland, coming to the Okanagan in 1863. Captain Charles Frederick Houghton claimed land (as a veteran of the Crimean War) in the northern Okanagan, choosing a site which he called Coldstream near what is now the town of Vernon, and wielding considerable influence as settler and magistrate. The two men became friends, enjoyed hunts together, and were eager to acquire good land for ranching. By the time Hester White was born in 1877, however, secure on her father's now established ranch in Osoyoos, Marie Brent's father had been absent for five years, and her mother, Sophie Nkwala, had died in 1872, the same year C.F. Houghton left the region. Sophie was the daughter of young Chief Nkwala, who died before Marie Brent was born, and granddaughter of the old Chief Nkwala, *xʷistsmx̌ayqn* or Walking Grizzly, a key mediator during the fur trade period in the Okanagan, from the 1811 to 1850 (Carstens 20, 37-41).[1] By school age, Brent was negotiating the complications of being a Syilx child in a settler society, living with her late mother's relatives in *kilawna?* or Kelowna. When Brent and White finally connected in the 1930s and began a correspondence that was to last twenty-five years, they were living quite different lives— White, the wife of a prominent doctor in her small community, Brent living in a cabin "on reverted land of 320 acres—fourteen miles (on the bench) from Vernon," doing some mining "in a small way" (Letter to Hester White, February 24, 1938). While their correspondence points to social and economic inequality in a colonial society, Brent's life provides a contrast that highlights the gentility that encased White's experience.

Yet, as Brent's letter suggests, they shared many similarities. Both had received some education (according to settler definitions; Brent also received a Syilx education, see Part One). White was taught by governesses at home and Brent at age seven or eight started attending the newly established public schools in the Kelowna and Vernon (then Priest's Valley). Both eventually went to convent boarding schools, White at age thirteen in Plymouth, Cornwall, after her father's death, and Houghton at age sixteen in Kamloops or *tk'mlups*. They both travelled, White to England for schooling and Brent to Montreal to live with her father in the early 1890s and then to New York City to nursing school. Both were later happily married, White to Dr. Reginald B. White, after a first marriage to settler Charles Lambly, and Marie Houghton to William Brent, also from a mixed settler and Indigenous family (see "Standing Between" in Part One).

Perhaps the most important link that kept them corresponding and then visiting over the years was writing. Their correspondence shows both were interested in writing local history and writing about their fathers who, because of death or absence from the region, were perhaps in danger of being forgotten. White published the biographical article "John Carmichael Haynes" for the British Columbia Historical Society in 1940, and also included aspects of her father's history in a series of columns "The Pioneer Trail: Reminiscences of the Early Days" in The *Penticton Herald* in 1947. Several shorter and more autobiographical pieces were published in annual reports of the Okanagan Historical Society (OHS) between 1948 and 1962. Brent, for her part, kept her father's role as a settler and builder of Canada alive through biographical articles in the *Vernon News* both in 1927[2] and, as part of the celebration of British Columbia's Centennial, in 1958. In 1956, in a letter to White, she states that her father was "destined to carry out a military career for many years in this country & went as high as one could go at that time." Both inserted their fathers into the typical narrative of the brave, resourceful and entitled pioneer. Brent, however, also wrote about settlement in quite a different story in her 1935 piece "The Indians of the Okanagan Valley" in the annual report of the OHS (see Part One). It is possible that seeing Brent's article prompted White to contact Brent in her own search for information about her father.

Brent published several articles in the reports of the OHS. Leonard Norris, a founder of that historical society and interested in Syilx history and culture, had been in touch with Brent about her knowledge of Syilx and settlers in the early years of its publication (Norris, Letter). Her articles appeared in the *OHS Reports* of 1927, 1930, 1931, 1935, 1948 and her last in 1966. In "Indians of the Okanagan Valley," published in 1935, she wrote bluntly, and, given her era, boldly about the consequences of the colonialism in which her father participated, stating:

The invasion of [the Okanagans'] country by the whites not only disrupted their usual mode of living and crumpled up and destroyed their old-established customs and usages which had endured for centuries, but it deprived them of their country as well. They were soon exiled to reservations. The Salish Indian of the Okanagan Valley today is an expatriate . . . although still dwelling in the land of his forefathers. It will be many years yet before these people fully recover from the shock of this double catastrophe.[3] (126-27)

Brent's language, when she speaks of invasion and exile, does not exaggerate the effects of establishing reserves in the Okanagan, which occurred only ten years before she was born. White's father, J.C. Haynes, importuned by Brent's father C.F. Houghton and other Okanagan settlers, played a big part in it.

Drawing Lines
In 1860, at the request of Governor James Douglas, W.G. Cox, then collector of customs and assistant gold commissioner for Rock Creek, marked out reserves for the Syilx of about two hundred acres per family at the north end of Head of the Lake, *nk'mapǝlqs* or Nkamapulks, and at *snpinktn* at the southern end of the lake, lands pointed out to him by the Syilx. In 1874, after his retirement, Douglas justified his relatively liberal land policy in the interior of British Columbia as "commensurate with the wants of these tribes; to allow sufficient space & range for their cattle in all seasons" (qtd. in Harris, "Native Land Policies": 115). When J.C. Haynes replaced Cox as the colonial government agent in 1864, and after he travelled the land with the newly arrived Irish immigrant Thomas Ellis in May of 1865, searching out good grazing land, he wrote to Douglas that in his opinion the reserves were "much too large" (qtd. in Thomson, "History": 119). He was granted permission to reduce them, if this could be done without provoking too much discontent among the Syilx (119).

In November of 1865, accompanied by surveyor James Turnbull, Haynes laid out new reserves at the Head of the Lake in the north and *snpinktn* in the south so that the Syilx reserves were reduced from two hundred acres for each family to forty-two to forty-five acres, much of it not cultivable (Thomson, "History" 119). C.F.

Houghton rode with Haynes on the northern part of the journey (Carstens 63) and Tonasket, Chief of the Okanogan south of the United States-Canada border, who also worked as a packer for Haynes, travelled with them and communicated with the Syilx. His assumption of authority in the north Okanagan at a time when *c'əlhic'a?* or Chelahitsa, then "the most prominent and prestigious Okanagan Chief," was absent, was later contested by the Syilx in their long fight to regain their lands (Thomson, "History" 120). Throughout the decades following the establishment of the Okanagan reserves by Haynes, a growing movement of the Syilx against settlement drove the provincial and federal government to form the Indian Reserve Commission in 1876 and propel it into action in the interior of British Columbia in the spring of 1877 (Harris, *Making* 119-20). This Commission and the one that followed it, the McKenna-McBride Commission (1913-16), did not resolve land issues. Neither recognized Indigenous title and both failed to obtain Indigenous final agreement to the drawing and re-drawing of reserve lines (see "Girlhood Days in the Okanagan" in Part One). The Syilx struggle over land continued, long and tortuous, up to the present day, with chiefs and spokespeople fighting for the right to keep Indigenous lands, hand in hand with the battle for the right to Indigenous title in British Columbia.

In the years following Cox's and Haynes's actions to define and limit Indigenous lands in the interior, attitudes and conditions changed rapidly. When Cox had first designated reserves, the Syilx had not been confined to reserve lands. In 1865, when they pointed out to Haynes particular lands that would be a priority for their needs, they had expected continued access to hunting and fishing, as well as compensation for use of Syilx lands by settlers as Douglas had promised would always be the case (Armstrong et al. 47-49). Instead, settlers began pre-empting land and building fences, so that the Syilx became literally barred from adjacent range lands and access to water. As well, with Governor Douglas's retirement in 1864 and the appointment of Joseph Trutch as Chief Commissioner of Land and Works, the rules changed. A view of Indigenous people as "a vagrant people," to use the words of Philip Henry Nind (qtd. in Harris, "Native Land Policies": 117), rather than as hunters, gatherers, land owners and stock raisers, became entrenched. Nind, gold commissioner in the Cariboo at Lytton, British Columbia, had recommended the reduction of the reserves laid out by Cox in that region just prior to Haynes's reductions in the Okanagan (Thomson, "History" 120; R. Fisher 162). Settler society outlawed the pre-emption of land by Indigenous people, which Douglas had previously permitted, and rejected Indigenous title to the land (which Douglas at least partially recognized). Significantly, non-Indigenous people began to view reserves as areas "to which Indians were restricted or confined, beyond which they had limited rights" (Thomson 122).[4] As the old Chief Chelahitsa's son Chief John Chelahitsa from the Okanagan and Douglas Lake later put it to Prime Minister Laurier in 1910,

> [I]n many places we are debarred from camping, travelling, gathering roots and obtaining wood and water as heretofore. Our people are fined and imprisoned for breaking the game and fish laws and using the same game and fish we were told would always be ours for food. Gradually we are becoming regarded as trespassers over a large portion of this our country.[5] ("1910 Memorial")

Was Hester White at all aware of this drastic shift in the lives of the Syilx? In her published biographical article about her father, his reduction of reserves merited only a sentence, echoing Haynes's own words:

> Thus in 1865, when it was found that the reserves which had been marked by W.G. Cox some years before in the Okanagan were far too large, it was Haynes who arranged with the Indians to have them reduced to reasonable proportions. ("John" 193)

In the first instalment of "The Pioneer Trail," however, White's next publication, we find this opening sentence: "Long before the whiteman trod the trails of the Okanagan and cast his disintegrating spell on its life and spirit, the Indian held sway and was monarch of all he surveyed" (June 26, 1947). Her wording suggests an awareness of the destructive effects of settlement on the Syilx which may have been partly influenced by her reading of publications by Marie Houghton Brent and Mourning Dove.

A letter from Mourning Dove to White in 1934 indicates White had also written to her to collect information about J.C. Haynes. Mourning Dove notes, perhaps diplomatically, Haynes's "kindness to the natives in the past" and that he was "very much loved," but admits she knows little about him. She also mentions that she is "honoured to have you interested in my effort as a 'writer.'" Mourning Dove had published the popular *Coyote Stories* in 1933 and *Cogewea, The Half-Blood* in 1927, a novel that dramatically illustrates the impact of settlers' appropriation of Indigenous lands. The novel must have impressed White, as nearly thirty years later she still recommended and circulated it as an important historical source. Writing in 1961 to Katie Lacey, a keen disciple of White in the amassing and documenting of local history, White says, "I will let you have [*Cogewea*] when it's returned [from a friend who has borrowed it] since it has a lot of information in it" (September 14, 1961).

Mourning Dove died in August, 1936, less than two years after she wrote to White, but there are signs of Mourning Dove's continuing influence in White's series "The Pioneer Trail" published twelve years later. In the early columns, White incorporates a grandmother figure, Stem-tee-ma, who has "the authority to import knowledge and self-discipline to the youth, and tell the stories and legends" (July 3, 1947); her name and role echo those of Mourning Dove's Stemteemä, a central character in *Cogewea*. The eleventh column (September 11, 1947) ends with a summary of the story of Green-blanket-feet, deserted by her fur-trader husband who had taken her children with him, a story which Mourning Dove tells at length in *Cogewea*. In the eighth installment, however, White incorporates Mourning Dove's writing wholesale into her column (August 14, 1947). In discussing the origins of the name "Okanagan," White recounts a Syilx story about three brothers, Choo'-pahk, Scra'kan and Nak-ka'-tuya, and the maiden Scoo'-malt, that reproduces a large part of the story "En-am-tues—The Wishing Stone," found in Mourning Dove's *Coyote Stories*.

These borrowings can be understood from many perspectives. They are not acknowledged, but neither are any other sources in her series: White gives no references for her information on the fur trade, the introduction of the horse to the Okanagan, and other topics. This casual attitude to sources was fairly typical of popular writing of her time: in *Cogewea* itself, for example, what exactly editor Lucullus Virgil McWhorter contributed to the novel as a whole is famously undocumented, and in some of his contributions he also borrows wholesale from other authors (D. Fisher xv-xvi). Perhaps a more significant appropriation is White's resituating along a "pioneer trail" land and landmarks that Mourning Dove is at pains to establish as part of pre-settlement Syilx history in "En-am-tues." White also leaves out of account the ways in which white settlement has ignored or desecrated traditional relationships to the land. The column ends with a complacent reflection on a contented and (literally) fruitful Okanagan valley. At the same time, White's borrowings suggest her immersion in Mourning Dove's texts, and could be seen to represent respect for and homage to Mourning Dove's grasp of Syilx history as well as her skill as a writer.

White's "Pioneer Trail" series also makes no reference to the taking of land or the reduction of the reserves by Haynes. Mention of her father stops short at 1864, after he had established a customs house at Osoyoos. The "disintegrating spell" of the settler seems to manifest itself in the changed ways of the Syilx people as White describes them:

> We will walk away with very deep thoughts, sad, knowing that through contact with and imitation of the Shoyahpee (whiteman) the Indian will soon forget that the Spokelitz, a fresh water ling, can be caught through a hole in the ice at Sooyoos, on the first sunny days in February .... ("Pioneer Trail," July 10, 1947)

In her columns, White draws a clear line between a pre-settler past and the Syilx community at the time of her writing. She reiterates the familiar settler story of the degeneration of the noble savage, who "will sacrifice his God-given birthright of priceless treasures for a miserable mess of pottage" (July 10, 1947). Sometimes blaming the Syilx people and at other times the interference of white settlement, White suggests an awareness of a real loss of Syilx cultural knowledge. At the same time, she demarcates a debased Syilx present from a vital culture of the past.

A different perspective on the relationship between Syilx

and settler culture surfaces in the work of another writer, Isabel Christie MacNaughton. She also published columns in the *Penticton Herald*. (ten years earlier than Hester White). The Christies, coming from Nova Scotia to the Okanagan's dry climate in 1917 in search of a remedy for James Christie's chronic lung problems, bought a ranch in 1918, which they named Meadow Vale. South of Penticton and north of Osoyoos, the ranch was situated between Vaseux Lake and Okanagan Falls. MacNaughton's mother was a university graduate and her father had been a lumber broker in Nova Scotia before trying his hand at cattle ranching in the Okanagan. By all accounts, their daughter Isabel Christie MacNaughton was a great reader and had aspirations to be a writer from her childhood on. Born in 1915, the second oldest of seven children, "Buddie" was teased by her younger sisters for being dreamy and uncoordinated in anything to do with sports or athletics, but she was looked up to as well. Her sister Joyce remembers Robert (their one brother) "as being the oldest child, so he had no problems with his identity, and Buddie, despite her many responsibilities, also had her own place" (Hobbs 40).

Performances

In 1936, MacNaughton found herself back in the Okanagan after training to be a nurse at Vancouver General Hospital. She had given up this career due to ill health, but this loss opened the door for her to accept an offer to be a writer for the *Penticton Herald* newspaper. Her regular columns appeared from 1937 to 1939, and among these were over twenty-five stories that were told to her by Josephine Shuttleworth (see Part One). The daughter of Chief Francois of Penticton, Shuttleworth was born in 1865, a contemporary of Marie Houghton Brent and Hester White. She and her husband Harry Shuttleworth ran their own pack train, and in 1895 settled on ranch land Harry Shuttleworth had earlier pre-empted near what became Okanagan Falls. When the Christies acquired Meadow Vale they moved next door to Josephine Shuttleworth, now widowed and living with three sons and a daughter.

Only traces of how and when Shuttleworth's stories were told to MacNaughton are documented; MacNaughton had listened to them as a child (Anthony Walsh, "Developing" 4), and again when she returned to the Okanagan from Vancouver in 1936 (MacNaughton, "Tribute to a Lady"). The sheer number of stories Shuttleworth shared suggests communication and trust between the two women developed over a long relationship. According to her friend, historian Jean Webber, MacNaughton was "a good listener, gentle and quiet" (Personal interview). An undated handwritten note in MacNaughton's papers describes her response to Shuttleworth's storytelling:

> The Indian folktales were my delight. They were told in the Okanagan language by my dear old friend, and translated into English by her daughter Louise; also translated by Mrs. Shuttleworth's most charming and lively hand-telling—almost a mime of the story with her hands. The Okanagan language is lovely and soft, and the charm of it, with her hands telling too, rather leads one to weave a bit of poetry around the bare bones of an English translation. ("Indian folktales")

Whether or not Shuttleworth actually knew if her stories were being published in the newspaper has not been documented, but it seems almost certain that Louise Shuttleworth would have known and informed her mother. MacNaughton was scrupulous in giving Shuttleworth the credit for the stories she published, omitting her own name and using the byline "as told by Josephine Shuttleworth" for most of the *Herald* columns. MacNaughton added her voice and interpretation to the story's "bare bones," yet her contribution was in part inspired, she suggests, by Shuttleworth's oral performances. The stories she published documented not only Syilx history, but a living Syilx culture that continued in the present. They created the possibility for remapping Syilx landmarks, perspectives, and more-than-human figures such as coyote on to an increasingly settled Okanagan land. Hester White, who clipped and saved some of these stories, was a reader who may have been encouraged to write by MacNaughton's columns and Shuttleworth's stories.

Another reader of Shuttleworth's stories as written by MacNaughton was Anthony Walsh, who contacted MacNaughton in 1938 "to ask if she could make one or two plays from her stories for my youngsters"; MacNaughton, along with Elizabeth Renyi, who was recruited for her experience in producing "playlets" at the Oliver Public School, agreed (Anthony Walsh, "Developing" 4). Walsh taught from 1932 to 1942 at the Inkameep Day School established by Chief Baptiste George (*cianut* or Che'nut), initially at his own expense, on the Osoyoos Indian Reserve in 1915 (Andrea Walsh 17). Both a progressive and a traditionalist, Baptiste wanted to give his sons and the children on Nk'Mip land (*nk'mip* meaning "door" or doorway of the lake system, a narrows in Lake Osoyoos) an alternative to residential school, and the chance to learn "new teachings alongside of the traditional Okanagan teachings" (Andrea Walsh 17) as well as the skills to cope with "'the avarice of the White Man'" (Baptiste, qtd. in Buell: 34). He would have been familiar with this propensity, given the recent fraught history of white settlement. In 1879, J.C. Haynes had obtained over 4,000 acres of prime Nk'Mip land on both sides of the Okanagan River for his own ranch, even though he knew it had been set aside by the Indian Reserve Commission for the Osoyoos Indian Reserve.[6]

Born in Paris and raised in England, Ireland and Scotland, Walsh came to Canada in 1923 after serving in World War I (Buell 16-26). He was hired at Inkameep after two years' teaching at Six Mile Creek School on the Head of the Lake Reserve in the north Okanagan. While teaching the required curriculum at Inkameep, Walsh, employing experimental childhood education practices (Andrea Walsh 9), and through accidents and serendipity, began to connect with the Syilx culture of his small group of students, from nine to twelve children (Buell 37). He became known for his encouragement of the artistic production of his students, especially in the visual arts, but drama also became part of the curriculum.

Walsh describes vividly the effects of two plays MacNaughton adapted from Josephine Shuttleworth's stories—*Why the Ant's Waist Is Small* and *The Crickets Must Sing*—on the children of the Inkameep Day School: "When I read the first play about the ant and its waist there was great commotion. It was as though there had been an invasion of acrobats. There was great joy in the eyes and much exaltation" ("Inkameep Indian School" 17). To hear these stories in the classroom from a settler was apparently astounding, marvellous. Such stories were not new to the community, of course. Mourning Dove tells Hester White in her letter of 1934 (published below) that she "gathered much

264

material from the Indians" for her book *Coyote Stories* while she was living at Nk'Mip during World War I; she had taught at the day school from 1917 to 1919. Walsh's development of drama at the day school, with MacNaughton's involvement, enabled stories to be transmitted—as dramatic performances—to settlers in the Okanagan region in the late 1930s, but the process was protracted. Walsh relates how, after a picnic for the schoolchildren that was rained out at Inkameep, Johnny Stalkia (Stelkia) approached him with an "Indian story." Walsh reports, "I was all ears. The others wished to squelch him for this was forbidden territory" ("Inkameep" 16). The stories were usually kept secret. For one thing, performing traditional dances was then outlawed under the Indian Act. As well, settlers were not trusted. As Walsh recalls in 1974:

> . . .[I]t was generally assumed by adults, and so was accepted by the children, that no matter how kind a white man might seem, he was always suspect. This attitude, which is easily understandable, was largely due to the many broken promises of the past, and the greed and disdain. ("Inkameep" 15)

Stelkia's rare performance that day galvanized Walsh: "Then a very strange thing happened, this small boy became like a bear—for his story was about a bear. And there before our eyes the bear walked and rolled and talked in the Okanagan dialect." Walsh was inspired: "There flashed through my mind the thought—here are the elements of drama" ("Inkameep" 16). In addition to MacNaughton's and Renyi's input, the children formed their own drama group, Can-oos-sez Skay-loo (*k'nusəs sqilxʷ*, Animal People) and wrote their own plays.[7] Ranging in age from six to fourteen, Johnnie, Jane and Frank Stelkia; Bertha, Irene, Gertie, Raymond and Harry Baptiste; Vincent Louis; and Edith Kruger performed locally at Nk'Mip, in Osoyoos, Penticton, Oliver and Summerland from 1938 to 1942 (Korpan 50-51), as long as gas rations allowed during the wartime years (Buell 45). Some of these performances brought settlers and Syilx, now largely "exiled" on reservations, to use Marie Houghton Brent's term, together in shared venues.

The plays also reached international audiences. In the summer of 1939, drama professor and folklore specialist Frederick Koch saw Walsh perform *Why the Ant's Waist Is Small* at Banff at a workshop he was leading, and later that year published MacNaughton's "playlets" of Shuttleworth's stories in *The Carolina Play-Book*, a publication of the University of North Carolina. Calling them "Canadian Indian Folk Drama," Koch fitted them into the context of a people's theatre drawn from the cultures of diverse regions, and expressing a "many-sided and multi-colored American life" (Koch 174). Focussing on ordinary people's traditions and experiences, the works were ideally "written and staged by the people on whom the plays were based" (Moore 4). If the Inkameep plays could travel internationally, however, the Syilx could not. Although some local performances were allowed, the restrictions of the reserve system hindered Syilx people from moving freely on their own land, or for that matter, anywhere off the reservation. Enforcing its laws on reserves through Indian agents, the Indian Act performed a stranglehold on Syilx political, economic and cultural choices and practices. To wear traditional costume and to travel to perform dance or theatre was forbidden, though exceptions were made by some agents looking the other way, as in the local performances by Can-oos-sez Skay-loo.[8]

Inkameep students did make a journey, however, to Victoria, British Columbia in 1941, partly through the influence of Alice Ravenhill and her support of Indigenous cultural production. Immigrating from England to Vancouver Island in 1910, she took on the project of "revitalization" of Indigenous arts and crafts in the 1930s (Wan 52). She and Walsh had begun corresponding in January, 1939 (Wan 61), and through her network of contacts, Ravenhill helped generate support and recognition for many of Walsh's and his students' efforts at Inkameep, including the drama projects (Smith 62-73). Ravenhill founded the Society for the Furtherance of BC Indian Arts and Crafts in Victoria in 1940 (its original name being The Committee to Promote the Revival and Development of their Latent Gifts among Native Tribes of British Columbia [Andrea Walsh 13]), and Walsh was a member. Modelled on this organization, the Okanagan Society for the Revival of Indian Arts and Crafts (SRIAC) was formed by Albert and Daisy Millar, with Walsh, in March of 1941. The Okanagan SRIAC took on activities to support the Inkameep plays, painting and art shows, and other artistic productions. They raised funds for the Can-oos-sez Skay-loo group to participate in the opening of Thunderbird Park in Victoria in May, 1941. Special permission had to be obtained from the Department of Indian Affairs, but an invitation was facilitated by Major L. Bullock-Webster (Korpan 51) who was a founding member of Ravenhill's Society, as well as director of school and community drama for the British Columbia Department of Education.

The performance at Thunderbird Park, which included *Why The Ant's Waist Is Small, The Crickets Must Sing,* and *The Chipmunk and the Owlwoman,* provided the Nk'Mip children with an exciting opportunity to travel and perform a version of their stories. Bullock-Webster introduced their plays as "a unique form of drama . . . Native Drama" (qtd. in Korpan:135). On provincial and national political stages, their performance could also be seen as an exhibition by the provincial government of a benevolent relationship with Indigenous people, a tableau of "the whole harmonious state" of Canada as a nation from its Indigenous roots to the present (Korpan 131), at a time when Canada sought to severely contain and control Indigenous peoples and cultures.[9] The Inkameep children themselves, in pictures they made later, included no sign of an audience. In one painting, they depicted their dancing before the totem pole and longhouse being celebrated on site, and the beautiful coastal environment, new to them, with a whale breaching nearby (136). Their acting and dancing demonstrated the living presence of Syilx culture not only in the stories of Shuttleworth, but in their own generation.

Not long after the exhiliaration of that performance, the conditions at Inkameep school began to deteriorate. Walsh resigned his post as teacher at the end of 1942 to work with the Legion War Services elsewhere in British Columbia. Chief Baptiste George had died in 1939. The Inkameep schoolchildren were left without a teacher until 1944. Finally, at the intervention of SRIAC appealing to the federal government, a new teacher was appointed, then another, in quick succession. A third "remained long enough to discourage all effort to develop Indian Native Art, by destroying all exhibits as adorned the schoolroom walls" (Millar 27), labelling the paintings, masks and drama costumes "'diabolical'" (qtd. in Buell: 46).[10] Those who supported Indigenous arts and crafts in the Okanagan were confronted by the lack of rights and autonomy on the reserve. The Okanagan

SRIAC, which according to its president Albert Millar was "[f]rustrated in its efforts to assist the Inkameep Indian children, and realizing the helpless position in which these wards of the Government live on the reserve," put its efforts into reforming the Indian Act (27), a "Rehabilitation scheme to be laid before the Government" (Minutes of SRIAC Council meeting January 18 [1942?]) that they had been thinking about since 1942. The organization submitted a brief, "Native Canadians: A Plan for the Rehabilitation of Indians," to Prime Minister Mackenzie King in 1944. The paper did not address Indigenous land issues but focussed on issues of Indigenous rights.

Its opening paragraphs comment upon the problem that, "while we [those involved in societies such as theirs] were fascinated by the past of a deeply rooted and highly developed culture" most Indigenous people in Canada lived in "deplorable conditions," and further, *they have no rights as citizens anywhere in the world* (3). Many of their demands are disturbingly familiar to Canadians today. Their paper called for, among other things, full citizenship without loss of land, self-government on reserves, more and better health care, economic security, and freedoms of speech, assembly and religion, as well as "a new system of education" (15-20). Reforms would include the replacement of residential schools by day schools, as well as the teaching of Indigenous cultures within these schools. Encouragingly, a joint committee of the Senate and House of Commons was formed in 1946 "to examine and consider the Indian Act" (Millar 28). Their proposed reforms, however, after three years of work, were mostly rejected by the government. A revised new Indian Act was announced in September 1951. It did grant certain human rights, lifting bans on the potlatch ceremony and traditional dancing, as well as on holding political meetings and raising money for land claims. However, it "was not a radical departure from earlier versions" (Leslie) and further undermined the rights of Indigenous women.[11]

MacNaughton was no doubt influenced by the thinking of Koch, Walsh and Ravenhill and was active in SRIAC from the beginning ("Minutes" March 9, 1941), supporting its goals to make a presentation to the federal government, working on subcommittees, but remaining in the background of this movement. The inherent paternalism of SRIAC's goals, initially proposing to work on "developing the latent Indian talent of the Inkameep reserve" ("Minutes of Meeting held March 1st, 1941") did not seem to be shared by MacNaughton. In an undated note from the SRIAC files in Osoyoos she suggests that aspects of SRIAC's work should be led by Syilx people themselves. Admitting she had been "woefully inadequate" in "'keeping in touch' with Inkameep and helping with art work," she recommends that such work could be better carried out "by a committee of Inkameep women" ("We").

MacNaughton's relationship with Shuttleworth had never been about "developing the latent Indian talent" among the Syilx, but rather was personal, longstanding, and reciprocal. As MacNaughton's plays received national and international attention, their link to Shuttleworth became faint. MacNaughton, however, republished *The Crickets Must Sing* and *Why the Ant's Waist Is Small* in her book of poems *Wood Fires* (1942), acknowledging that they are "adapted from the Okanagan Indian folk-tale as told by Josephine Shuttleworth" (9). In her versions, MacNaughton attempts to retain the integrity of the stories Shuttleworth told her, not always the case among her contemporaries. Elizabeth Renyi, for example, rewrote *Why the Chipmunk's Coat Is Striped* into the longer play *The Chipmunk and the Owlwoman*.[12] Her adaptation introduces a theme of Christian forgiveness of Owl-Woman, at odds with the traditional message of Syilx coyote stories in which Coyote rids the world of monsters or "people eaters" in order to prepare the world for human habitation (Armstrong, "Constructing" 96). Christian messages also surface in the childrens' plays, not surprising since Inkameep was a Catholic school.

By the early 1940s, MacNaughton's life was changing rapidly. She had married Carleton MacNaughton in 1939, they had built a home, and her first child, Sheila, was born in 1941, the same year her brother, Robert, joined the RCAF. His plane was shot down over Germany in 1943. *Wood Fires* was published partly to raise money for the Red Cross's war effort. Many of MacNaughton's short, vivid poems focus on nature in the Okanagan. The opening poem, "'Incantation,' RCAF," addresses those fighting overseas. Out riding with her brother and her father some time before 1939, MacNaughton had made sketches of pictographs they had observed ("Deed of Gift"). She wrote in a note about them that "most authorities . . . claim they are Power signs. In the old days when an Indian boy was nine or ten part of his training was to be sent out on a lonely trail in the night." During that time, "some animal, bird, or tree would speak to him and grant him a 'Power' which would stay by him and help him throughout his life" ("Indian Paintings").[13] Her poem "'Incantation' RCAF" speaks of what "They," the fighter pilots, have known, and calls up elements of home, but particularly of plants and animals of the Okanagan land: "White Olalla, wild syringa / Voices of home, pine trees . . . " and "Wild goose and eagle / On distant, tireless wings." The poet asks the "God of all these remembered things" to grant "the strength / The infinite beauty of these / To all Thy men of the sky." While the poem could be seen to invoke a Christian God, perhaps MacNaughton, with her "incantation," was also calling upon the powers of the Okanagan land and its living beings to accompany her brother and other volunteers from the Okanagan.

MacNaughton's writing became more occasional after her marriage as her time was taken up with family (three more children) and orcharding with her husband. Two other works, however, attest to her connection with Shuttleworth—her poems to Shuttleworth in "Tribute to a Lady," appearing in the *Penticton Herald* following Shuttleworth's death in 1950, and a new edition of *Wood Fires* published in 1948 that included MacNaughton's play *The Greasewood Tree* written when she was developing plays with Walsh (Korpan 65). The play is not attributed to Shuttleworth, but is clearly influenced by her storytelling. The relationship in the play between the failing old woman and her young granddaughter could echo the importance to MacNaughton of her relationship with the older Josephine Shuttleworth; eventually, in the play, the older woman is transformed into a greasewood tree (also known as black sage or antelope brush) and thus never has to leave the girl or the Okanagan land.[14]

Secrets and Testimonies

Correspondence shows that Hester White was also involved in working to support the Nk'Mip children, helping to organize art exhibits in the spring of 1938 and a concert in June, for which she was recruited to "interpret the Chief's talk, as well as give a talk in the Chinook language" (Anthony Walsh, Letter to

Hester White, June 4, 1938). When she came to publish her series of articles "The Pioneer Trail" some ten years later, however, White included none of the experimentation in art and drama and tentative bridging between Syilx and settler communities that took place during the 1930s and early 1940s. The Syilx community she describes in her opening columns is an ideal, pre-settlement one in which "the Indian" lived "a carefree, natural, wholesome life," albeit with hints of impending disruption (June 26, 1947). In many of the articles and reminiscences she writes over the next fourteen years, White also envisions an ideal time or golden age in her own life: the peace and security of childhood, before the sudden death of her father when she was eleven years old, and the disintegration that occurred through the loss of place, land, and status for the Haynes family. In White's reminiscences and letters about those early days, Matilda Kruger emerges as a significant figure.

Matilda Kruger had been with the Haynes family as "our nurse and dear friend," according to White ("On Okanagan Lake" 42), since about 1881 or 1882 (Fraser 200; White "First Memory"). Hester would then have been four or five years old and Kruger seventeen or eighteen,[15] and she stayed with the Haynes's until at least 1890; by that time the family had moved to Victoria, living there for just over a year after J.C. Haynes's death. In the fall of 1890, five of the six Haynes children, including White, were sent to boarding school in England (White, "Off to England") where they stayed until January of 1895 (White, "Plymouth Devon 1890"). Kruger remained in Victoria for part of that time, looking after Susan, the youngest Haynes child.

White's writing suggests that Kruger was vital to creating the sense of security she enjoyed as a child. Kruger was "Mother's right hand and my ideal," she says in "Over the Hope Trail," and in a handwritten, undated note, White describes Matilda Kruger as "a splendid all round help and 'teacher' to Mother and we children" ("First Memory"). Kruger's contributions as teacher are also implied in a passage from a letter White wrote to Ann Briley, an acquaintance and fellow local historian living in the Okanogan, south of the Canada-United States border: "I rode many miles with her when a child. Her knowledge of the hills, plants, birds, etc. was beautiful" (February 18, 1959). Clearly, White looked up to Kruger; an echo of youthful admiration for an older teenager can be inferred in her description of Kruger in *The Story of Osoyoos*: "tall, slight, lovely olive skin and nut-brown hair, she could do everything" (qtd. in Fraser: 200). In "We Cross the Columbia in an Indian Canoe," printed below, White depicts Kruger as fearless, describing a scene when the Haynes family is travelling back to the Okanagan by train in 1883 from a trip to New Westminster. When they stopped in Sprague, Washington, White recollects, "We got out of the train on the side away from the hotel and were told to go round the end, but Matilda took two of the children and crawled under the train. Nothing daunted Matilda" (37).

Writing to Katie Lacey in the early 1960s, not long before her death in 1963, White reveals how Kruger's strength and courage were crucial in a time of upheaval. Looking back at her father's funeral, White says "I think that was the night I found my strength—to meet what ever happened—Poor Val [her older brother] & Mother had none! Matilda was a marvel" (Letter to Katie Lacey, "a.m. Wed." [July or August, 1961]). In another letter to Lacey, she writes that Matilda "certainly kept us together after my father died—and in Victoria—she kept the home going!!" (October 18, [1960]). Around 1895, Kruger left Canada to live on the Colville reservation in Washington state. She died in 1935, but it seems she remained a vivid part of White's interior life. In the same letter to Lacey, White wrote she "would love to get a picture of Matilda Kruger—must write about her one of these days."

White never wrote a piece featuring Matilda Kruger, but Kruger's appearances in her published writing both expose secrets and maintain silences. Matilda Kruger first appears in a piece White wrote described as an installment of "The Pioneer Trail" published in the "Miscellany" section of George Fraser's *The Story of Osoyoos*. Here, White identifies Kruger as "Mr. Kruger's native daughter and mother's right hand" (200). Theodore Kruger had settled in the Osoyoos area in 1866 to run the Hudson's Bay post there and the Krugers were neighbours of the Haynes. To actually name a Syilx descendant of a pioneer crossed a line that few settlers dared to breach. Indigenous people were mostly absent from the pages of the OHS's annual reports, and a particular silence was kept about the Syilx wives and children of settlers who had later married settler women of European heritage. Except for Hester White's descriptions of her in various articles about her childhood, Matilda Kruger does not appear in the OHS's publications until 1996, when historian Jean Barman published a ground-breaking article documenting and discussing Okanagan settlers' relations with Syilx women and their descendants.[16] In 1935, Chrestenza Kruger recounts her husband Theodore's history in Osooyos in the *OHS Report* with no mention of his relationship with a Syilx woman from the Colville reserve and their children Matilda and Mary. Theodore Kruger also had a son, William (Billy) Kruger, who was a younger half-brother to Matilda and Mary (White, Letter to Ann Briley, February 18, 1959). White would have known, from Mourning Dove's letter to her in 1934, that Matilda Kruger's mother was Mourning Dove's great aunt, her grandmother's sister on her father's side (November 5, 1934).

With the exception of her article in *The Story of Osoyoos*, White, like Chrestenza Kruger, makes no mention of Matilda Kruger's parentage, and thus creates recollections that reveal and conceal at the same time. For example, in "On Okanagan Lake" White mentions that her family travelled "with Matilda Kruger, our nurse and dear friend, to help us," while at the same time recalling "Theodore Kruger and his eldest daughter Dora" passing them in another boat (42-45).[17] Matilda was, in fact, Kruger's eldest daughter, and Dora was one of the four children Kruger had with Chrestenza after 1873. In the unpublished reminiscence, "Over the Hope Trail," Kruger is recognized as an active and important participant in the Haynes family. At the same time, White's enumeration of the many chores and responsibilities that fell to Kruger make it clear that she is not regarded as an equal member of the family, but rather as a nanny and maid of all work. In that same reminiscence, White seems comfortable in acknowledging Lucy Richter, their friend Francis (Frank) Richter's Syilx wife with whom he lived openly in his ranch in the Similkameen for at least twenty-five years. White describes how, as the family passed through Richter's ranch on their travels to New Westminster when she was a child, "Lucy Richter, Frank Richter's native wife, came with butter and milk for our supper." She goes on, "Lucy was a very fine character and always a great friend of mother's. She had five small sons Charlie, William, Joe, Edward, and Hans" ("Over the Hope Trail"). Perhaps Frank Richter's own acknowledgement of and continued relationship with Lucy enabled White and her mother to recognize her and their children, or perhaps, if the piece had been published, this reference would have been omitted.[18]

White's writing suggests her intimacy with Kruger, someone White regarded as a trusted and, at times, sole ally. It also testifies to the distance between them, no doubt resulting from what Janet MacArthur in her essay in Part Two identifies as racial and settler "contracts" which White absorbed. Even as an adult writing her reminiscences in the 1960s, White fails to acknowledge the inequality and hardship of Matilda Kruger's life among the Krugers and the Hayneses. The only recognition we have of that in writing appears in Kruger's letter to White in 1934, included below, when Kruger, like Mourning Dove and Marie Houghton Brent, answers White's enquiries about her father's history. Kruger's lack of belonging among the settlers is marked by her references to her father and stepmother as "Mr. Kruger" and "Mrs. Kruger." Her letter implies she responds to questions White has sent her, and she also fills in some blanks in her own life, ironically in a sentence in which she apologizes for things not told:

> we lef lots of stories out because it was hard & unplesant memery of our young days it was nothing but hard work & no schooling. When we came to Uncle Sam we were treated like a human being and went to Chemawa school through our Mother because she belonged here.
> (November 20, 1934)

In 1934, it seems, Kruger can disclose to White some of her feelings about the privation of her youth, speak of her mother, and acknowledge her own full existence. She had gained some education at schools in the United States such as the Chemawa Indian Industrial School in Oregon, and had been living on an allotment adjacent to her sister Mary's on the Colville reservation near Omak for seventeen years. Her brief obituary in 1935 adds a new dimension to White's portrayals, describing Kruger as "well-known in this district and possessed [of] one of the most valuable collections of Indian art work in the region" ("Death" 1). White had some contact with Kruger in the United States,[19] and Kruger's letter printed in this section mentions recent communication, but White is most interested in writing about the Matilda Kruger who was so important to her own childhood.

Matilda Kruger no doubt also represented something that

White strove to keep secret during her lifetime—the existence of White's own Syilx half-siblings. J.C. Haynes, like Theodore Kruger and many other pioneers, had had a relationship with a Syilx woman, Julia (Julie) Abraham, also from Colville, who lived with Hayne's when he first arrived in the Osoyoos region in the 1860s. They had two children, Mary Ann Haynes, born in 1866, and John Carmichael Haynes, born in 1868, the year that Haynes met and married his first acknowledged wife Charlotte Moresby, and he and Abraham parted ways (Hayes, "Haynes-Moore Story" 81).[20] After Charlotte Moresby's death in 1872, Haynes married White's mother, Emily Pittendrigh, in 1875.

White's longstanding silence about her father's relationship and her Syilx half brother and sister is indicated in a letter she sent to Katie Lacey in the 1960s:

> I am enclosing a Baptism Certificate which will surprise you? Mother was very good to Little Julie—the mother of Johnny & Mary Haynes—she told me that my Father was very, very ill and that Little Julie nursed him through it— and cared for him—Johnny & Mary are both mentioned in his will—as his "reputed" children and received the money willed to them—its more than we got.[21] ("Many thanks for Thursday" [circa 1960-63])

Both Mary Ann and John Carmichael (Junior) are listed on the Canada Census of 1881 as members of the Haynes household, so it is possible they were living there at that time.[22] Little is recorded of their childhood;[23] in 1882, at sixteen years old, Mary Ann Haynes married Charles William (C.W.) Hozier and moved to Vernon and then to pre-empted land near Camp McKinney in 1894, where their ranch, "on the old stage road between the Okanagan and Boundary Country," was a familiar stop for refreshment "for freight teams and wagons and passenger stages" (Lacey, "Hoziers" 143). Later, they moved to the Fairview or *txʷltiʔiws* district near Oliver, British Columbia. Hester White would have been five years old in 1882, and this would have been about the time Matilda Kruger came to live with the Haynes family. John or "Johnny" Carmichael Haynes "was educated by priests in New Westminster," according to his wife, Christina Moore (Utley, "Keen Minded Woman" 3); before their marriage in 1892, she tells us, he was "riding for Lequime" on his ranch in the Mission (3).

275

John and Christina Haynes established a farm in the Benvoulin area of Kelowna (Hayes, "Haynes-Moore" 83). They had seven children. John Haynes died in 1948, and Christina Moore Haynes lived on to become a celebrated pioneer. It seems that not only White, but her five full siblings also maintained a silence about the existence of their half-siblings, including her older brother Valentine (Val) Haynes, who had married a Colville woman, Elizabeth Runnels. Her mother had been a sister to Nespelem George (1863-1929) (Lacey, "Valentine," 117-18), a well-known chief of the Sanpoil Nation, one of the Confederated Tribes of the Colville reservation.

It is doubtful that Lacey would have been "surprised" by White's revelation of Syilx relations, given that Mary Ann and John Carmichael Haynes, Jr., had continued to live in the Okanagan region as adults. In the *OHS Report* of 1963 Katie Lacey eulogizes Leonard Hozier, Mary Ann Hozier's son, saying that he "[inherited] his keen instincts and quiet, unassuming ways from his Indian forbears," her own recognition and simultaneous effacement of his mother and his grandmother Julia Abraham ("Hoziers" 143). C.W. Hozier died in 1919 at Lake Marron, British Columbia, and the date of Mary Ann's death is not known. The Hoziers' daughter Gertrude (1892-1937), J.C. Haynes's grandchild and one of four siblings, became part of the story of the Inkameep Day School. Department of Indian Affairs records show that Gertrude Hozier from Fairview succeeded "Miss Christina McLeod" or Mourning Dove as a teacher at the Inkameep Day School from late 1919 to 1923 (Fleming, Smith and Raptis 8). She was considered eminently qualified as she had a high school certificate, "a substantial credential held by only a small number of provincial teachers of the time" (8).

Histories of J.C. Haynes or his family before articles by Barman and Hayes are almost completely silent about Julia Abraham, Mary Ann, and John Carmichael Haynes, Jr. When White sent out letters in the 1930s, one of the few people to acknowledge the existence of White's half siblings as part of J.C. Haynes's history was Eleanor Laurence Saucier. Saucier was the youngest daughter of Cyprien Laurence, often spoken of as the first settler in Kelowna, and Theresa Laurence, the daughter of old Chief Nkwala and a great aunt to Marie Houghton Brent (see essay "Standing Between" and Brent's "Indian Lore" in Part One).

Born in 1868, Saucier was about the same age as Marie Houghton Brent, and went to convent school in Kamloops with her; she had also attended the Okanagan Mission Valley School with Christina Haynes, who was Christina Moore then. A 68-year-old woman in 1936, Eleanor Saucier wrote back to White's enquiries about J.C. Haynes, saying

> I was six weeks old when my father [Cyprien Laurence] died, I do not know him and have not even a photo but I remember your father quite well. He had only one child with his first wife that he married[,] Fairfax[;] he had two other children before[,] John and Mary[,] your father claimed [them] as his children provided and educated them, this is all I know of your fathers family. . . .
>
> (August 9, 1936)

Saucier would have felt connected to Julia Abraham and her children—at the time of her letter, her son Daniel Saucier was about to marry Johnny Haynes's daughter Isobel. Saucier's letter creates a more complex portrait of J.C. Haynes than White's own writing and many other more recent histories provide.

No doubt Marie Houghton Brent knew of White's Syilx relatives, given that Brent's Laurence relatives had close relations with them. It is possible that White and Brent talked about these relations during their visits. In one letter written in 1955, White fills Brent in on her family and friends; here, she mentions Christina Moore Haynes, but makes no reference to their family relationship. Perhaps her half-siblings were left an open secret between Brent and White.

Brent's letters and the unpublished memoir "My School Days" show that she had always connected to both sides of her family. Her ability to embrace them may be informed by the philosophy of inclusiveness typical of the Syilx. Concepts of race did not figure in Syilx thinking, and although Brent utilizes terms such as "race" and "blood" in her essay "The Indians of the Okanagan Valley" (124), she attributes the strength of Indigenous people to cultures based on a long history of respect for the autonomy of the individual. Family ties are extended and important, as Jeannette Armstrong demonstrates in her essay "Standing Between" in Part One. Brent's father C.F. Houghton, European heritage or not, had "married in" to her Syilx lineage and was to be as respected as Pelkamulox or Nkwala. Brent's attitudes contrast with White's relationship with the Syilx side of her family, stifled and restricted by racist colonial fears and hierarchies. Perhaps White's relationship with Brent, which developed into the mutual recognition of equals, gave White some awareness of the potential she had forfeited in her relationship with Matilda Kruger and with her half-siblings, John and Mary Ann Haynes. Brent also appreciated her relationship with White, writing in 1956 that "I have no one with that warm link else where—always have to be on diplomatic terms else where—" (Letter to Hester White, Xmas night, 1956).

The crossing lines that were sent in letters, transmitted in conversations and stories, written down as memoirs, histories, novels, plays and poems, performed, published and left behind by the women in this section, help to retrieve some of the connections between Syilx and settler women of that time. They reveal a network of contiguity and crossing paths, and also communication and continuity—Hester White and Marie Houghton Brent share their abiding interest in history, Syilx and settler; Syilx stories travel across the friendship and mutual appreciation of Isabel Christie MacNaughton and Josephine Shuttleworth, and cross boundaries recently drawn around the Osoyoos Indian reservation to reach the Inkameep school, where the stories coincide with those told by and to Mourning Dove. The interdependence between Syilx and settler emerges in White's record of Matilda Kruger's vital influence in keeping the Haynes family together. Ruptures, difference and dislocation are evident: Kruger's revelation of her alienation from colonial society throws into relief White's inability to comprehend the personal toll in her own time of the "disintegrating spell" of colonialism. Mourning Dove's letter, however, draws a line to connect Kruger's family to her own, and Kruger crosses the international line to find a place of belonging with her mother's people, while at the same time the restrictions of reservation lines and policies drawn there affect her life.

These writings reveal, in my mind, not a redeeming narrative of relationship that overcomes the exploitation and attitudes of superiority visited upon the Syilx by colonialism, attitudes that continue to this day, but rather networks in which bonds and ruptures, understanding, incomprehension and ambiguity weave. Hester White can admire and depend on Matilda Kruger and at the same time be unable to cross the line drawn by colonial society against intermarriage between settler and Syilx. MacNaughton can be receptive to stories shared by Shuttleworth, but the fullness of Syilx cultural understanding will elude her. Nevertheless, amidst the constraints of colonialism and differing ways of knowing, these writings allow us to reclaim connections between Syilx and settler women that histories written by and for the colonizing power have often been blind to or dismissed as insignificant. The connections are at times brief and tangential, at others day-to-day, year-to-year patterns of mutual care, exchange of knowledge, respectful attention, and inspiration—and many more relations that can be drawn. They are an important part of Okanagan history.

Haynes family portrait, c. 1889-1890. [G.H.E. Hudson].
Hester is seated in front with Sherman.
Back row, L-R: Irene, Will, Valentine.
Courtesy of Penticton Museum and Archives.

Hester Emily White
1877 - 1963

Though in her time known as "Mrs. Doctor White," a socially prominent figure in the small town of Penticton, British Columbia, Hester Emily Haynes White was also esteemed in the Okanagan as a local historian. A contemporary views her as writing "with decision. Mrs. White is a decisive woman. . . . Tall and spare and upright even now [at seventy-three years old] she is a force to be reckoned with in the community" (Phillips 5). "Indomitable spirit" and "gallant" are words used in her obituary published by the Okanagan Historical Society ("To Hester" 136-37). Her chronicling of her family's settler history in the southern Okanagan creates a detailed picture of early settler days and inadvertently points as well to the blank spaces of what was excised from that picture by her and other white settlers.

Born in Osoyoos in 1877, Hester Emily Haynes, second of six children, was the eldest daughter of one of the earliest and most influential settlers in the south Okanagan, John Carmichael Haynes, and his second acknowledged wife, Emily Pittendrigh Haynes. She travelled from Malta to New Westminster, British Columbia, with her father, Captain George Pittendrigh, and his family in 1872. In 1875, she married Haynes, an emigrant from County Cork, Ireland, then a widower as his first acknowledged wife, Charlotte Moresby, had died in 1872. Haynes had arrived in British Columbia in 1858 and, after a time at Rock Creek and the Similkameen as an aide to W.G. Cox, established himself in Osoyoos, British Columbia as a collector of customs in 1862 (White, "John" 187-88; for his early years in British Columbia, see White's columns below from "The Pioneer Trail"). With the additional appointments of assistant gold commissioner, member of the colonial legislature, and County Court judge (he was often referred to in the district as "Judge Haynes"), Haynes had become, as White simply puts it, "responsible for law and order and acted as the general agent for the Government" throughout the Okanagan ("John" 193). In that capacity, he recommended and carried out the reduction of Syilx reserves in the Okanagan in 1865 (see the essay "Crossing Lines"). Haynes himself began pre-empting land after that, and raised stock, primarily beef cattle, in partnership with W.H. Lowe until Lowe's death in 1882. Lowe had come to the Okanagan in 1860 from San Francisco (White, "W.H. Lowe") and had served as a constable under Haynes in the Similkameen ("John" 195). At the time of his death in 1888, Haynes owned one of the largest cattle ranches in the region, accumulating over 20,000 acres of land. The stability and comfort White experienced as the daughter of Judge Haynes came to an end when Haynes died at a stopover at the Allison ranch in Princeton, having suddenly been taken ill on his way home from Victoria, British Columbia. White's piece "[July 6, 1888,] Osoyoos" printed below describes this turning point, momentous for Hester Haynes.

White's mother moved the family to Victoria and then, in 1890, to England where she placed White in the Convent of Notre Dame in Plymouth, Cornwall, with her sister Irene, and her brothers Valentine (Val), William (Will) and Sherman in Beaconsfield College nearby (White, "Plymouth"). White returned to Osoyoos in 1895 (her mother had returned two years earlier) to find that the Haynes ranch was for sale; J.C. Haynes had taken a mortgage in order to buy out Lowe's widow in 1884, and it had been foreclosed. The land and property were acquired by Thomas Ellis, another early settler from Ireland who had been taken under Haynes's wing when he had arrived in the region in the 1860s, and who had settled in the Penticton area. It is said he benefited from Mrs. Haynes's confidences when she told him of her financial difficulties in keeping up mortgage payments in 1893 (Koroscil 33). In the article below entitled "May 1, 1895, Osoyoos" White's feelings of being betrayed by Ellis are evident.

In the next few years White and her family had to improvise, pressured by changing circumstances. The family moved into Henry Nicholson's old ranch house, at the time owned by Francis Richter, at Rock Creek. White reminisces that they lived on venison all winter and were glad of chickens laying in the spring ("Nicholson's Creek"). They had no carriage or team and had to depend on borrowing them from Susap who had worked as a ranch hand for Judge Haynes, and was the brother of Chief Baptist George at Nk'Mip. Her mother bought the Lancaster Restaurant in Midway, British Columbia, in 1896 with gold mining shares, a "disastrous" investment (Koroscil 33). Val Haynes, who had been "cowboying since he was 8 years old," went to work for Thomas Ellis as a ranch hand, and after that for the Okanagan Land Company which bought Ellis's land. He later acquired the Swan Lake Ranch (at Vaseux Lake, as it is called today), land at "The Meadows" at the head of Osoyoos Lake, and at Kruger Mountain in the southern Okanagan (Lacey, "Valentine" 117).

Given the precarious family finances, it is not surprising that White, at the age of nineteen, married Charles Anderson Richardson (C.A.R.) Lambly in 1897. Twenty-five years her senior, he held the post of government agent at Rock Creek, Camp McKinney, Osoyoos, and Fairview. She moved into quarters in Osoyoos that were part courtroom, part private living quarters, and part jail. In November, 1897, she gave birth to her son Wilfred. He was delivered by Dr. Reginald Brant White

(1875-1950), a young man who had moved to the region from Pembroke, Ontario, that same year. In 1898 White and her husband moved with the government offices to Fairview, then a booming mining community (near present day Oliver, British Columbia) where Dr. White was also based, and where a second son, Charles, was born in 1906. White also had a daughter who died in infancy ("To Hester" 136). In 1907, C.A.R. Lambly died unexpectedly of pneumonia, leaving White with Wilfred and the one-year-old Charles.

In 1908, the year her mother died, Hester married Dr. R.B. White, now based in the small settlement of Penticton incorporated as a municipality that year with a population of about six hundred people. The townsite had been laid out in 1892 on Syilx land that had been pre-empted by Thomas Ellis. Dr. White established a practice, and they both by all accounts devoted themselves to the welfare of their community. White had two more sons, W. H. (Bill) White and R.V. (Jack) White; W.H. White followed in his father's footsteps and became a doctor, joining his father's practice in 1938. Hester White helped found the Women's Institute, the local IODE,[1] and a cottage hospital, as well as serving on the school board and the Children's Aid Society ("To Hester" 136). A social worker who came to the area in 1947 named White as one of five people who were instrumental in the "development of social services in the South Okanagan" (Bennest 21). Dr. White died in 1950. He was liked and respected by the Syilx community and recognized for contributions to the settler community, receiving Penticton's first "Good Citizen" award two years before. According to the Okanagan Historical Society's tribute upon his death, the unassuming doctor "tried to avoid attending" the ceremony for the award (Andrew 46).

In her fifties, White began writing for publication. Knowing of her interest in family history, editor W. Kaye Lamb encouraged her in the 1930s to write a piece on her father J.C. Haynes for the *British Columbia Historical Quarterly*. This protracted effort involved White sending drafts to Victoria, where the editors of the British Columbia Historical Society had easier access to the provincial archives. They augmented her text and sent drafts back to White to be rewritten (Lamb, Letter to Hester White, December 4, 1936). "John Carmichael Haynes" was published in 1940. Meanwhile, White pursued her own research on her father and the early days of settlement, establishing in the process the correspondence with Mourning Dove, Marie Houghton Brent, and Matilda Kruger published below. Matilda Kruger's letter in response in 1934 entitled "History of early days" gives us one of the few histories from that time in existence written by a Syilx woman. White's correspondence with Brent allows readers to glimpse a more informal and unguarded White and trace some of the dynamics of the relationship between these two women over time. Both took their historical writing seriously. Like Brent, White became an early member of the Okanagan Historical Society founded in 1925. That White is referred to as a source of information in its first reports indicates that she was a respected historian in her community.

White's biographical article on Judge Haynes was followed by a more popular history of the South Okanagan, a series of anecdotal newspaper columns entitled "The Pioneer Trail: Reminiscences of Early Days," published in the *Penticton Herald* newspaper from June to December of 1947. The columns, some of which are printed in this section, demonstrate White's intense love for the region in which she grew up and her attempt to place her knowledge of the southern Okanagan in a wider history not only of settlement but also of the Indigenous Syilx people and their culture.

The *OHS Reports* became a major outlet for White's writing. She began publishing for the Okanagan Historical Society in 1948, when Margaret Ormsby took the position of editor, and in that year White joined the editorial committee on which she served for the next ten years. She was the first president of the newly formed Penticton branch of the OHS in 1948 and attended their meetings virtually to the end of her life. White published fourteen articles with the Historical Society in the fourteen years between 1948 and 1962. In "Mail Day" and "We Cross the Columbia in an Indian Canoe," published in this anthology, White tells the story of a family trip, which offers the perspective of her six-year-old self and also describes the complexities of travel in the interior of British Columbia in 1883.

In the early 1960s, when she was in her mid-eighties, White wrote or rewrote pieces that were never published. Some were begun decades earlier. In a letter to Katie Lacey in 1961, White says "I have found an article I had written a long time ago—of the time of my father's death—it is not typed[,] badly written but a good account and good description of the home life—of that time I cry when I read it. . . . But I will have to finish it—" (September 7, [1961]). That article is printed below under the title "[July 6, 1888] Osoyoos." White's correspondence with Lacey from 1959-1963 suggests that Lacey's interest in Osoyoos and her determination to create a museum there (which opened in 1963) encouraged White's reminiscences and confidences. White was relieved to be passing on her papers—"all the material (Historical) that I have in 'bits & pieces' scraps of writing" to Lacey and the museum (Letter to Katie Lacey, September 7, [1961]). Although twenty-three years younger than White, Lacey died in 1964, only six months after White's death. White's papers were later inherited by the Penticton Museum and Archives.

Hester Emily White, c. 1960.
Courtesy of Penticton Museum and Archives.

White's unpublished reminiscences describe her impressions through personal perspectives and vivid language. Feelings are rarely expressed, unless they are cheerful or appreciative; White implies but does not state her grief and loss at her father's death. Her writing often demonstrates qualities her friend and contemporary Mrs. Elizabeth Daly, a settler in the Similkameen, saw as typical of "the pioneer": "downrightness, . . . pride in what they have achieved, . . . hatred of show and affectation" (135).

In her writing, White refers to Syilx people who are intimately entwined in her life and its important moments. White is described in the notes on contributors to the *British Columbia Historical Quarterly* of 1940 as someone who "has long taken an interest both in the history of the Okanagan and in the Indians of the district" (219), which, while true, does not convey White's personal connections to Syilx people. Some of these appear in her writing about Matilda Kruger, such as in "Over the Hope Trail" below. The mixed heritage daughter of Haynes's neighbour Theodore Kruger and a Syilx woman, Matilda Kruger worked for the Haynes family for at least eight years, from the time White was four or five until she left for boarding school at age thirteen, and probably beyond that, into the early 1890s. Susap, who was present in White's childhood, was another important figure (see "Susap," below). White learned much from Marie Houghton Brent, daughter of

Irish settler Charles F. Houghton and Sophie Nkwala (see Part One, and Brent's correspondence below). Another source of Syilx history and culture in White's writing is Maggie Victor, daughter of Chief Edward of Penticton, who worked as her housekeeper, and White was well acquainted with Victor's sister Louise Gabriel, who also helped White with housework and was active in local Syilx politics (Webber, Personal interview). White also incorporated Mourning Dove's work into her writing (see "Crossing Lines").

White's writing shows her to be curious about and interested in Syilx culture, and letters among her papers suggest she was willing to intercede with Indian agents when Syilx friends came to her for help. Her perspective, however, remains strongly influenced by the values of colonial white settler society. White's connections with Syilx people, furthermore, are juxtaposed with a lifelong public silence about her father's first wife, Julia or Julie Abraham, and their children.

J.C. Haynes and Julia Abraham had two children together, a daughter, Mary Ann, born in 1866, and a son, John Carmichael Haynes, in February of 1868 (see "Crossing Lines"). In September of that same year, J.C. Haynes married Charlotte Moresby, and Abraham and Haynes separated (Hayes, "Haynes-Moore Story" 81). Because of the Haynes family's silence, and that of most other settler families, there are few records of the childhood of Mary Ann and the young John Carmichael. The Canada census for 1881 lists them as living with the Haynes family in Osoyoos, when White was four years old. In 1882, Mary Ann married Charles William (C.W.) Hozier, a settler from Ireland, and they lived in Vernon where he was "head cattleman" at Coldstream Ranch (Lacey, "Hoziers" 143). From there they moved to a ranch near Camp McKinney and then the Fairview district. They had four children. C.W. Hozier died in 1919 in British Columbia, but the date of Mary Ann's death is not recorded. Young John Carmichael was educated in New Westminster "by the priests" (Utley, "Keen Minded Woman" 3). Back in Kelowna in 1890s, he worked on the Lequime ranch (3). In 1892, he married Christina Moore and established his own farm in the Benvoulin area of Kelowna. They had seven children (3). Haynes lived there until his death in 1948, except for the three years he served in World War I (Hayes, "Haynes-Moore Story" 83). Even with her step-brother and step-sister living in close proximity, White, like so many settlers in Kelowna, chose to disown her connection to her Syilx family. Along with the devotedly recorded details of White's memoirs and histories, this erasure has continued in the histories of the Okanagan non-Indigenous community, including in many records and publications disseminated in the present time.

From "The Pioneer Trail: Reminiscences of Early Days"

June 26, 1947

Come with me on the Pioneer Trail,[2]
You may ride my cayuse small.
I will tell you the story of long ago
As we canter and jog along.

We will hobble our horses,
And pitch the tent,
I will bake bannock,
And you sit content.

Hudson's Bay blankets,
Whiffs of camp smoke,
Pungent green fir boughs
Will comfort invoke.

The whispering silence
Will lull us to sleep
But howls of coyote
May make your flesh creep.
Up in the morning,
Breakfast at six,
Horses all rearing,
Secure diamond hitch.

T'will be tough round the Skaget [Skagit],
Tho' the summit will bloom
With flowers to greet us,
As we ride down through the gloom.

Then it is Whipsaw;
Just nine miles to go
To where Allison's log house
Once stood in the snow.

Now it's called Princeton,
Where fine people live.
There we will meet Angus,
Alec and Gib.

Along through the valley
The Similkameen flows,
There used to be Walkers,
Cawstons and Lowes.

Down in the bottom,
Daleys had hay;
Now we ride past
For they are away.

Over the pass
By Richter's corral,
Then down to Sooyoos
Where we will meet Val.

The Krugers and Haynes
Were the first to live here.
They'll soon be forgotten,
So why shed a tear?

Now it's Osoyoos,
Busy and sound,
With Co-ops and counters,
But they ride a Greyhound

We'll cross over the bridge
And up on the east
We will seek Susap
At old Inka-Meep.

Long before the whiteman trod the trails of the Okanagan, and cast his disintegrating spell on its life and spirit, the Indian held sway and was monarch of all he surveyed. He lived a carefree, natural, wholesome life, roaming at will the length and breadth of this lovely valley, which, as now, has always been bountifully blessed. He lived close to mother earth, possessed the secret to this bountiful treasure trove, for his every need, physically, mentally and spiritually.

The Okanagans' *Illahee* (country) extended from four miles north of Okanagan Lake to four miles south of the Okanagan river where it flows into the Columbia river. It is now cut in half by the International boundary line, between B.C. and the State of Washington.[3]

It is a far cry from the yester-years when the Indian, lithe, agile, and unfettered with the ways of civilization, with an easy natural grace, clothed himself in buckskin, left his hair long, painted his face, and lived in a tepee, to the Indian of today in whiteman's garb, living in shacks or frame houses on pitiful reservations.

The outstanding trait in the character of the Indian (individual) was independence and love of freedom, but the tribe was made up of a number of small bands headed by a chief, elected by its members to whom they allowed a nominal authority.

The medicine man performed certain spiritual rites, used magic in healing and judging by the beautifully-made arrow-pointed, peculiar shaped agate knife, performed operations when necessary.

They worshipped a Great Spirit, their principal religious ceremony consisting of the chief's calling his people around him in solemn conclave and then taking the pipe of peace, a small black or green stone pipe to blow whiffs of kinikinik[4] smoke towards the four points of the compass and three towards the heavens in salutation and acknowledgement of the invisible and invincible power above.

To have known the character of the old Indians of yesterday is to understand that their strength proceeded from their forefathers whose nobility was nature-born surrounded as they were with the beauty of the mountains, clad with evergreen fir and pine, bunchgrass covered hills, trickling streams, bordered with an endless variety of trees, with foliage of every hue.

They travelled trails neath pine and cedar, crossed mountains and flats, rode by, or paddled dugouts along a chain of four most beautiful lakes, linked together by a winding quiet flowing river, feeling its way through grassy meadows; its waves glistened like diamonds, into whose depths were reflected ever changing marvellous cloud effects.

The mornings and evenings, with their sunrisings and glorious sunsettings, speak to those who can hear and reveal untold beauties to those who will "be still and know."[5]

It is almost impossible to recapture the atmosphere of that day but those like "old Sooyoosians" can hear the coo of a wild dove at eventide; the drumming of a grouse at dawn; the call of a curlew, the hoot of an owl, and the honk of wild geese; hear a rush of wings and see trumpeter swans light on the placid water of Sooyoos lake; hear the lonely cry of a loon, the laugh of a coyote, and the gossipy chatter of a pair of divers, echoed and re-echoed into the mysterious stillness. Those who hear will have caught just a glimpse of that never-to-be-recovered "Presence" into which the first trader penetrated in 1811.[6]

July 3, 1947

Hast-hala-halt (greetings), this morning, for we find the Okanagans, two thousand of them, camped beneath and through the pines on the flat near Sa-ha-nit-que meaning "falls," now Okanagan Falls.[7] They are ready, with willow traps, baskets, and drying racks, to catch and dry the beautiful blue-green Ste-ween (small salmon) and, as an immediate delicacy, the salmon fry or Stutz-a-wain taken from the stream.

Great preparation and forethought have preceded this June (See-ah-tan) fishing. It is the "service berry moon." The berries have been picked, dried and stored in grass sacks, made from strands of the silver willow bark, and these put into larger receptacles made of cotton-wood bark.

This was part of the women's work to whom fell the task of making the ever moving camp life comfortable. Fire wood a continual chore, as fires smoldered always while in camp. Matting, the summer covering for the teepees in which they lived, was made from the tullies (Tule) or round rushes, sewn together with silver willow threads, which they got at Sooyoos. These mats were re-enforced with slender willow rods.

Teepees were of different sizes, one set of poles for a small family, two sets for a large, and three sets for the council and dance teepee.

Small bone needles were hard to make, the most prized being one made from the small bone in the swan's leg.

Sinews, horsehair, and willow strands for thread, dyed with natural dyes. Baskets for berries and roots, and baskets and wooden pots (no-lo-luaks) for cooking had to be all carefully made.

Hemp, grass, willow, birch and cottonwood bark filled the need.

Cooking with heated stones placed in the pots or baskets, containing food, was the usual method. A bread "Skuleep," made by soaking the moss found hanging from the fir, pine and tamarack trees, was shaped into cakes and baked on flat heated stones, laid on the grass.

Meat and fish were prepared and dried, then stored in caches for winter use. These caches were made by removing stones from the required size hole. To keep mice out it was lined with dried pine needles, on which the meat or fish was placed in separate caches, covered with pine needles and stones placed on top.

Summer garb for the men was a buckskin breech cloth and a small skull cap or band round the head. Women's summer garb was a grass or slashed buckskin skirt, and buckskin band around the head in which was placed a small bone with which to scratch themselves, never using their fingers.

They had beautiful black hair, and would travel for miles to Spotted and White lakes [in the South Okanagan] where they washed their hair in the chemical and alkaline water.

To Stem-tee-ma, the grandmother, was left the authority to impart knowledge and self discipline to the youth, and tell the stories and legends, relating to the lives and customs of the Indian people.[8] Its history and its inherited traditions were as wide in their character as the experiences of the people.

Story telling was known as Chip-chap-tiqulk. It told of the animal people and of legendary times [see Part One]. Some of the women were noted as story tellers and they went from camp to camp to tell them, many of them centering around Sin-ka-lip (coyote) revealing his cunning guile. He was accused of piling stones at the foot of Skaha Lake, and also on the Similkameen river, thereby preventing the salmon from getting up the river, or into the lake.

The legend of Stuan-aw-wkin [Stenwyken, sc̓wanytmx], the hair-covered giant, who lived in caves at Tul-meen [Princeton] was told. His size, tho' he had never been seen, was imagined by enormous tracks found near their food caches and molested fish traps, and whose smell "as of burning hair" created panic among hunters and berry pickers, and tales of which sent children scurrying under the bed coverings.

Stories of the In-cha-mas-ski-lu-ak [ncəcmaʔsqilxʷ], small cave men living in the mountains to the west of Okanagan Lake, were also told.

Na-ha-ha-itque (snake in the water)[9] now given the meaningless name of Og-o-po-go,[10] has according to legend, existed in Okanagan Lake for many moons whereby Indians would not bathe or paddle a canoe or dugout on the lake.

The adolescent boy or girl was subjected to severe training, often being sent off into the hills or mountains alone for days and nights to live on berries and roots and to bathe in cold water, by which means they gained courage, physical strength, and knowledge of the ways of nature.[11]

A custom which might explain the peculiar paintings found on many rocks through the country, required that a young "would-be brave" go out at night to a certain rock some distance from the camp, where he painted on the rock an interpretation of the idea which was foremost in his mind.[12]

The paint he used was crushed rock got at Tulameen, and some say mixed with dried red salmon oil. This secret is remarkable in that it has stood the weather test of years.

Let us now leave Stem-tee-ma with her tales of hairy giants, little cave men and cunning coyote, and saunter through the pines to the council fire where we will see the older Indians sitting about, their stone pipe filled with Kin-ic-ka-nick and being passed from one to the other.

Kin-ic-ka-nick smoke is pungent and soothing and conjures up soughing pines, quiet, trickling water, the distant beat of the tom-tom, and the slow soothing dirge, like humming, of the Indian song.

The younger Indians are lying on the ground, firelight playing over their keen bronzed faces. A riffle of concern is sensed tonight, and as we listen we know. Rumour has come from far down the "big river" by the moccasin grapevine that some palefaces have a camp there. Two Indians have gone down the Okanogan to the Columbia in a dugout, and it will be late fall before their return.

We see Yak-um-tic-um, the chief from Inkameep, and Tenas-ket from farther south. Stel-kia, too, and Susap. And over there is Sin-sa-nat-kin making signs to Su-sa-pkin.[13] We will steal away and leave them to their quiet content, happy in the thought that the paleface will pass them by.[14]

July 10, 1947

It is late September. The trees are clothed in their lovely autumn tints, the day is clear and bright, the air tinged with a threatened early frost. A feeling of loneliness prevails which, through the stillness, is echoed in the cry of Tuk-le-nu-it (loon). The last silvery leaves on the Quaking Aspen seem to whisper and sigh, as we ride along the trail to mouth of the Similkameen where it joins the Okanagan River [just south of Oroville, Washington].

These old trails are friendly trails, and to know them is to grasp their hidden meaning. They amble just where they please, up hill and round a hill in single file, or double, where space permits. There will be many trails abreast, though not so well defined as the main double trails, which later became the first "waggon road."

They were leisure roads, giving one time to realize the hidden beauty of nature, its perfume, and its song. The horse took his time and seemed to know his way, but expected a tightened rein and help from the rider when the trail became difficult.

We ford the river at the foot of Sooyoos Lake and make our way to the camp. Teepees are seen spread over the flat where Oroville stands today.

There are many Indians, for they are busy taking the last of the salmon, the Ta-an-nia, which is not so fat as the St-e-ween they caught in June, but it has turned red. The occasional large red salmon caught in September is the Su-Wa-im, caught in June it is the En-de-de-eque.

Soon it will be time for the hunt, when the deer will require all the attention, for the flesh means food, the skins, coverings for the Teepees, buckskin for clothes and moccasins and gloves.

For the hunt, many weapons, traps, knives, arrow heads and shafts, were fashioned from flint, stone, bone and wood. Thongs from buckskin and the sinews of animals.

The pliable and strong Syringa (whaa-whaa-hai-aalp) [Mock orange or *Philadelphus lewisii*, an indigenous shrub in the Okanagan] and Juniper wood was used for bow and arrow shafts.

The Indian stalked, ran down, or snared his game, also killing with stone shots thrown with a buckskin thong. Spears, harpoons, stone axes, spoons and drinking horns occupied the men's time. They hunted the mountain goat near Tulmeen (Princeton) the hair being beaten and made into a warm blanket.

To make buckskin, the deer skins were soaked in the creek or lake, then stretched on a wooden frame and the hair scraped off with a flint. It was then soaked in deer's brains, then put onto the frame and scraped with the flint.

The result was a soft white chamois like buckskin. It was after the trader came that the Indian women learnt to smoke the skins over rotted wood, which turned "yellow" and gave it a peculiar smell.[15]

A low murmur is heard around the council fire and many of the older Indians have a look of grave concern. The two Indian scouts have returned from the "big river" where they worked all summer at the Trading Post[16] and on their return brought a pair of scissors and a tin cup. The scissors had caused a great commotion and there had been war-whoops and dancing much to the old chief's disgust.

The next year three Indians made the journey and returned with a knife and some white calico.

We will away with very deep thoughts, sad, knowing that through contact with, and imitation of the Shoyahpee (whiteman) the Indian will soon forget that the Spokelitz, a fresh water ling, can be caught through a hole in the ice at Sooyoos, on the first sunny days in February; that clams will bask in the sun in early spring on the shores of Vasseaux [now Vaseux] Lake, where the Indian women will gather them in baskets, spread them on the ground, cover them with dried pine needles, set fire to the whole, and the clam shells would open.

They will not spend days searching for a "hard to find" sugar pine tree, from which gum like sugar will hang or drip from its boughs, and has a peppermint flavour.

Many occupations and customs will pass and, because of his negative sense of values, he will sacrifice his God-given birthright of priceless treasures for a miserable mess of pottage,[17] consisting of trumpery trinkets, red blankets, coloured glass beads, useless muskets and whiskey.

The old chiefs will shake their heads and mutter sadly "Gust, Gust" meaning "it is no good."

But Stem-te-ma will build her sweat house with slender willow rods, cone shape, cover it with cotton wood bark, put earth on top, and a tule mat for the small entrance. She will heat the right number of stones, roll them into a small pit just inside, to one side of the entrance, reverently place balm of gilliard [Gilead][18] leaves and cedar sprigs on top of the hot stones, then sprinkle with cold water, an aromatic steam will rise.

Stem-te-ma will bathe in the cold water and then enter her sanctuary, draw the tule mat over the opening where in meditation, quiet, and solitude she will commune with the Great Spirit and find healing for all her needs.

Though no one can authentically tell of his origin, or speak for certain of his past, it is known that the Indian has inhabited the Okanagan for many, many years before the trader invaded his realm. There are still many interesting facts relating to the life of the Indians, and as we travel the Pioneer Trail, many of them will come in to the picture.

September 11, 1947

On the old trail from Sooyoos to Hope, after one had passed the Frank Richter ranch in Boundary Valley,[19] and the horses had had a drink and a rest at the small creek that ran over the trail with a welcoming trickle on a very hot day, the trail ran down the hill to the valley. The Similkameen River flowed east here for just a short distance, made a sharp bend, and went west again.

Here near the north bank stood a lonely log cabin of rough logs, chinked and daubed with mud, a dirt roof on which dried dead grass and weeds waved in the breeze, a stone and clay chimney was at the far end, a whipsawn lumber door, facing east, stood ajar and creaked on its rusty barn door hinges.

It stood there all alone amid the sage brush on dry baked earth; glimpses of rippling water could be seen through the trees that lined the river bank.

This unimportant hut was at one time a most important post, for it was the first Colonial Government Revenue Station on the Similkameen, the site having been chosen by Lieut. H. Spencer Palmer, an officer of the Royal Engineers, instructed by Governor James Douglas to make a careful survey of the country lying between Fort Hope and the 49th parallel of latitude, a strategic point at which customs officers could intercept persons bound for the Fraser River gold diggings, who would come by the inland routes, from Colville, Walla Walla, in the Columbia district or up the Okanagan or Similkameen rivers from the Washington territory.

This was in September, 1859, and just a few days after, in October, a sergeant attached to the United States Boundary Commission discovered gold on the Similkameen River just south of the 49th parallel. The two commissions had been surveying along the line for some time previous, and H. Bauerman, geologist to the commission, did geological work in the southern part of Similkameen in 1859-61, when the boundary line was being defined.

It was to this place that the writer's father, John C. Haynes, was appointed in the late summer of 1860 as the first officer in charge.[20] He had come out from Ireland via the Panama,[21] to San Francisco, and to Victoria on the boat Panama, which arrived at Victoria on Christmas Day, 1858. Colonel Richard Clement Moody (who was to be in charge of the Royal Engineers) and his wife were travellers on the same boat.

Chartres Brew, who had been an officer in the Irish Constabulary, and had been appointed inspector of BC Police, introduced Haynes to Governor Douglas, and when he asked for an appointment in the new BC Police force his application was accepted.[22]

He left Brew early in January and went to Yale where the "Ned McGowan War" caused alarm; [23] Colonel Moody with twenty-five Royal Engineers, and a hundred marines and bluejackets [enlisted sailors] from H.M.S. Satellite had been dispatched there.

Thomas Elwyn, W. G. Cox, and John Haynes remained with Brew at Fort Yale which was the centre of population and of mining, and Brew was chief Gold Commissioner as well as superintendent of police.

In November 1859 Haynes was appointed chief constable at Yale, which position he held until Governor Douglas sent him to Similkameen as an officer in the Customs Service, Deputy Collector, at a salary of £250 per annum.[24]

Gold had been found at Rock Creek and W. G. Cox was appointed Justice of the Peace and Gold Commissioner there.

Douglas visited Rock Creek, where he found five hundred miners at work and at "Similkomeen" there were a hundred more, many of them engaged in putting up huts; but the earliest settlement of miners was at Black Foot, on the South Fork of the Similkameen, about six miles south-west of Princeton of today, and two miles past Allenby.

Here there were forty miners' cabins, and Theodore Kruger built a store and stopping place across the river, which was known as "Kruger's Bar."[25] It was not long before he had all the trade. Miners leaving the Fraser River were now coming over the trail from Hope headed for the Similkameen and Rock Creek.

Much to Kruger's annoyance a Chinese opened a store and had the cheek to sell rice at $5.00 a sack cheaper than Kruger; he took the matter up with his Indian packer, Kusa-tas-ket,[26] who nodded his head and suggested the matter be left with him. The Chinese had two horses which he took into Hope and brought back loaded with goods.

The Indian went one night to where the horses were tethered, cut them loose, filled his mouth with grass and chewed the ends of the ropes so it appeared the horses had "cut" them. The horses were driven across the river and the store was out of business for a long time.

Kruger came out from Germany in 1854 to San Francisco, and from there to the Fraser where he mined on the "Boston Bar."

The only record of Black Foot is a bill in the writer's possession dated May 6, 1861, and addressed to Marshall and Company from Theo. Kruger. The first item on the bill is "1 bottle rum, $3.00." Later, "another bottle rum (sinking a shaft, good prospect)," then "1 bottle rum (house raising) $2.50," and of course, candles, butter, coffee, etc.

Blackfoot Indians were said to come to trade at Yak-Tulameen [Syilx word for the Tulameen Cliffs] for red paint which may have accounted for the name.

So almost over night our part of the country came suddenly to life after years of quiet and calm, for the Fur Brigade had discontinued its trips down to Fort Okanogan [in 1847] and sent the furs from Kamloops to Hope via the Similkameen and Coquihalla.[27] Except for the Indians going to and fro, the trail was deserted.

Fort Okanogan was being closed this year, 1860,[28] for on June 17 a number of Indians were at the fort assisting the factor to pack up the goods for removal to Keremeos, where a farm and trading centre was to be established [by the Hudson's Bay Company];

stock raising and horse breeding was also in mind.

The goods were being packed in "parfleches" [bags] made of rawhide, and loads made ready for 150 horses. Francis Deschiquette was to be in charge. He built a small log building and farmed on a small scale. Dying two years later he was succeeded in 1863 by Roderick McLean.[29]

So the old fort became a memory. Chinese mining at the mouth of the river and the bars of the Columbia raided the place for its logs and lumber, and the flood of 1894 swept the site clean. So ended the life of the post where the Indians came with loads of priceless furs which piled equal in bulk to the object of their fancy, and called an even swap, thus for a flintlock of the musket type, six or seven feet in length the company received a pack of finest skins stacked to the height of the firearm.

And the story of "Green-blanket-feet," the little Indian girl who married one of the traders, and had two children. The father left, taking them with him and leaving the mother behind. She tried to follow them and went for miles on foot, her moccasins wore out and she tore strips from a green H.B. [Hudson's Bay] blanket she carried. She gave up the quest finally and when she returned, broken hearted, to the fort she had torn all but a remnant of the blanket, hence her name "Green-blanket-feet."[30]

October 2, 1947

"Strawberry Creek" — One wonders who named this little stream that ran across the old trail from Sooyoos to Boundary Valley, though in a very dry season the trickle ended in a cool refreshing pool.

The name conjures up the thought of red ripe berries growing on the grassy banks of the little creek, where perhaps in the long ago some weary thirsty traveller, whose diet had been "bacon, beans, and bannock," rested, spied the luscious fruit, and holding some in his hand, with tender "homing" thoughts blessed the little brook.

We will ride up the creek, about half a mile to where, years ago, the first "lumbermen" plied their trade.

They were two Chinese, Chesaw and Ah Tuck. They camped here, dug a pit, placed the logs over this, and one man standing in it, and the other on top of the log, with a long saw, ripped the planks off the log; this was lumbering the hard way, the "whipsaw way."

At this time they were cutting lumber for the first customs house at Sooyoos, which was being built on the high ground, where Mr. Hanbury's orchard flourishes today. In fact it was the very first building in the Sooyoos district, and was a little more imposing than the little log, dirt cabin on the Similkameen [the first customs post in the southern interior noted in the previous column]. Here Mr. Haynes came as the first officer in charge late in 1861, for he had not remained long at Similkameen. The picture had so changed, that from having just the one post, in April his jurisdiction was extended to include the trails to the interior which boarded [bordered] Okanagan Lake.

Work had not been strenuous for to date only 356 horses, 92 mules and 625 cattle had passed through.

But suddenly the news came of the riches of Cariboo having been uncovered and the rush northward depopulated the Rock Creek-Similkameen area.

Re-organization was necessary, hence the district headquarters were transferred to the more central location on Sooyoos Lake. So began Mr. Haynes' long term of office in the lower Okanagan.[31]

Mr. Cox, in charge at Rock Creek, was transferred elsewhere, and Mr. Haynes had that district included, but in the Spring of '62, the post was closed, and where four constables had been on the staff, only two remained.

The "historic safe" weighing twelve hundred pounds, which Cox had packed in from The Dalles, was moved to the customs house at Sooyoos. . . .

Life at Sooyoos must have had its joys and its sorrows for Mr. Haynes.[32] The beauty of the lake over which the sun would rise and paint the glistening waters either silver or gold was always an inspiration; the days were hot in summer and sometimes extremely cold in winter.

The summer evening breeze wafted coolness and comfort, but the winter north wind, "caribou" as the Indians called it, rose with a gust and made one shiver and fear that it might last for days.

[1947]

Mail Day 1882

The arrival of mail for the Okanagan in the '70's and 80's was an exciting event, to be looked forward to for months. The mail did not come dropping from the sky on swift aeroplanes, or even by slower trains and buses. It was carried over rough and hazardous trails on the shoulders of the tough and hardy mail carriers; such men as "Bristol Bill [Bill Bristol]," Sinsinnat-kin, the Indian, "Ranald," and Jim Wardell [Wardle] of Hope.

I remember particularly the first mail to arrive via the Hope trail, in the spring of 1882. The sack was carried into the dining-room; every one stood round tense with excitement; the seal was broken and out poured the mail on to the table. Official letters for my father were tied with red tape and sealed with large blobs of red sealing wax, personal letters tied in bundles with tape or string, copies of English papers and magazines sent out by Father's aunt, wrapped and tied securely as only she could do, The Illustrated London News, the London Times, Tit Bits, Punch, and the Ladies Home Journal, on the cover of which was a "Lady" complete with huge leg-of-mutton sleeves and an enormous "bustle." Then the bundles of the Victoria and New Westminster papers. All work was suspended while letters and papers were read and discussed.

In one of the coast papers was an announcement which greatly excited my Mother; it read as follows:

> Lord Lorne, Governor-General of Canada, and Her Royal Highness The Princess Louise, daughter of Queen Victoria, will visit British Columbia, travelling by way of Niagara and Chicago to San Francisco, arriving there on September 13. Thence they will embark on HMS 'Momus' for Victoria and then to New Westminster.

My Mother, like so many of her generation, loved Royalty; as a little girl, she had been at Aldershot when Queen Victoria reviewed the troops on their return from the Crimean War. The Queen stopped and spoke to her, for, with her mother and father, Captain Pittendrigh, she had been at Scutari, where the Captain was wounded and suffered the ravages of cholera.[33]

My Father was persuaded that the family must be in Victoria

and New Westminster to enjoy the festivities attendant on the Royal visit, so we all journeyed over the Trail to Hope and thence to Victoria, remaining at the coast for a year.
[1961]

Over the Hope Trail

This unpublished piece by Hester White is undated, but could have been written in the 1950s, as her handwriting, which changed over time, is similar to other pieces written in the 1950s. White wrote about this trip in several drafts—each slightly different from the others. This one was probably meant to describe a trip taken in 1886, judging from the Hayneses visit to Mrs. Cawston along the way, who had just arrived in the South Okanagan in December, 1885. On the other hand, if White's little sister Irene Margaret was only two, that would have situated the piece in 1883. It probably represents an amalgam of many trips taken over the Hope Trail from Osoyoos to New Westminster, and it fits well between two published pieces included here, one describing the family's invitation to Hope in "Mail Day 1882" and the other depicting the return journey in "We Cross the Columbia in an Indian Canoe."

One morning in the early summer mother, Matilda[34] & some of the children were in the kitchen. Busy of course with the early mornings work. My father appeared at the kitchen door and said "Em don't you think we should be getting ready to leave for Hope—the weather is fair—the morn is new—and the trail is said to be in fair shape." I wonder what mothers thoughts were—for she knew after many trips what was required of her in the way of preparation for the actual trip with a family of 4, [what] the 150 miles to Hope meant. There were five of us children [now] who called for clothing for the trip and for New Westminster.

But next morning all was activity in the kitchen and on the veranda. The Hudson's Bay Blankets had been put out to air—the ground sheets unrolled & spread in the far end of the veranda—Matilda was at the little old Singer sewing machine, the very first that had come to Osoyoos in Charlotte's time.[35] It was a chain stitch and made a great "to do" over the stitching. Matilda was patching the large tent, the one we all sleep in—with a piece of yellow soap. She "soaped" the heavy duck or canvas so the needle would go through without breaking. "Jinny" the little Indian woman was sewing the "tent ties" firmly into the little tent—it was new and white—this was my father's and mother's "abode" on the trail & was always set apart, with a small fire lighted outside. Little "Jinny" had very knobbly fingers that curled up. The writer thought it was from washing for she seemed to be always over the washboard, and one day she told us her fingers had been frozen when she was a little girl. There was an Indian war at Sooyoos and her mother had escaped on her horse—holding the baby in front of her and little Jinny had ridden behind (with her arms [around] her mother) the weather was cold and her fingers had frozen. Jinny always had a funny little green fly—with wings—looked like a tiny sail boat—on her shawl so we named them "Jinny flys."[36] And the kitchen box stood over near the corner cupboard—it was about the size of the present day apple box but of strong boards & well maid. It always smelt of Pepper & Bacon & beans. The black Kettles, the Billy Can, frying pan & the cups were on the floor beside it. Matilda had made the Sacks of different sizes of unbleached linen calico—a tape sewn in each near the top. These were for flour, beans, sugar, coffee, tea, oatmeal, etc. & were loosely tied—so when they were thrown into the kitchen box—they "flopped" in and were secure. Of course the side of bacon & the sweet condensed milk can & the syrup tin & the baking powder all went in too. The mantou [manteau] was the cover over the top[37] —clothes, for five children, boots and stockings, all packed in carpetbags—and I don't think mother would forget the syrup of Squills, Castor oil & paregoric and Steadman's powders, and the Quinine & "Charlie Dean" as we called "chloredine."[38]

Meanwhile Pa was arranging which Indian packers would go to Hope, which saddle horses especially the one for mother were to be used, and which and how many packhorses were needed—& did they need shoeing—saddles and cinches, bridles, pack saddles, saddle blankets all to be checked.

At last, tho' rather late in the day the saddle horses were led up to the front of the house. Sin-sin-atkin had already left with the packs, the bell faintly tingling heard in the distance. Mother was to ride "Bee's Wing," Jim McConnell's buckskin,[39] with the black stripe along its back—it was gentle and safe but had lost an eye! Bee's Wing was led up to the South West Corner of the veranda—which was just the right height for mother to put her foot into the stirrups and get into her side saddle. Mother tho' perhaps always a bit nervous on a horse, always looked a picture in her grey broad cloth London made riding habit, felt hat with plume, riding crop and gloves. At last we were off, Val on Rattler, Will & the writer for the first time on horses of their own—to go over the trail. Will's was "Mousie," mine "Small Bones." Matilda was carrying Irene, Susap had Sherman.[40] Soon we were leading our horses over the H.B. Bridge [Hudson's Bay Company bridge over the narrows at Osoyoos Lake] their hoof sound on the rails echoing a "woody rhythm" out over the calm blue water—mounting again we went up the hill to the side of the Kruger's house. Mr. and Mrs. Kruger & family came out to "wish us well." Mr. Bash the U.S. Customs office from "Smiths"[41] was riding with us to the "Hill." He was always kind and considerate of us all. It was evening of a very hot day when we arrived at the Richter Ranch in Boundary Valley—Camp had been made up the draw beside the creek, a short distance behind the Double Richter Cabin. It was cool & shady, such a treat after the heat. Presently Lucy Richter, Frank Richter's native wife, came with butter and milk for our supper.[42] Lucy was a very fine character and always a great friend of mother's. She had five small sons Charlie, William, Joe, Edward & Hans.

Camp was struck quite early—the morning was hot—& the trail dusty—but refreshing was the riffling water of the Similkameen seen through the trees as we rode along. We lunched at Cawston Creek—mother enjoyed the cold water. We called on Mrs. Cawston[43]— the first time we had had the pleasure since her arrival from the East the Christmas before. Percy [the Cawston's first son John Pearson] was about three months old and Mary Jane Gartrell[44] carried him to the sitting room—the long beautifully made & freshly laundered gown hanging nearly to the floor. Our visit was short and on we went, camping that night [at] Keremeos Creek—the High Mountains towering over us! & the sun seemed to be rising over the wrong mountain top the next morning. And so we trekked up along the Similkameen, enduring the heat and dust until we got to Allisons—where we stopped for a visit. I sat demurely in a kitchen chair while mother chatted to Mrs. Allison.[45] The Allison children were playing with the "tame-wild cayotes" & a small boy rode a white colt right through the house. On we went & up to the summit, where we rode along trails on either side of which were beautiful flowers and shrubs—Heather, Rodedendron, Spiria—& Musk.[46] Mother got some plants to take to friends in Victoria— & we camped later near a creek. This always was a favourite camp with the family. Susap had fresh brook trout for supper—and soon after we were soon tucked away for the night.

The camp fire crackled, sparks danced up into the dark, and the flames cast strange shadows on the side of the tent where five of us drowsy, cozy and warm, lay between Hudson's Bay blankets, on a deep fir bough mattress, as only Sin-sin-natkin, our Indian camper, could make. Matilda, "Mother's right hand and my ideal," was on my right, and beside her on the outside so she would not be disturbed was Baby Irene, nearly two. On my left was Will, three and a half, to his left was Val, the eldest, seven. Over at the cook's fire where Susap had just finished baking "bannock" in frying pans tilted against a log to catch the heat—Sin-sin-nat-kin and Pierre lay on their blankets, smoking their small stone pipes filled with kin-nic-ka-nic, talked quietly in the drawl of the Okanagan tongue.

The tinkle of the pack horses, and the clang of the hobble chains on some of the other horses—came through the trees from where the horses foraged for their supper after a long day on the trail. Then foot steps and my Father was making a round of the camp before he retired into the small tent which he and Mother occupied. He came first to our tent, spoke to Matilda, tied down the flaps of the tent, it would soon get chilly and heavy dew would fall and the fire would go out. He went over to where the Indians lay, in low tones gave them instructions for the next day, when we should break camp, the distance we would travel etc. Before entering his tent he spoke and patted "Toots" the black spaniel dog who lay at the door of the tent.

Then all was quiet, the creek sang its soothing lullaby, an evening breeze came whispering through the trees ladened with mountain fragrance, soon dispelling the many camp smells and blessing us all with quiet peaceful slumber. Chopping of wood for the different fires were the first early morning sounds. Then Pierre was lighting our camp fire. Matilda was soon up & dressed and off to the creek to wash and comb her hair. She would soon be back with the tin basin of cold water, get us up, wash and dress us. Soon we were 'round the mantau [manteau] having our breakfast. Pierre & Sin-sin-nat-kin would get the tents down, blankets rolled—roped—Horses were in—saddled. Soon the "gnawing of the ropes of the diamond hitch"[47] were heard—the horses bracing themselves, puffing out their bellies and grunting in protest.

[196?]

We Cross the Columbia in an Indian Canoe

It was late October, 1883, and the Haynes family were in New Westminster, a long way from our home in Osoyoos.

We had been in New Westminster since June, 1882. At that time my father had come down to attend officially, the visit of the Marquis of Lorne and Princess Louise, Mother and the children to enjoy the gala occasion. Then, owing to an outbreak of smallpox at Osoyoos, we were obliged to remain. On September 8, 1883, Baby Sherman made his appearance and there was further delay until Mother was able to travel.

With great hope my father made all preparations to return over the Hope Trail, but word came from Jim Wardle, express, postman and storekeeper at Hope that the Indian Sin-sin-at-kin had arrived from Allison on snowshoes to say that the Trail was closed because of a blizzard, that he had left the pack train at Allison's, and what should he do? After much discussion of ways and means it was decided that we should return by way of Portland and Sprague [Washington]. Word was sent to Sin-sin-at-kin to return to Osoyoos with the pack train and to send the ranch wagon with the camp outfit to Sprague to be there on a certain date.

Plans were soon made to travel by boat to Port Townsend [Washington] and thence by train to Portland, so began a memorable journey.

Memories of the voyage are hazy as I was sea-sick all the way but after landing at Port Townsend I remember climbing a long flight of stairs with Matilda who carried Baby Sherman wrapped papoose-fashion in a light gray shawl; we would stop now and again on small platforms to rest and look out at the ocean.

On arrival in Portland we stayed at a large hotel, all somewhat confused by the noise and tall buildings . . . Matilda had a bad toothache so Mother took her to a dentist who said the tooth must come out, in preparation he gave her a large drink of brandy and waited for it to take effect, but the result was not quite what he expected, Matilda felt so much better, she got off the chair, put on her hat and coat and walked out.

Memories of the trip by train from Portland to Sprague are of a day coach very bare and not too clean, the only passenger I remember was Malcolm Sproat who sat across the aisle and further back in the coach; he was Commissioner of Indian Affairs.[48] About lunch time he came and asked me, a small girl of six, to share his lunch with him, we were nicely started when he unrolled a small packet, it smelt so horrid I knew I would be sick if I stayed so I ran back to Mother. Matilda laughed and said the stuff was "pumpernickel" a German cheese, but the dictionary says that it is a bread of unbolted rye, whatever it was I can still smell it when I get on a train.

The track followed the banks of the Columbia for some distance then stopped. By this time I was back with Mr. Sproat and was horrified to notice that the engine and part of the train were on the other side of the river. Mr. Sproat explained that it with some cars had crossed on the ferry and that our coach would soon be ferried across, coupled on, and we would once more be on our way.

It was evening and dark when we reached Sprague, then the terminus of the railway, though construction was being carried through to Spokane Falls. Much to Mother's horror it was learned that the better hotel had been burned down a few days before and the only place to stay was a navy's resort. We got out of the train on the side away from the hotel and were told to go round the end, but Matilda took two of the children and crawled under the train. Nothing daunted Matilda.

The large room we entered was a general purpose room, dining, waiting and lounge, a narrow stairway led up one wall with no railing and a narrow balcony also without a railing, ran round the four sides of the second floor, the bedrooms opened off this. Matilda was kept busy herding us up and down these stairs. As the wagon had not arrived we spent two nights in dirty, uncomfortable quarters. Pa was busy gathering provisions for so many people for a long journey and feed for the horses. At last the wagon arrived but then arose further difficulty and delay; the wagon would not hold the family, baggage and provisions;

another team and a light buggy had to be purchased.

The team, small white cayuses were named Pancake and Patsy, it was rumored that they had once been with a circus; they were extremely wild. When Pancake's heels were up, Patsy's head was down or he reared up on his hind legs, but, as Pa remarked, "the load would soon take the devil out of them." At last everything was ready.

Though it was late in the day Mother begged to make a start, to travel a short distance and camp where it would be clean and quiet. A few miles out a camping place was found on the banks of a small stream. Val, Will, Irene and I slept in the covered wagon, Mother, Pa and the baby in the lighter one, the two drivers some distance away, and the horses tied to trees. Mother said she did not sleep as the wagon was on a slope and she was afraid it would slide down into the creek. Pa told her not to be silly as, of course, the brake was on.

At nine next morning we were ready to start on what was to prove a difficult and tiring journey. Mother, Pa and the baby led the way in the light wagon, Pancake and Patsy prancing and rearing; Matilda and we children followed in the heavy ranch wagon. The going was slow for the trail was rough and dusty and the loads heavy, 20 miles a day was good going.

On the 4th day out we came to "Wild Goose Bill's" place. Pa had known this character on Wild Horse Creek in 1864, when he was a miner and packer; his real name was Samuel Wilbur Condit, born in 1840 near New York. He came west in 1852 with an uncle and from then on his life was one of adventure. At one time he fought in the war against Chief Joseph.[49] He married an Indian woman and had three sons. It was evening when we arrived and camped near a stream; slight misfortune followed for Pancake got loose in the night and found the oat sack. After eating his fill he drank from the stream. In the morning he was dead. A horse was purchased from Wild Goose Bill and broken to harness before we could go on which caused quite a delay.

Now the road was up and down steep hills. Sometimes the two ponies would balk and refuse to pull up hill; the ranch team would have to be unhitched, hitched to the light wagon and pull it up the hill and then back to take us to the top. Camps were poor, water scarce and wood even scarcer except for sage brush here and there.

Finally we came to Grand Coulee and the Columbia River could be seen far, far in the distance but many miles and many hazards had to be overcome before we reached the river. The so called road was the most difficult yet encountered, down into deep ravines or gullies then up the far side. The trail so steep, that going down the hind wheels had to be "rough locked," that is, a chain was wound around the hind wheel and fastened to the front axle which caused the wheel to drag and act as a brake. Going up again the teams had to be double hitched. In many places it was considered safer for us to walk.

Thirty miles out from Coulee was a camp which had been started by a band of U.S. soldiers on their way to Lake Chelan where a fort was planned in 1887 as a defence against Indian aggression, but was abandoned as unnecessary after the Nez Perce war. Here we found cord wood which must have been hauled for some miles. We camped to rest and clean up, for remember we had a small baby with us and in those days there were no disposable diapers.

Proceeding again, the ravines were, if possible, deeper and more frequent, the worst aptly named "The Three Devils." But, by rough locking and doubling, we finally reached the bench land from where we could look down on the river. Several Indians were on the bank, by "moccasin telegraph," they had heard of our approach.

There was the river, our goal for many weary miles, but what a terrifying sight it was. The wide swirling waters, four frail canoes drawn up on the bank, the Indians dressed in buckskin, their long hair in plaits and their faces painted. Somehow, we, the goods and wagons must reach the other side.

Pa went ahead and talked to the Indians in Chinook, after much "wa-wa" [talk, consultation] it was decided that the family all go over in one canoe, blankets, provisions, etc., in the other. The Indians protested that there were too many people for one, but Mother would not think of the family being divided, so in we got, first an Indian in the bow with his paddle, then Matilda with Will and Irene, then Mother. When she was seated Pa gave her the baby wrapped like a little mummy in his warm gray shawl. Pa got in and took me, I sat between his knees. Val was in the stern with the other Indian paddler. The canoe was shoved off into the swirling waters, the other Indians shouting that we would never make it. Pa cautioned us to be very quiet and to keep our eyes on the far bank, not on the rushing water. Mother grasped the side of the canoe, as she did so her fingers were in the water. She made the sign of the Cross, blessed us all and prayed for a safe crossing.

Pa in a low voice began to tell us the story of the river, how it rose far up in the mountains starting as a little stream, and, as it was fed by other streams, became the great body of water we were on; then that it was 1,200 miles long out to the Pacific Ocean where the water was salt; how David Thompson a fur trader with the Hudson's Bay Co., like Mr. Kruger, was the first white man to come down in a canoe.[50] We heard of the million of dollars worth of furs bought from the Indian trappers for beads, shawls, etc.; of gold discovered at Wild Horse where he had been sent for the government. From a mysterious source a biscuit was produced for each of us which we were told to munch slowly, so the time passed and we forgot our fear.

The Indians paddled with all their might, the canoe going forward but at the same time drifting down stream, at last the bank was reached and one by one we got out on shaky legs and made our way to level ground where soon a camp would be set up as it would be some time before the two wagons could be brought across. It took two canoes to ferry the wagons. A log was placed to brace them the right distance apart to permit a front and back wheel in either canoe. The poor horses had to swim. At last Matilda was able to make up the beds in the wagons, and a weary family tucked away for the night, Pa being the last to retire. The Indians were camped some distance away and seemed friendly but he wanted to be sure that all was safe.

Next morning the small wagon train was on its way, and after what seemed to be hours and days of endless treking through sage brush, cactus, sand and dust, up hill and down, shut up in a springless wagon, we came to the Okanagan River which had to be forded twice. At long last we sighted Hiram Smith's ranch at Oroville, he came out to greet us and wanted us to rest, but Mother thanked him and said we were very anxious to get home; three and a half more miles.

Coming to the Boundary fence, the sound of the gate bars being thrown one by one on the ground, the first woodsy sound of "Home" along through the pasture and past the little grove of aspens all aquiver in the afternoon sun, and as we rounded the grove, the home bars of the big corral appeared and a flock of "barnyard biddies" came to greet us. They must have heard the creaking of the wagon wheels. As we came through the bars Justinian Pelly (a brother of Mrs. Sillitoe)[51] who had been left in charge of the ranch greeted us and at the kitchen door was Susap to help us down from the wagons, the first to make their way up through the Okanagan Valley. The house was nice and warm, the white cat Tom and the red one Fixy rubbed gently against our wool stockinged legs, purring with content. How good to be home at last.

All was not joy in our home coming for several of our Indians had died of smallpox brought in by some Indians who had been in Hope, where they had picked up a tent belonging to a white man who had died of smallpox.

The disease spread rapidly; there was no one to care for the poor Indians except one or two of their own people who had had the pox. Mr. Cawston wired to Victoria for vaccine and vaccinated many with a buckskin needle. The Indians were buried at Joe Creek on the east side of the lake.

So ends the story of one of the many journeys of the Haynes family.
[1961]

The following extended conclusion to White's story, recounting more about the smallpox epidemic at Nk'Mip in 1882, is taken from a typewritten draft of the same article, entitled "We Cross the Columbia in a Canoe."

But there was sadness when we arrived home for small pox had taken a number of our old Indian friends, they had been cutting rails up on Haynes Creek for my father the year before, were camped there in fact, when the "pox" struck with all cruelty and eighteen of them had died, without medicine or relief.

It was in the fall of 1882 that Cultus Jim, Joe Galagher, Agath, known as Crooked Nose Sophie were in Hope, there they found a tent which had been tied up and thrown in to the bush. They brought it to Sooyoos in to the Indian camp on Haynes creek, where the eighteen were cutting rails for Mr. Haynes.

This tent had belonged to a whiteman who had small pox, so the infection came and eleven died, without vaccine, or care, for all were afraid to go near them. An appeal was sent to Victoria, and vaccine was sent in, R.L. Cawston volonteered to vaccinate them, putting "buckskin needles"[52] in cork he scratched their arms with this, he was granted $200 for his heroism, bought a gold watch with part of it and often related the story of the scene across the lake, where the unfortunate souls were dying with out aid, except that rendered by Susap, Batist[53] and one or two others; they had the pox in '63, when twenty-five had died at the head of the Lake.[54]

Poor Alexander who had been left in charge of our house gave Cawston the key who took it from his sticky hand.

Mrs. Kruger told how Old Soo-yoos, Mary Smith's father, came to the bridge and called to her to give him some "hy-ui lumigen'hum" meaning "bad smelling medicine" the poor Indian meant Carbolic Acid, and she had none, not even a dose of physic. Jim McConnell had the contract to supply the sick camp with provisions, and Mr. House [A.E. Howse] the Indian Agent was sent down from Nichola to do what he could.[55]

Then the Kruger children, Dora, Rika, August and Theodore, were taken very ill. Cawston had taken serum from Su-mae-qu-lix an Indian woman, and vaccinated Mrs. Kruger and the children. August was the worse, for hours she cared for them, her anxiety greater for Mr. Kruger was away at the coast; Bill Schoonover[56] who was over at Grand Prairie (Grand Forks) heard of her plight and rode over to help, he stayed up all night with the children to give her much needed rest.

Those Indians who died of small pox were buried at Joe Creek, on the east side of the Lake, north of the Haynes home.

[July 6, 1888,] Osoyoos

It was late afternoon of a very hot day, the sixth of July 1888. Mother and I sat on the south east shady side of the house; not a breath of wind came from any direction—the lake as calm as a mill pond. A loon called away across the water and echoed into the beyond. Gossippy divers chattered as they swam, leaving a long fan-like ripple behind them glistening in the late sun. The sky, not a cloud to mar its beautiful blue, was reflected, together with the mountains and the sage-brush covered hills, into the very depths of the lake. Happy children's voices came from the shore where Will, Irene and Sherman paddled near the shore. Matilda was with them so they were safe. The baby, Susan, just eight months old was asleep in the green room. Mother had been reading a letter from Pa—written from Victoria June 15th, where he had gone on Government business the month before, in which he mentioned he would arrive home today. The letter had been carried to Osoyoos by Hayes Van Volkenberg, buyer, who had come to buy sheep from drovers taking 12,000 sheep through to the upper Okanagan and the Nicola. The flock had spent a day in our upper pasture and Mother had received twelve head as pasture levy. An air of happy anticipation prevailed as Pa was expected home this evening from his trip over the Hope Trail, and my brothers Fairfax and Val who had been at the Rev. Percy Jenns' school in Victoria[57] would be with him. With Pa home we always felt safe and he always thought of us all with kindly gifts so that his homecomings were doubly joyous. Mother looked particularly nice today, she wore her hair, very black in a four strand plait and pinned in such a way as to almost represent a coronet. She was wearing the pink "peek-a-boo" blouse as my wee brother Sherman called it—a white Swiss muslin—real muslin of those days—Sherry would peep through between the dots and say "Peek-a- boo." We then shelled some peas, lovely tender, green ones grown in the lower garden.

Mr. Turkey Gobbler had sauntered up from the corral—he seemed to know "shelling pea" time. He would swallow the pods until he had had his fill then in spite of the heat would fan his tail, drag his wings and strut off showing all his beautiful toleage [a style of painting pottery and tin] colors—bronze, green and turquoise blue painted over the black— his buzzard [breast beard] showing his age and great importance. Back he would go to the corral—later to roost on top of the fowl house as it was beneath his dignity to perch with the cackling barnyard biddies, dressed in varied hues, who were as independent as you please, laying just when they felt like it—in the early spring when the grass got green and the days warmer—then they were broody and nothing would change their minds not even to being thrown in the lake. Then there was Rooster who traded around. He would grow his spurs and become quite aged before finding himself in the pot. When it got dark someone had to catch Gobbler and put him in as an owl had got his predecessor [sic], which, together with two hens had been packed over the Hope Trail—Mother was so proud as no doubt they were the first turkeys in our part of the Okanagan. But they were doomed—early in the Spring the hens would wander off into the pasture to lay, and we children hunted in vain for their nests—one day to find only a few eggshells and some feathers, Mother cried over the loss—this last trio had been got up from Walla Walla in Washington—these places stood out in my child mind—Hope—from where our H.B. Company goods were packed—where we rode to on our way to the Coast and where the beef cattle were driven.—Walla Walla—from where my father got the teams of horses and where the organ had been bought and brought to Osoyoos—and a huge hand washing machine which Mrs. Noah must have used in the Ark—Then Colville to which place a packer had been sent with packhorses to bring back the wheat, oats, oatmeal and flour for the ranch. Johnny Pierre, the Indian boy came slowly up from the Corral, playing a native air on his Jew's harp, plaintive and sweet.[58] He went into the woodshed—came out with an armful of wood and into the summer kitchen with it—came out again with two buckets which he took to the lake to fill. When he returned he came to the verandah to say he was going for the cows—which would be at the north bars waiting to come in to the big corral, below which in the little pasture their calves were kept—Matilda would milk them later.

As the cows passed along in single file I noticed Peghorn, Lottie, May and Spotty followed by Johnny with his jews harp. Mother would go over to the Kitchen often to see how the dinner was progressing as after camp fare Pa would expect something special—then she would take the field glasses and go to the north side of the verandah to see if there was dust on the trail down from Richter pass. Dust meant travellers—but none rose on the breeze. The children had their suppers and were put to bed—the milk was brought in, put in covered pails and lowered into the well as was meat, butter, water. This well had been dug 80 or 90 feet down before the house was built, but it seemed impossible to get below the blue clay, so the little water in it was not good.

No travellers arrived so Mother spent a lonely disappointed evening—next morning about eleven o'clock my half-brother

Fairfax rode up and without getting off his horse said Pa had sent him on ahead to let Mother know he would be delayed as my Aunt, Connie Pittendrigh, ... was coming up to visit and they would arrive later. We spent a busy day as usual and about six o'clock mother and I were alone on the verandah when R. L. Cawston rode up on his horse, Dirty Bill. Mother was surprised as she knew he should be at Princeton preparing to take a beef cattle drive down to the Coast. She said "How's John?" Without answering her Cawston rode on down to the corral. Mother called to me to get the office key. I ran into the house and took down the key which was about six inches long and hurried down the path to Pa's office—opened the door and Mother was prostrate in my father's chair, Cawston standing by. They had come in by the other door. I went to her and child that I was poured out my strength and courage to her. I seemed to know by instinct that my father was dead. I got mother up to the house, gave her some wine. A hush seemed to descend on the whole household. I sat with mother on the verandah overlooking the lake—she and I were too stunned to speak but thoughts must have crowded her mind as they did mine. As night descended on the lake a late moon rose over the mountain casting shadows across the still waters of the lake—out near the long island as we always called the spit of land across the lake a riffle appeared in the moonlight, an occassional duck swam in the light. It was to the far side of the long island Pa would row in the "rocking boat" about 5 a.m. undress and dive into the deep blue water off the shore.

What did his death mean to us as a family? Just nothing short of disaster. Our home had been a home protected and guarded by a loving, kind, generous father who was planning a secure future for each one of his six children. We had freedom in every sense of the word. The whole outdoors as a playground, the lake to bathe in in summer, to skate and sleigh ride on in winter—horses to ride, green pastures to roam in, trees to climb—good food, good clothes and a good father and mother.

Would mother live up to the responsibility imposed on her? For thirty years Pa had endured hardship, loneliness and sorrow to provide this home for us. Was it to be swept away?

I got Mother to bed and stayed with her all night—patted Florida water on her head and arms and fanned her for the night was hot. Rubbed her knees as I had so often done before and no one came. Matilda was busy with the children, Johnny Pierre with the milk dishes etc. The first to arrive were Mr. and Mrs. Daley [Daly].[59] Mr. and Mrs. Kruger were in California. The blinds were all drawn in the large dining room and there we all sat. Not a word was said.

About 3 P.M. a waggon with the black coffin on it pulled up on the east side of the house. Tom, my father's lovely sorrel horse was tied on behind with my father's saddle on and his riding boots reversed in the stirrups—Val got off his horse for he had ridden from Allison's and ran into the dining room to Mother, all was quiet and then we were all in the green room, the black coffin there with the Immortelles,[60] candles in the brass candlesticks lighted. Mr. Henry Nicholson[61] reading the service, room hot and close, odor unbearable, and then we were at the graveside, numerous people many, many Indians.

Then all were gathered in the dining room, the large door in the hall was open and I was on the corner behind it—reduced to tears. Joe McKay found me put his arm around me and took me to the Blue room to comfort me. He was Joe McKay, the Indian agent, and a very wonderful man.[62]

R. L. Cawston was there, Harry Pittendrigh, Henry Nicholson, Bob Stevenson, Hiram Smith, of course Gregoire (chief),[63] Susap for he told me he had received a letter from my father to meet him at Osoyoos at that time. Susap had been herding cattle at Grand Prairie then. He said he never worked for anyone again. [1888, 1960]

May 1st, 1895, Osoyoos

Yes, it was the 1st of May so many years ago. I had been out from England, at least back from England where I had been at the Convent of Notre Dame at Plymouth, Cornwall. Today Mother had received disturbing news from Victoria, no doubt from the administrator of our estate (the Haynes estate) E.A. McPhillips, to the effect that the property was to be sold—20,000 acres of range land—and our cattle which did number 3,000 head when my father died in 1888.

I was to drive Mother and little Susan over to Krugers where they would catch the stage at 8 a.m. It was a lovely May morning and as we drove along I noticed the hawthorne was all in bloom, so beautiful and fragrant. I returned to the old home and realized that I was to be in charge of the domestic affairs of the house. Irene, who was 13, was with me, but she had always been excused from household duties so the responsibility was all mine. James Stuart was staying in the house. He was the new manager appointed by the Trustee. Louis Cuppage[64] shared his room and Tom Curry and George Inglis were part of the ranch. Of course Val, Will and Sherman were home too, so my household consisted of nine for me—so inexperienced.

My first problem was yeast to be made with potato water, flour, sugar, salt and hops tied in a little muslin bag and let boil. Then the starter must be added when it was lukewarm. I placed the butter keg near the stove to be kept warm, waited and wondered. It foamed and bubbled but did not rise to the top of the wooden keg, so I sent Sherman, then 12, with a note to Howard Bullock Webster[65] asking his advice—should the yeast rise to the top of the bucket, etc. I think he rode back with Sherman to tell me if it foamed and "worked" it was ripe—just put it away in a cool place and use a cupful when I had to make bread. He told the tale on me many times, always with laughter. So my days were full with cooking three meals a day and keeping the house clean—washing and ironing. One evening after the "men" had been fed and Irene and I were in the kitchen, a man arrived at the side door and asked if he could get a meal and stay the night. Lo and behold he was riding a bicycle the first to venture into that part of the country. He was one of the Smith Brothers, stationers at Vernon. Next day an Indian came to tell Val Smith had ridden down through the reserve and to their amazement it had only two wheels—one here—"you-wa" and one there "you-wa"—pe yakka courie coupa oyhoit.

I rode down to Okanagan Smith's with Irene to see the orchard in Bloom. Susap, Johnny Stilkia [Stelkia] and Baptist came one day from Inkameep to ask me to order some fruit trees for them— so I made out an order to Laritz Bros. for them,[66] also ordered 50 trees of various fruit for ourselves.

When I came from England I had a precious gold sovereign given to me by a very dear friend at Saltash [in Cornwall, England]. My wise brothers advised me to buy three little pigs which foolishly I did—one broke its leg and someone stole the other; one was Stubbs for he had no tail and he loved the gingerbeer we made, which was no good—could drink it out of the bottle. Another day Irene, Sherman and myself were rummaging in the old cellar, storehouse, where once had been stored provisions of every discription, wines, liquors, Cross and Blackwells' jams etc etc. Now it was empty but we found a mysterious stone bottle, took it up to the house and pulled the cork. It was sweet and delicious, so we each had two or three drinks—then we went to the lake and got in to an old boat—Sherman at the stern—Irene and I were rowing. All at once the boat filled with water. Sherman jumped off into deep water his cowboy hat floating on the water top. Just then Mr. Dick Sidley rode up and rescued us. We had been drinking "Curoco" [Curaçao, a liqueur]. Sidley asked me if I could teach school and would I go to Sidley.[67]

Then one morning we noticed a hack drive past the house towards the corrals, shortly after a Mr. Dick Lowe, deputy sherriff came to the door and asked to take an inventory of the furnishings etc, in the house. I calmly told him I was in charge as Mother was away and could not allow him in. I realized then that he was the deputy sherriff and that we were being sold out. Irene and I pulled Mother's buggy to the back of the house. This and the contents of the house were all that were saved. Our own saddlehorses were driven down in to the pasture but curiosity made them wander back to the stables and they were sold, Sherman's for $4.00.

Pemberton, the sheriff sat in the hack, having had more than a plenty and Windy Dick Lowe was the auctioneer. There had only been the early roundup so the count of 1,300 head were sold for $13.00 a head—no calves were counted nor yearlings, and the land 20,000 acres for the mortgage, $90,000.00.[68] At lunch time I walked to the stables to tell Val lunch was ready. In his good-hearted way he asked Tom Ellis to come to lunch. As we walked back to the house Sherman ran up beside me, tears in his eyes, and said "—Hess ask Mr. Ellis if I can have my horse"—I turned to Mr. Ellis and asked if Sherman could have his horse. Tom Ellis answered "yes, until I need him." Tom had had 'more an plenty' too and it was rather amusing to see the butter smeared over his grey beard when he sat at our lunch table. And so we were penniless and homeless and were required to move by the 1st of

October—no wagon, no horses, no nothing but some furnishings and a buggy.

While Mother was away the trees arrived from Laritz—50 of them, the Indians had picked theirs up at Krugers and believe it or not Irene and I dug the holes carried pails of water from the lake and planted them. Our little orchard was to be between the house and the office. Each evening we carried a pail of water to each tree.

Irene and I had gone to bed quite early one evening and were soon fast asleep. I was awakened by a terrible "hullabaloo" downstairs. The clink of bottles and glasses made me realize the "men" of the household were on a spree. I got up and stood with my back to the door, for there was no key, and prayed. I did not disturb Irene for she would be more frightened than I. Then I heard the men coming upstairs for there were three other bedrooms. Val and Will were away, Sherman aged 12, slept in the far room. I stood in the dark and listened and prayed and was thankful the four went to their rooms. Next morning as I came down stairs Mr. Stewart was telling Sherman to remove the bottle and mess before Miss Haynes came down, but Miss Haynes was already down and said "yes, Mr. Stewart, better remove the mess yourself." He very humbly set to work.

Mother arrived home to hear that the worst had happened—we were sold out—though she had obtained an "injunction" against the sale, but the messenger from Penticton had been waylaid with a bottle and the telegram had never arrived. We soon had notice from Tom Ellis to vacate our home. Irene and I were sent with a note up to Boundary Valley to Frank Richter asking him to rent us the Nicholson ranch at Rock Creek—the Henry Nicholson place—which my Father had had the first mortgage on, but had never registered it, having too much respect for a valued friend. Frank Richter had the second mortgage and had foreclosed. It was decided that I was to ride over with Dora Pittendrigh and August Kruger[69] to Rock Creek to prepare the cabins, which had not been occupied for three or four years, except by horses trying to get away from the flies and by bushrats.

It is years since this all happened but since then I have evidence that our home at Osoyoos with the 150 acres of land was held under a Military Grant (the Thos. Forgey) which was good for 99 years, and then ours by Possession. Mr. Patterson had surveyed it and it was not included in the mortgage and those who conducted the sale that day in May 1895 were all trespassing for it was not until later that a great friend of ours "inveigled" my Mother into signing a "quitclaim" to our home and land for $300.00; and he had been influenced to do it after Ellis had approached two others who had refused to stoop so low.[70] My one worst friend, Tom Ellis, who immediately we left put in his pre-emption stakes. And this had happened to the family of J.C. Haynes, who had so honorably lived a just true life for thirty years at Osoyoos.

It was Dan Driscoll who lent us a team and wagon to haul our effects to Rock Creek and Susap, the Indian, who lent Mother a team to take her in the buggy to Rock Creek.

Signed,
Hester E. White

One afternoon when things seemed so hopeless and forlorn I said to Mother, "I would love a chicken dinner." She replied "catch the chicken, kill it, and I will cook it." I caught the poor thing, got the block and the ax. Irene was to hold it. When the time came I failed. Irene said "mother and I will do it," so she took the ax, Irene held the poor victim—shut her eyes—turned her head. Down came the ax, Irene let go and away ran the chicken with its head awry, cut in the neck and blood running out. Poor thing went into the chicken house. George Inglis came along later and caught it and one or two others and killed them, and we had chicken dinner after all.

[196?]

Stenwyken

This story was told to me by an Indian called Susap. He was a wonderful man and I was proud to call him "friend."[71] In 1872 as a young man he went to work for Mr. Barrington-Price near Keremeos and in 1888[72] he came to work for my father, Judge Haynes, at Osoyoos. He helped with the cattle and served as guide and packer when we travelled over the Hope Trail to the Coast. He also guided Bishop and Mrs. Silitoe [Sillitoe] over the

Hope Trail to Osoyoos in 1880 [and in 1883] and in consequence he was sometime called "Silitoe."

He came to see me one Christmas in Penticton and related the following tale.

"Stenwyken, The Hairy Giant who smelt as of burning hair, left large tracks near the Indian caches from which he helped himself to the dried meat, fish, roots and berries stored for the winter.

"He was often seen at the mouths of creeks catching fish. He was a peaceful man and never harmed the Indians.

"However, one day in the long ago at berry time a young Indian maiden disappeared; it was feared that Stenwyken had carried her away. After a long time she returned to her tribe and told the following tale. Stenwyken had seized her and carried her to a large cave, the floor of which was covered with skins of bear, deer and mountain sheep. She was given roots, berries, dried fish and meat to eat and was not molested or harmed in any way, but a large stone was rolled across the mouth of the cave making her a prisoner.

"When alone she made moccasins of some of the hides, hoping somehow, sometime, to escape. One night when the moon shone bright she noticed that the stone was not quite tight at the cave mouth and she slipped out. After travelling many miles and for a long time she found her people.

"Some years after this episode, a maiden of a north Okanagan tribe vanished from the camp. Three years later she returned and related the story of her capture. Stenwyken had seized her, put pitch on her eyelids and carried her to a large cave. Sometimes afterwards she gave birth to a baby but it died. In due time pitch was again put over the eyes and she was carried back to a spot near her people's camp. There the pitch was removed and she was released. Stenwyken remained hidden and watched her safe arrival."

The cave in which Stenwyken lived is supposed to be a large cave near Princeton. Miners on their way to the Fraser goldfields sometimes hid in the cave when they feared the Indians the story goes.[73]

A. E. Howse, who had a general store in Princeton, used the cave to store his merchandise, and before the Hope-Princeton road was built the mouth of the cave could be seen from the

Kettle Valley trains.

A Japanese, working in a mine at the north end of the Valley was awakened one night when something heavy brushed against his tent. Thinking it was his employer, he went to the door and there stood Stenwyken with his hands out making signs for something to eat. He was given food and left. Again near Lumby [in the north Okanagan] Stenwyken came to a tent with hands out asking for food and left peacefully when satisfied.

No doubt the Susquatch of Harrison Lake and Stenwyken of the Okanagan are one and the same. As he has done no harm he deserves consideration and his freedom to roam at will.[74]

[1962]

Susap

Time has changed the ways of the Indians in the Okanagan Valley, and taken its toll of the many old friends we used to know, and almost the last to pass is Susap, at Inkameep, in his ninety-seventh year.

To have known Susap all one's life was indeed a privilege, for he was a noble character, honest, trust worthy, industrious and a willing worker.

He was one of three brothers, the well remembered Chief Batiste [Baptiste], of Inkameep, was one.

Susap first worked for Mr. Barrington Price, on the old Hudson Bay Place at Keremeos, in 1872, where Mr. J. C. Haynes first got to know him, and asked him if he would care to come to Sooyoos (Osoyoos) to care for his band of horses. Susap did, and remained working for Mr. Haynes, until the latter's death in 1888 after which he never worked again for anyone.

Susap was renowned as an outstanding rider, and could handle and break the most difficult horse.

He was a reliable packer and guide, and was sent twice over the Hope Trail to Hope to bring to Sooyoos, Bishop and Mrs. Silito [Sillitoe], this was in the year 1882 [1883], when General Sherman also went through to Hope. They came a second time,[75] and Susap was the guide and packer, after which he got the name of 'Silito.'

That same year he carried the writer over the Hope Trail, on his horse. She was a very small child, and he had many ways of amusing her, he would pick bits of bark off the golden pines along the trail, and explain in Chinook the different forms and figures; he had a small baking powder tin with a string attached, and when we came to a creek, he would lower the tin into the water, and give her a cool drink, this saved getting off the horse.

One summer morning Will, then a small child, fell into the lake, the waves were washing over him, no one was near, but Susap far out on the lake saw the accident, and immediately jumped into the water and swam to shore. Rescued the child, held him up by the legs and ran to the house with him. Susap was rewarded for many years with a suit of clothes, shirts, etc. by Mr. Haynes.

Sophie his faithful and kind wife died last winter, and of his sons and daughters, Manual and Margaret, who is now Mrs. Billy Kruger,[76] are well known to the writer. Twenty years ago Susap was thrown from a wild horse onto a stone, and his hip was broken, after many days Dr. White was sent for, the leg was set and weight attached, but it was soon removed, for Susap believed in a "nature's cure," consequently he never walked again without crutches.

Faithful to Church for he was one of Father Pandozie's followers, his memory will live on through time, and our prayer is that the "Saghalie Tyee kwonesum kloshe nanitch nesika skookum Tillicum [God forever take care of our strong spirited relative]."
[1949, 196?]

Correspondence with Mourning Dove

In preparing in the 1930s to write a biographical article about her father, J.C. Haynes, for the British Columbia Historical Society Quarterly, *Hester White sent letters to many sources for information including Mourning Dove (Christine Galler) and Matilda Kruger. The letter below from Mourning Dove, written in 1934, is the only one White received from her; Mourning Dove died in 1936. See "Crossing Lines" for a discussion of White's connections to Mourning Dove and Part One for information about Mourning Dove and her writings.*

Inchelium, Washington,
Twin Lake Camp, Nov 5-34 [1934]

Mrs. RB White
Penticton, BC

My Dear Mrs. White;
Your letter recently reached me forwarded from my home
town Omak Washington, which was rather a surprise to hear
from you. I feel honored to have you interested in my effort as a
"writer."

I have frequently heard of your family. If I am not mistaken
you are Val Haynes sister and the wife of Doctor White who has
charge of the Indians in your locality. I know Dr. White and also
Val and his family but never had the plasure of meeting you.

The history of your father is very interesting to me. In my
research work among the Indians I have talked to the old people
many times about Judge Haynes and his considered kindness to
the natives in the past. He was very much loved by the Indians.
Cheif Batise [Baptiste] and other old timers of Inkameep Reserve
still remember when he first became in charge of the Custom
office at Osyoos in 1860. The old people have good memories and
anything you wish to know I am sure they will tell you of your
father. They could tell it to you better than I could. Because my
information is from the old Indians and book history.

I knew Father DeRouge ever since I was a small child attending
his church at the old Colville Mission when he was a darked
haired and full bearded man till he died at the Omak Mission an
old man with his good faithful work done for the Indians. Father
Pandoza was another charcter that is very interesting in the
Okanogan country of the early Missionaires.[77] The old Indians
still talk of him in kind tones.

I know Matilda Kruger and her sister Mary [see letter below].
In fact they are first cousins to my father. Her mother was a
sister to my grandmother who was part Nicola Indian, and
we have many relatives around the Penticon and Smilkameen
Reserve including Inkameep. I use to live at Inkameep, teaching
the Indian children from the year 1914 to 1918. I gathered much
valuable material from the Indians while there to write my latest
book "Coyote Stories" legends of the Indians. It is mainly to suit

children interested in animal stories that the natives tell their children. It is written just as they related the legends to me.

My other book is a novel based on facts and written in Montana while I lived there in 1912. It is called "Cogeawea" and sell for $2.50. "Coyote Stories" are priced at $2.00. This last book sold out the first edition in three months last fall after publication by a Western Publishing House in Idaho. Many of the schools are buying them for White children to read, so I am very thankful with its success. Being the writer of the books I have no comment to make but leave it to the reader to be the critic of my efforts. I am hoping that I will be able to produce another book this winter if my time and health is spared me, to continue my work.

I am sure that you can produce valuable historical information about the early history of your country. You are in a position to do so, and if I can be any help in a small way I shall be happy to help. But as I said, the Indians that are old and have the first hand information could help you much more than I can. They may not know exact dates but could give you accurate information by searching their thoughts.

I am forwarding your letter to Mr. Guie of Yakima who has charge of my affairs in filling orders in the book list.[78] My reason for this is, that I am afraid the International Line Customs will not allow us to send books across the line without some tangle of "red tape."

With best wishes for your success in your chosen work, I wish to remain,

Sincerely yours,
[signed] Christine Galler
(Mourning Dove)

[1934]

Correspondence with Matilda Kruger

Matilda Kruger [1864?-1935] lived with and worked for the Haynes family from about 1882 until at least 1890, when Hester White and her siblings were sent to school in England after their father's death in 1888. The "we" in this letter no doubt refers to both Matilda Kruger and her sister Mary Kruger Crook. See "Crossing Lines" above for more on Matilda Kruger's relationship with Hester Emily White.

Matilda was the daughter of Theodore Kruger and a woman from the Colville reservation whom Mourning Dove identifies in the letter to Hester White above as her grandmother's sister. On death certificates for both Matilda and Mary Kruger Crook, the mother is named Mary Lambert. She is enrolled by the Colville agency from 1893 until her death in 1928. Her birth date, based on her age recorded in the rolls, is estimated as 1855, which would have made her too young to have been Matilda's mother, but these dates are estimates and they fluctuate, as do Matilda's dates.

Listed as seventeen years old on the Canadian census of 1881, Matilda Kruger would have been born in 1864, and her sister Mary three years later. When Matilda moves to the United States in the 1900s, her birth dates change according to the estimated ages she gives or is given.[79] William (Billy) Kruger, who does not appear on the 1881 census, was born in 1872 ("William" 110). According to White, he was a half-brother of Matilda and Mary (Letter to Ann Briley) and, through Chief Francois, was given land in Penticton, where he became a well-known horse breeder and racer ("William " 110). Mary and Matilda Kruger are listed in the 1881 census as members of the Kruger family, which also included as head of household Theodore Kruger and Chrestenza Kruger, whom he married in 1873, and their children Dora, Fredericka and Johann August Kruger. Another son, Theodore ("Babe") Kruger was born in 1883. The two parents and the children, including Matilda and Mary, are listed as "German" under "Origin."

Hester White remembers that around the time the Haynes family moved into their new home in Osoyoos in 1882, "Mary [Kruger] left then and Matilda came to be all round help and 'teacher' to Mother and we children" ("First Memory"). She also believes Matilda as a child received some education from the school run by Mrs. Glennie (Susan Allison's mother) in Hope (Letter to Ann Briley).

As Matilda notes in her letter to Hester, she and Mary gained some education at the Chemawa school. They are listed as students at the Chemawa Indian Industrial School in Salem, Oregon, in 1895. It seems neither were in the best of health. Both Matilda and Mary are recorded as having "scrofula," a glandular swelling that is often associated with tuberculosis; it can also refer to any type of skin disease (Marion County Oregon Census, 1895 2:41). A local directory for Salem City, Oregon, lists them as working at Chemawa in

1896, Mary as a seamstress and Matilda as a laundress ("Chemawa" 131), and they maintained these positions through 1897 (Official Register of the United States 1897, 1: 802).

The two sisters continued to work for the Indian School Service for about ten years, though they parted ways. By 1899, Mary Kruger was working as a seamstress at the Siletz Indian Reservation Agency in Oregon. She became a matron there from 1901 until at least 1905. Matilda Kruger worked as a seamstress in Covelo, California, in 1899, and then at Hoopa Valley, California, from 1900 or 1901 until at least 1905. [80] In 1907, both are listed on the Indian census rolls at the Colville agency as with the United States Indian School Service.

Matilda Kruger in regalia portrait, c. 1901,
Hoopa Valley, California [Augustus Wlliam Ericson].
Courtesy of the Clarke Historical Museum, Eureka, California.

In 1909, both sisters are registered on the rolls for the Colville agency as "accepted claimants of Moses Columbia." The Colville Indian Reservation was established in 1872. In 1884, the Moses band of Columbia Indians joined the nations on the reservation, including the Colville, Arrow Lakes, San Poil, Nespelem, Okanogan, Chelan, Entiat and Methow people: all had unilaterally been designated Colville Indians (Arnold, "Bartering" 4-7). Matilda remained on the rolls for the rest of her life. Mary, too, is on the Colville rolls, but she is also listed from 1908 on at the Siletz Indian agency in Oregon as the wife of Jesse Crook who is enrolled there. Mary Kruger probably met Jesse Crook at the Siletz Indian Boarding School, where Crook had been a student in 1900, according to the United States Census for that year. The United States Census of 1910, which shows both Mary and Jesse Crook living on the Hoopa Valley Indian Reservation in California then, describes Crook as having been born in California, as was his father. Jesse Crook's occupation is "shoemaker" and Mary Kruger's is "Matron." Crook's mother is from Oregon. On the Indian census rolls for Siletz of 1933, Jesse is further described as being a member of the Smith River tribe of the Confederated Tribes of Siletz. United States City Directories show that Matilda Kruger is also at Hoopa Valley from 1910 to 1916, working as a seamstress.

The United States Census of 1920 shows Matilda and Mary Kruger living in Omak, Washington, on the northwest border of the Colville Reserve, with Jesse Crook recorded as a rancher and head of household, and Matilda as "sister-in-law." Jessie Crook, the daughter of Jesse and Mary Crook, born in 1908, is living with them and attending school. The Indian rolls for Colville of 1920 show both Matilda and Mary had received allotment numbers for land acreages. A policy of allotment had been in the process of being implemented on the Colville reservation since 1900, following the Dawes Act of 1877 (for more on the effects of allotment, see the note preceding Marie Houghton Brent's correspondence with Hester White, December 14, 1959 to February, 1960). The United States Census of 1930 lists Matilda as sister of Mary K. Crook who is head of household, and records her daughter, Jessie. They own their home and live on a farm (probably their combined allotments), according to this census.

About a year after the letter below to Hester White, Matilda died on October 27, 1935. Only a few months earlier she had married Alex Nicholson, a mixed heritage son of Henry Nicholson (White, Letter to Ann Briley), on July 21, 1935. Henry Nicholson, a British settler in the Similkameen, had known both Susan Allison and Hester White. Jesse Crook died on Oct 2, 1936. Mary Kruger Crook lived with her daughter Jessie and Jessie's husband Harry Watson on her Colville allotment until her death on March 3, 1945. White reports to Marie Brent in a letter in 1955 that Jessie "comes up to see Babe [Kruger] quite often" (October 20, 1955), suggesting family relations reconnect and continue.

Omak Washington,
November 20, 1934

Mrs. Doctor White

Dear Hester,
I received your letter. We did the best we could in answering all your questions. We lef lots of stories out because it was hard & unplesant memerry of our young days it was nothing but hard work & no schooling. When we came to Uncle Sam we were treated like human being and went to school, had a very nice time we went to Chemawa School through our Mother because she belonged here. The History what Mrs. Kruger told is very good for her age, its all true what she told, only one thing she was mistaken about the white woman.[81] Mary is a little better she had to sit up a little while at the time & write, she has been at the Hospital 2½ months. Hope the History will be good. You'll have to correct the spelling. Please send the Paper some time.

Dear Hester did you know your mother owed me $250 she borrowed in Victora just a little befor you all went to England she promised to pay intrest never mind the intrest I will be very glad to get the $250. There is enough of you all to pay this little sum, as I am really in need of it, I wanted to ask you for a long time I thought you knew of it. I wrote to your mother at Sooyoos & no answer. We must thank you for the nice groceries you [sent] up in July.

> With much love from both of us,
> Matilda Kruger
> Star Route
> Omak Wash.

Omak Wash.
Nov. 14, 34

History of early days

> Yes Solders with the officers
> American soldies
>> Genaral Miles
>>> "Sherdern [Sheridan]
>>> "Shermen [Sherman]

328

They were intained [entertained] by Mr. Haynes & then by Mr. Kruger.[82]

Heard tell of Indian fights with white people, the battle field was on Sooyoos flat where Hudson Bay Building [was;] it must be built after the war, it was Mr. Kruger's home after the [that;] stood on the grave yard. *[Matilda Kruger may be referring to conflict between miners and Syilx around 1856. See Part One, "Indian Lore"]* The Indian Races were most interesting they came from all parts of the country & white people too, They were dressed in gay costums & they were very orderly. The women were gayly dressed & they took par in the races. The race track was commenced from your last home up to the Creek the races lasted about 3 days. Yes we hear Mr. Kruger telling about a Steam Boat coming up from America up to Sooyoos lake in Hudson Bay time.[83] Mr. Kruger was over seer of the Hudson Bay Co. The Co. traded in furs with the Indians, Mr. Kruger an expert in judging furs. Yes the Indians use to count with sticks & stones, the Indians used a string to tell the days of the week 1 big knot for Sunday and small knots for week days, they knew all about the moon[,] the changes of the moon to make 1 month. When an Indian woman expects the Stork to come she quietly with her nurse go up the Creek or River & when the newcomer comes they bathe it in the creek & after walk home, she was considered not brave if she dident do this— You can leave this out if you want to.

About the earth quake we heard the Indians talk about it, Mr. Kruger said there were a quite a crowd came from America asking about earth quake & tell about a big mountain a terrible fire & smoke coming out of it, then Mr. Kruger explained all about it to the Indians, Some Catholic Church gathering on this side we don't know just where. A Priest we don't know who was telling the story about old Cheif Tonasket, he had 9 wives and the Priest told him to choose one of those women & marry her & he said no, I am a cheif I can have as many wives as I want, the Priest told him he must support the other women & children. Well the earth quake started at mid night the same day, he went to his camp alone & that night when he got home, he lit fire in his large tee pee he was sitting by the fire, when he heard a great rumbling noise like thunder[;] in a few seconds the [ground] opened wide his Tee Pee fell in the open ground he & the fire went down he was up to his armpits he was held there and another Shock came

329

& opened the ground he clung to the Tee Pee poles & got out, he was very much frightened for he remembered what the Preist told him about his wives, he hurried & got on his horse & went to the Father & told him, he will marry one woman.[84] He was a fine looking man & a good leader as a Cheif, he was well to do, he had lots of cattle and horses. & a great worker among the Indians in his tribe were well behaved.

Mr. Kruger traded with the whites, Indians & Chinman, when the gold rush was at Rock Creek. We never heard the Indians bring gold, its was all way furs they brought very expencive furs, the black Cross fox very rare, he gave from $60 to $75   there were the silver and red fox were not so expencive.[85]   In early days Mr. Haynes was gold commistioner for Koodney.   Mr. Haynes was a married man at that time his wife [from] New Westminster her maden name was Miss Mosby [Moresby], she was beautiful woman with golden hair blue eyes and pink and white completion a lovely figur she was tall & graceful. She was the first white woman [in Osoyoos region] after the Indian war, she was the first to have hand stand sewing machine.[86] We heard he [J.C. Haynes] was governer & he was Judge and Customes officer, he had a 1000 head of cattle & very fine blood horses. Mr. Haynes was a perfect gentleman & a perfect man, he was well liked by every body, & he had a nice home.

Later he married Miss Pittendrigh [Emily Pittendrigh, Hester White's mother] from New Westminster, she was a very nice young lady & highly educated she played the paino & a nice singer & spoke good french and latin. They had 6 children and she was a good mother and a good maneger. She was a small woman about 5 foot 2 inches, she had aburn hair & large gray eyes & she was very pretty. When Mr. Haynes went on business Mrs. Haynes took charge of the office. Mrs. Haynes understood a great deal about medicines & very kind to her neighbours all ways ready to help in sickness. We dont know when you were born. Mr. Low [W.H. Lowe] was a constiable. He was in pardnership with Mr. Haynes in cattle, he came from Canda [Ontario], he was a good rider hunter & sportmen and he was well liked by every body. Mr. Causton [R.L. Cawston] he was Mr. Haynes's forman in your times.[87] About the bridge, the government built it during the Hudson Bay Times.

We forgot this the Indian War was before the Hudson Bay times at Sooyoos. Hudson Bay Store was moved to Smilkmeen for a while then the Hudson Bay Co. moved the Goods to Kamloops on pack train they located the Store at Kamloops where they had a big trade. Mr. Kruger was manager at Sooyoos Smilkameen & Kamloops. In later years he came back to Sooyoos & bought the [HBC] buildings and started his own general merchantdise, he continued in trading in furs with the Indians, he went to Victora once a year to get his goods for the year. One year he met a very nice german young Lady she was very fair & with a pink & white complecation with large blue eyes, she sang beautiful german songs & was well educated in German. She was a good house keeper & a splendid business woman, and a good mother.[88] Mr. Kruger was a good size man he was fair with blue eyes, strong & healthy in his young days they had a nice comfortable home. [1934]

Correspondence with Marie Houghton Brent

Hester White carried on a long correspondence with Marie Houghton Brent, initiated, as well, from White's need for information about her father, J.C. Haynes, while preparing a biographical article on him. See the essay "Crossing Lines" for discussion of White's and Brent's relationship and Part One for more information on Marie Houghton Brent and her writings.

Lavington, BC
Sept. 8th, 1936

Dear Mrs. White,
Thank you indeed for your most kind letter rec'd in due time and I will say that by name you are far from a stranger to me. Tho' I have never met you, we are truly kindred spirits as if it were of an old tie that I did not know you even dreamed of. Our fathers were old friends who respected each other very much, such an acquaintance is not made to-day—and the children of the old timers are the strangers to-day, they do not push themselves any where. I am glad you take enough interest in our country to take up some bits of history left and both Mr. Brent and I would gladly assist you if we could. I think we may be able to give you

a little but we need time and if you could only come up to see us a day or 2. We are in a rough old cabin now tho' once a good house, but it would be camping for you and may do you good to tough it for a short space. I have a comfortable enough spare room tho'—it sure is a lovely country here too. Wonderful change from Penticton. Lavington store-people would direct you to us. We have no way of going any where, we wouldn't fix up our old car so we gave it away.

I always wanted to look up all the oldest Indians still living & take up what they say first hand & translate it into English, but I have never been able to do so.[89] No way to go now—it is a pity for they are dying off too. If you care to, come hunting time and let us know before time—with kindest regards

> yours very sincerely
> Marie Brent

Lavington P.O. BC
Feb. 24th, 1938

Dear Mrs. White: -

Your most kind & nice letter came some time ago for which I thank you very much.[90] Its good to have a real talk with some one of same mutual interest as ourself—there are but few left now. I am glad you are writing a book on your father's life, it was of much worthy interest. I only knew of him from my father, he thought a great deal of him and used to like to talk about him, I think he must have been a real man, a quality not always to be found nowadays.

Yes, I can be of much assistance to you, truly their lives were closely linked to-gether—a sort of tie, not understood to-day, and you are so good to think of it too. And it sort of fills a gap of much to be desired—

I have clippings of father and doings of what worthy men wrote in the papers of him different times, as well as first hand information. I would long to tell you everything, people were jealous of him and tried to give him a black eye whenever they could.[91] Men of his type always had enemies, ever the world began, I guess—but he also had staunch friends—that never wavered. Norris even a tenderfoot like that, in trying to help Vernons, he even knocked him.[92] I must ask you to patience it would take time. We wrote the history of the [word omitted] but the Vernon news wanted it, it's a long thing—in it was a nice piece about Judge Haynes and all the people we could think of—its been in [with] the Vernon news for nearly a year.[93] I don't know why, they are not using it, or what they intend doing with it. The Historical Society wants it, but I think we should publish it in book form—how I wish you could have been here with me last summer. I was at the mercy of others, all & all. We are on a most beautiful place but I think I don't want to be cut out of the world another year. I hardly know where or what we will do, but we are mining all the time in a small way—this was reverted land [land returned to the Crown] of 320 acres, 14 miles (on the bench) from Vernon—not far, in summer good roads, but I can let you know where we are or if we are still here, you surely could have a lovely holiday here. I have a nice spare room—this is so different from anything down there [in Penticton].

I will be happy to come & see you if ever we come there, who knows what we may be doing or when. I must close with kindest regards from us both. Willie is sickly often—it's discouraging. One thing, he has an army pension now and helps out.

    Believe me

        Yours very sincerely

        Marie Brent

Willie may be going down this spring. If so I may go with him, tell me if your always home or away sometimes. It may be in April around the 1st or 2nd week.

June 13th, 1946
Marie Brent
Tonasket Box 309
Washington

My dear Mrs. White

I come to surprise you, and do not know why I did not do so before this. In my loneliness, I have often thought of you, and now this Centennial business of the Boundary Line makes me think of many things, but only one shall I mention to you—as our fathers were so closely connected in many ways. Add whatever you like down below here.

Capt. Houghton (at that time) & Judge Haynes, brought the first cattle to go over the Boundary Line at Osoyoos in the late 60's as partners in this purchase; but Captain Houghton, went down here looking for cattle & bought them from Mr. Splon [A.J. Splawn, see note in previous letter] of Oregon, later of Yakima, then Loomis afterwards—½ of these cattle went to the Coldstream Ranch, Capt. Houghtons Army Grant of 1400 acres from Her Majesty Queen Victoria from the Crimean War. These Cattle grew to a big herd—Judge Haynes ½ grew to a very big herd also—He was custom officer and everything else there was—so few capable of taking office at that time, he was a grand man too. Mr. Splon often wondered what became of the young English Capt. who quoted Shakespear by the yard. But he was destined to carry out a military career for many years and went as high as one could go at that time in his country.

Let me know if you get this.

Kindest regards, Sincerely

Marie

Penticton, BC

RR 845 [94]

Oct 20th [19]55

My dear Maria Brent,

Greetings and cheers from Dog Lake this beautiful morning sun shining on a calm blue lake—I live right on the beach. Tho' it is very rough and windy at times the lovely times make up for it—I cannot tell you how happy I am to receive your letter this morning & how suprised I am to know that you are <u>well</u> and comfortable—It is some time since I drove through Republic and I always wonder where you are—now I know[95] —I drove through there in June going to Castlegar with a friend of mine. I suppose your husband Billy Brent went with his brother Johnny Brent to the Spanish American War—that was in 1897 or 8 was it not. Johnny Brent died about a month ago in Vancouver at the

Shaughnassy [Shaughnessy Veterans] Hospital.[96] He was buried at Lumby—Caroline and Ellen Arnott [note in pencil: Ellen Basset (Arnott)] went up to the funeral—there was a great gathering there! Fred Bassett-Ellen's brother died the night before. He was the last of the old freighters who I remember in the old Fairview and McKinney Road. Yes the Pioneers of our Valley are getting very scarce—Val Haynes [White's older brother] was named the Good Citizen this year at [unclear]—he will be 80 on the 21st of December. We Haynes; 6 of us are all still living—Susan the youngest a Mrs. Gardom lives in Vancouver. She comes up each year in August to stay in Dr. Bill Whites home[97]—Sherman Haynes my youngest brother was up a year ago July from San Diego—so we were all together for a dinner—Mrs. Tweddle who was Mrs. Frank Richter [Richter's second wife, Florence] has been laid up for such a long time broke her hip—and being so heavy has not done so well—I go over often to see her. Her son Frank Richter is MP Social Credit for Similkameen. Ed Richter and Joe Richter[98] both live in Penticton. Billy Kruger and his wife Margaret were in this afternoon he is a fine old man. Babe Kruger[99] is a great friend of my brother Will and Val-I often cook a meal & go down and have it with them—they are all alone each living alone! Is your brother Ed. Haughton with you its years since I saw him. I was present at the Kelowna Birthday dinner Caroline Renshaw—& Christine Haynes[100] cut the birthday cake & Old McDougall lighted the town cake. Let me hear from you again for I am always interested in you! Our Valley's too noisey now in the summer months—tourists & visitors keep it busy! I liked it better in the old days when we could ride quietly along the trails! Mrs. Saucier[101] died this last summer she was a grand person—had weathered many sad difficulties! Mary Kruger's daughter[102] comes up to see Babe quite often—I must try to see her next time. I would be very pleased to have notes of historical interest from you—I am supposed to be writing in the Boundary that is Midway, Greenwood, Boundary Falls & Phoenix. I must close now and tell you again how happy I was to hear from you.

> With very kind thoughts
> best wishes & love
> very sincerely
> Hester E. White

Mrs. R. B. White
Xmas night 1956

dear Hester:

Sorry I could not write sooner to thank you for your nice letter and sweet little hankie you sent me Dec 13th but Ames wrote to or sent you a Xmas card from this house anyway—Every thing is in same [position] as you saw it—all at a stand still.[103] We were glad to hear from you. I was trying to write to you.

Well the big day Xmas is over and the house full are all gone home 5 kids just the noisy age—house is dead now.

I was reading your precious letters and I saw again, where you said at your fathers court house, in 1876—Osoyoos—my father's picture was taken with your father and mother when Vall [Valentine Haynes] was a baby. Now I do wish you would have 6 taken from it for me, would you. I could give you one of them, I will pay for them, you must have a good photographer there. I have never had one of father taken in Okanagan it must be [have been] some [someone?] going thro there with a rare camera. I told you I had my fathers whole life history. Friend got all his military life in the Crimea, England, and Ireland all from the Canadian Encyclopedia, and all what I know will make a book along with his ranching & expeditions. He was lst member of parliament for Canada [for Yale-Kootenay], then got attached to his old military life again, sent from one end of Canada to the other building Esquimalt Harbor as naval station then called to the Trouble in Saskatchewan,[104] got stationed at Winnipeg, recruited, built up armies in Esquimalt, Winnipeg and Saskatchewan after this all over was sent to the largest military station in Canada, which was Montreal, city, & surrounding country 3 Rivers even [Three Rivers, now Trois-Rivières]—building up Army stuff until he had a large Brigade of different Regiments, ever so many to each Regiment. I had that picture of Massed Brigade, here in Republic but some one either stole or destroyed it just before I came to this house, when I was sick in the hospital, can you then wonder. I feel bad at times—seemed all the way, that people thought I should not have this or that & helped to destroy or take away from me. These Invitation cards I showed you here were going to be destroyed after my fathers death, but I suddenly saw them in the kitchen & redeemed them again, but I did lose some of them, any way there were enough of them left to show a lot of things. I don't know the object of doing all this to me, by people I was good to, too—always. I never said a word but they saw me pick these things out and take away—

I am going to have one of fathers pictures taken over by Crescents store, I asked them last year. If I get them, I'll give you one of them—in memory of your father's friendship with father. They thought a great lot of each other, had so much in common of the 1st days of Okanagan country—I had so much to say to you but there'll come a day—I have no one with that warm link else where—always have to be on diplomatic terms else where—or else be pulled to pieces—

Think I told you not to send that piece of my great great grand fathers history [Pelkamulox's history]. My friend told me to keep this, she has another copy of it—I have another big bunch of that. It was chief N'Kwalas father & his own enough for book too, some from Tradition not in book Ethnology, some from Ethnology, Smithsonian by Mr. Tate, dear old Historian, only for him, there would have been no record of these precious people,[105] born to rule and got killed (Pelkamulox, N'Kwalas father) for befriending the 1st White man—the Hudsons Bay factor Kamloops called his son NKwala (my great grandfather) Chief Nicola, who was a great friend to them—When Governer Black was killed Lady Black sent for him by courier to Head of Lake Okanagan to come at once to her & family. NKwala did & took whole Entourage & sons with him & took care of Mrs. Black & family for one year before help came from their headquarters.[106] I would like to get memoirs of Hudson's Bay, is this what you are sending for? Give me address please so I can send for one too. They knew people there, Kamloops, took Nicola for a Shuswap I think—I got one of the business books of H.B.C. years ago, they knew nothing of the real History of their Governers death. I have not the book now. Governer Black was killed in 1840—Taite—N'kwala died in 1858—or 9—Taite in Smithsonian Institute. I have more from Tradition than he has. Poor dear old man worked hard, but sometimes got the wrong people, being no other—as I think or recall I jot down.[107] Got a book full I guess—when I get into brighter room, I can really go on with it—think I have all— I really must stop. These people are going to town at once, send, there it goes again too—please excuse mistakes & all. Please send

me address of Smithsonian—Name of Book–No. of Volume—
love—Marie Brent

Republic Washington
March 26th, 1957

Mrs. (Dr.) White
Penticton

Dear Hester: –

I hope you are well, I wrote to you around New years and I have not heard from you, then I thought possibly you may be with your sister Mrs. Gardom [Susan Haynes Gardom] for a while, I think you said she was in Vancouver. However, we will all feel better now that the snow is gone. Tho' cold, is still nice. Republic and us here were all froze up all Winter. Republic water pipes were busted, but not much here only no water. But we, in our country, have nothing to cry about have we? Some places still bad. We had no blizzards or anything else. Republic is a high cold country, we look for that, but lovely in Summer—a long, long winter this year and dark weather, that's what gets me—every body well here. Ed— [Brent's brother Edward Houghton] said it was a long drought. One morning after raining all night cats & dogs, stopped, sun came out a few minutes just the time he came to breakfast—he looks well.

People are all busy on making history here, I gave them & Tribune, Tonasket, good stuff about old chief Tonasket they wanted. [*She adds a note:* My great grandfather chief of all Okanagon made Tonasket Chief as a young man as a helper here—from Bk of Ethnology—Smithsonian—Washington D.C.] They are all thinking of going to his grave with some flowers, decoration day—and a plaque later on sometime.

The dark winter kept me from writing much this winter, too bad. I could not see from eyes tearing from pain in my arm & back. I could not see—

Do you know about general Sherman, maybe you do. They, here, would like to know or find the old trail he came on, I don't know. Your brother was called Sherman, your people must have known him or of him well. Please, tell me just as soon as you can or write to Mr. Kelly & tell him all about what you know of Sherman, tell him I asked you to —will you please, dear Hester— write

Mr. Alvin Kelly
Manager of the Bank of Republic
Republic P.O.
WN.
your old friend Maria Houghton Brent

lots of love, <u>write</u>
Marie

April 30th 1958

My dear Hester: -
It's time I Thank you for nice little card received Eastertime, glad to get it. I was just about to write you when it came saying you were to write in a few days. Now, I have been looking ever since but none yet—and I am bubbling over with so much to say—
First of all: I want to tell you Mrs. Ames would like you to say when you are, or, I mean intend coming. She wants to be home when you do come, because they Mr. and Mrs. Ames intend going to Seattle to see their sons over there and families this Spring— she wants a good visit with you this time, so do I. Tell her soon, so she will know what to do—some times she gets a houseful here too, and we want you to ourselves, no one else here to bother— and before I forget will you bring my Fathers photo, may be we can get a copy of it, a snap shot from it here. I would sure like to see it. I don't tell Mrs. Ames completely every thing, there are so many of them, I don't like being discussed, and when things get into all their different opinions, babies & all, it is a very different article. Are you writing much? I feel you are, what are you doing for the Centennial of BC? I am writing lots or at least friends are copying, typing lots for me, heaven bless their hearts—
Can you send me address of Province—Victoria paper? Very

soon? Or just address—do you still have the Hotel Incola in Penticton? Incola was supposed to be named after a great chief of long ago. That was my great grandfather and should have been (chief) Nicola. His name was NKwala. Hudson Bay Head men called him chief Nicola and Teit called him both but in the Smithsonian Institution, Washington D.C. —they called him Chief Nicolas. Headquarters at Ne-comop-lex Head of Okanagan Lake and King George III gave Him that Reserve, Okanagan No. 1. Reserve—and gave him medals to seal the good faith as such home for him, his descendants and His people and people's descendants, for all time—the dear old man died pleading for the welfare of his children, their descendants, and that of his peoples. He died in Grand Prairie, on his way to Kamloops for conference with the Hudson's Bay Governor—as was their custom always. I have more of this, you can see it when you come. He made his younger son chief on his death bed, young Nicola, my mothers father, to take his place when the old man died. They sent word by a courier, to announce his death at Hudsons Bay Head quarters. The Governor sent their messenger to meet the cortege and bring the body on to the H.B.C. Head quarters, Kamloops, which they did on 2 horses. Upon arrival there the officials ordered his burial near Govt. House, gave him a military funeral and ordered a big camp made near by, so they can all take turns to guard the Body. Hudson's Bay people as well—so nobody can cause any ill doing—all winter. When Spring and good weather came they exhumed the body & took it home to his own Reserve and head quarters Head of the Lake (Na comaplex) accompanied by some of H.B.C men—he was buried with some of his medals, given by King George III. They [laid? hewed?] Timbers and put a large cross on his grave. I remember seeing it, was still all right, but I heard since I came here it fell down. Some wanted to put it up but some did not want to bother, they were strangers and squatters any way—they were jealous of me too, he [Nkwala] had some more medals but everybody of his died[,] his nephews took possesions of them, Chilihitchas. NK'walas own only Sister's children of Nicola Valley, Salista, and his brother Alexander Chilihitcha, took them and said they were made heirs to the Okanagan too. No such thing I reported them to Ottawa, they [the Chilihitchas] did not get [the] Okanagan [chieftainship of Head of the Lake reserve] but I did not say, who I was.[108] Lots more to say please write to us very soon I'm still looking for long letter you were going to send me cold here yet it is very high here you know, last day or 2 grass is growing—below the house here south side was all a lake, but going down now. Lots of love from me dear pardon hasty scribble—love from Mrs. Ames—everything in the world happened to us since you were here but we are all getting better. I even had a little operation on my nose I think hurt it when I fell that time affectionately—

Maria Houghton Brent

May 11th/[19]58

My dear Maria,
Greetings this quiet Sunday morning and I wish to thank you for your most interesting letter received Friday evening on my return from Victoria where I had been for a week—my son Jack & Shirley took me as a birthday present—Victoria was lovely with all the beautiful gardens—flowers—shrubs—trees—especially the Pink May—& the Dogwood & the Azaleas—I have never seen the Dogwood so lovely all the way from Hope to Victoria. Bucharts [Butchart] Gardens are a wonder made in an old Cement Quarry. I simply cannot get down to see you and Mrs. Ames sooner than two weeks—this week is the Historical [Society] Annual meeting at Osoyoos with Banquet on Wednesday & Thursday the Pioneer Dinner here over 400 people expected. Then the Parade on Saturday. Mrs. Ames better take her trip I would not like to interrupt that—will let you know when I can.—Oh! I saw the Stage Coach with the six horses parade in Victoria—with all the outriders—starting on its trip to Barkerville—It's all trucked between towns[109]—and also I was at the ceremony by the Indians at the Totem Pole in front of the Parliament Bldg.—crowds of people—many Indians—the Pole is 116 feet long and weighs 13 tons.[110] I have not been able to write much for I have had a lot to do with Will Haynes wife. She was dumped on my doorstep right out of Hospital in January—nearly died one night—then was in hospital for six weeks—then back here again—I then got her into Valley View Lodge but getting her things & her clothes & going to see her and take her out is all I can do, I was <u>81</u> in April

341

From Hester White to Marie Houghton Brent, with clipping enclosed dated June 8, 1958

The PROVANCE. VANCOUVER. BC

The COLONIST. VICTORIA. BC

Yes the Incola [Hotel] is still running in Penticton too bad they did not name it NICOLA. A friend of mine TRUDY JACKSON has just named their little baby daughter NICOLA because it is the Centennery year and she is anxious to get the story [presumably of Pelkamulox and NKwala]—she is coming down one day to get it. I have to type it all out again as you have given me more to think about—"NE-COMOP-LEX" means the "head of the Lake Okanagan" [indecipherable]? Ellis diary written in 1865—Mr. Haynes and Mr. Ellis with Chief Tonasket—rode from Osoyoos to the Mission and then to the Head of the Lake—Mr. Haynes had some work to do with the Indians there—Capt Haughton asked them over to his place for dinner—The head of the Lake was where the trail hit the lake from Kamloops—then down the West side in low water—on the East side in high water they went up the East side & Mr. Ellis said the trail was the worst he had been on.[111]

I am mailing you a Province, the week end Edition. I will have to stop now my right eye is sore today so with all my love and the very best to Mrs. Ames and family

affectionately,
Hester White

Encl. Clipping entitled "Penticton Beaches are Pouplar [sic]" from The Spokesman-Review, *Sunday, June 8, 1958.*

Republic, WN
June 10th, 1958

c/o Mrs. Ames Sr.
Keller Route WN.

Dear Hester!—
Pleased we have a little princess again <u>Nicola</u>. How sweet
of Mrs. Jackson your friend to name her baby Nicola, chief of
all the Okanagan—a grand, most colorful history of a long line
of natural borne rulers. Hudsons Bay head officials called him
Nicola. Was very fond of him and had much dealing with him
all his life. I had this written at once on receipt of your letter but
thought you may come, so I send it now—I would not give it all
up. Can be coppied would be better but hold it. I have lots more,
but I have one more move yet and that is slower—you will learn
why when I see you. I am worried so much you did not tell me
who & where this friend is, not one of the people who bought the
Brent place is it, please tell me <u>very soon</u>.
    What I want to ask you is about your Centennial activities,
when & all about it because my great grandfather Nicola's birth
and history as you see is around Penticton, Similkameen. His
mother was borne of Nacoma-plex [Head of the Lake]. Her father
was chief there long, long before great grandfather got his own
reserve from King George III (3rd) for his own home place at
16 mile post from Vernon town now. He was chief Nicola of all
Okanagan, when the line got drawn up.
    See if you and I can get all this history into Penticton paper for
your Centennial, we must work fast now, Editor used to be Mr.
Harris, who is it now[?] I guess you know him have everything
only to copy—Mrs. Ames is going right now. Let me know very
soon, please. See <u>at once</u> please.
                    love Marie—

Thursday [summer, 1958]

My dear Maria,

Blessings this horrible hot day. It really takes all the starch and energy out of me. Thank you for your letter with all the historical facts. I am doing my best with it—articles for the Report have not to be in until August—One question I would like to ask you is what was your Mother's name? And when did she die? Did she live up at the Head of the Lake?[112] I had hoped to be able to go down & see you but it has been too hot I cannot endure it— Went up to Kelowna for the Dedication of the old Father Pandozi Mission [indecipherable] a very nice service—many Chiefs and Dignitaries there—Kamloops School Choir sang—1500 people there.[113] I intended going to the unveiling of the Cairn to Chief Tonasket[114] [but] too hot—then I would have gone on to see you.

Forgive this short note but I am not in a writing mood— Very best wishes to the Ames

much love

Hester White

Penticton, B.C.
RR2 845

Friday [early December, 1959] [115]

My dear Maria,

Greetings this very lonely cold windy evening!! How fortunate you are to be with such friendly kind people to care for you. Living alone as I do is very "ALONE"—but as I love my freedom and independence it has to be!

I am sending you under separate cover the Penticton Herald with the article re the Dunsmuir Home—which was known as the Dunsmuir Castle[116] in the old days. We the Haynes family lived just over the fence and south in the "Joe McKay" House in 1888 and 1889 & saw the building of the Castle—it was all manual labour in those days—and I remember the huge block of granit that went into the building. We moved away in the fall of 1889—but Robt Dunsmuir died before then for I remember the huge funeral procession pass along Belcher Street—And do you know the "Chain Gang," the prisoners that worked on streets or else—would pass too with the ball and chain attached to them?! And we could hear them coming. In 1929—my son Bill White attended there for two years for it was Victoria College and later as now the School Board office—what a wonderful Museum it will make!! When did your father marry a Dunsmuir Girl? And what was her name? Did she die soon after she married—you said once she was lame! Where were you in Victoria? I have enjoyed the article so—Robt Dunsmuir and his wife and family were very poor when first they were at Nanaimo—and at first he was a great gambler!

Christmas seems like a nightmare to me this year—my brother Will was always so vital a part of Christmas—he would arrive & go into the dining room and look with great pleasure at the table which I took such great pains & care to lay! I did it for Mother when I was very little. Will would stand and admire it and then come and say to me "Hess it is too nice to spoil." He always had such humorous stories to tell.[117]

Have you given up all attempt to claim or gain your right to property which you went to Nespelem for, when we saw you? Can I help you in any way am willing to give evidence if given the true story! Ask Mrs. Ames to answer this question! I mean Ernestine!!

Must close—much love & best wishes not forgetting & the family

love
Hester E.

*The question Hester White asks Marie Houghton Brent about claiming her "right to property," above, begins a series of letters on that topic that carries on through February, 1960. Below are selections from that series, as many reiterate the salient details. Brent is claiming that she is the only living heir of Anshanin or Sepetsa (sipica, power-blanket) and her allotment S-1212. Anshanin, Brent tells us, was the full sister of Brent's grandmother, Kughpetcha (x*ulk*pica? or whirlpool blanket) or Suzette, who in turn was Sophie Nkwala's mother. Thus Anshanin was Brent's great aunt on her mother's side. Anshanin's siblings and her two children had died, according to Brent, without descendants.*

The land in question is in north-central Washington state, nearer Chesaw, where Mary Ann Lake is located, than Molson. It is close to the Canadian border, in the "North Half" of the Colville reservation. The reservation was formed in April, 1872, by executive order of President Ulysses S. Grant, spreading over both sides of the Columbia River up to the Canadian border. In July, it had been reduced after an outcry from settlers. By 1892, the north half of the reservation which extended to the Canadian border was ceded to the United States by an Act of Congress after a "disputed land sale" (Arnold, "Bartering" 8) and the reservation took its current dimensions. By 1900 the area was opened up for settlement, though 660 Colville people were allotted land on the north half and hunting and fishing rights were guaranteed there for all Colville people. This is where Brent's great aunt Anshanin had her allotment, according to Brent. Shortly after the turn of the century, the policy of allotment was imposed on the south half of the reservation.

The policy of allotment, supposedly an attempt to give Indigenous people the right to individually own and control 160 acres (or less) of land, was also intended to dissolve reservations. The land on reservations that was not allotted was declared surplus and was opened up to homesteading by settlers and purchase by speculators. The policy was a substantial factor in a massive transfer of Indigenous land to settlers, estimated at sixty percent, between 1887-1934 (Carlson 18). The allotments themselves could also be sold and leased to non-Indigenous people, although numerous rules and regulations encumbered Indigenous people's ability to effectively control their allotments. Indian agents, persuading people on reserves to take allotments, could then oversee leasing and sales, and even control money obtained by the lease or sale of allotted land (Carlson 15). The numerous restrictions and regulations enabled agents and others to take advantage of Indigenous owners. At the same time, many agents were lax in record-keeping, accounting, and oversight that would promote the interests of Indigenous people.

In 1934, the Indian Reorganization Act, under President Franklin Roosevelt, ended the future allotment of Indigenous lands and established policies that could restore the "surplus" land that remained unallotted or was held in trust by the United States government for Indigenous peoples. Allotted land could be sold by some Indigenous people, if granted the right (as the laws continually changed), for fee simple, or direct sale. Other allotments could be held for twenty-five years in trust before the person who owned the allotment could sell it. It appears from the correspondence below that one of Anshanin's allotments was sold by heirs for a fee simple, and the other was held in trust, and then restored to the Colville Confederated Tribes in 1934.

Marie Houghton Brent's letters to Hester Emily White speak to many of the issues concerning land that plagued the Syilx people of the Okanagan and Colville after boundaries were established between Canada and the United States, including the effects of unilateral appropriation of Syilx land by *governments on both sides of the border and the division of the Syilx nation; the lingering effects of the Dawes Act; the difficulty of establishing records of inheritance for Indigenous people; and the intimidating authority of Indian agents.*

Republic, WN
Dec. 14th, 1959

Dear Hester!—
Thank you for your kind letter of four days ago, you are always so kind—& as usual I am always in a hurry—its the surroundings I guess—always behind—

Yes, you may be able to help some where in this case, its mine yet cannot get at it—too <u>valuable</u>, I guess. You may find some body there, some old person, who knew my grand mother [Kughpetcha or sister of Anshanin] or of her, perhaps at InKamip—but be very, very careful you don't get up against the wrong person, don't go near Sissie or any of them—Brents— they know nothing & don't care. This property comes from Edward's two daughters my grandmother's mother['s] <u>side</u>. Not N'Kwala's side, my grandmother was married to young N'Kwala, old Chief Nicola's son.

My grandmother's father was Edward, father also of Gabrian, Chief of Penticton long ago, you must have remembered him, he's got children yet living in Penticton. Mother['s] brother [was] Chief Edward of Penticton also. After that, all it was by Election to any body; our folks were all gone.[118] The Edwards lived here by W. Oroville. I have all this history—will tell you some other time—

This property [the allotment Brent wishes to claim] lies beside Molson, between Molson and Chesaw on U.S.A. side on the Boundary Line—it is 240 or 60 acres, virgin timber & soil, no owner now, a LAKE on it, Mary-Ann Lake. Very valuable now— why they won't give it to me is because Anshanin was also called Sepetsa & she took, they said, the other adjoining 110 acres in her second name, Sepetsa—said they took that away from her because she can't have 2 allotments, they said, and now that is in trust, for the Govt.—then they claim [remaining pages missing].

347

The following undated fragment found among Hester White's papers may be from the same letter, but judging from a pen that blots often in this letter but not the former, it could be from another following. It is headed "Anshanin continued."

Finally when I was called to Nespelem in 1933, I was to have had an old man as a main Wittness for the case viz. above. He knew all of our family through and through—even Ed. [Marie's brother, Edward Houghton].—Ed and I knew him too.

His name was Andrew Tilson of the Boundary Line, and well known on both sides. Inkamip—Oroville was his home, but the Okanagan up & down—was his stamping ground—Tonasket— all on boundary around there, Palmer Lake—that's where my grandmother & Anshanin were raised—until my grandmother got married to her distant cousin Chief N'Kwala's son whom he named young Nicola—

This poor old man [Tilson] was anxious for Ed. and I to get Anshanin Allotment S.1212 between Molson and Chesaw when she died in 1905[,] and long after Ed. came to Republic. He [Tilson] came to Republic to see Ed—told him to tell me at once that he could win that place for us easy, but Ed. was too dum[b] to understand.

After a long time, he got word to me & he must have put my name in the Anshanin list of business you know how that is, "In the Matter of—." All at once I got word or notice after a long time, I woke up, so here we are with 2 Sepetsa's, that's what we got to prove now—you see Penticton you found out did not have that name [Tilson], anyway, you found that out. I never did think there was, Inkamip was next door to Palmer Lake and Oroville, the Line, that's why I asked you to get in touch with Inkamip then, too. There may be one some one or relative of Tilson's who would hear him talk about all that, he may still live, but very old now & feeble there. He had been at Molson district when I came looking for him [in] '33, but some one hearing I was on the way, [it] seems, took him away across the Line—so I missed him and no time.

[Her letter ends here with no signature.]

Penticton BC
R.R.2 845
December 27, 1959

Re: Allotment S1212 and Maria Brents Claim
The Superintendent of Indian Affairs
The Colville Agency
Nespelem, Wash. U.S.A.

Dear Sir,

A few days ago I had a letter from Maria Brent asking me to help her verify her claim to Allotment S 1212, as I was in Hospital at the time I could not attend to it at once, but can now if you will defer the hearing from January 3rd, 1960, for at least two months. I request this [as] a great favour for I have known her and her People for many years.

My brother Val Haynes of Oliver B.C. will assist in obtaining evidence to support her claim.

I am enclosing $5.00 with the request that you give me a few particulars of her Claim, she mentioned a hearing of 1933, of which I would like a few facts, and some of the names.

If the enclosed amount is not sufficient, kindly advise me.

Maria Brent and her brother Edward Haughton [Houghton] are old and very poor and I feel they should be given every consideration possible.

May I offer you and your Staff the Compliments of the Season
very sincerely,
Hester E. White
Mrs. R.B. White

Superintendent Elmo Miller returned White's cheque on December 30, 1959, stating that "there is no charge for the information you have requested." See his full response on February 2, 1960.

Jan. 8th, 1960

Dear Hester—

With all my heart I thank you for doing so much to help me out of some body else's blunder. Agents don't want to take too much trouble about inquiring too far into any thing, easier way is what they do.

Thank you over again & Val—tell him it is wonderful. I thought I did not have a friend—I have here evidence, I am the only relative, Ed. & I, left of Anshanin S.1212. Whatever you spend on me I'll pay back if even in another year—& Trudy dear girl.

> Hester dear, bye just now. Got yours & all last
> night[119] —
> affectionately, Maria Brent

Republic, WN
Jan. 9, 1960

My very dear Mrs. White

First off, please may I have your forgiveness for my broken promise to you. This has been such a hectic past 3 months I hardly "know from nothin." <u>I am so glad</u> you and your dear brother are helping Marie to gather the data and information she will need if she ever gets to the place where she will have to make a court appearance. In October after the notice was served to come to Nespelum, & I had Mr. Hutton (att [attorney]) come with us, I said that I would drop you a line as to the out come. I didn't do so because I felt I could not accept their verdict at the hearing and rather than confuse you any further, I bided my time for some thing more definite to go on. The hearing lasted about ½ hr. At this time a typed record of the hearing in 1933 & which Marie had testified was brought out. She gave no evidence or testimony that Anshanin was her mothers <u>full sister</u> and that Marie was the only living heir. Why she did not reveal this I don't kno. In any event Mr. Montgomery who conducted the hearing said Marie had never registered[120] when she came to America or Republic, therefore she could not expect to get her inheritance from Canada or the U.S. Marie has been so confused & I fear she in her confusion

350

has mislead the people at the agency. The fact still remains and can be <u>proved</u> by Marie's living presence <u>she</u> is the only living <u>heir</u> to her grandmothers (Sepetica) inheritance so why can't something be done. she as you kno has never had a cent, I believe the allotment of Anshenin S1212 is valuable therefore the agency wants to hang on to it until Marie's death.

I hope to bring Marie up to see you as soon as the weather breaks, if anything I can do to help her I'm certainly willing to do. I've written letters, called upon people, talked on the phone but I can't seem to penetrate the curtain of mystery. Was sorry so sorry to hear you had been in the hospital again—do eat carefully my dear. All of my patients are very well thank heavens. I could do with a bit more rest & hope to get it one of these days.

Christmas was a busy time but if you felt an extra guest at your Christmas table it must have been I, because I walked out in the night and looked up at the stars thinking of you. I always do think there is too much material things connected with such a holy time. I like the peace of the great outdoors at Christmas time so it makes my friends and dear ones seem much closer. Your lovely card & sweet letter came just at the right time. I had five or 6 pkges to get off in Dec to various members of the family. There must always be a little spot of mothers kitchen in the package. Then I made 5 beautiful little red velvet muffs for my five little granddaughters, bless them. Thanksgiving I had 22 for dinner here at the house & on Dec.4 I had the Golden Age Club meet here for their Christmas party there were 27 present, I served hot plum pudding Coffee and Tea—had a small tree with gift exchange. Their joy and happiness was a great inspiration. All of the guest were in their 80s and two in their 90s. I was the baby at 60! Wish you could have been here & I hope to have you some day in the summer. Christmas day I had 14 of the family here <u>all day </u>so you can well imagine it was no time for letters! Today my husband is working on the dining room, doing the paneling which I have been wanting him to do for 3 years! Now my dear if you can forgive my broken promise I shall love you more & more. It has not been intentional, I assure you. I do thank you for aiding Marie. And I wish you and your family a most Happy & Peaceful New Year. May God Bless & keep you in His care.

> Lovingly,
> Mrs. Ames,
> Ernestine

Fragment of a letter from Hester White to Marie Houghton Brent written probably after January 9, 1960, since Brent refers to having her baptism records in the following letter.

... him that is interested in the Plaque to be placed for N'Walla-His term as Chief runs out this year-[121]

I will write the Priest in charge of St. Mary's Mission—near Omac. re Baptisms—marriages and Deaths of the names of Indians you have [given] me. I got my sister, Susan Haynes [records?] of Baptism there in 1887—she was able to get her pension with it—and Kamloops may have some information—I will write these letters when I hear again from the agent at Nespelem—so don't worry and I will let you know as soon as possible—Mrs. Jackson is willing to help me—

> PRAY that will help me
> love   Hester E.

Republic, WN
Jan. 14 1960

My Dear Hester

I am sorry dear you are working & worrying so much for me, when you have not been so well. I only hope this business will turn out right in the end. I can never repay you for the great trouble. I really wish I could get one [allotment] for you & Val. There are really 3 of them, one they took away from Anshanin S. 1212, touching S. 1212, of 110 acres, another Muskrat Lake and one I was told that day at Nespelem. Allotment of Grace Kelley[122] down in South Okanagan somewhere. I suppose—sold too. Grace Kelly been dead a very long time too—no heirs—

I was afraid to say a word I am so green—Examiner of Inheritance in 1933— Mr. Rahler—said that too—I was going to apply for that too but Willie [Brent's husband, William Brent] was ill at the time—and everything else came like a whirlwind at that time & I did not have examiners address. Then when Willie died in 39 [1939] I was sure in a daze—trouble all came so fast, I found my self all alone and did not know what to do—

What I want to say now is this: I have my baptizam certificate from Kamloops. I was born in 1870 Dec. 5, North Okanagan Reserve in BC—it was all Reserve at that time—

Must close love—Mrs. Ames going now—trust I made myself clear. I am so slow forgive me—bye now

     Marie Brent

Mrs. Marie Brent
% Mrs. Ames
Keller Route, Republic WA
Jan 25, 1960

dear Hester,

Do you think you should write to the agent at Nespelem again to say you wrote to them in lots of time before my 60 days was up asking for 2 months or more extension of time for hearing on Anshanin/Sepetsa S1212 case of Marie Brent, Republic WN

[saying] you got no answer—please answer—to
Mrs. R.B. Hester White, Penticton BC, South Beach Dr, RR 2.

Republic P.O. WN
Marie Brent
25th Jan/60

Dear Hester:

Please write to the agent at Nespelem saying you asked for 2 months or more before January 3—fix this up; I was to have 60 days from Nov 3. You wrote them before 60 days were up [see letter above, of December 27, 1959] but No answer from them. In case you have not hear from Nespelem I give you the Inheritance Examiners name and address behind this—

You see there were 2 Sepetsa's. This is the important part. Mother and daughter. OLD Sepetsa and Anshanin (Sepetsa) S 1212.

I was given the original information in hand writing by an old man who knew all of our folks always—given in 1925 at Vernon, Okanagan BC, Komasket of Reserve No. 1. [for more on Komasket, see headnote "Marie Houghton Brent" in Part One].

    W.J. Montgomery
    Examiner of Inheritance
    Bx 3537 Portland 8
    Oregon   353

Some time in Inkamip Andrew Tilson was to be my main witness but they spirited him away—night before hearing in 1933—

You see there are 2 Sepetsas Mother and daughter. That's where the agents office made a big mistake. I tried to make this clear I hold this little old piece of paper of full information until it is needed, made in 1925 to dictation of an old Indian in Okanagan Reservation. [The] old man's name [was] Komasket
[no closing]

United States Department of the Interior
Bureau of Indian Affairs
Colville Indian Agency
Nespelem, Washington

February 2, 1960

Dear Mrs. White,
Thank you for your enquiry regarding Marie Brent's interest in Colville Allotment No. S-1212.

We have checked our records regarding the Colville Allotment No. S-1212. The records indicate that An-sha-in, Colville Allottee No. S-1212, was the same person as Se-pe-cha (Mrs. Red Bull), Colville Allottee No. C-86.

The heirs of Se-pe-cha (Mrs. Red Bull) were determined by the Department under the date of April 24, 1914, to be as follows:

Amelia Tomtusel, widow of subsequently deceased brother, ½
Mattie Hope Kelly, daughter of subsequently deceased brother, ½

Under the date of September 8, 1919, the sale of Colville Allotment No. C-86, by the abovementioned heirs, was approved by the Assistant Secretary. Fee Patent No. 914713 was issued August 22, 1923, to Marion Warren purchaser of the entire allotment of Se-pe-cha or Mrs. Red Bull.

Since An-sha-in or Se-pe-cha (Mrs. Red Bull) received two allotments and Colville Allotment No. C-86 was sold by the heirs, trust patent covering Colville Allotment No. S-1212 was cancelled under the date of March 24, 1934, by T.A. Walters, First

Assistant Secretary, and the allotment reverted to the Colville Confederated Tribes.

Since the heirs to Colville Allotment No. C-86 have been determined and Colville Allotment No S-1212 has been cancelled, there will not be another hearing held regarding Colville Allotment No. S-1212.

Sincerely yours,

Elmo Miller
Superintendent.

Sunday
[February, 1960]

My dear Maria,

Greetings and blessings this lovely sunshine morning and I am wondering how you are! I am enclosing the letter from Nespelem which I think is very sad and bad news for you!! Allotment S1212 was cancelled in 1934 that is 26 years ago and reverted to the Confederated Tribes—what I cannot understand is the delay in your claim being put forward—or presented at that time. Val Haynes was saying the other day that the Government was doing its best to buy back these allotments and giving them back to the Indians. Alice his daughter[123] has one near Moses Mountain—which her husband Louis "logged off" last year— someone was trying to buy it from her!! Well my dear I feel I have been little help! to you! but it would cost a mint of money to fight the U.S.A. Government for this seems to have been "settled" long ago! We old timers have been denied our rights—me for instance over the Haynes Estate which was a steal[124] [and]—when Chas Lambly died leaving me with an infant one month old & a small boy—no home no nothing—& a few hundred dollars—and my Cousin in England dying without a will & £51,000 pounds went into Government Treasury—but I am still happy & content. Lets us plan our trip to the "Head of the Lake" for the unveiling of the Cairn—& the story of N'Qualla[125] —with all my love to you and Ernestine God bless you
Hester

March [2nd? unclear] /[19]60

My dear Hester,

I've been looking for a letter from you to hear word of how you are. Did you get mine of 2 weeks ago and I asked if you found any thing of what is going on at the head of the Lake. I just don't know how to put it, maybe please give me Chief Bower's address. I would like a word with him—too. My prayer of years has been answered, or going to be, not too long now.

My worry was a great man lies in an unmarked grave, no one to think of him and I could do nothing about it. Willie and I spent our own money to save his place—ranch at 16 mile post on Okanagan Lake, No 1 Reserve.

Chief NK-wala's own Reserve, given to him, his descendants, his own people and descendants by King George III known as Reserve No 1-Head Okanagan Lake, N'Kam-ma-plex, and he died pleading for his descendants & peoples welfare [. . .] [no closing]

Penticton BC
702 South Bend
Sunday, [August 14, 1962] [126]

My dear Ernestine—

Greetings this lovely & stormy morning and wish you were here to watch the STORM creep up the lake—now too angry waves are all trying to tell us something but tourists are such Cowhards they bang the doors of the cars and speed away! There's Thunder to the East and I always think "and God spake these words."[127] Mother always so afraid of thunder, & gathered all around her, but I always slipped away to join my Father and enjoy the wonder of it—The storm blew over but the Lake is still rough—and a little sail boat battled with the waves! I thought it would tip over but it made it—

Jack, Shirley and I went to Kelowna to Mayor Parkinson & aldermens Garden Party[128] in a beautiful Garden. The home of Mr. Williamson whose brother was a Diamond Millionair and died a few years ago and left his Fortune to the brother! It was by invitation only and a Guard was at the Gates to check the Guests. Last year many "crashed the Gates." It was all very nice—one old lady with the frilliest mauve tulle hat a Mrs. Simpson sat by me—she was so pleased to see a number of Guests wearing hats—it was so much more dignified! Hers was not for a very old Lady! We went to the Capri for dinner all very grand—dining room too dark one could not see to enjoy! Seeing is one of the most important senses.

Oh the Crowds that were on the Beach the last weeks—but less today because of this lovely Lake wind—it blows the dust too the other way. The Rogers Pass new Highway has certainly made the Okanagan Valley a "throughway."[129] A Pity in a way! All our Privacy gone! I hope to get down to see you in Sept—after the holidays are over—have been nowhere on my own since last year when I drove all the way home on a Prayer—but it was a long drive.[130]

We had a wonderful Pioneer Gathering during the Peach Festival—900 invitations sent out. Glad I lived in those lovely old days—knew the quiet friendly trails—the woodsy cheerful wail of the "BARS" when let down to let us through-there were no Gates then! and knew the Hoof Beats on the old Hudson Bay Bridge at "Sooyoos"—knew the security and value of HOME—of Family & Friends—of FRESH PURE WATER—of which there is none in the Valley today!

I often think of Maria how comfy she was on my Chesterfield the night we saw her asleep & thought how like a warrior Chief she looked in a Tee-Pee. I have often thought of it as such![131] Our dear old friend Babe Kruger died last month of Cancer! I sat for over an hour by his bedside the night he died—he was the white son of Theo. Kruger the H.B. Trader at Osoyoos. He was a wonderful friend—he, my brother Will and I were such old happy Pals—

> All my love
> Hester E.

The preceding letter is the last we have been able to find in the correspondence between Hester White and Marie Houghton Brent among their papers in the Penticton Archives and Vernon Archives. Hester Emily White died in November, 1963.

[1936-1962]

Isabel Christie MacNaughton at MV Ranch, c. 1932.
Courtesy of MacNaughton Family Collection.

Isabel Christie MacNaughton
1915 - 2003

During her long life in the southern Okanagan, Isabel Christie MacNaughton was a writer and poet, a local historian, and, alongside her husband, Carleton MacNaughton, one of the early environmentalists of the region. She was born in River Hebert, Nova Scotia, in 1915 and brought to the Okanagan in 1917 to join her parents James and Helen (Gunn) Christie who were looking for land in the area. In 1918 they purchased a ranch near the small settlement of Okanagan Falls, located in the Syilx traditional territory. The falls, *sxʷəxʷnitkʷ* or "little falls" to differentiate it from Kettle Falls, a site shared by all Syilx people, was protected by the Nk'Mip people. The Christies named their home Meadow Vale (MV) Ranch, and settled into a house that had belonged to the foreman on Thomas Ellis's ranch. Their daughter Gladys "Skip" Christie Alton, born in 1926, remembers the "tall narrow two story building" (Alton 1), to which rooms were gradually added, and which had no electricity "until I was well into my teens" (Alton 3). James R. Christie, who had been a lumber-broker in Nova Scotia, began cattle ranching. He became one of the founders of the Southern Interior Stockmen's Association in 1942 (Morrie 90) and was its "tactful, capable and almost perennial President" ("James" 154). MacNaughton's mother Helen Christie, a graduate of Dalhousie University (1911), had been an elementary school principal in River Hebert, and in the Okanagan became a charter member of the Women's Institute in 1921. Both were active in support of the local school and the United Church. Isabel Christie, or "Buddie" as she was known, with one older brother and five younger sisters, was the second eldest of seven children.

MacNaughton's childhood friend Cora Chase remembers that the Christie family in both Nova Scotia and the Okanagan were "educated and had careers," unlike most of the people Chase knew. MacNaughton went to high school in Penticton, boarding with relatives. Chase gives some idea of the significance of high school in the settlements of the British Columbia interior in the 1920s and 30s: "High School was higher education. . . . In those days if you wanted highschool you gave up ideas of having fun. Evening and weekends were for studying, and some girls worked for their room and board" (2).

MacNaughton's "original ambitions" after high school were to be "a writer or a doctor," as asserted in a compilation of family recollections entitled "Family Reunion" put together for a reunion of the Christie family in 1992 by Janice Hobbs (17). She was receptive to the stories and history of the Okanagan land told by settlers and Syilx in her community, and she was a reader: some of her favourite childhood books included the works of L.M. Montgomery and Nellie McClung (Hobbs 17). Chase describes camping out overnight with MacNaughton, "soothing to two girls from big families and small houses." According to Chase, "Buddie had her own knoll where she could meditate and compose poetry. No one else was welcome there. That seemed romantic, in those Anne of Green Gable days" (1).

After high school, MacNaughton, discouraged from becoming a doctor "because of the tremendous work and prejudice toward women in the medical field" (Hobbs 17-18), studied nursing at Vancouver General Hospital in 1935-36, but, after earning her cap, she returned to the Okanagan because of "problems with her feet" (18). Once home, she turned to writing, and began publishing columns in the *Penticton Herald* from 1937 until shortly after she married Frederick Carleton MacNaughton in April, 1939. Originally from New Brunswick, Carleton's parents came to the Okanagan in 1922 from Winnipeg, where Carleton, born in 1910, had grown up. His father, John Beverley MacNaughton, had been a freight inspector for the Canadian Pacific Railway. Carleton remembers that first summer in British Columbia, when the family lived in a tent while his parents worked the fifteen acres they had acquired for orcharding near Oliver in the South Okanagan and built a small house. The twelve-year-old boy "fished and hunted, chased bugs and snakes and wild flowers all of which stood me in good stead when I became a naturalist" (F.C. MacNaughton 80). Chase remembers Carleton MacNaughton who "hopped around like a jumping bean" as being unsuitable for the "quiet, studious" Isabel, but later, "his talents became obvious":

> He had a good singing voice, he could preach a sermon
> as well as a trained minister [Carleton was a lay minister
> who had a lifelong association with the United Church]
> and he built a good sized house on his own land. And
> he made most of their furniture out of material at hand.
> I didn't see any other young fellows doing those things.
> (2-3)

Between the fall of 1937 and the spring of 1939, MacNaughton did some of her most important writing. Her columns for the *Penticton Herald* chronicled settler reminiscences and history, but the bulk of them reflected another important relationship in her life—her friendship with her neighbour Josephine Shuttleworth, born in 1865 (see the essay

"Standing Between" and Part One). Over twenty-five of MacNaughton's columns retold, in English and in writing, Josephine Shuttleworth's oral stories, *captikʷɬ* as well as Syilx history. Shuttleworth lived on her ranch next door to Meadow Vale, and MacNaughton frequently visited, absorbed by Shuttleworth's oral stories, translated by her daughter Louise, who also helped out at the Christie ranch, as did Josephine's son Tommy. MacNaughton attributed Shuttleworth's stories to her, and some can be found in Part One of this volume. Sometimes MacNaughton wrote a column in the third person, and she did not always sign her articles. The unsigned article which appeared in the *Penticton Herald* in 1937, "How an Ancient Indian Woman Taught Her People Wisdom," tells a story of Shuttleworth's grandmother. It was clearly written by MacNaughton, informed by Shuttleworth and perhaps other sources, and stands as an example of the other histories not only of early settlers but also of Syilx people from before settlement that MacNaughton published in the *Herald*.

Shuttleworth's stories published by MacNaughton (then I.M. Christie, or Isabel Maud Christie) caught the eye of Anthony Walsh, who had been teaching since 1932 at the independent day school on Nk'Mip land near Osoyoos. In late 1938, Walsh brought together Isabel Christie and Elizabeth Renyi, a student at Oliver Public School, originally from Hungary, who had experience with playwriting and acting. Shuttleworth's stories, such as *Why the Chipmunk's Coat Is Striped* and *Why the Ant's Waist Is Small* were adapted, among others, into dramas (Anthony Walsh, "Developing" 4). *Why the Chipmunk's Coat Is Striped*, included in this section, suggests collaboration between the two women. It differs from the story "How Chipmunk Got Markings" which Shuttleworth previously told to MacNaughton, reprinted in Part One of this volume, particularly in its stage directions and addition of the Great Spirit and Coyote. As well, the Chipmunk character, a female in MacNaughton's original rendition of Shuttleworth's story, as is traditionally the case, is here a male character.

While there was collaboration, the written plays and program notes from performances in the south Okanagan community of the time also credit specific plays to single authors. The two plays *The Crickets Must Sing* and *Why the Ant's Waist Is Small* are attributed to Isabel Christie. *The Chipmunk and the Owlwoman*, a playlet based more closely on Mourning Dove's rather than Shuttleworth's version of the chipmunk story (see "Chipmunk and Owl-woman" in Part One) is attributed to Renyi (Korpan 47-48; 167-72).

Partly due to a growing interest in folklore in the 1930s, MacNaughton's plays received perhaps the greatest exposure and acclamation of all her writing. Walsh performed them at a summer drama conference in Banff in 1939 where they were seen by visiting professor Frederick Koch from the University of North Carolina and published that December in *The Carolina Play-Book*. The version of *Why the Chipmunk's Coat Is Striped* printed below comes from this issue. They received more attention at a conference in September, 1939, at Hart House Theatre in Toronto, where Walsh again went on stage. In these venues, the connection to Shuttleworth was often attenuated, but where MacNaughton had control, such as in her columns in the *Penticton Herald*, she made sure the stories were attributed to Shuttleworth. Her collaboration with Shuttleworth suggests her respect for Shuttleworth's voice and knowledge, and her desire to make them known to the settler community.

The plays were also performed locally by students of the Inkameep Day School where Walsh had encouraged—albeit after regular school hours and through much trial and error—graphic arts, weaving, and other crafts, as well as local Syilx history and story-telling. In 1939, the students formed a group called Can-oos-sez Skay-loo (the Animal People; *k'nusəs sqilxʷ*) and wrote plays; they performed dances, songs, and plays locally to great acclaim in Osoyoos, Oliver, and Penticton from 1938-1942 and were invited to perform at the opening of Thunderbird Park in Victoria, British Columbia, in 1941. At this event, *The Crickets Must Sing* and *Why the Ant's Waist Is Small* were on the program (with the titles *The Ants and the Crickets* and *The Partridge Mother*) (Korpan 55). Through her connection to Shuttleworth and Walsh, MacNaughton participated in this cultural resurgence.

The Crickets and *Ant's Waist* also appeared in 1942 in a book of poems published by MacNaughton entitled *Wood Fires*. They are reprinted below from this text. *Wood Fires* was dedicated to MacNaughton's brother Robert Christie who had joined the RCAF in 1941 and was killed in an air strike over Mannheim, Germany, in 1943. Profits went to the Red Cross as well as to the BC Indian Spitfire campaign, as did those from the performance of the Can-oos-sez Skay-loo children in Osoyoos in 1942. MacNaughton's poems are unpretentious and rarely flowery, though some employ conventions and hint at the sentiments of popular nature poetry of her time. Others, such as "Okanagan Winter," suggest the influence of modern imagist techniques. A reissue of *Wood Fires* was printed in 1948, with the addition of three new poems and the play *The Greasewood Tree*. It was probably inspired by Shuttleworth's storytelling, though MacNaughton is careful to differentiate this play from Shuttleworth's traditional stories, calling it "a fantasy playlet in verse and mime." Two later poems published in the *Penticton Herald* shortly after Shuttleworth's death in November, 1950, in an article called "Tribute to a Lady," both reprinted in this section, convey through imagery MacNaughton's bond with Josephine Shuttleworth. The poems included in "Tribute" were reprinted and slightly revised as "Desert Portrait" and "Portrait of an Old Lady in an Orchard" in the *OHS Reports* of 1984 and 1985. MacNaughton published poems in these reports and other publications such as the *Province* newspaper (Vancouver) and *Chatelaine* magazine throughout her life.

Isabel and Carleton MacNaughton worked at orcharding on land near Carleton's parents' homestead during the 1940s, raising four children born between 1941 and 1953 and eventually moving into the MacNaughton family home in the 1950s. Walsh had left the Inkameep Day School for war work in 1942, and Isabel MacNaughton worked for a time with the Okanagan Society for the Revival of Indian Arts and Crafts (SRIAC) which Walsh had helped found in 1941 before he left the region. This group not only supported the activities of the children of the Inkameep Day School, but also made efforts to encourage the reform of the Indian Act. SRIAC presented a brief entitled "Native Canadians: A Plan for the Rehabilitation of Indians" to Prime Minister Mackenzie King in 1944, but their suggested reforms were for the most part rejected (see "Crossing Lines" in this section.)

Isabel Christie MacNaughton with husband Carleton,
as they embark on hiking the Old Hope Trail
from Princeton to Hope, c. 1943.
Courtesy of MacNaughton Family Collection.

In 1958, to contribute to provincial centennial activities, Isabel MacNaughton, with her father James Christie, wrote *The Story of Okanagan Falls* published by the Okanagan Falls Centennial Committee. In the opening, MacNaughton's self-deprecating humour is evident. The paragraph cites a glowing projection of Okanagan Falls in the local newspaper of 1893 as the "Geographical, Industrial, Agricultural, Mining, Manufacturing and Railroad Centre of the Southern Interior of British Columbia, Delightful and Healthful Climate," which is followed by the wry comment: "While a great many of these predictions have not yet been fulfilled we still at times have a delightful and healthful climate" (7). Also in 1958, she and Carleton MacNaughton created the Grey Sage Museum, a wildlife park south of Okanagan Falls that housed over two hundred different indigenous birds and animals. After it was sold in 1964, Carleton MacNaughton became one of the province's first park naturalists, a position he held for the next seven years.

In 1969, MacNaughton and her husband built their house Rim Rock into the cliffs of Vaseux Lake on land that had been designated a migratory bird sanctuary in 1919. Carleton MacNaughton died in 1999, and Isobel Christie MacNaughton in 2003. Throughout their lifetimes, they shared Rim Rock and another acreage they named Tamarack not only with the region's wildlife but also with Boy Scouts and Brownies, environmental and community groups, Historical Society gatherings, town picnics, and interested visitors. MacNaughton's children have remarked on the comfort of her homes, in which housekeeping and material possessions were unimportant (their parents' first home had no running water until after their first child was born), but books and home grown food, found objects, plant specimens, Carleton's wood carvings and a space to read and write took priority. Her gentle, reciprocal approach has influenced her relationships, her writing, and the physical enviroment of the Okanagan region.

How an Ancient Indian Woman
Taught Her People Wisdom

June 10, 1905, marked the death of Francois, chief of the Indians of the Penticton Reserve.

Although the old chief has been gone from the valley these many years, his name is yet recalled with pride among his people and with respect by all who knew him.

A tale is told of Chief Francois' grandmother, who lived with her people at Tonasket in the days before the white man crossed the mountains to the Great Blue Waters, or ever set foot in the long narrow valleys between.

She was a thrifty woman and a hard worker. Every spring she gathered cottonwood bark, which comes off easily when the sap is running. By putting an end and a cover on to the peeled ring of bark, the Indians made little barrels in which to store their dried meat, berries, fish, roots, etc. Sacks woven of tulles were also used for this purpose.

The barrels and sacks belonging to each family were stored on a little pole shelter built up on a pole foundation on some high rock or hill. Few animals could reach the food stored in this manner.

The grandmother of Chief Francois worked through all the seasons, gathering food for her store-house. She went on long journeys for roots, seeds and berries, and knew all the places where they grew in plenty. She smoked and dried meat and fish on smoke-racks of green willow, intertwined in a lodge-shaped manner, with a fire built inside.

It often happened in seasons when the salmon were scarce, and other food supplies for some reason or other were not plentiful, or perhaps when the winter was very long, that the Indians ran short of food.

It so happened one long, cold winter among the people at Tonasket. Before the winter was over, the chief's grandmother, who was a young woman at that time, was the only one who had any food in her store-house.

She fed the people as best she could, doling her berries and roots and other food out day by day. When sickness came, she nursed the sick ones and gave them medicines from her stores. In gratitude they made her chieftainess of the tribe.

By the time spring had come, many of the Indians, weak with hunger and privation, were dead or dying. More of them, eating the sunflower arrowleaf [balsamroot] shoots, which were too strong for bodies so weakened, died. At last only a few dried salmon remained in the store-house, and the people were weary and sad with living.

Then the chieftainess dreamed a dream of deer-hunting. She dreamed she saw four deer close to the camp. In the morning when she wakened she told her husband where she had seen them, and bade him go to bring them in.

Her husband was a big man, so strong that in happier hunting days when he shot a deer the arrow would go right through its body and fly far out beyond. Now, however, he was weak with hunger.

Taking the favorite of his four bows, he chose some arrows and started out to find the place where his wife had dreamed of seeing the deer. Almost dragging himself along, so often he had to rest, he finally came to the little glade where the four deer stood.

Four arrows flew from his bow, one after another, and one after another the four deer dropped dead. Strong with excitement, the man strode back to his chieftain-wife. She came and skinned the deer, and when the carcases had cooled, carried home every edible part.

The Indians had small cottonwood baskets to boil their meat in. They heated stones red-hot in their camp fires, then lifted them into the bucket of water and meat, and soon had savory stews boiling. Some of the meat they cooked on sticks.

The chieftainess' word was law among her people from that time on, and they let all matters of importance abide by her decision.

She taught them a religion which previously they had either forgotten or never understood. Under her guidance they learned to give thanks to the Power that cared for them, to ask for what they wanted and to discuss matters as freely and trustfully with that Power as with a comrade.

She taught them happier ways of living, and more skillful methods of hunting, so that they lived in peace and contentment for many years in their valley home.

[1937]

Children rehearsing plays at the Inkameep Day School.
Courtesy of Osoyoos Museum Society and the Osoyoos Indian Band.

Why the Chipmunk's Coat Is Striped
An Okanagan Indian Folk Tale
Recorded by Isabel Christie and Elizabeth Renyi [132]

*The scene is the Inkameep Reserve in the Okanagan Valley of British
Columbia. A sheltered berry patch among the evergreens. A teepee in one
corner of the clearing. The mountains above the trees.*

The time is sunset.

The characters are Little Chipmunk, The Grandmother Chipmunk, The
Owl, and The Coyote.

Prologue

THE COYOTE:
We bring you a tale of the long ago, when the Animal People
lived in the land, before there were any White Men and
even before there were any Indians. It is the tale of "Why the
Chipmunk's Coat Is Striped," as it happened in the long ago,
when the Chipmunk and his Grandmother made camp for the

367

picking of the berries and the Ceremony of the First Fruits, at sunset.

[Little Chipmunk and the Grandmother, with two baskets, poke their heads out of the tepee door, look all around, and dart over to the berry patch. Grandmother sits down. Chipmunk goes on slowly and picks several berries on a curl of birch bark, then returns to The Grandmother. He takes the curl of bark with berries in upraised hands, turns to the South, and speaks.]

CHIPMUNK:

O Great Spirit above the mountain,
I am going to eat of your berries.
[Turning to the North.]
O Great Spirit above the mountain,
My grandmother is going to eat of your berries.
[Turning to the East.]
O Great Spirit above the mountain,
We are going to eat of your berries
Before this sun goes down the trail to the West.

[He hands the berries to the Grandmother and seats himself. They eat three or four berries each, then sit with arms uplifted towards the East while the sun sinks behind them. Grandmother sits and picks berries around her into a large basket. Little Chipmunk darts about picking into a small basket. They chatter excitedly, but in rather low tones.]

THE OWL:

Whoo! Whoo! Whoo! *[Softly in the distance.]*
Whoo! Whoo! Whoo! *[Louder.]*
Whoo! Whoo! Whoo! *[Very loud.]*
Who is picking my berries?"
                    [Appearing from among the trees.]

THE CHIPMUNK:

"The Owl! My Grandmother, we must begone!"

THE GRANDMOTHER:

"The Owl! The Owl!

[*Both run for the teepee. The Grandmother gets inside. The Owl, in swift pursuit, claws the little Chipmunk's back just as he is getting inside the door. The Chipmunk screams wildly, but escapes into the teepee. He moans.*]

[*Just as* The Chipmunk *falls inside the teepee door,* The Coyote *appears on the scene from among the trees nearby.* The Owl *runs off in terror.*]

THE COYOTE:
The Owl! Even the Owl is swift to go when the mighty Coyote comes. But his trail is not for the Coyote's feet today— and the way is long before me. [*He trots off.*]

[The Grandmother *and* The Chipmunk *poke their heads out of the teepee door and come out. The Chipmunk moans.*]

THE CHIPMUNK:
My coat, O Grandmother, the Owl had torn my coat!

[*The Grandmother turns and raises her arms to the sky and stands so for a moment or two. Then turns to The Chipmunk.*]

THE GRANDMOTHER:
The Great Spirit above the mountain has spoken, O Chipmunk. The Owl has torn the coat of the Chipmunk. The tears will be mended by the Great Spirit, but the marks he must leave. From this time on, as long as the sun rises, and as long as the sun goes down the trail to the West, the coat of the Chipmunk will carry those three great stripes. The Great Spirit above the mountain has spoken.
[1939]

From *Wood Fires* (1942)

The Crickets Must Sing
(*Adapted from the Okanagan Indian folk-tale as told by Josephine Shuttleworth*)

ANT:
O lazy ones, up with the morning!
The cobwebs woven in the ways are broken.
The sun is far above the hills, and still you lie and sing.
What need have you of singing?

CRICKETS:
What need have we of singing?
We have need of singing, Ant, as you have need of work.

ANT:
Your work is yet undone!
See! We have wood to carry for winter
          and dry grass and leaves.
We have honey and fruit stored up for the cold.
But you—your work is yet undone!
You sing, and songs are only cinders blown in air,
And just as soon forgotten.

CRICKETS:
Not cinders, Ant,
But little flames to light the dark,
Or smoke wreaths rising high among the trees.
For songs have warmth and gladness of the fires,
And songs are sweet remembered
          as the blue smoke trails
Seen from afar on some clear day,
Slow climbing to the sun.

ANT:
The fires and smoke of summer
And the fires of spring and fall are little help when
          winter comes.
Who wants to eat in winter must work before the snow.

Up, Lazy ones, and work!

CRICKETS:
Gladder are we when winter comes,
To sleep and rest safe in the dark,
Beyond the fast blown snow
Than to half wake, and fumble in the greyness
For bits of a summer's hoard.
Gladder are we to live along the trails, and sing,
Than to be hurried so, and spent with living,
That no songs come to us in any season.
Better a winter lost, to cricket folk,
Than spring and summer and fall pass by,
And we not see the star flowers come,
Or sing the white olalla bloom along the trail,
Or watch the crimson sumac on the hill.
O, ask us not of singing, Ant
        For we have need of singing,
        As you have need of work.

[*1939*, 1942]

Why the Ant's Waist Is Small

(*Adapted from the Okanagan Indian folk-tale as told by Josephine Shuttleworth*)

PARTRIDGE MOTHER:
O small one, awaken, awaken!
Gladness has gone from our tepee,
As leaves from the tree in the autumn.
O small one, awaken!

ANT:
He cannot awaken, O Partridge Mother.
He sleeps as the leaves that have fallen,
He sleeps as the leaves of the autumn.
We must cover him over with earth for a blanket above
      him.

PARTRIDGE MOTHER:
O, but he must awaken! He is my small one.
He only sleeps as the flowers sleep, to waken in the spring.

ANT:
He sleeps as flowers the deer have trod on sleep,
      O Partridge Mother,
Let the earth lie over him lightly.

PARTRIDGE MOTHER:
He MUST awaken!

ANT:
My heart has known your grief, O Mother Partridge,
And grief but grows with weeping, as the meadow grass
      with rain.
Come, ask it of the Coyote.

COYOTE:
O Partridge Mother, the Ant speaks with wisdom,
The small one sleeps to awaken again in the land of the Spirits,
But not to awaken to you,

And grief but grows with weeping, as the meadow grass
    with rain.
We must cover him over with earth for a blanket above him.
The earth will lie over him lightly.
Look to the Ant—
She has pleaded so earnestly with you,
And pulled at her belt in her pleading,
That her waist is now small.

So shall it be in days after, that you may look,
And looking, remember.
Always the waist of the ant shall be small,
And always the ant shall be working;
For as the snow falls soft on the dead tree,
And brings it new beauty in winter,
So does work soften the sorrow,
So is grief eased in the working.

[*1939*, 1942]

A drawing by Frank Stelkia (*Showkame*), c. 1939
illustrating Coyote with Partridge Mother and Ant.
Courtesy of Osoyoos Museum Society and the Osoyoos Indian Band.

"Incantation" R.C.A.F.

They have known blue mountains
And loved familiar hills—
White olalla, wild syringa,
Voices of home, pine trees, sunshine and rain,
Green river meadows, and new plowed fields;
Quiet evenings,
Lilacs against the cabin wall;
And wings soaring above—
      Wild goose and eagle
      On distant, tireless wings—
God of all these remembered things,
God of the higher hills they soar above,
Grant thou the strength,
The infinite beauty of these
To all Thy men of the sky.

Okanagan Winter

If I were painting a picture of winter
I'd paint
A hillside of white,
With an old snake fence
Zig-zagging its grey pole length along

To a group of pines.
(And a snow bird's song,
And little grey gusts of the fitful breeze
To show me the outstretched arms of the trees
Cradling the snow).

And then I'd paint
Some dappled horses,
Plodding one by one,
In eager line

To where the tufted
Bunch grass shows

Gold-brown and rusty
Through the snow.

(And a snow bird's song,
And little grey gusts of the fitful breeze
To show me the outstretched arms of the trees
Cradling the snow).

Old Timers

You who rode across the gold-brown Okanagan hills,
Many singing years ago, with glory in your eyes,
Packing down the long trails sweet with sage and grey with
      dust,
Dreaming of great ranches spread beneath the blue, blue skies;
You who built your homes in little corners in the hills,
On meadows green, and by the lakes, in happy days of old—

Are these things you dreamed for us,
These tidy rows, these orchard plots?
Or are you seeing still
The rolling hills, the wide brown lands
Before the fences came—
The white-face herds and the wild horse bands
That roamed their way down a lonely land
In the fading years of old?

Lord of all the pioneers,
Lord of all the old-time folk—
However little be our lands,
How rushed and crowded be our lives—
Grant that our views may be as broad,
Our hearts as warm our minds as free,
Our hospitality as kind,
As theirs in days that used to be—
As theirs still is in little homes
Where they can sit when lights are low
And tell the tales of long ago.

Wild Geese

He stands and watches as the wild geese go
Honking adown the southern sky on slow
        Unhurried wings.

His hand upon his plow, he looks and smiles;
His soul has travelled with them, miles and miles
Beyond the dim, blue mountains, over all
The trackless waste just crimsoning with Fall,
Where the winds meet and the roaring storms are born;
Where each new day glows red to greet the dawn.

His hands have turned these furrows, brown and bare;
His heart has loved these fields, this evening air;
But his soul has wandered on with the birds
Where they have gone—flying out to meet the day
        And what it brings.
[1942]

From *Wood Fires* (1948)

Oh Tell Me Do the Wild Geese Fly

Oh tell me do the wild geese fly
Across the German skies in spring?
And does their honking fill the night
With far away remembering?

Brown hands that loved the fields of home,
Hands that in German valleys lie,
Will surely rest more gently there
To hear the wild geese going by.
[1948]

The Greasewood Tree [133]

A fantasy, played in verse and mime.

[Indian music. The Tree Chorus, several figures in dusty green robes, enter from left and right, forming an arc at the back of the stage, standing on a raised dais to suggest the tree-line on a hill-top, with arms upraised.]

FIRST SEMI-CHORUS:
Greasewood trees are always old
And gnarled and twisted, where
They crouch along the hilltop
With ragged limbs in air.

Greasewood trees are dusty green
And dull and tiny, still
Greasewoods carry cheer enough
To brighten all the hill.

SECOND SEMI-CHORUS:
Greasewood bloom is neat and gay
Like elf-lamps burning high,
Like little yellow candle-wicks
Alight against the sky.

Greasewood trees are always old
And gnarled and twisted, so
They crouch along the hill-top
With ragged limbs bent low. [134]
> *[They bend slightly, rhythmically and droop their arms slowly, raising them before one the Chorus begins.]*

ONE OF THE CHORUS:
But once in far off story days
The greasewoods were not here—
And where they stand, a woman stood,
On her brown face a tear.

*[Chorus let arms fall slowly. Lights gradually dim. As last verse
is spoken, Old Indian Woman, in buckskin robes and shawl, followed
by her small granddaughter, Morning Star, enters from center back,
slowly comes to centre stage and stands looking up. She raises her
arms and speaks pleadingly.]*

OLD WOMAN:
Oh must I leave this land I love?
These brown hills of my heart?
Who in all that spirit land
Would have me from them part?

[She indicates hills with a sweep of her arms.]
Why take me from these piney hills
And the dear things they hold?
What need have they to trouble with
A woman lone and old?

[Puts hand over her heart.]
Too old to live! The spirits say
A woman as old as I should go
Away to the distant shadow land,
The land the spirits know.

[Raises her arms again.]
The land where the Spirit Chieftain sits
And looks on our little hills,
Watches us walk our little trails
And calls us as he wills.

*[She gradually lets her arms fall and stands dejected, with
slightly bowed head, her hands over her eyes.]*

TWO OF THE CHORUS:
The voice of the Spirit Chieftain calls—
There are none can stay when he bids them go.
The spirit land is happy too.
Old woman, why do you worry so?

[The Chorus glance at Old Woman questioningly.]

[Raising her head...]

OLD WOMAN:
He calls me now; but the brown old hills
Have been calling me night and day
For many and many a waking moon,
And I cannot go away.
[She spreads her arms to indicate hills.]
Not only the hills I love so well
Not only the hills are keeping me—
There is another who calls me too,
Who needs me still—oh spirits see.
[She indicates Child. Chorus look at Child.]
Who will care for my Morning Star,
My little shining one
Who plays all day in the tepee door,
In the days when I am gone?
[Hand and arm gestures with right arm going forward to represent one walking a lonely trail.]
She might walk on the lonely trails
Tired and hungry and cold,
No one she has to care for her,
But me so lone and old.

[She starts and stands listening intently, with fear; head upraised, voice sharp.]
[Chorus listen intently.]
Listen! Oh listen! The spirit braves!
Over the hills they tread!
And I cannot go—I cannot go—
To that far land of the dead!
[She makes as if to hide.]
I'll hide—but no, the spirit braves
Come swift to those who huddle and fear,
Where can I turn—where can I go?
They're coming so near—so near.

Listen! I hear their falling feet!

Perhaps—perhaps they'll pass me by.
I'll crouch and dig for the speetlum roots,
O brown hills hear my cry!

> *[She looks wildly around, then crouches and digs. The
> Child watches a moment, then crouches down beside
> Old Woman and digs likewise.]*

ONE OF THE CHORUS:

> *[As if addressing the Spirit hovering close.]*

Oh spirit braves from the spirit land,
The one you seek could never be here,
Only a woman who works and digs
For speetlum roots as the dusk draws near.

ANOTHER OF THE CHORUS:

Perhaps 'twas an older one you seek—
Who sits and nods in the sun—
'Twould never be such a one as this
Who works till the day is done.

> *[They indicate Old Woman working. Chorus with
> arms lifted to left and slightly upward, stand looking
> off to the left as though watching spirits vanish, as they
> speak.]*

CHORUS:

Over and over the hills they tread,
Farther and farther away,
Old woman stop your digging and rest,
For dusk is following day.

> *[Old Woman rests, sitting with feet tucked under her
> and swaying from side to side. Child does likewise.]*

OLD WOMAN:

> *[Speaking first to Child then looking up.]*

The spirit braves have come and gone,
Small Morning Star. Will they come once more?

> *[Sighs deeply.]*

Oh brown earth arms, cradle me now,
Rest an old woman whose heart is sore.

Let the wind whisper and softly caress me,
Let the dark pine trees sing me a song,
Rest in the dusk time, soft swaying rest time,
While the grey shadows slip gently along.

[Suddenly springs to her feet, listening with fear.]
Listen! Oh listen! They come again!
Over they hills they run!
And I cannot go. I cannot go,
To that land beyond the sun.

[Child springs up too.]
What can I do? They passed before
While I was digging so,
But it grows too dark for digging now,
Where, oh where can I go?
                [Hand movements swiftly upwards.]
If I were a bird to fly away—
Or a deer to be over the trail—
A deer! –Oh little Morning Star
Follow and do not fail!

'Tis long that the deer have been our friends.
We have walked the trails in the dawn.
They taught us to walk as the wild deer walk,
Gracefully, daintily, on—
                [Woman and Child start to walk the Indian Deer Dance.]
We'll walk the way the little deer walk,
Walk while the braves are nearing,
The dusk is deeper, the spirit ones may
Think we are deer in the clearing.

[They walk the Deer Dance: Both hands are raised to forehead, just above eyebrows, fingers extended. Start off with right foot, raise right hand up, out and down to forehead, then left foot and same hand movements with left hand. To be done with rhythm and grace.]

Two of the Chorus:
                [With graceful arm movements, first to point out the deer, then as if pointing to spirits.]

Gracefully, daintily, so the deer walk
In the dusk on the trails on the hill.
And nearer and nearer the spirits come
Through the pines so sombre and still.

A SECOND TWO OF THE CHORUS:
Closer and closer their falling feet—
Hasten old woman, walk softly away,
Walk as the deer walk, proudly and swiftly—
Will they pass by—oh who can say?

A THIRD TWO OF THE CHORUS:
                    [Chorus pause and peer in rhythm.]
They pause and they peer in the gloom
Through the pines so sombre and still.
Pause and peer and stop and start,
Searching the trails on the hill.

A FOURTH TWO OF THE CHORUS:
                    [Chorus look from side to side questioningly.]
Where and where can the old one be,
The lone old one they seek?
Yonder are only two little deer,
Walking down by the creek.

ONE OF THE CHORUS:
Listen! The spirits start away,
They are going—now they are gone!
They saw in the dusk just two little deer.
They are going on and on.
                    [Chorus watching the Spirits depart.]
CHORUS:
Over and over the hills they tread,
Farther and farther away,
Old woman stop your walking, and rest
Where the dark night shadows play.

OLD WOMAN:
                    [Coming back with Child. Chorus sway arms as she speaks.]
Sway little tree friends, sway on the hilltop.
Be glad with an old one the spirits passed by,

382

And help me, hide me, if they're returning,
Returning once more from that land of sky.

Let the wind whisper and softly caress us,
Let the dark pine trees sing us a song,
Rest in the dusk time, the soft swaying rest time,
While the grey shadows slip gently along.

Let the small night bird nestle beside us,
Let the white ollala our candle be,
Let the pines sing us a song of the mountain,
Let the wind tell of the far away sea.

*[Woman suddenly starts up, holds Child close to her and
listens with fear and terror.]*

Listen! Oh listen! They come once more.
Over the hills they fly!
So tired I am, but I cannot go
To that land beyond the sky!

'Tis long and long I have lived with the rocks,
I have loved them many a year.
I would that the rocks could give me strength,
Could hide me in my fear.

If I were but as strong and sure,
As grey and hard as they,
I'd never be hiding and huddling here,
Frightened to go away.

[She crouches as in fear.]

Huddling in fear among the rocks,
The grey old rocks on the hill—

[Idea comes to her with enthusiasm.]

Let's crouch down under my buckskin shawl
And lie all hard and still.

*[They both crouch under shawl, hurriedly, pulling it over
themselves to resemble a rock.]*

TWO OF THE CHORUS:

[With rhythmic movements pointing at rocks.]

So hard and still the grey rocks lie,

383

May be the spirit ones will see
Only another rock on a hill
Where many a rock should be.

ANOTHER TWO OF THE CHORUS:
And it may be that they will go
So swiftly through the cool night winging
Nothing at all will meet their eye,
But a rocky hill and a soft wind singing.

> [Throughout the following verses arm and hand movements,
> such as Indian story tellers use to express various actions
> and moods, are to be done in rhythm by the Chorus. These
> movements are hard to explain, but they come when
> one lets one's arms and hands "tell the story too," simply
> and naturally. Throughout this verse-play it is intended that
> the hands be as important a medium of expression as the
> voice.]

ONE OF THE CHORUS:
But the spirit ones are weary too,
Weary with looking and looking so long.
They pause by the rocks on the brown old hill,
Pause where the pine tree is singing its song.

A SECOND ONE OF THE CHORUS:
Its song of the mountain—
And sweetly they rest,
By ollalas perfumed,
By night winds caressed.

A THIRD ONE OF THE CHORUS:
Crouching under the shawl so low
And huddled together tearfully,
The old one and the small one wait,
Half hopefully, half fearfully.

A FOURTH ONE OF THE CHORUS:
Oh, will the spirits never go?
Why do they wait so long and so long,
Glancing about from rock to rock—

Watching the pine tree singing its song?

A FIFTH ONE OF THE CHORUS:
So still the two 'neath the buckskin shawl,
Never a move they show.
Silent and still as stone they crouch.
When will the spirits go?

A SIXTH ONE OF THE CHORUS:
                    [*Very clearly.*]
But suddenly as she listens there
The small one stirs with a happy thrill.
                    [*Child gives tiny quiver.*)
It is her song that the pine tree sings!
Her song up there on the wind-swept hill.

The happy, laughing song he sings
That she may dance as the shadows fall—
Smiling and gay, and reaching up
For the velvet sky as a dancing shawl.
            [*Chorus members sway in rhythm and reach up as for the sky.*]

TWO OF THE CHORUS:
                    [*Sharply, hands stretching forward.*]
Don't move! Don't move! Oh hardly breathe!
If you quiver she must go!
Don't move! The spirit ones will see!
If you move they will see—they will know.

A SECOND TWO OF THE CHORUS:
                    [*Drawing back.*]
So still they crouch, all filled with dread—
So still they crouch, and low.
But alas for that one happy thrill—
The spirit braves see, they know.

A THIRD TWO OF THE CHORUS:
                    [*Hands raised to cheeks in dismay.*]
They know, and now they have lifted the shawl,
They bid the old one stand,
And one on either side they are

Taking her by the hand.

[Woman gets up from under shawl as though it were removed and her hands being held by spirit braves. She stands almost leaning back with arms held forward, as though she is resisting the spirits' hold. The Child hides her head in her hands and weeps silently as the Woman speaks.]

OLD WOMAN:
[Pleadingly.]
Oh leave me! Leave me! Spirits, pray!
Leave me here with my Morning Star.
Keep all the glories of shadow land
I'd rather be where the brown hills are.

Oh take me not from the long grey trails,
From the flowers and the sun.
My soul will still go walking down
The hills till time is done.

[With deep anguish.]
Oh but my heart grows weary and sore.
Why do you lead me away?
I never wanted your shadow land.
In the hills I want to stay.

[She goes off slowly, as though forcibly led by spirit braves. Child still sits weeping.]

ONE OF THE CHORUS:
[Softly.]
The dusk grows deep as she walks away,
So old and wrinkled and brown.
And the little one weeps helplessly
As the night falls darkly down.

A SECOND ONE OF THE CHORUS:
[Softly.]
Tired and hungry and all alone,
Alone on the lonesome trails—
Never an old one to hold her close
When the thin Coyote wails.

A THIRD ONE OF THE CHORUS:
>   [*Softly.*]
Never an old one to still her fears—
To feed her and sing her to sleep—
Frightened she is, and lost she is,
She can only lie and weep.

TWO OF THE CHORUS:
>   [*With arms upraised and speaking with particular*
>   *expression.*]
There is a tale the old ones tell
That if one's love is strong and true,
In some strange way the soul may come
Back to the winding trails it knew.

ANOTHER TWO OF THE CHORUS:
Darkness falls as she walks away,
That woman old and brown,
And as she goes a little tree-soul
Slips swiftly and softly down.
>   [*A figure clothed in the dusty green robes of the Chorus*
>   *enters.*]
She runs to where the small one weeps,
She holds her to her heart,
And whispers, 'Little shining one,
We never more shall part!'"
>   [*The figure runs to Child and kneels beside her holding her*
>   *close. Then they stand together in centre of stage.*]

FIGURE IN GREEN:
>   [*Speaking at first to Child, then to audience.*]
Because I loved the brown hills so
My soul none else could keep,
The old hill trees have taken me in,
O small one—do not weep.

The kind hill trees have taken me in,
And I'll forever be,
In sun and rain, on the brown old hill,
Now known as the greasewood tree.

And half the world will never know,
And half will never care,
That an old brown woman in dusty green
Is really standing there.

Or that she holds small Morning Star
Still close beside her, so,
As she did in the far-off story days,
Those days of long ago.

> *[She holds the Child close. The Chorus raise their arms and look up.]*

FIRST SEMI-CHORUS:
Greasewood trees are always old
And gnarled and twisted, where
They crouch along the hilltop
With ragged limbs in air.

Greasewood trees are dusty green
And dull and tiny, still
Greasewoods carry cheer enough
To brighten all the hill.

SECOND SEMI-CHORUS:
Greasewood bloom is neat and gay
Like elf-lamps burning high—
Like little yellow candle-wicks
Alight against the sky.

Greasewood trees are always old
And gnarled and twisted, so
They crouch along the hilltop
With ragged limbs bent low.

> *[Chorus let arms fall slowly as curtain falls.]*

[1948]

Tribute to a Lady

Portrait of a Lady in an Old Orchard

She is my friend
This little Indian woman—
Old and brown is her face,
And purple her silk head shawl,
And soft and gentle the fall of her little feet
Down the green and brown of the old, old orchard path.

These are her own hills rising beside us,
On yonder blue mountains the trails that her forefathers knew.

But her I shall always remember,
Coming so softly down
To her tall log house,
With the blue spruce trees
On either side of the little gray gate.

She is my friend,
This little Indian woman—
She is very old
And straight as a fine fir tree—
And I think that I'll never forget
The welcoming grace of her smile,
And the soft dark light of her eyes,
And her little silent footsteps
Over the green and brown of the old, old orchard path.

A year or more ago I wanted to make with words some pictures of my friend Mrs. Josephine Shuttleworth. This first picture "in an old orchard" was to be the first of four; and it carries my earliest recollections of her. My last glimpse of her was almost identical. She seemed ageless.

One can hardly imagine that she is really gone—it would seem that she has merely rounded a bend in the trail, or topped the next rise in the hill.

Her dignity, her sympathy, and her twinkling-eyed love of fun are unforgettable.

The courteous and loving care with which her family at all times surrounded her are unforgettable too.

Having known Mrs. Shuttleworth in her home; having loved her stories and been fascinated with her story-telling; having heard of her fishing-lore since early childhood, and known in these last years how beloved a fishing companion she was; having watched her often at community gatherings, and in the dusty hustle and bustle of Stock Sale time at the Falls, memory-pictures of her are clearly etched.

The valley has lost a lovely and gracious lady, and a most interesting personality.

Some time ago, with water-colors I tried to paint from memory the face of my friend—but not being skilful with colors and brush I could capture no likeness.

Working with words again I painted this little picture. It isn't particularly good poetry. Neither is the first of my as yet unfinished "series of four" for that matter.

Perhaps, however, it may express some of the feeling of those of us in the Okanagan who knew and loved her.

Portrait

If I could paint you
I should like to use
The colours that we live among—
The lovely Indian brownness of your face
Could be the brownness of these desert hills
That purple silken head shawl
The petals of a fragrant shooting-star [135]
Or tints of far blue mountains, dimly seen.
And the darkness of your eyes,
Could be done with the midnight skies.

And for the gallant grace of you
I'd blend my colours as artists do,
A blending of the three to show
Strength of the hills,
Beauty of the hills,
Beauty of the purple star-flower,
And the dark mystery of skies at night.
They are all part of how
My heart can see you now.

[1950]

Notes

Introduction

1 See Jeannette Armstrong and Lally Grauer, *Native Poetry in Canada: A Contemporary Anthology* (2001).

2 Many researchers on the Okanagan have been important to us. We would like to mention some works focussed solely on the Okanagan that have been key to our understanding: Frank M. Buckland's early account of settlement in the Okanagan, *Ogopogo's Vigil* (1948), which preserved much history; John Goodfellow's early history of the Similkameen, entitled *The Story of the Similkameen* (1958); Margaret Ormsby's work on Susan Allison, *A Pioneer Gentlewoman in British Columbia: The Recollections of Susan Allison* (1976), as well as her articles on early Irish settlers in the Okanagan; Duane Thomson's seminal research embodied in his dissertation "A History of the Okanagan: Indians and Whites in the Settlement Era, 1860-1920" (1985); Harry Robinson's stories as recorded by Wendy Wickwire in *Write It On Your Heart: The Epic World of an Okanagan Storyteller* (1989), and other works by Robinson; Shirley Louis's *Q'SAPI, A History of Okanagan People as Told by Okanagan Families* (2002), and Jeannette Armstrong's Syilx-centered dissertation "Constructing Indigeneity: Syilx Okanagan Oraliture and *tmixw* Centrism" (2009), as well as an earlier work edited by Armstrong and Delphine Derrickson, Lee Maracle, and Greg Young-Ing, *We Get Our Living Like Milk from the Land* (1994).

3 Hereafter we refer to these reports as the *OHS Reports*. The Okanagan Historical and Natural History Society was incorporated on September 3, 1925, and published its first annual report in 1926. The first five annual reports were published under title of The Okanagan Historical and Natural History Society. From 1935 onward, the name changed to the Okanagan Historical Society. The annual *OHS Report* is one of the oldest historical journals in British Columbia.

Part One

Essay: "Standing Between"

1 *ha?mismƏs* (Mourning Dove) is Christine Quintasket's name to the Syilx. The custom of taking a new *nsyilxcn* name when a significant life change occurs is still in practice and the one name is both first name and surname. I therefore use Mourning Dove to refer to her throughout the essay.

2 Donald M. Hines, who edited Mourning Dove's *Tales of the Okanogan*, provides in his Foreword a list of members of her family and community who provided stories she collected for publication.

3 The word *snaqsilxʷ* translates as "relatives" in English; in literal translation, "members of one skin," indicating members of one house or one family.

4 Marriages referred to as *à la façon du pays*—in the custom of the country, have been referred to as marriages of convenience by some historians. Sylvia Van Kirk has argued against the concept in her essay "Women in Between" 1977.

5 Eleanor Leacock mentions intermarriages particularly among *coureurs de*

bois (her spelling) during the fur trade period (qtd. in Chance, "Influences of the Hudson Bay Company": 132). David H. Chance mentions that some voyageurs—French Canadians, or half-breeds or Iroquois, who accompanied the HBC as brigade labourers—came back to Colville to marry and have descendants in the thousands (Chance, "People of the Falls" 83-84).

6 While scholars cannot explain its origins, F.W. Howay says that Chinook Jargon, as reported by the earliest European contacts, grew naturally out of the contacts of the maritime traders with the coastal tribes, and was made up of several Indigenous languages followed by French (246-47).

7 *sux^wnmicin* is commonly translated as "interpreter"; however, the literal translation should be "person who is language-adept in truth-knowledge" (knowledge of both Indigenous and non-Indigenous cultures) and so must also be accomplished in the deeper cultural contexts of languages external to *nsyilxcn*. Such persons held positions of privilege and are recognized by all Syilx as knowledge keepers.

8 *captik^wł* are passed down from generation to generation from ancient times by storytellers gifted in the art of oral transmission. The stories all together form a story world and have been described as "a cycle or a complex of myths" found in a particular culture (Mattina and DeSautel 22). Most Syilx storytellers describe them as philosophical teaching stories meant for each new generation to use to situate the choices they face on a personal as well as on a societal level.

9 Eric Sismey incorrectly writes that she is Francois's granddaughter ("Maggie" 183).

10 *sx^wǝx^wnitk^w* is the name of Okanagan Falls meaning "little falls" to differentiate it from the place name of Kettle Falls called *sx^wanitk^w*, which refers to the roaring sound of the falls and to the Columbia River.

11 The is the same Chief Francois who worked for Thomas Ellis, the first white settler in Penticton, packing over the Dewdney Trail (Sismey, "The Shuttleworths" 136).

12 This Colville Chief is identified as *six^wilxkn* or See-whehl-ken, maternal great grandfather of Mourning Dove. He was located at Kettle Falls in Syilx territory which included both sides of the Columbia and both sides of the Canada/US border. Mourning Dove identifies one of his daughters (her grandmother's sister) as having married Shuttleworth who in later years fell heir to a lordship. (*Mourning Dove* 8).

13 Scripts rely on the use of common knowledge of very well-known social customs to suggest implications or to set expectations for subsequent significant outcomes further in the story (Rubin, "Memory" 24).

14 *sma?may?* are historical stories of community and individuals containing detailed accounts including the genealogy of the teller and identifying source tellers (whom they were heard from) with significant events and specific geographic information included (Armstrong, "Constructing" 103).

15 The Dominion government disallowed the British Columbia Land Act of 1874 to consolidate previous land legislation in British Columbia because it ignored Indigenous land rights that were established by English policy regarding acquisition of Indian lands in the Royal Proclamation of 1763 (Harris, "Making" 91).

16 The Joint Indian Reserve Commission 1876-1878 had a dominion government Commissioner, a provincial government Commissioner, and a Commissioner jointly agreed upon by both governments (Armstrong et al *We Get Our Living* 53).

17 Marie Houghton Brent used the spelling "Laurent," but according to Edmond Rivère her last name was spelled Laurence (70).

18 Brent's great aunt Theresa was old Chief Nkwala's daughter and the sister of her grandfather, young Nkwala, who died circa 1860. See Brent's "Indian Lore" for more on young Chief Nkwala.

19 Brent's assertion that her mother was present when she was seven years old contradicts "Indian Lore," Brent's final memoir, in which Brent says that her mother died in 1872, when Brent was two years old. Oral knowledge also reported that Sophie Nkwala died in 1872, right before Brent's father, C.F. Houghton, left the area.

20 For more on Chief Chelahitsa and his sons Alexander and John or Salista, see notes to Brent's letter to White, April 30, 1958, in Part Three.

21 Brent's story "The Legend of Shuswap Falls" was included in Clark's *Indian Legends of Canada*, and also first appeared in *OHS Report* in 1948.

22 In his volume *Tales of the Okanagan* (1976), Donald Hines used the preface Mourning Dove had originally written for *Coyote Stories* (1933). This preface was edited by Dean Guie for *Coyote Stories*, but Hines published it unedited.

23 *swaŕak̓xn* means the common frog in *nsyilxcn*.

24 A common word among Plateau tribes, *suyapix* or Shoyapee refers collectively to non-Indigenous people.

Josephine Shuttleworth

1 Genealogy chart provided by Hereditary Chief of Penticton Adam Eneas, grandson of Chief Francois.

2 The town of Colville is south and east of Kettle Falls, Washington, an important salmon site. Its name comes from Fort Colvile, a Hudson's Bay Company fort established in 1825. Both Kettle Falls and Colville are within Syilx territory. For more on Syilx territory, see the Introduction.

3 The entire title of the article printed by Isabel Christie MacNaughton is "How Chipmunk Got Markings and Why the Loon Laughs." The chipmunk story here is excerpted from the longer piece.

4 "Snu" could be the beginning syllable of the Syilx word for Owl, *snina?* (sneena or snee-naw) adding drama to indicate the child's level of fear (she is so afraid she can only repeat the first syllable) and grandmother's slowness to understand her.

5 Rock rose or *Lewisia rediviva* is also known as bitterroot. See Eliza Jane Swalwell, "Girlhood Days in the Okanagan".

6 See essay "Standing Between" for more on Chief Francois.

Eliza Jane Swalwell

7 The first wagon road of any length, known as the Okanagan and Mission Valley Wagon Road, was built in the late 1870s from Pandosy's Mission in the south, through Priest's Valley (later Vernon) to settler Cornelius O'Keefe's ranch at the north end of Okanagan Lake. It was 38 miles long (Buckland,

Ogopogo's Vigil 53-4).

8 "Corky core" refers to internal browning and lesions at the core of the apple and "single disk" could refer to the single disk plow or harrow used by orchardists.

9 Spanish "vaquero" traditions arrived via Mexico to British Columbia, as well as "cowboy" traditions from Texas, according to Ken Mather in *Buckaroos and Mud Pups*.

10 George William Simpson was a Presbyterian; the priest at the Mission (in what is now Kelowna), founded by Father Charles Pandosy, would have been Roman Catholic.

11 Canadian geologist John William Dawson published *Fossil Men and their Modern Representatives* in 1880.

12 Dawson was referring to the Bible, Acts 17:22.

13 From "An Essay on Man," Epistle I, by Alexander Pope (1688-1744), an English poet and scholar.

14 The Head of the Lake, *nk'mapəlqs* is the territory of the Syilx people at the northern end of Lake Okanagan.

15 The Consolidated Land Act of 1874 or "Act to amend and consolidate the laws affecting Crown Lands in British Columbia" consolidated previous land acts giving rights to settlers for pre-emption without any recognition of Indigenous title to land. British Columbia having entered confederation in 1871, this act was declared void in March, 1875, by the federal government. Swalwell is quoting from federal Justice Minister T. Fournier's Report. Changes were later agreed upon by the federal and provincial governments that did not completely ignore aboriginal rights but largely avoided issues of title and reserves (see Cumming and Mickenberg 199-200 and "Standing Between" in Part One of this volume).

16 The first two decades of the 1900s saw a concerted effort on the part of Indigenous peoples in British Columbia to address their land concerns, title and treaty rights which had been overridden by the British Columbia Government and left largely unaddressed by joint provincial and federal commissions. Chiefs representing their peoples' interests made various attempts to directly address the Canadian government and the Privy Council in England, which, as they saw it, upheld Indigenous right to the land unless ceded by treaty or compensated for as enshrined in the Royal Proclamation of 1763.

In August 1910, Sir Wilfred Laurier, as part of a pre-election tour, met with a number of delegations of Indigenous people, including a deputation of Chiefs from the Syilx (Okanagan), Secwépemc (Shuswap) and Nlaka'pamux (Thompson) nations in Kamloops. Laurier assured them that he would prepare a set of questions concerning Indigenous title, size of reserves and other issues that would be submitted to the courts (Armstrong et al. 60), including the Judicial Committee of the Privy Council (Tennant 88). British Columbia Premier Richard McBride blocked these submissions by refusing to go to court. Laurier lost the election in 1911, and the British Columbia interior nations, the Syilx among them, then submitted a request to the new Conservative Prime Minister Robert Borden. Borden, instead, formed a Royal Commission (the McKenna-McBride commission) which proposed to make "a final adjustment of all matters relating to Indian Affairs in the province of British Columbia." It dealt only with the issue of reserves, and not with "title, treaties or self-government" (Tennant 88). The Commission was empowered to both cut off and add to Indigenous reserves in consultation with but, in the end, without final agreement from Indigenous people. In the Okanagan close to 19,000 acres were cut off and 2,600 added (Thomson, "History" 157).

In 1913, the Nisga'a coastal Indigenous people prepared a ground-breaking petition to the Privy Council of England, advised by Arthur O'Meara, a lawyer from Ontario who had become an Anglican missionary in British Columbia (Tennant 87). Basing its arguments on the Royal Proclamation of 1763, the petition demanded the right to representation in any ongoing reserve process, as well as the right to land that had been sold by the provincial government, and compensation for lands they may choose to cede (Tennant 90). The Nisga'a helped form the coastal Indian Rights Association and the interior nations joined in a group called the Interior Tribes of British Columbia. Both joined in the Allied Tribes of British Columbia to respond to the McKenna-McBride commission in 1916.

The Allied Tribes held a meeting at Spences Bridge in 1919 and prepared a lengthy petition to British Columbia Premier John Oliver voicing their concerns about the McKenna-McBride recommendations, including the lack of recognition of Indigenous title, proposed cut-offs, and issues such as water rights, stating that they would "'continue to pressing our case in the Privy Council'" (Tennant 99). In 1927, in hearings before the Canadian parliament's special joint committee, seen as a step toward reaching the Privy Council, the claims of the Allied tribes were rejected, and, furthermore, raising funds for claims was outlawed under the Indian Act on the committee's recommendation. This action undermined for the time being further activity by Indigenous peoples in British Columbia to make legal claims concerning title.

17 Laurier is reputed to have made this statement before a sympathetic delegation of Friends of the Indians of British Columbia, an organization formed by Arthur O'Meara (Tennant 87) on April 26, 1911 (Harris, *"Making"* 378, n. 51). According to Cole Harris, the statement is cited in Duncan Campbell Scott's "Report on the British Columbia Indian Question" to the House of Commons (1926). Clearly, Swalwell was intently following issues regarding land and title in British Columbia.

18 George W. Johnson, "Why the Okanagan is a Dry Belt" (25-6).

19 Edward, William and Alfred Postill, originally from Malton, Yorkshire, England, arrived in the Okanagan in 1872 with their family via Ontario. They acquired ranch land from George William Simpson (originally owned by Frederick Brent) and continued to operate the sawmill Brent had established there and expand the cattle ranch to about 5,000 acres. Alfred Postill became the first Okanagan member of the British Columbia Fruit Growers Association. Edward died in 1888, and, in 1895, William moved to Alberta to become a stockraiser. Alfred died in 1897.

Marie Houghton Brent

20 Marie Houghton Brent or Marie Brent is Brent's chosen name later in life, from around the time she moved to the U.S. During her childhood and early adulthood she was called "Maria." As she states in an article published in OHS in 1927 about her schooling in the Okanagan in 1884, "I was then Maria Houghton" ("The Priest's Valley" 27).

21 This story was originally untitled, handwritten in a notebook, probably gathered between 1919 and 1926. It begins with the note, "Indian fables translated by Marie Brent." It ends with a comma, as if to indicate it continues on. The ellipses are added. Caribou and reindeer are the same animal; caribou is the name usually used today in North America. According to James Teit, in pre-settler Syilx history, caribou herds were abundant on hilly terrain east of Lake Okanagan (213).

22 For more on the occasion of this story being written and told, see the essay "Standing Between" in this section.

23 Alexander Ross (1783-1856) was born in Scotland and emigrated to Canada in 1804. He published *Adventures of the First Settlers on the Oregon or Columbia River* in 1849 (London). It documented his voyage from New York to the Columbia River in the west where he helped to establish Fort Astoria at its mouth in 1811 and in the same year, Fort Okanogan at its junction with the Okanagan River. (See also Hester White, "The Pioneer Trail," June 26, 1947 in Part Three.) There he traded with the Syilx for the next few years. He and Sally or Sarah (circa 1798-1884) likely married according to Syilx customs in 1812 and established a household. They were later married in the Anglican church (1828) after Ross, Sally and their children settled in the Red River colony, Manitoba, in 1825. Much of Ross's information on Indigenous traditional ways recorded in *Adventures* and his other books may have come from Sally (Daniells).

24 Father Pierre-Jean (Pieter-Jan) de Smet (1801-1873), a Jesuit missionary, came to the US from Belgium in 1821 and established schools and missions in Missouri, Iowa and Montana. In 1845-46 he took on a difficult exploratory journey to the Canadian Rockies to attempt to broker peace between the Blackfoot and the Flathead community in Montana. His extensive travel amounted to hundreds of thousands of kilometers, including nine trips to Europe to fund his missions. His most known works published in English are *Western Missions and Missionaries* (1863) and *New Indian Sketches* (1865).

25 Father Adrien-Gabriel Morice (1859-1938), an Oblate missionary who arrived in British Columbia from France in 1880, lived at Fort St. James on Stuart Lake in north-central British Columbia from 1885-1903. Here, Father Charles Pandosy was his Superior from 1885 until 1887, when Pandosy returned to the Okanagan. Morice is best known for his work on the Carrier language, for which he developed a syllabics system, and his *History of the northern interior of British Columbia formerly New Caledonia, 1660-1880* (1904).

26 Simon Fraser (1776-1862) was born in Mapletown (near Bennington, Vermont), to which his Scottish highlander family had emigrated (Lamb). After the American revolutionary war, during which his loyalist father died, the family settled in Montreal, where Fraser joined the North West Company

as an apprentice to the fur trade when he was sixteen. He was charged with operations west of the Rockies for that company in 1805, and established Fort McLeod and Fort Fraser in what he named New Caledonia, now British Columbia. With James McDougall he created a post at Carrier's Lake (Stuart Lake) where Fr. Adrien-Gabriel Morice later lived (Fort St. James, British Columbia). Fraser is well-known for his voyage down the Fraser River in 1808, mapping its mouth at 49° latitude after a harrowing thirty-six-day journey from Fort George (Prince George, British Columbia) to the Musqueam village at the mouth of the river. His discovery was of no use to the fur trade then, but it later helped establish Canadian claims to the 49th parallel as a border.

27 Thomas Carlyle (1795-1881) was a controversial and influential Scottish essayist and historian. The reference Brent is making comes from his book *The French Revolution: A History* (1837).

28 The purported autobiography Long Lance, from which Marie Brent is quoting, is in fact the work of Sylvester Clark Long, born in North Carolina in 1890, of Croatan (Lumbee), Cherokee, European and perhaps African ancestry (according to his parents), but perceived and treated as African-American (his parents had been born slaves). As a youth, he presented himself as a Cherokee, but at the time of his autobiography, published in 1928, he claimed to be a Blackfoot chief. Moving to Calgary after WWI, having served in the Canadian Army, he was, in fact, adopted by the Kainai (Blood) Nation of the Blackfoot Confederacy in 1922 and named Buffalo Child. Working for the *Calgary Herald* and claiming Blackfoot heritage, he published articles critiquing the Indian Act and often reporting Indigenous issues in the west. He moved to New York in 1927, and according to Donald B. Smith, attempted to publish Long Lance as historical fiction, but his publisher insisted it be labelled autobiography. It, and he, received great acclaim, but over time rumours of his fabrication of identity began to circulate, gaining force after his death in 1932. They had apparently not yet reached Marie Brent in the Okanagan.

29 American author William Henry Johnson (1845-1907) published *French Pathfinders in North America* in Boston in 1905.

30 Brent inserted a note here with the reference "'The Romance of British Columbia' by A. Anstey, page 51" for this quotation. Matthew Baillie Begbie (1819-1894) became the first Chief Justice in the Crown Colony of British Columbia in 1858 and subsequently in the province after Confederation in 1871 until his death in 1894.

31 This manuscript was found, undated, among Marie Houghton Brent's papers in the museum and archives in Vernon, British Columbia. It appears to be a first draft in note form. The quality of the handwriting suggests it was written late in life, perhaps in 1957 or 1958, as does internal evidence in the manuscript—e.g., Brent estimating the population of Kelowna to be 10,000.

32 In "Indian Lore," Brent tells us that her mother Sophie Nkwala died in 1872, so it is unlikely that she would have been alive when Brent was seven years old in 1877. However Brent could be refering to an earlier statement of her Mother's. The "elderly" and "handsome" woman was Brent's great aunt Theresa (Thérèse, Teresa) Laurence (1837-1892). She was young Chief

Nkwala's sister and the daughter of old Chief Nkwala, chief of extensive Syilx territories, and important in the fur trade in the Okanagan. See the essay "Standing Between" and Brent's "Indian Lore" in this section for more on Nkwala. Theresa Laurence married the settler Cyprien [Cyprian] Laurence.

33 "[T]his woman" probably refers again to Theresa Laurence, and her "little daughter" could be Laurence's youngest daughter Eleanor, who was about Brent's age, or it could refer to Laurence's older daughter Mary, who was married to Donald Nicholson, a Euro-Canadian from Ontario. In Chinook, a "Boston Man" usually refers to an American but can signify any white man.

34 Here, Marie Brent is traveling from Syilx land at the Head of Lake Okanagan, near what is now Vernon, where she was living with relatives after her father left in 1872 according to "Indian Lore," to Mission, part of what is now Kelowna.

35 The Okanagan Mission Valley School was established in 1876 in the area near Mission Creek that became Kelowna (Buckland, *Ogopogo's Vigil* 57), located "close to the present-day school board offices on Underhill Road" ("Benvoulin").

36 Most likely Brent is referring to Miss M. Coughlan, a sister of Mrs. Thomas Greenhow, who taught in the school from 1878 until 1882. William Brent notes in his memoir that she later joined the "Cloistered Nuns of Quebec" (3).

37 Brent went to Montreal to live with her father Colonel C.F. Houghton, from 1893-1897.

38 William Smithson donated his log house to the school, but it needed to be expanded, reconditioned and furnished (Buckland, *Ogopogo's Vigil* 52).

39 William Brent mentions that Joseph Christien, a French-Canadian settler, was one of the first trustees of the school when it opened and also a pupil at the age of forty-five (45).

40 In fact, Theresa Laurence did not die until 1892. Later in her narrative, Brent refers to "sickness and deaths" at that time.

41 Mary Laurence was Therese Laurence's oldest daughter. Her father, Cyprien Laurence, died in 1868. Mary Laurence married Donald (Dan, Daniel) Nicholson in 1880.

42 Donald (Dan) Nicholson came to the Okanagan in 1876 from Madoc, Ontario, hired as a blacksmith to work on the road being built between Okanagan Mission and Priest's Valley. He bought a quarter-section from Eli Lequime as well as additional land of over 700 acres in total. He sold his land in 1891, but around 1892, after briefly returning to Ontario, he bought the Benvoulin Hotel, which he ran for eleven years and sold after his wife Mary Laurence's death in 1904. He travelled briefly to the Klondike during the first gold rush there, and lived in the Cariboo, British Columbia from 1915-1919. He died in 1927 ("Dan Nicholson"). His obituary comments that "He was kind-hearted and generous, too much for his own good. . . ."

43 "My grandfather" would be young Chief Nkwala, who died circa 1859.

44 According to William Brent, William Peon's property situated east of Kelowna passed to Eli Lequime who sold it to "an Indian named Niqualla" (another spelling of Nkwala, probably young Chief Nkwala), then Lequime retrieved the land and sold it to "Dan Nicholson" (65). William Peon from the

Colville area had come as a packer to the Okanagan with Father Pandosy's party in 1859. Kelowna historian Frank Buckland asserts that William Peon's deed to this land was stolen when he was away in the Colville area in the 1860s (having been outlawed by J.C. Haynes) ("Peon" 42). Marie mentions "William Peon his [Brent's father's or young Chief Nkwala's] brother-in-law." There is a connection through marriage between young Chief Nkwala and the Peons, in that Louis Peon, William's father, was probably married to Old Chief Nkwala's daughter Mary Sukome'lks (Teit mentions she married "one of the Peones" [268], and Buckland surmises this was Louis Peon). William Peon married Julie, apparently a half-sister of Mary (Buckland, "Peon" 40), and thus he would have been a brother-in-law to young Chief Nkwala.

45 August Gillard and Jules Blondeau, early francophone settlers, arrived in the Mission area of the Okanagan from France via California in 1862 (Buckland, *Ogopogo's Vigil* 38-9). Frank Buckland tells the story that "some Indians passing" Gillard's dugout in winter saw smoke rising, and paused to find out more. Gillard emerged, and his unkempt hair and beard put them in mind of a black bear, or "Kim-ach-touch" (*kəmxstus*) (39). Brent had noted in an article she published in 1935 that the name "Kelowna" stemmed from the name "Kim-ach-touch" which "the Indians had given to August Gillard," meaning "bear's face" or "bear face." It was decided by a committee in 1892 that this name would be too difficult for settlers to pronounce, and so they chose the related name Kelowna, meaning grizzly bear (Brent "The Name Kelowna" 162-63).

46 Sisters of St. Anne Convent in Kamloops, British Columbia.

47 The Sisters of St. Anne's school, later known as St. Ann's Academy, was opened in Kamloops in 1880 after similar schools had been established in Victoria, Cowichan, New Westminster and St. Mary's Mission on the Fraser, British Columbia (Rink 8-32). "Maria Houghton" is listed as a boarder from 1886-1887 in the *Registre des Noms, Entrées et Sorties des Élèves qui ont fréquente le Convent des Soeurs de St. Anne a Kamloops depuis 1880 jusquà 1930* (Student Register of the Convent of the Sisters of St. Anne in Kamloops 1880-1930). However, Brent is listed in the *Livres des Élèves* 1882-1906 (Student Accounts) as being paid for until April, 1888 (although in the year 1887 it says she is attending "*à raison de charité*," which could mean the institution waived fees, or possibly donated a scholarship). "Lena Laurent" is also listed from 1886-1887. The latter is probably Eleanor Laurence, Mary's younger sister and Theresa Laurence's youngest daughter. Maria Houghton Brent received her first communion in January of 1887 and her confirmation in March of that year. "Eleonore Laurent" was also confirmed in 1887 at St. Anne's (Sacramental Records, Convent of the Sisters of St. Anne).

48 Brent could be referring to the superior general of the Sisters of St. Anne, Mother Mary Anastasia, who visited the western missions in 1885, according to Deborah Rink. It is possible this visit extended to 1886. Mother Mary Anastasia encouraged the use of English and the change of the name in the west from St. Anne to St. Ann (Rink 32-3).

49 Brent is probably referring to Juneau, Alaska, where the Sisters of St. Ann established a school in November, 1886 (Cantwell and Edmond 26).

50 Brent's teacher could have been Sister Mary Peter, who was transferred from St. Anne's in Kamloops to be the first teacher in the Juneau school in 1887. She spent fifteen years in Juneau. She taught instrumental music including piano, guitar, mandolin and banjo (Peter). The accounts book (*Livres des Élèves*) from Sisters of St. Anne convent in Kamloops shows that payment was made for Brent to study music.

51 Autumn, 1888 or 1889.

52 Brent could be referring here to the past from the perspective of 1893 or the present of her writing of this memoir. She is probably referring to her mother and her mother's line—her grandfather and great-grandfather Nkwala. Theresa Laurence died in 1892, but Mary Laurence was still alive in 1893. She died in 1904.

53 C.F. Houghton was elected as a member of parliament for Yale-Kootenay in December, 1871 (Ormsby, "Houghton"). In an interview with Marie Houghton Brent in 1958, Elsie Turnbull tells a probably apocryphal story of Houghton's election: ". . .[T]wo persons turned up at the nomination meeting, a blacksmith and a barroom roustabout. The blacksmith offered the name of gentleman-farmer, Captain C.F. Houghton, who had paid well for the services to his horse. The other man seconded the nomination and Houghton thus became a member by acclamation . . ."(22). A similar story of only two voters nominating and acclaiming Captain Houghton as the representative for the Yale District is told by B.R. Atkins in "First Federal Election at Yale" (42-3).

54 After serving in Parliament, Houghton had support for an application to the Canadian militia. He attended the gunnery school in Quebec in the winter of 1872 and in March 1873 became deputy adjutant general for District 11 (British Columbia), stationed at Victoria (Ormsby, *Coldstream* 6.)

55 After retiring in 1897, Houghton died in Victoria in 1898 (Ormsby, "Houghton").

56 There is no record of Marie Houghton Brent attending Mount Sinai School of Nursing, which opened in 1881. However, they did not record names of students who did not graduate (Niss).

57 This is the original editor's note. Sources for some of the material in this article, particularly on the history of Chief Pelkamulox, are James Teit's "The Salishan Tribes of the Western Plateaus" in the 45th Annual Report of the Bureau of American Ethnology (1927-28), and George M. Dawson's *Notes on the Shuswap People of North America* (1891). In her section "Events of the Life of Chief Pelka-Mu-Lox," Brent incorporates Dawson in word-for-word passages and paraphrases, but the speech Pelkamulox gives is from Brent. In "Events of the Life of N'Kwala As I Remember Them," the story of N'Kwala's attack on the Lillooets is taken from Dawson. Brent acknowledges this source in this article, saying "MacKay [Indian Agent J.W. McKay] gave Dawson this story pieced together from several sources of information. I knew Mr. MacKay when I was a little girl." Here, Brent could be suggesting that McKay's information passed on to Dawson originally came from her people, and therefore is hers to be used. Ella Clark, an English professor at Washington State University, had sent Dawson's *Notes on the Shuswap People of North America* to Brent, apparently after Brent had told her the story of

Pelkamulox. A note written by Brent at the bottom of Clark's letter reads "This letter has been copied in its entirety to prove that Marie Houghton Brent did know the facts she states before they were found in the Archives in Ottawa . . . by Ella Clark . . ." (August 7, [circa 1956-57]).

58 Irish settler Charles Frederick Houghton.

59 Grand Chief Nkwala, Brent's great-grandfather, died in 1858 or 1859, which Brent notes in her letter to Hester White, Xmas, 1956, printed in Part Three of this volume. His son, Isaiah Moses (Chilkposemen, Five Hearts, Moise Cinq-Coeur), became Chief at Head of the Lake in 1865 (Carstens 115).

60 When the forty-ninth parallel became the border between Canada and the United States in 1846, it divided Okanagan Syilx territory. North of the border, the word "Okanagan" was used and south of the border, the word "Okanogan." Brent, who had lived on both sides of the border, uses these spellings interchangeably in this article.

61 Brent is citing section 3.4 which refers to the description of Pelkamulox in James Teit's "Salishan Tribes of the Western Plateaus," p. 265-67.

62 This is George Dawson's spelling.

63 A version of this speech, and of Pelkamulox's death and Nicola's revenge, was also published by Brent entitled "The first white men and the revenge of Chief Nicola" in *Indian Legends of Canada* by Ella E. Clark (1960).

64 The Seton Lake chief's speech is partly paraphrased and partly taken directly from Dawson's *Notes on the Shuswap* (24).

65 The Nicola country is in the southern interior of British Columbia, west of the Okanagan. It encompasses the basin of the Nicola River. The river, Nicola lake and the valley, as Brent indicates, were named after Chief Nicola (Nkwala).

66 As this sentence acknowledges, most of the information in this paragraph and the one above it describing the attack on the Lillooet is taken from Dawson (28). Joseph William McKay (1829-1900) was a valued advisor to both Syilx and settlers throughout the Okanagan and indeed British Columbia given his experience as fur trader, explorer, businessman and Indian agent. His parents, William McKay and Mary Bunn were both of mixed Indigenous and European heritage. McKay aided Governor Douglas in negotiating with Indigenous peoples in the Fort Victoria treaties of 1850; from the 1850s to the 1870s he worked for the Hudson's Bay Company in Victoria and Nanaimo, Thompson's River (Kamloops), Fort Yale (Yale) and the Cassiar and Stikine mining districts. In the 1880s, no longer with the HBC, he worked for the Canadian government as an Indian Agent for the Kamloops and Okanagan agencies. He was a source of information on the Syilx for both George Dawson and James Teit.

67 *Archeology of the Thompson River Region, British Columbia* was published by Harlan Ingersoll Smith (1872-1940) for the Memoirs of the American Museum of Natural History series in 1900.

68 Most of the description and wording in this paragraph and the one following comes from James Teit, "Salishan Tribes of the Western Plateaus," p. 269.

69 Conflict between miners and Indigenous people of British Columbia occurred in the Okanagan as well as the Fraser River area. In 1858, as reported by miner H.F. Reinhart, a series of skirmishes took place between

miners coming from the Colville area, where they had been in hostile Yakima territory, and the Syilx of the Okanagan-Similkameen, causing loss of life on both sides. The Robinson party had invaded the Syilx winter village in Penticton, taking food supplies and killing ten to twelve people. When they arrived in Kamloops they were chastised by Chief Nicola who threatened them with severe reprisals if they did not mend their ways (Thomson, "History" 214-15).

70 Samuel Black (1780-1841), after a long career with the North West Company, joined the Hudson's Bay Company after the two fur trading companies merged in 1821. In 1837 he was assigned to the "inland posts of the Columbia," including the Thompson's River Post, which turned out to be his last (Woodcock). For more of Brent's comments on the Samuel Black family, see her letter to Hester White, written on Christmas night 1956, in Part Three.

71 Grand Prairie was a stopping point on the Hudson's Bay Brigade Trail at present day Westwold, British Columbia, between Head of the Lake and Kamloops. It was on the Barnard stage coach route Brent took to go to school in Kamloops.

72 This description of Chief N'Kwala's death can be found in Teit, p. 370.

73 Irish settler Edward J. Tronson (1841-1909), rancher and farmer, pre-empted land between Priest's Valley and the arm of Okanagan land in 1867, going on to acquire holdings at the Commonage (near what is now Vernon) and Armstrong, British Columbia (Louis 159). He also lived at Okanagan Mission in 1878 (Martin 159). He became an important settler in Vernon, laying out the townsite of what was then called "Centreville" in Priest's Valley in 1885, and building the Victoria Hotel, which he sold in 1889 (Martin 159). He married a Syilx woman, and Edward Houghton attended school with their children.

74 Peter Carstens holds that Tonasket was named a "Captain" or sub-chief by Old Chief Nkwala in 1858 after his successful handling of contentious white miners at the border and that "after Nkwala's death [in 1859] Tonasket styled himself chief." He also mentions that Tonasket had been an orphan "who had been taken into one of Nkwala's southern households as a child" (46).

75 See Brent's letter to Hester White, December 14, 1959. Apparently, there were two Chief Edwards. One was the father of Suzette Sepetsa and the other was the brother.

76 The Moses Agreement was officially termed "Agreement with the Columbia and Colville," drawn up on July 7, 1883 and ratified July 4, 1884.

Mourning Dove

77 See Swalwell's "Girlhood Days" above and "Crossing Lines" in Part Three for more on the McKenna-McBride Commision.

78 The title page of *Coyote Stories* claims that the text is "edited and illustrated by Heister Dean Guie." Settler Hester Emily White, however, writes to her friend Katie Lacey that the "splendid" sketches were done by her brother Valentine's wife, Elizabeth Runnels of the Colville reservation. "Lizzie" told her that personally (Letter to Katie Lacey, "Sunday, At last I have been able,"

[circa 1961]. See Part Three.

79 In 1988, Alanna Brown gave this original transcription to Jeannette Armstrong, "cousin to Mourning Dove," in thanks "for helping me to locate the family elders Charlie Quintasket and Mary Lemery" (Brown, "House" 60).

80 *The Giaour: A Fragment of a Turkish Tale* (1813) was written by George Gordon, Lord Byron (1788-1824), British Romantic poet and satirist.

81 "Thou art weighed in the balances, and found wanting" is from the Bible, King James version, Daniel 5:12. Daniel interprets this writing on the wall in the sumptuous court of King Belshazzar in Chaldea (Babylon).

82 *The Song of Hiawatha* (1855) was written by American poet Henry Wadsworth Longfellow (1807-1882).

83 Shoyahpee (many variant spellings) is a Syilx word that denotes non-Indigenous people in North American at the time among western nations such as the Okanagan, Spokanes, Yakima and others.

84 Mourning Dove leaves a footnote here indicating that traditional stories referred to in *Cogewea* will appear in her next publication. See the Swa-lah-kin story, "Gods of the Sun and the Moon," from *Coyote Stories* (1933) in this section.

85 We learn later in *Cogewea* that the letter is from Densmore's fiancée Livinia, warning him about "that savage squaw girl" but encouraging him to continue his "game" to "get her money" (228).

86 An Aeolian harp, named for Aeolus, the ancient Greek god of the wind, is built so that it can be played by the wind. It is also a symbol of inspiration popular among the English Romantic poets. See Samuel Taylor Coleridge's "The Eolian Harp."

87 In Greek and Roman mythology, Harpies are flying daemons or lesser deities, with half-bird, half-human features. They have female faces and the talons and wings of raptors. The personification of storm winds, harpies were the providers and dividers of destinies, the deciders of fate.

88 In a note here in the original *Cogewea*, Mourning Dove associates the Thunderbird with the Syilx Owl-woman.

89 In Norse mythology, Thor is a powerful god associated with storms. He is the god of thunder and lightning.

90 Mourning Dove's note: "The service berry, *Amelanchier alnifolia*, also known as Saskatoon Berry. The fruit resembles the black currant but has a sweeter flavour. The Indians gather large quantities and sun-dry them for winter use. The berries are also used in the making of pemmican" (*Coyote* 51, n 1).

91 The Syilx heated food in watertight baskets into which hot stones were placed for heating.

92 Mourning Dove's story continues with Owl-woman encountering Coyote. Through cunning and trickery, Coyote causes her death.

93 In every tepee there was a blanket or robe reserved in a specific spot for the man of the house. A visitor would sit in a place by the door.

94 This note accompanied Mourning Dove's original story.

95 Marcus, Washington, is near Kettle Falls, northeast of the Colville Reservation.

96 Kelly Hill is in the area between the Kettle and the Columbia Rivers in

Washington state, northeast of the Colville Reservation.

97 Inchelium, Washington, is in Ferry County on the Colville Reservation.

98 Chief Antoine Nachumchin (*nx̌əmcin*) was a chief in Keremeos in the Similkameen.

Part Two

Essay: "Something Very Real"

1 Susan Allison published a series of recollections of the 1860s-1880s in the Vancouver *Sunday Province* in 1931. In 1976, University of British Columbia historian Margaret A. Ormsby published them as a book entitled *A Pioneer Gentlewoman in British Columbia: The Recollections of Susan Allison*. Hereinafter I will refer to them as the *Recollections*. All quotations in the essays are from Ormsby's edition.

2 Racialization and ethnicization are terms used to describe the ways in which a consciousness of racial or ethnic difference is constructed in a particular culture.

3 I use the phrase "subject position" to account for the way one is defined in a culture by one's age, ethnicity, class, race, occupation, ability or disability, gender, and other aspects of identity. While not erasing the role of individual features of our identity, or of our own agency in determining who we are, the phrase "subject position" also comprehends the role of things beyond individual disposition and effort.

4 Allison writes, "At the time I am writing of [1869], the tribe living at Chu-chu-ewa were under Quiniscoe . . . the Bear Hunter, and numbered nearly two hundred (today [circa 1930] I doubt if they number ten)" (Ormsby, *Pioneer* 27). See Thomas King's *The Truth About Stories: A Native Narrative*, pp. 32-33, for a discussion of how this belief shaped white narratives, art, and photography focussed on Indigenous people in the late nineteenth and early twentieth century.

5 This term is used in studies of autobiographical and biographical work to characterize the biographer's or autobiographer's desire to leave a trace or an account of people and events from the past. Such writing can be useful in responding to a past that has been "dis-membered" by trauma, injustice, false histories, or oppression.

6 Hyphens are used in these names, as Susan Allison often included them, likely to convey the enunciation of them in the Syilx language. Hereinafter, hyphens will not be used except where they appear in Allison's original work.

7 Much work in contemporary studies of settler colonialism emphasizes the "unsettled" psychosocial condition of the settler and settler descendants, and the unsettled legacy of settler colonialism in the present. Members of the dominant culture in Canada—past and present—are said to be haunted by the unresolved history of interaction with Canada's aboriginal people. See Arthur Manuel and Grand Chief Ronald M. Derrickson's *Unsettling Canada: A National Wake-Up Call*, Between the Lines Press, 2015.

8 Chuchuwayha [*cuʔcuʔwixaʔ*] is adjacent to the site of present-day Hedley,

British Columbia. Chuchuwayha Indian Reserve No. 2 borders Hedley. This reserve is part of the Upper Similkameen Indian Band comprised at present of about two hundred people. Many mixed heritage descendants of John Fall and Susan Allison are buried in the cemetery at Saint Ann's Roman Catholic Church on this reserve land. *cu?cu?wixa?* is an Okanagan word meaning has many springs or small creeks.

9 Ashnola [*ʕaysnulax*ʷ] is eleven kilometers west of Keremeos, British Columbia, where the Ashnola River flows into the Similkameen River.

10 Yacumtecum was a nephew of Quiniscoe and the brother of Nora Yacumtecum. He was also known as Tuctac or as "Charlie Yacutecum" (John Goodfellow 138). He died on May 25, 1930, apparently due to injuries sustained after being hit by a car. See Susan Allison's letter of November 28, 1930, to her daughter Louisa.

11 Suggesting Cockshist's close relations with the Allisons, Allison recounts that in 1881 her husband "took his Indian Cockshist" ("Early History," 9 Mar. 1923, p. 3) to find a man in a suicidal mental state wandering in the mountains. In another place, recounting the 1870s threat of Indigenous reprisal against Canadian settler encroachment, she states, "our old Indian travelled sixty miles to warn me to take my children and put off to the mountains" ("Early History," 5 Jan. 1923, p. 3). Identified as Cockshist, he is said to have stated that, in the event of a fight between Syilx and settlers, he would "go to the mountains and keep out of it. The whites are my friends, I could not harm them, nor could I strike against the Indians who are my brothers" ("Early History," 5 Jan. 1923, p. 3).

12 John (Johnny) McDougall (1827-1903) was a Metis from Red River and a Hudson Bay Company employee. After he left the company, he became an early pre-emptor of a considerable amount of land in the Kelowna area. He was married to Amelie, a Syilx woman, with whom he had a lively family of ten sons who became well-known ranchers and guides in the central Okanagan.

13 In various records, Nora is referred to as Nora Yacumtecum, Nora or Norah Baptiste, Julienne Baptiste, Julienne, or old Julienne. On a private genealogical website, she is referred to as "Nora (XAYLXATK)," daughter of "Francis Skius Kikitasqt" [Kikitasket]. He was likely the medicine man and elder Susan Allison calls Dr. Scuse and a brother of Chiefs Incowmasket and Quiniscoe. Harry Robinson, Syilx storyteller, mentions that she was married at one time to a man named Baptiste (*Nature Power* 114). This is confirmed by the 1891 census for the Princeton district where she is listed as Norah Baptiste, wife of Baptiste. They are listed as the parents of Daniel, age seven, and Felicite, age one. In the 1921 Canadian Census, Nora Baptiste is living with her older brother Alex Skeuce and his family on the Lower Similkameen Indian Reserve.

14 Lily was with her father's second family much of the time, spending winters at Hope in the early 1870s with Susan and her children. Here Lily went to school. Lori Thomas writes, "For many years there was much controversy as to whether Lily was an Allison. When she married, she was pressured into using the surname Thomas (we are not sure why that name) so that the Allison name would not appear on the marriage announcement. Today

she is accepted as being an Allison—either by birth or by adoption as she lived with the Allison family until she left to be married. She married John Norman [a French settler] in Penticton in 1902" (204). Caroline Allison, Susan and John Fall's seventh child, was her maid of honour.

15 Rachel (1873-1957) is variously identified as "Rachel," "Rachael," "Arcell," "Ashell," or "Arsel." Her name appears on private genealogical websites as "Arcell Rachel Matilda Sxwultkw" and as "Rachel Matilda Ashell Pierre Allison." She is "Rachael" in the 1901 census.

16 Notions of blood quantum are central to Euro-western constructions of "race." The quantification of the proportion of blood inherited from ancestors identified as belonging to various racial categories has long been used to position people legally and socially. There has been some movement away from this view in Canada, particularly since the civil rights movements of the last half of the twentieth century to the present.

17 See *The Sexual Contract*, Stanford UP, 1988.

18 "Passing" here connotes "surpassing" other peoples although she may have intended other meanings.

19 This was her father's and her brother's name.

20 Multiple references to the presence of Cosotasket and Tatlehasket at the Allisons' home in Susan Allison's writing indicate their closeness to the Allison family. Cosotasket was a healer and a knowledge keeper. The grandsire is likely modelled on Tamtusalist, son of her friend Shlawhalakan. Tamtusalist may have been father not only to Shlawhalakan, but also to Quiniscoe, Incowmasket, Tatlehasket, and Scuse. All members of this generational cohort are identified as brothers in many places in Allison's writing.

21 Ethnographer James Teit names the chiefs in the southern interior in the early nineteenth century, stating "some say that at the same time Skeu's was chief of the Upper Similkameen" (262). This may indicate the high rank of Susan Allison's friend Dr. Scuse and his family.

22 In a conversation on July 11, 2016, at En'owkin Centre in Penticton, British Columbia, Jeannette Armstrong and Greg Younging first called my attention to this possible meaning of Allison's term "Souie Appoo."

23 This phrase, then and now, has frequently been used to describe them.

24 The McLeans were sons of a white Hudson's Bay Chief Trader and rancher Donald McLean and his Indigenous wife Sophia Grant. After committing a number of crimes in the summer of 1879, including the murder of Johnny Ussher, a constable in a posse pursuing them, they were apprehended, tried, and hanged. This has become a "wild west" legend in British Columbia history.

25 Disclosure of white descent could jeopardize the treaty status and therefore the entitlements of Indigenous women and their descendants: "until 1985, the Indian Act removed the Indian status of all Native women who married individuals without Indian status (including nonstatus Canadian Indians and American Indians, as well as white men)" (Lawrence 8).

26 That there were Indigenous and non-Indigenous branches of the Allison family appears to have been common knowledge of longstanding in the Similkameen, though not part of public histories until the late twentieth

century. For example, regional historian Bill Barlee refers to the two branches of the family on the popular British Columbia television program "Gold Trails and Ghost Towns" in 1987. (See the "Princeton" episode). This predates Jean Barman's discussion.

27 The "Klootchman's Race" was a popular community event in early Princeton. This was a horse race engaged in by Indigenous women. "Klootchman" was a Chinook term for an Indigenous woman. It came to be used pejoratively.

28 A case in point is this statement: "The mountain streams, instead of perpetuating the names of the hardy pioneers who discovered them at the risk of their own lives, have been re-named after so-called pioneers, who came into the country in stage coaches" ("Early History," 9 Feb. 1923, p. 3).

29 Allison states that the victim was Killeketza, a Syilx man. In another account of George Jim's story, Syilx storyteller Harry Robinson states that the man who died was Harry Shuttleworth (*Write It* 246). In both versions, George and the other man were in a physical fight while drunk. A piece of inward correspondence to the British Columbia Attorney General's Office dated 1886 states that Ashnola George murdered "Isbakitza" and shot "Shuttleworth," but not fatally (Tunstall). Susan Allison also wrote a narrative about the immediate aftermath of the death of Killeketza entitled "The Mother of Killeketza."

30 See Library Archives Canada, http://www.bac-lac.gc.ca/eng/collectionsearch

31 Joseph W. McKay (1829-1900) was a "very dear friend" of Susan Allison (Ormsby, *Pioneer* 7). Allison often refers to him as someone who had insight into the Indigenous people that many other officials and settlers did not. McKay was Metis. For more on McKay, see Marie Houghton Brent's "Indian Lore" and Hester White's "Osoyoos" in this volume.

32 Robinson calls the aunt and uncle, who he says are cousins, Mary and John. He does not provide their Indigenous names. Ghenac may have been Ashnola Mary, sister of an important chief named Ashnola John or Johnny Chuchuaskin (Parsons and Laurence 53). She was said "to be 116 when she died in 1944" (Wickwire, "Introduction" 12).

33 There is no record of a Charlie Harvie (or variant spellings of this name) from Canada in the records although the Library and Archives of Canada website states that 7368 men served in the second South African War, but only 5935 service records remain. http://www.bac-lac.gc.ca/eng/discover/military-heritage/south-african-war-1899-1902/pages/service-files-south-african-war.aspx See also http://www.veterans.gc.ca/eng/remembrance/history/south-african-war http://www.warmuseum.ca/cwm/exhibitions/boer/boerwarhistory_e.shtml

34 In the early twentieth century, Krishnamurti was born in British India and taken under the wing of British theosophists as a boy. He eventually forged a somewhat divergent path from that of his British mentors.

35 The website of the Westbank First Nation explains: "*nx̌aʔx̌ʔitkʷ*, commonly referred to as 'Ogopogo,' is recognized today as a metaphor for sustainability. Known as the Sacred Spirit of the Lake, *nx̌aʔx̌ʔitkʷ* lives in the water but can also move to the land and air. *nx̌aʔx̌ʔitkʷ* reminds us to

be mindful of our resources; if *nx̌aʔx̌ʔitkʷ* disappears due to pollution and misuse of the water, so do the plants, medicines, trees, and foods that sustain us" ("Public Art").

36 Jeannette Armstrong explains that *nx̌aʔx̌ʔitkʷ* means spirit of the lake.

37 In the British Columbia Archives, there are a number of letters in the Susan Allison Family Fonds from Will and Rachel's eldest son Henry Allison (1894-1918) to Susan Allison. These were written from England and France. Henry was a Canadian soldier who died in France one month before the end of World War I. They reveal a close personal relationship between grandmother and grandson. Henry also gives accounts of his visits while stationed in Britain to his English relatives on his grandmother Susan Allison's side.

38 Mary Rose Allison McFarland (1913-1963)

39 Wilfred Allison, Jr., or Buck Allison (1902-1977)

40 Life writing is a term used for various genres of autobiographical writing, for example, book-length autobiography, memoirs, letters, diaries, journals, blogs, and email.

41 See Celia Haig-Brown and David A. Nock, *With Good Intentions: Euro-Canadian and Aboriginal Relations in Colonial Canada*. UBritish Columbia Press, 2006.

Susan Louisa Moir Allison

1 See note 1 to "Something Very Real."

2 See note 12 to "Something Very Real."

3 In a letter to Major J.S. Matthews, archivist for the City of Vancouver, Allison's daughter Alice O.A. Wright attests to her mother's disinclination for romanticizing: "...an MLA [Member of the Legislative Assembly of British Columbia] in suggesting she write a romantic account of her life, said 'But Mrs. Allison you are such a stickler for the truth;' he didn't care for her plain style of writing" (23 April 1969).

4 In the typescript of this essay at the top of the first page, in handwriting, is the following attribution: "This was written in the 1870ies—about 90 years ago. A.O.A.W." These initials are those of Susan Allison's daughter Alice Olivia Aurelia Wright.

5 This is a description of a baby swaddled and tied to a cradle board. This could be secured to the mother's back, a sled, a travois, or a horse for travel. Cradleboards were often beautifully decorated.

6 Susan Allison's prosody (line lengths, metre, rhyme, stanza form) echoes that of Henry Wadsworth Longfellow in his popular poem *The Song of Hiawatha* (1855).

7 See note 20 to "Something Very Real."

8 Semminatcoe may be based on Suzanne Cole, a sister of Chief Quiniscoe, who lived near the Allisons, acting as mid-wife in the delivery of Allison's first child Edgar (Ormsby, *Pioneer* 28). According to Allison, Suzanne was the mother of a boy named Hosachtem. Allison also identifies Johnny Suzanne, who worked for the Allisons, as Suzanne's son. Whether or not Johnny and Hosachtem are the same person is not clear. At some point, Suzanne married Thomas Cole, a white settler in the area.

9 This is present-day Mount Chopaka in northern Washington State.

10 The evil spirit of Mount Chippaco is identified by Allison as the "Souie Appoo," her rendition of a Syilx term often used for the white man.

11 Chin-Chin is mentioned as a young wife of the actual Incowmasket (Ormsby, *Pioneer* 57).

12 Allison identifies Penquinac (or Penquenac) as the daughter of Incowmasket (Ormsby, *Pioneer* 57-58). She was also known as Julia, the name given her by the priest, or Princess Julia. Margaret A. Ormsby states that she was "Princess Julia, the last hereditary chieftain of the Similkameens" (*Pioneer* 123 n56:29). See Allison's "Kind Penquinac or the Princess Julia" in this volume.

13 This is the Syilx name for the rocky area located at the mouth of Arcat Creek where it flows into the Similkameen River. Half way between Princeton and Hedley, it is now the site of Bromley Rock Provincial Park. The Syilx word refers to the deep holes or dips in the land in that area.

14 These are the names of two young men whom Allison first saw in the spring of 1869 when the Chuchuwayha community rode by her house.

15 See note 20 to "Something Very Real."

16 See note 9 to "Something Very Real."

17 This character is likely based on one of the many French Oblate priests who were part of a Roman Catholic mission in the Okanagan and Similkameen. Most famous was Father Pandosy (1824-1891) from Marseilles who established a mission in 1859 on Mission Creek in what is now Kelowna. He was revered by many of the Syilx people.

18 Allison describes an earthquake in the fall of 1880, which precipitated the conversion of many Similkameen people (Ormsby, *Pioneer* 57). On December 15, 1872, a major earthquake of 6.8 magnitude occurred in the region ("Important"). Northern Washington and southern British Columbia are prone to seismic activity.

19 The red ochre culled from the cliffs near the confluence of the Tulameen and Similkameen Rivers and other parts of these valleys was used for dye and other purposes. It was a trade item for the Similkameen people.

20 The coyote (sank'l'ip) is a central trickster figure in Syilx culture. Coyote is a complex sacred figure difficult for non-Indigenous people to understand as Coyote embodies creative and destructive forces, the spiritual and the material. These forces are generally opposed in western culture.

21 In the recollections, Susan Allison states that, after conversion, "In-cow-mas-ket sent pretty Chin-Chin away and kept the mother of his boy and Pen-quin-ac" (Ormsby, *Pioneer* 57).

22 Quiniscoe, who died some time in the 1870s, was the older brother of Incowmasket.

23 See note 13 above.

24 This is another Syilx word for owl. Some owls are considered Owl Monsters, as seems to be the case here. See Mourning Dove's "Chipmunk and Owl Woman" for a depiction of the dark deeds of Owl.

25 See note 10 to "Something Very Real."

26 As traders/storekeepers, it is likely that the Allisons had a secure safe. Susan Allison often indicates that they were trusted by the local Indigenous people.

27 See note 29 to "Something Very Real."

28 See note 13 above.

29 See note 9 to "Something Very Real."

30 "Tyee" is a Chinook term for a chief or someone in a position of power. In this case, the tyee was likely Arthur H. McBride, the warden of the New Westminster Penitentiary.

31 Based on the birth dates of the people depicted below, this episode likely took place in 1904 or 1905.

32 With Susan Allison at her ranch at this time are her eldest son Edgar (Ed), born 1869; his wife Marguerite, born 1879; their son Percy, born 1901; her grandson Wilfred, Jr., (Will) or Buck, born 1902; her daughters Angela, born 1889; Alice, born 1892; and her granddaughter Babs (Constance Thomas), born 1904, to Allison's eleventh child Grace, born 1884.

33 Louisa is from the Nicola area north of Princeton. Today the Syilx people who live in this area have reserves at Quilchena Lake (Nicola Lake) and Spaxomin (Douglas Lake). They are part of the Okanagan Nation Alliance.

34 This is a reference to the Cariboo Gold Rush (1860-1863) in central British Columbia.

35 The Fountain people are from the Lillooet area. Today, the government offices of the Fountain First Nation or Xaxli'p are located ten miles up the Fraser River Canyon from Lillooet.

36 The 1891 census for the subdistrict of Princeton lists the "Moise" [Moses] family. Moise is listed as the father and his occupation as "Indian Chief." His wife is listed as Elizabeth. Their eldest child is Julie, aged seventeen. Susan Allison states in her "Recollections" that Incowmasket was called Moses by the priests.

37 This is likely a reference to the 1850s or 1860s before much white settlement. Allison may therefore have written this in the 1920s or early 1930s.

38 The excerpts from the "Recollections" in this volume are based on the handwritten manuscripts in the City of Vancouver Archives.

39 For more about Edgar Dewdney, see "Something Very Real." Jane Moir Dewdney was two years older than Susan and became a well-known politician's wife in early Canada, residing with her husband in New Westminster, Victoria, Regina, and Ottawa. Many of Susan Allison's daughters spent extended time with her in Victoria. Storekeepers George and Marie Landvoight, Marie in particular, were Susan Allison's good friends at Hope.

40 Cockshist was a "well-known [Similkameen] Indian guide" (Ormsby, Pioneer xxviii-xxix) who had led Edgar Dewdney and others on the trails into the Similkameen when they were looking for routes for wagon roads and trains. See note 11 to "Something Very Real."

41 See note 8 above.

42 See note 10 in "Something Very Real.

43 The story "The Big Men of the Mountains" appears as one of the "Tales of Tamtusalist" in her handwritten manuscripts. The story was published in the OHS Report of 1927 and as an appendix in Margaret A. Ormsby's A Pioneer Gentlewoman in British Columbia: The Recollections of Susan Allison.

44 This was likely Nora Yacumtecum (1847-1926). See note 13 in "Something Very Real."

45 See note 13 in "Something Very Real."

46 A Balmoral petticoat was usually made of wool with stripes, often red, and worn under a dress. The skirt of the dress could be looped up and the petticoat exposed during physical activity.

47 Tatlehasket, Toupes, and Whylac are all characters in her sequence of long poems based on the lives of Incowmasket and Quiniscoe.

48 See note 20 to "Something Very Real."

49 A shift or smock generally worn as an undergarment or as sleepwear.

50 Thomas Cole pre-empted land in the Similkameen on July 5, 1873 (Some Early 35). He is listed as a stock raiser from Keremeos in the 1882 "Directory of British Columbia" (Ormsby, "Directories" 186).

51 Mourning Dove states that Syilx mothers-to-be followed a strict program of physical exercise, slept less than others, and while in labour did not moan or cry out since this was seen as detrimental to the baby (Mourning 70-72).

52 See note 14 to "Something Very Real."

53 The character Cosotasket speaks against conversion to Christianity and becomes alienated from the community after the Chief and many others convert in "In-Cow-Mas-Ket, Part Two." Tatlehasket and Cosotasket are firmly allied in the poem. See note 20 to "Something Very Real."

54 The Skagit River Valley is south and east of Princeton.

55 Reverend John Booth Good was an Anglican priest who worked at Nanaimo and Yale. In 1867, he established a mission (St. Paul's) at Lytton (Fisher 137).

56 Ashnola John was a Similkameen Chief who lived in the Keremeos area. Often caricatured by the settlers and considered difficult by officials, he was a strong advocate for his people. His grave is near Keremeos (Rhenisch). See note 32 to "Something Very Real."

57 This is an American repeating rifle first made in the 1860s.

58 Arthur Wellesley Vowell (1841-1918) was superintendent of Indian Affairs for British Columbia from 1889-1910 (Ormsby, *Pioneer* 115 n.35:2).

59 John Carmichael Haynes (1831-1888) was stipendiary magistrate, gold commissioner, and county court judge residing at Osoyoos. See Part Three of this volume.

60 See note 31 to "Something Very Real."

61 Wilhelmina (Mina) Wade married Thomas Ellis (1845-1918) in Dublin in 1872. Ellis was from County Tyrone, Ireland, and became one of the first settlers at the foot of Okanagan Lake where the city of Penticton stands today. He acquired large holdings in this area beginning in 1866. See Part Three of this volume.

62 See note 13 and note 21 to "Something Very Real."

63 Allison is referring to the widespread dissatisfaction and organizing among Indigenous people in Canada and the United States in the 1870s in response to displacement and settler appropriation of land. The most famous of the battles that comprise the American "Indian Wars" took place in June, 1876, between the Sioux and the American army at a site known as Little Big Horn in Montana.

64 Allison often expresses great respect for British Columbia's first leader, Governor James Douglas (1803-1877). She describes him as a "fine far-seeing man", for his understanding of Indigenous people (Ormsby, Pioneer 13).

65 This is Green Bay in West Kelowna.

6 See note 17 above.

7 Therese Laurence was married to Cyprien Laurence, one of the early settlers in the Kelowna area. She and her husband were part of a small settler party led by Father Pandosy who came into the Canadian Okanagan from the United States in 1859. Her uncle, Chief Paqlpitsa, or Capeau Blanc (aka "Chapeau" Blanc), from the Penticton area, was hostile toward the group, but she convinced him to allow them safe passage (Rivère 70, Buckland 29). She was also the daughter of Grand Chief Nkwala, and the great aunt of Marie Houghton Brent. (See "Standing Between" and notes on Brent's "Indian Lore" in Part One of this volume).

8 In 1863, Chief Joseph (1840-1904), following his father Tuekakas, or Joseph the Elder, resisted the removal of the Nez Perce people from their reservation in present-day Oregon and parts of Washington and Idaho, to a much smaller one in Idaho. Joseph stayed on his Oregon land. In 1873, he negotiated a treaty for his band to stay in the Wallowa Valley in Oregon, but in 1877, federal authorities gave him 30 days to move to the Idaho territory. Instead, Chief Joseph and about 750 Nez Perce travelled over three months to seek asylum with Chief Sitting Bull in Canada. Their encounters with a pursuing United States Army are called the Nez Perce War. They finally surrendered after a five-day battle in 1877. In 1885, the Nez Perce were placed on the Colville Reservation in Washington State.

9 Margaret A. Ormsby suggests that Allison may have meant the Americans (*Pioneer* 45).

0 See note 24 to "Something Very Real."

1 The gang consisted of Allan, Charley, and Archie McLean, and their mixed heritage friend Alex Hare (not Nick).

2 This is John Andrew Mara (1840-1920) who was an important rancher, businessman, and politician in the Shuswap and north Okanagan area at this time.

3 Allison mistakenly dates her encounter with the McLean brother and his sister as the summer of 1876, disrupting her chronology.

4 Susan Allison recounts Mr. Hayes' ill will toward her a number of times in the "Recollections." The fact that he had an Indigenous wife may explain his negative attitude toward her. He may have seen this middle-class British woman as a harbinger of a white civility that would put an end to the way of life of many up-country white men.

5 Cole Harris states that Sproat's attempt "to find what he considered to be fair, just space for Native people . . . was a virtually impossible task" because of "the tangle of settler property rights and prejudices" (*Making* 144). Harris' book dedication for *Making Native Space* reads: "In memory of Gilbert Malcolm Sproat, a colonizer who eventually listened" (v).

6 Scots Gaelic for a boy or young man who attends a chieftain on a hunt or a fishing trip.

7 Animals including deer and coyote were often domesticated pets of the Allisons. They often came and went inside the house. Remembering a visit to the Allisons in her childhood, Hester White recounts the children playing with their coyotes and a boy riding a pony through the house. (See"Over the Hope Trail" in Part Three)

78 Barrington Price and Henry Nicholson were middle-class English friends who had income from family remittances ("Remittance Men"). They came to the Keremeos area in 1872. Both acquired land, ranched, and started a flour and grist mill there in 1876 (Manery 73). Price had two mixed heritage daughters. One was Millie who married Charlie Allison. After he died, she married Daniel or "Wichy," another of Nora Yacumtecum's children. Henry Nicholson had a son of Syilx heritage, Alex Nicholson, who married Matilda Kruger in 1934. (See "Hester White's Correspondence with Matilda Kruger" in Part Three of this volume).

79 See note 18 above.

80 Susan and John Fall Allison had nine children at this time: Edgar (Ed), Wilfred (Will), Beatrice (Bea or BJ), Louisa, Rose, John (Jack), Caroline (Carrie), George, and Elfreda (Frida), ranging in age from 11 or 12 years of age to infancy. Lily, about 19 years old at this time, likely did much child-minding and domestic work, along with Susan's older girls. Lily appears to have moved between her father's and mother's families.

81 This was probably an outbuilding for lodgers such as cowboys and miners.

82 Howse (1855-1938) was Indian Agent for the Okanagan Agency from 1880-1884. He also held land in the Nicola Valley where he ranched. He was the manager (1905) and then owner (1906-1911) of the *Similkameen Star* newspaper in Princeton (Ormsby, *Pioneer* p. 125, n.64:16) where Susan Allison published many articles.

83 General Sherman gave Jack (John Stratton Allison) a sword which is in the possession of a descendant.

84 This address is close to what is now Pacific Spirit Regional Park. Allison lived here with her daughter Alice Olivia Ashwick Perkins Wright and her family from 1926 until her death in 1937. All letters bear this address.

85 This is Susan Louisa (Allison) Johnston, Susan and John Fall Allison's fourth child who lived at this time in Princeton.

86 See note 15 to "Something Very Real."

87 "Will" may be her son (Robert Wilfred) or his son and her grandson Wilfred Jr., known as Buck Allison (1902-1977). These letters indicate that she was in correspondence with him and that he tried to visit her one day. "Henry" may be another son of Will, Sr., and Rachel--Henry Allison who was killed in France in World War I. See note 37 to "Something Very Real."

88 Mary Rose Allison McFarland (1913-1963), Robert Wilfred and Rachel's daughter and Will, Jr.'s, younger sister.

89 Angie is Aurelia Angela Allison McDiarmid (1889-1982), Susan Allison's thirteenth child.

90 Edgar Moir Allison (1869-1943), Susan Allison's oldest child. He appears to be estranged from the family.

91 Her five eldest children: Edgar Moir, Robert Wilfred, Beatrice Jane Allison Bruce-Mitford, Rose Isabella Allison Sandes, and Susan Louisa Allison Johnston.

92 Albert Johnston, Louisa's husband.

93 Albion was Alice's first husband, Albion Everett Perkins (born 1879). This letter does not indicate the year of writing, but must have been written some time before Albion's death on July 18, 1931.

64 This is Thomas Glennie, Susan Allison's mother's second husband. This dinner scene likely took place on their land ("Hopelands") near Hope, British Columbia, in the 1860s before Glennie deserted them in 1864.

65 This is Jane Shaw Moir Dewdney, Susan Allison's sister.

66 This could be Mrs. Elizabeth Daly. Her husband Thomas purchased the Barrington Price ranch near Keremeos in 1885.

67 Sir Oliver Lodge (1851-1946) was a physicist who researched electricity and wireless transmission. Allison and her daughter Alice were interested in his work on spiritualism and psychic communication for which he is better known.

68 This may be another of Will Sr.'s, sons, Hugh Allison (1900-1956).

69 This could be the Kamloops Indian Residential School opened in 1893, or St. Ann's Academy in Kamloops. For generations, Syilx children were forcibly moved to the Residential School. Mary would have been about 17 at this time. She also had a younger sister Maggie, 12 years old in 1930. "Asel" may be the girls' mother Rachel Allison, also known as Arcell.

70 Valeria Helen Grace Allison Thomas (1884-1969), Susan and John Fall Allison's eleventh child.

71 "Some Recollections of a Pioneer of the Seventies"

72 See note 10 to "Something Very Real."

73 See note 72 above.

74 See note 31 to "Something Very Real."

75 The Convent of the Sacred Heart (1913-1979) was a Roman Catholic school for girls in Vancouver.

76 Susan Allison's granddaughter, daughter of her tenth child Alfred Edward Allison (1883-1954).

77 Margaret or "Maggie" Allison (born in 1918), youngest child of Robert Wilfred and Rachel [Arcell]. She died on March 3, 1932.

78 "Cheer, Boys, Cheer" was a song written in 1850, which became very popular in the British army in the Victorian era.

79 Susan Allison wrote an essay entitled "The Eternal Now."

80 The "rows" are likely the unrest in the downtown area of Vancouver as the Depression deepened into the 1930s. Many homeless, unemployed people came to Vancouver from other parts of Canada for the warm climate. There were many marches, demonstrations, riots, some looting, and violent confrontations with police.

81 Beatrice Allison Bruce-Mitford, Susan and John Fall Allison's third child and oldest daughter, who lived in England from 1912 until her death.

82 Sympathy for Shylock was hard to find in literary criticism until after the Holocaust prompted a critique of anti-Semitism in western culture.

83 No year. The references to poverty suggest the 1930s.

84 This could be Rachel (Arcell), her daughter-in-law.

Part Three

Essay: "Crossing Lines"

See Marie Houghton Brent's "Indian Lore" in Part One for more information on the old Chief Nkwala and his son the young Chief Nkwala.

2 Although this article was not signed by Marie Houghton Brent, internal evidence suggests she contributed much of the material for it.

3 This excerpt is from the 1935 article. Versions of this article were also published in the *OHS Report* of 1930 and 1931.

4 For a detailed discussion of land issues in the Okanagan during this period, see Duane Thomson, "A History of the Okanagan: Indians and Whites in the Settlement Era, 1860-1920," pp. 111-167. Other important studies include Jeannette Armstrong et al., *We Get Our Living Like Milk from the Land;* Peter Carstens, *The Queen's People: A Study of Hegemony, Coercion, and Accommodation Among the Okanagan of Canada;* Robin Fisher, *Contact and Conflict: Indian-European Relations in British Columbia, 1774-1890;* Cole Harris, *Making Native Space: Colonialism, Resistance and Reserves in British Columbia,* and Paul Tennant, *Aboriginal Peoples and Politics: The Indian Land Question in British Columbia, 1849-1989.* See also "Girlhood Days in the Okanagan" by Eliza Jane Swalwell in Part One of this volume.

5 Chief John Chelahitsa (Syilx), Chief Petit Louis *Hli Kleh Kan* (Secwépemc) and Chief John Tetlanitsa (Nlaka'pamux) met with Wilfred Laurier in Kamloops when he was on a pre-election tour of Canada and presented their Memorial to him regarding land and rights for interior Indigenous people. For more on this, see notes for Eliza Jane Swalwell in Part One.

6 For a full discussion of Haynes's encroachment on Nk'Mip lands, see Duane Thomson, "A History of the Okanagan" pp. 143-47.

7 Synopses of the plays produced at the Inkameep School can be found in Cynthia Joanne Korpan, "Authentic Culture: The Inkameep Plays as Canadian Indian Folk Drama" pp. 63-67.

8 See Lisa-Marie Smith, p. 49, for an indication of the approving attitude of Indian agent James R. Coleman of Walsh's work at the Inkameep Day School.

9 The tangled and contradictory agendas involved in Canadian support of Indigenous artistic and cultural productions has been written about by many. For an overview of some of the positions in British Columbia, see Lilynn Wan, "A Nation of Artists: Alice Ravenhill and the Society for the Furtherance of British Columbia Indian Arts and Crafts," passim. For a discussion of conflicting contexts and perspectives involved in the Inkameep children's performance at Thunderbird Park, Victoria, in 1941, see Korpan, "Authentic Culture," pp. 129-36.

10 Many of the paintings were saved by Katie Lacey (1900-1964), who donated them to the Osoyoos Museum in 1963, but they remained under her bed for twenty years (Johnson 2). The Osoyoos Museum and Archives and the Osoyoos Indian Band are currently joint stewards of the collection. An "Inkameep Day School" Exhibit is housed in the acclaimed Nk'Mip Desert Cultural Centre, established by the Osoyoos Indian Band in 2007.

11 Bonita Lawrence points out that the 1951 Indian Act "heightened colonial regulation" over Indigenous women, particularly those who married non-native men (*"Real" Indians* 53). They not only continued to lose their Indian status, as had been true since the Enfranchisement Act of 1869, but furthermore were "compulsorily enfranchised," which meant they lost

"band membership, reserve residency, . . . any property they might have held on the reserve, but also access to any treaty monies or band assets" (51). After ongoing challenges from Indigenous women, this situation was finally addressed in 1985 with Bill C-31, and even then only partially (see Lawrence, *"Real" Indians and Others*, Chapter 3).

2 The script of that play is printed in *The Carolina Playbook*, volume 13, number 4 (December, 1940). It is also reprinted in Korpan, pp. 75-81.

3 No doubt MacNaughton's "authority" here was her friend Josephine Shuttleworth, as this description matches the Syilx explanation, according to Jeannette Armstrong. A note with the annotated drawings of the pictographs (not in MacNaughton's writing) says "these designs were read by Frederick A. Botsford archeologist and Pioneer and Chief M. Mountainhorse of the Blood of the Blackfoot Confederation."

4 In discussions with Jeannette Armstrong, I learned there is a well-known story about two girls who disobeyed their brother and their grandmother and were abandoned. The greasewood appears in the story as the place that through its roots transforms into a portal to another world, where the girls' grandmother and village had gone. Unlike in MacNaughton's play, this world could not be reached by the girls.

5 I am going by the 1881 Census of Canada listing Kruger as seventeen, which would mean she was born in 1864, but dates for Matilda and Mary Kruger in various United States censuses fluctuate, usually portraying them as younger, and sometimes giving the same year for both their births. See the headnote to "Correspondence with Matilda Kruger" in Hester White's section in Part Three.

6 This article was entitled "Lost Okanagan: In Search of the First Settler Families," *OHS Report* 60 (1996), pp. 8-20.

7 Jean Barman cites White's reference to "Theodore Kruger and his eldest daughter Dora" to assert that "in public Matilda did not exist" ("Lost" 14). I am trying to show here that Matilda Kruger's existence was both affirmed and denied in the same article written by White.

8 As this piece was undated and unpublished, it is not certain when it was written, but its subject matter fits chronologically between two published reminiscences of White's childhood, "Mail Day" and "We Cross the Columbia in a Canoe," both of which were published in the *OHS Report* in 1961.

9 In a letter to Ann Briley, White mentions that she "went twice to [Kruger's] home in Omak" (February 18, 1959).

0 See Robert M. Hayes's article "Haynes-Moore Story Deserves to be Told" and its information on J.C. Haynes's and Julie Abraham's children. It was published in 1997, a year after Jean Barman's article.

1 It is unclear whether White was referring to a baptism certificate for John Haynes or for Mary Ann Haynes. In her papers, she kept a baptism certificate for "Marianne" Haynes, dated July 11, 1866, stating that Marianne was "three months old" and signed by Father Richard, OMI. The certificate was sent to her by the Oblate Fathers in Kamloops, British Columbia, in 1941.

2 Censuses, however, are well known to be unreliable and could have listed

the children as descendants of John Carmichael Haynes, without them actually being present.

23 One tantalizing detail of John Haynes's childhood comes from Kathleen Dewdney. She claims that Francis (Frank) and Lucy Richter's sons had attended Father Pandosy's Mission church school which preceded the government-run Okanagan Mission Valley School established in 1875. Dewdney implies that Johnny Haynes was also present in her listing of the members of Father Pandosy's school band, which included "Joe Richter, B-flat cornet; John Brent, E-flat cornet; Bill Brent [later to become Marie Houghton's husband], trombone; Joe Brent [William Brent's older brother], alto horn; and John Haynes, B-flat cornet" ("Francis" 85). This particular band was probably not at the Mission church school which closed around 1866, but rather the Okanagan Mission Valley School which was established in 1875. According to F.M. Buckland, Father Pandosy (adept on the French horn as well as other instruments) formed the first brass band at this second school (*Ogopogo's Vigil* 53).

Hester Emily White

1 The Imperial Order Daughters of the Empire (IODE) was founded in 1900 in Canada in support of Canadian soldiers in the Boer war and, more generally, of the British empire and its values. Now an international charitable organization, it continues today.

2 White's poem is describing one of the trails from Hope to the interior of British Columbia. She mentions various settler families, landmarks and outstanding features of the landscape. See the excerpts from "The Pioneer Trail" and "Over the Hope Trail" in this section for more detailed information. See also the Introduction and "'Something Very Real'" in Part Two for the information on Syilx trails as the foundation for settler trails and roads. Susan Allison would have been very familiar with this trail, and John Allison took part in mapping and developing it. In this poem introducing "The Pioneer Trail" series, White suggests the record of her family is disappearing, along with much of local settler history.

3 White's description does not encompass the full extent of the Syilx land. See the Introduction and the Map for more on the territory of the Syilx.

4 A dwarf shrub indigenous to the Okanagan that creeps along the ground, of the family *Arctostaphylos*.

5 The quotation is from "Be still and know that I am God," from the Bible, Psalm 46:10.

6 In March 1811, fur trader Alexander Ross (1783-1856) helped establish Fort Astoria for John Jacob Astor's Pacific Fur Company (PFC) at the mouth of the Columbia River (now Astoria, Oregon). With David Stuart (1765-1853), accompanied by Ovid deMontigny of the PFC, and David Thompson of the North West Company, among others, he travelled in July 1811 further up the river to set up the trading post Fort Okanogan at the confluence of the Columbia and the Okanogan Rivers (near Brewster, Washington). David Stuart travelled north through the Okanagan to the Thompson River district, now Kamloops, helping to establish a fur trade route which came to be known as the Okanagan Brigade Trail. In 1813, Fort Okanogan was

purchased by the North West Company which was assimilated into the Hudson's Bay Company in 1821. The fort was then relocated on the banks of the Columbia River.

See notes for "Standing Between" in Part One for more on Okanagan Falls. Stem-tee-ma, grandmother, in this column of "The Pioneer Trail" and the next, also figures prominently in Mourning Dove's novel *Cogewea* (1927). See the essay "Crossing Lines" in this section, and "Under the Whispering Pines" in Part One.

In *nsyilxcn*, the lake creature is *nx̌aʔx̌aʔitkʷ*, sacred being in the water.

0 See "'Something Very Real'" in Part Two for a discussion of the lake creature and the origin of the name Ogopogo.

1 Much of the material up to this point was reprinted in the *Okanagan Historical Society Annual Report 33* (1969), pp. 100-01, as "Notes on the Okanagan."

2 See Isabel Christie MacNaughton's description of "Power signs," likely received from Josephine Shuttleworth, cited in the essay "Crossing Lines."

3 White imaginatively situates her friends and acquaintances—Syilx chiefs and figures whom she knew of in her lifetime—into the era before 1811 when contact was made with white traders. Gregoire (Gregor, also Krewar) Yacumtecum (*yaqmtiqm*)was a Chief at Nk'Mip until 1907. Tonasket (circa 1820-1891) was a Chief in the Colville region, and a packer for White's father J.C. Haynes. See more information in Marie Houghton Brent's "Indian Lore" in Part One. Stelkia was a family name at Nk'Mip, familiar neighbours to White. Susap (1843-1949) was a brother to Chief Baptiste George (*cianut*)(circa 1846-1949) of the Nk'Mip, and worked for J.C. Haynes as a ranch hand. Sin-sa-nat-kin (1824-1894) also worked on the Haynes ranch.

4 This final statement is ambiguous: is it the Syilx young men who are "happy," or is it the observer, who knows what dislocation is to come for the Syilx people, but, for the moment, can put it out of "our" minds? White's columns in "The Pioneer Trail" go on to describe and imagine the arrival of explorers and fur traders in the region of the Columbia and Okanagan rivers. Interaction between Europeans and Okanagans initiated a period of rapid change for the Syilx. This column and the next are two of the rare places in "The Pioneer Trail" where the disruption of Syilx ways of life are suggested.

5 Much of the information about Syilx language and practices in "The Pioneer Trail" in this column and the one preceding it may have come from White's housekeeper and friend Louise Gabriel. Gabriel's "Food and Medicine in the Okanakanes" published in the *OHS Report*, vol. 18 (1954). It was "compiled by Hester E. White" (24) and contains similar (though more detailed) information.

6 This post is Fort Okanogan on the Columbia River.

7 White refers to the Bible, Genesis 25: 29-34. An ambiguous figure, Jacob deceived his twin brother Esau into giving up his birthright (as the eldest son of Isaac) for a meal of "red pottage."

8 White probably means balm of Gilead. Indigenous people in the British Columbia interior made ointment from the sticky buds of the black cottonwood tree (*Populous balsmifera ssp. trichocarpa*); both the ointment and the tree itself were called balm of Gilead by the settlers.

9 White refers to the area where settler Francis Richter established his second

ranch along the lower Similkameen River near the Canada/United States border.

20 In fact, as White points out in her biographical article about her father, J.C. Haynes was appointed first officer in the Similkameen in November, 1861 ("John" 187).

21 This would have been before the building of the Panama Canal, 1885-1914. Susan Allison decribes the arduous train ride across the Panama Isthmus in her recollections of the 1860s (Ormsby, Pioneer 2-3).

22 J.C. Haynes's position was facilitated by relatives at home in Ireland, according to White in her biographical article, "John Carmichael Haynes." He had the assistance of "his influential uncle, James Carmichael, of Hyndford . . . a personal friend of Chartres Brew" as well as a "strong testimonial" from the Mayor and Magistrates of Cork (183).

23 The Ned McGowan "war" consisted of disputes between San Francisco miner (and former lawyer) Ned McGowan, who occupied Hill's Bar in the Fraser River, and American leaders in the nearby town of Yale. It involved challenges to the British judicial authorities and was resolved peacefully.

24 In September 1860, Haynes was appointed Deputy Collector of Customs to assist W.G. Cox. Cox had been placed in charge of the Rock Creek-Similkameen area close to the United States border, where gold had recently been discovered. Up until this time, Yale had been the only port of entry into British Columbia from the United States, but with the discovery of gold in other places besides the Fraser River, Douglas provided the legislation to open up other border posts where necessary (White, "John" 186-87). White says that Haynes was "associated all his life" with the Customs Service (186), which not only provided him with a stipend, but was advantageous when he began ranching. As White tells us, "[Haynes and his partner W.H. Lowe] got their start in cattle by buying from Drovers [crossing the border near Osoyoos] sufficient to enable them [the drovers] with the money realised to pay the duty on the remainder of their stock." She goes on to say, "[Haynes and Lowe] also added to their herd by the purchase of foot-sore animals" which could be had cheaply (qtd. in Fraser: 79).

25 Theodore Kruger was born in Hanover, Germany, in 1829 and died in 1899 in Osoyoos. He came to British Columbia in 1858, and engaged in freighting between Victoria and the Fraser River, and placer mining on the Fraser and in the Cariboo. He arrived at Blackfoot "a rip roaring camp on the south fork of the Similkameen" in 1860 (Fraser 90-91). Later, he opened a store in Princeton. In 1867 he arrived in Osoyoos to manage the Hudson's Bay Company post, which he bought in 1873 and ran as his own store until 1897 (Chrestenza Kruger 76, 79). In 1884 he opened the first post office in the region, with himself as postmaster. He and his family were one of the very few close settler neighbours to J.C. Haynes and his family in Osoyoos. After Haynes's death in 1888, Kruger became Customs Collector in Osoyoos from 1889 until his own death in 1899. For more information, see notes in this section under "Correspondence with Matilda Kruger."

26 This is very likely the Similkameen hunter and knowledge keeper Cosotasket. See Part Two.

27 After the Oregon Treaty in 1846 which established the current Canada-

United States border as the boundary between American and British territories at the 49th parallel west of Rockies, the fur trade trail was rerouted through British territory in 1847. See Jean Webber, "Fur Trading," for more information on fur trade.

8 Even though the fur trade route through Fort Okanagan was terminated in 1847, the Hudson Bay Company continued to assert ownership of the fort, only removing Francis Desquichette from that post to relocate in the Similkameen in 1860. In 1967, its location was flooded by Lake Paternos resulting from the construction of the Wells Dam.

9 Francis (Francois) Deschiquette (Dechiquette) had been the manager at Fort Okanogan. Roderick McLean was the husband of Mary McLean, Josephine Shuttleworth's sister.

0 In Mourning Dove's novel *Cogewea* (1927), the grandmother, Stemteemä, tells the story of Green Blanket Feet (165-77). It is ironic that White mentions Green Blanket Feet here, perhaps to supply a note of drama, since she keeps hidden the fact that both her father, J.C. Haynes, and Theodore Kruger had had children with Syilx women previous to marriages to settler women. See essay "Crossing Lines" in this section.

1 In April 1861, Haynes's jurisdiction widened to trails into the interior from Okanagan Lake, and, as Cox was transferred to other areas, Haynes was placed in charge of the Rock Creek-Similkameen-Okanagan district in November, 1861. Haynes transferred the district headquarters from the Similkameen to Sooyoos (*s?wiws*, or Osoyoos) Lake, close to the international border, where he eventually settled. For more information on John Carimicheal Haynes, see Hester E. White, "John Carmichael Haynes," and Margaret A. Ormsby, "Some Irish Figures in Colonial Days." For detailed information on Haynes as settler, stockraiser, Judge, legislator and colonial official, see Duane Thomson, "A History of the Okanagan: Indians and Whites in the Settlement Era," throughout.

2 Likely during this time J.C. Haynes lived with Julie Abraham, a Syilx woman from Colville, as he had two children with her, MaryAnn in 1866 and John Carmichael in 1868. See essay "Crossing Lines."

3 Scutari was a district of Istanbul, Turkey, now known as Üsküdar, where Florence Nightingale had been based at the Selimiye Barracks during the Crimean War (1853-56).

4 Matilda Kruger lived with the Hayneses. For more on her, see the essay "Crossing Lines" and White's "Correspondence with Matilda Kruger" in this section.

5 Charlotte Moresby (1850-1872) married J.C. Haynes at Fort Hope in 1868 and came with him to Osoyoos. She died in 1872, three months after giving birth to their son, Fairfax.

6 An undated, handwritten note in White's files entitled "Jinny, an Indian Woman" adds this information about Jinny: "(Tee-qualt) small, alert—and was famous for her chip-chap-Tiqualk story telling—tribal storytelling—she lived in one of the cabins and used to wash out in the wash house or down at the Lake—for our family." In a later, unpublished reminiscence about the early days of her marriage to C.A.R. Lambly, White says "It was shortly after my [first] baby came [in 1897] that Jinny arrived with Chief Gregoire and three or four friends . . . sat down on the floor . . . lit the little stone pipe of Peace passing it from me to the others . .

. a sign of respect. . .which I have never forgotten" ("Jail House"). She also describes visiting Jinny when the latter was very old and blind: "I went into the cabin [. . .] and on the floor lay Jinny. I took her hand and said 'Jinny' and she immediately said 'Hashie'[;] she knew my voice" ("Jail House").

37 White probably meant "manteau," a "pack saddle cover" according to Mary Ann Cawston (122).

38 White is listing a number of medicines of her childhood, stimulating concoctions such as Squills, a powder from a plant of the lily family [Scilla, Drimia maritima] which can be a heart tonic and expectorant; and the laxative castor oil. She also lists soothing remedies such as paregoric or camphorated tincture of opium, and Steadman's (Steedman's) powders which contained opium and mercury and was used for teething. "Chloredine" or Chlorodyne, a patent medicine invented in 1857, contained a mixture of laudanum, tincture of cannabis, alcohol and chloroform.

39 James McConnell was manager of the Haynes ranch (Mather 88) and "worked for Judge Haynes in the 1880s in Osoyoos" (Dewdney, "Driving" 10).

40 "Val" was White's older brother Valentine Carmichael (1875-1963); her younger brothers were "Will," William Barrington (1879-1959) and John Sherman (1883-1957); and her sister was Irene Margaret (1880-1965).

41 Hiram F. Smith, known as "Okanogan Smith," was "the first permanent settler in the Okanagan" region in 1858 (H. Splawn, "Land of Giants" 25), obtaining land from Chief Tonasket just south of the international boundary before the Colville reservation was established in 1872 (Lacey, "Chief Tonasket" 23-24).

42 Francis Xavier Richter, born in Friedland, Bohemia [now the Czech Republic], arrived in the Okanagan in 1864 after ten years in Texas, Arizona, California and Washington. He established the R ranch on Similkameen land in 1865; he later acquired 10,000 acres of farm and rangeland, including homes at Lower Ranch (near the boundary), where he moved in 1885, and Inglewood in Keremeos where he lived in 1898. At Inglewood he established a thriving orchard and is credited with being one of the founders of the Okanagan fruit industry. He and his Syilx wife Lucy Simla (Sumlahw) (Louis 118-19) married circa 1868 (Dewdney, "Francis Xavier Richter" passim). Francis Richter and Lucy separated in 1894, when Richter married Florence Loudon of Loomis, Washington, with whom he had five daughters and a son. Lucy continued to live on the R ranch and, according to Florence Loudon's brother, "died in about 1903 or 1904 in the cabin she lived in on the original Richter ranch" (qtd. in Barman, "Lost Okanagan": 13). Francis Richter died in 1910.

43 Richard Lowe "Dick" Cawston arrived in the south Okanagan in 1874 from Stratford, Ontario. He was engaged "to take on the management of the cattle" on the ranch owned by J.C. Haynes and his partner W.H. Lowe, Cawston's cousin (White, "Cawston" 1). In 1884, in partnership with Mrs. Lowe (W.H. Lowe had died in 1882), Cawston bought Frank Richter's ranch in Keremeos where he became a successful stockman. Cawston brought his new wife Mary Anne Pearson Cawston from Ontario to the Okanagan in 1885 (Fraser 104-106). Upon their arrival in the Okanagan, the newlywed

Cawstons spent Christmas at the Haynes ranch.

4 Mary Jane Gartrell was the daughter of James Gartrell who brought his family to Penticton from Ontario in 1885 and pre-empted land on Trout Creek Point in today's Summerland in 1889 (Maisonville 62-63), land that was "reserved as a common pasturage for whites and Indians" but then thrown open to pre-emption in 1889 (Andrew 54).

5 For more on Susan Allison and her family, see Part Two of this volume.

6 White is probably referring to Rhododendron Flats, located in what is now Manning Park, in the Cascade Mountains about half-way between the Okanagan and Vancouver. This is one of the few locations in British Columbia where the Pacific or western rhododendron (*Rhododendrum macriphyllum*) grows wild in such abundance. Her reference to "Musk" may refer to musk monkeyflower or *Erythranthe moschatus*.

7 The "diamond hitch" is a form of roping used to lash a load onto a pack saddle.

8 Gilbert Malcolm Sproat had served as one of three appointees to the provincial–federal Indian Reserve Commission from 1876 to 1878. He then served as the sole Commissioner from 1878-1880, when he was perceived by both provincial and federal levels of government to be too sympathetic to Indigenous concerns and forced to resign. At the time of Hester White's journey around 1883, he would most likely have been travelling to the Kootenay where he worked as a government agent in various capacities until 1889. See also Susan Allison's "Some Recollections of a Pioneer of the Seventies" in Part Two.

9 For more on Chief Joseph, see Susan Allison's "Some Recollections of a Pioneer of the Seventies" in Part Two.

10 David Thompson (1770-1857) apprenticed to the Hudson's Bay Company at the age of fourteen. In 1797, he joined the North West Company (NWC). Walking and canoeing 80,000 kilometres or more, he surveyed and mapped much of Canada west of Lake Superior. In 1799 he married in traditional Indigenous fashion Charlotte Small, the mixed heritage daughter of NWC partner Patrick Small (Nicks); they were together for fifty-eight years. Between 1807 and 1811, he completed a survey of the Columbia from its source to its mouth (Nicks).

11 Violet Emily Sillitoe was the wife of Acton Windeyer Sillitoe, who was born in New South Wales in 1840 and educated in England. She came with him when he visited Osoyoos in 1879 and in 1883 when he became the first Anglican bishop of the Diocese of New Westminster.

12 Buckskin needles are needles used to sew buckskin.

13 Baptiste or Batiste George was Susap's brother, and was Chief at Nk'Mip from 1907-39. For more information, see the essay "Crossing Lines."

14 A smallpox outbreak spread widely throughout British Columbia in 1862-63. Robert Boyd estimates that the epidemic killed 20,000 Indigenous people (28).

15 In the *Annual Report of the Department of Indian Affairs*, 1883, A.E. Howse, Indian Agent for the Okanagan Agency, reports to John A. Macdonald, the Superintendent-General of Indian Affairs, that in 1882 smallpox had "broken out at Sooyoos Lake, or among the Indians of Een-kee-mip [Inkameep,

Nk'Mip]." He had arrived to help from Nicola (an area to the north and west of the Okanagan, essentially the basin of the Nicola River, where many Syilx lived). At Osoyoos, he left James McConnell "with written instructions" while he himself, feeling ill (with measles, also prevalent in the area), returned to the Nicola. He writes that a total of thirteen people died and the outbreak was contained because it was restricted to the small camp on the shore of Lake Osoyoos. He had given "strict orders" to quarantine the area "under pain of severe punishment" if not observed (50). His report suggests that not only those with smallpox suffered, but also those who had been quarantined without adequate food and clothing during the winter months that followed the outbreak. He himself had brought some cloth and blankets from Nicola in November of 1882, and local women from Nk'Mip "cheerfully" complied with his request to make clothing (50). Those quarantined informed him that the clothing and blankets were not sufficient. Howse's report concedes the point and also justifies his inaction: "This was too true, but as I had no definite instruction what to get, and a large amount had already been expended in various ways, I felt that I could take no more responsibility upon myself . . ." (51). For more on Howse, see Susan Allison's "Memoirs of a Pioneer of the Eighties" in Part Two.

56 William Schoonover herded cattle in the meadows around Chute Lake (between Vaseaux Lake and Osoyoos Lake) in the winter for J.C. Haynes (Goodfellow 134).

57 The Reverend Percival Jenns (1834-1915) was the rector of St. John the Divine Anglican Church in Victoria, British Columbia from 1868-1914. His daughter, Sylvia Jenns, had been a governess to White in Osoyoos in 1886 (White, "Governesses" 47).

58 Findlay and Violet Munroe, early settlers in Summerland, say that Johnny Pierre, who had worked for the Haynes in Osoyoos, became "the first real settler in Summerland." Before 1886, he staked 320 acres "on the flat where West Summerland now stands [which became known as Siwash Flat]" and "recorded the land as an Indian reserve, built a cabin, arranged irrigation from Aeneas Creek to his hay meadow and large potato patch" (63). According to them, James Richie [Ritchie], a developer who arrived in the Okanagan from Manitoba in 1903, convinced Johnny Pierre to trade for "inferior hillside" land, "telling him that whitemen did not want him for a neighbor" and Ottawa "helped the deal along." This allowed Ritchie to subdivide the land into what became West Summerland (68-69).

59 Mr. and Mrs. Daly arrived in Keremeos in 1885, having bought Barrington Price's property (see note below). Mrs. Elizabeth Daly ran a small store and was the postmistress, so the Daly property was a well-known stopping point in the Similkameen-Okanagan region.

60 A type of daisy that retains its colour after being dried.

61 Henry Nicholson, an Englishman, arrived in Keremeos in 1872 and leased the Hudson's Bay Company Post as a stock range with his partner Barrington Price (Nicholson 13-14); for more on Nicholson see "Memoirs of a Pioneer of the Eighties" in Part Two. After losing the Haynes Ranch in 1895, the Haynes family moved to Nicholson's former ranch at Rock Creek, then owned by Francis Richter.

2 For more on J.W. McKay, see Marie Houghton Brent's "Indian Lore" in Part One. See also Part Two, "Something Very Real," Susan Allison's "Recollections of a Pioneer of the Seventies" and "Letters to Louisa (Allison) Johnson, 1930s."

3 Chief Gregoire was Chief at Nk'Mip from approximately 1862-1907, when his son-in-law George Baptiste succeeded him.

4 Louis Cuppage was a provincial constable at Osoyoos.

5 William Howard Bullock-Webster (1866-1945) was a constable at Camp McKinney and Fairview at the time. He and his brother Edward had emigrated from Oxford, England, and lived on a ranch near Keremeos.

6 Baptist is Chief Baptiste George. According to R.O. Hall, John and Peter Stelkia of Nk'Mip were some of the early fruit growers in the southern Okanagan near where White lived, planting "an orchard of several acres" at the mouth of Inkameep Creek on Osoyoos Lake in 1890. They had obtained trees from Murray's Nursery near Brewster, Washington (106).

7 Sidley, British Columbia was a tiny settlement near the United States border founded by Richard G. Sidley, an Irishman, who held the job of postmaster and customs collector in the Boundary area in 1889. He held "advanced political views" and was frequently referred to as an anarchist (Fraser 186). Anarchist Mountain in southern British Columbia may have been named after him. The town of Sidley folded in 1912.

8 In *The Story of Osoyoos*, George J. Fraser gives the figure of $65,000 for sale price of the Haynes ranch to Thomas Ellis (130). This is also the figure cited by Paul Koroscil in *The British Garden of Eden* (33).

9 Dora Pittendrigh was Theodore Kruger's daughter, married to Charles Pittendrigh. He was White's mother Emily Pittendrigh's half-brother from her father's second marriage. August Kruger was a son of Theodore Kruger.

0 White indicates in a note in her files that this "great friend" was R.L. Cawston, who "obtained Mrs. Haynes' signature to a 'quit claim' to the homestead, which was not in the mortgage. . . .The Haynes family were evicted without a horse or a waggon from the home which had been the proud possession of John Carmichael Haynes" ("R.L. Cawston").

1 See note on Susap (1843-1949) in "Pioneer Trail," excerpt from July 3, 1947, above.

2 As 1888 was the year of her father's death, White must have meant 1878 or even earlier as the date when J.C. Haynes hired Susap. See "Susap," below, in which White, born in 1877, mentions having known Susap since birth.

3 This cave could be what was once known as "Allison's Cave," used as a stable by the Allisons (Ormsby, Pioneer xxvii). Later it was dynamited during the building of the Highway 3 (Hope-Princeton) in British Columbia.

4 Susan Allison also wrote a story of giants in the Okanagan, called "The Big Men of the Mountains," written in the 1870s.

5 The Sillitoes had also come through Osoyoos in 1880.

6 See "Correspondence with Matilda Kruger" in this section, below.

7 Father Stephen Etienne de Rouge (1860-1916), a younger son of a French count, was a Jesuit priest in the Colville region admired by both Hester White and Mourning Dove. That Mourning Dove's view of him was conflicted and complex is evident in *Mourning Dove: A Salishan Autobiography*, pp. 24-27. Father Charles Pandosy was born in Marseilles, France, in 1824, and arrived in Fort Walla Walla, Washington in 1847 as an Oblate missionary. In 1859 he established the

Immaculate Conception Mission in the Okanagan Valley (now the Mission district of Kelowna); he also spent much time in the south Okanagan in Penticton where he died in 1891 (Thomson, "Pandosy").

78 Heister Dean Guie, introduced to Mourning Dove by her friend and editor L.V. McWhorter, edited and illustrated *Coyote Stories* (although see White's opinion on the provenance of the illustrations, in Mourning Dove's biographical note in Part One).

79 Later records in the United States for Matilda's and Mary's ages are inconsistent. As a student of the Chemawa school on the Marion County, Oregon, Census of 1895 Matilda is listed as twenty-three, which would make her born in 1872. Her younger sister Mary is also listed as twenty-three. It is possible, for reasons of entry into the school, that the two sisters gave younger ages for themselves. The Indian census roll for the Colville agency has Matilda Kruger listed as forty-two years of age in 1910, which would mean she was born in 1868; in the rolls of 1929, she is listed as born in 1872, and the United States Federal Census of 1930 lists her as sixty-one, which would have meant she was born in 1869.

80 The names of Matilda and Mary Kruger listed among the employees of the Indian School Service during these years can be found under Department of the Interior in the *Official Register of the United States*, 1901, p. 983; 1903, p. 996; and 1905, p. 952.

81 Hester White may have sent to Matilda Kruger a draft of a reminiscence by Chrestenza Kruger entitled "Early Days at Osoyoos." It was published in 1935 in the *OHS Report*. There is no mention of a white woman in the published account.

82 General William Tecumseh Sherman visited Osoyoos in 1883, while he was stationed south of the border, and General Nelson A. Miles was on his staff. In 1877, General Miles intercepted and defeated Chief Joseph in Montana Territory as he was making his way to Sitting Bull in Canada. In negotiations, Miles agreed that Chief Joseph could return to the Nez Perce Reservation in Idaho Territory, but General Sherman overruled him and sent Chief Joseph and his people to Leavenworth, Kansas. Eventually Chief Joseph was permitted to return to the west, but not to the Nez Perce Reserve. He settled in the Colville Reservation in 1885. Hester White wrote about General Sherman's visit to Osoyoos in 1883 in the *OHS Report* of 1951. Sherman also visited the Allison family in 1883, recounted in "A Memoir of a Pioneer of the Eighties," Part Two of this volume.

83 Both Chrestenza Kruger in "Early Days at Osoyoos" and Hester White in "The Pioneer Trail" (*Penticton Herald*, October 2, 1947) mention an American, Captain William H. Gray, who engaged in 1861 in building a steamboat at Osoyoos Lake for freighting between the Columbia River and Okanagan Lake for the mining camps at Cherry and Mission Creeks. His project never came to fruition.

84 An earthquake took place in the Okanagan and northern Washington state in December, 1872. See Susan Allison's "In-cow-mas-ket, Part Two," in Part Two of this volume for a similar story.

85 White inserted this information on the price of furs in her article "Charlotte Haynes," published in 1952 in the *OHS Report*.

6 White later quoted this description of Charlotte Moresby, J.C. Haynes's first acknowledged wife, in the article "Charlotte Haynes," recognizing Matilda Kruger as the source.

7 For more on R.L. Cawston see "Over the Hope Trail" above.

8 Chrestenza (Christanze) Kruger (1857-1939) was born in Schleswig-Holstein in 1857 "when it still belonged to Denmark" and identified with being Danish rather than German ("Early Days" 76). She married Theodore Kruger in 1873 at the age of sixteen and became well known as an early settler in the region, admired by later immigrants such as Isabel Christie MacNaughton. It is poignant and ironic that Matilda Kruger refers to Christanze as "a good mother," when neither she nor her step-mother can acknowledge their familial relationship.

9 Manuscripts of stories about Coyote and place names in the Vernon Museum and Archives suggest that Brent was collecting and writing down Syilx stories in 1923.

0 We have been unable to recover this letter from Hester White.

1 In his book *Ka-m-iakin, The Last Hero of the Yakimas*, A.J. [Jack] Splawn, then a young American cattle dealer, refers to meeting "Captain Horton" and taking him to Yakima on a cattle-buying trip for himself and George Simpson in 1869 (see "Eliza Jane Swalwell" in Part One). He says Simpson advises, "'Take Capt. Horton along and give him as little money to spend as possible. He will be of little use to you, so do not depend on him for work'" (246). While Splawn is not always reliable—he describes Houghton as an English remittance man who is "past middle age" and Houghton was around 29 years old at the time (245)—other records point to Houghton's excessive drinking and incompetency. See Margaret Ormsby's "Houghton, Charles Edward" in the *Dictionary of Canadian Biography*.

2 Brent is probably referring to Leonard Norris, founder of the Okanagan Historical and Natural History Society as it was then called. Captain Charles F. Houghton had arrived in the Okanagan from Ireland in 1863 with his friend Lieutenant Charles Albert Vernon and his brother Lieutenant Forbes George Vernon (for whom Vernon, British Columbia, is named). The Vernons bought Houghton's land at Coldstream in 1873, after Houghton had left the region and needed funds to settle in Victoria, now a lieutenant-colonel, as deputy adjutant for District 11 (British Columbia) (Ormsby, *Coldstream* 6).

3 Brent could possibly be referring to her husband William Brent's unpublished manuscript "The History of the Okanagan."

4 Unless otherwise indicated, all the subsequent letters from Hester White bear this address.

5 Marie Houghton Brent moved into a home for the elderly with Mrs. Ernestine Ames in Republic, Washington, in 1952 or 1953, and Brent wrote to White shortly before this letter, perhaps to tell her the new address. Brent's letter to White has not been recovered.

6 William Brent fought from 1900-1901 in the Boer War, and then shortly after enlisted "at Fort Wright, Spokane, for the Spanish American War in Cuba." That war had ended in 1898, but troops were still being trained in Presidio, California, where Brent became a drill sergeant ("William Brent" 10). John Brent, William's younger brother, also fought in the Boer War with the Canadian Mounted Regiment.

97 Dr. Bill White is Hester White's son W.H. White.

98 Ed and Joe Ritcher are sons of Francis Richter and his first wife Lucy. See "Over the Hope Trail" above.

99 For more on Billy and Babe Kruger, see headnote for Correspondence with Matilda Kruger" above.

100 This is one of the very few times White mentions the John Haynes family, descended from J.C. Haynes and his Syilx wife, Julia (see Hester White headnote and the essay "Crossing Lines"). Christina Moore Haynes was the widow of White's half-brother, John Carmichael Haynes, Jr. Both Christina Haynes and Caroline (Brent) Renshaw, William Brent's sister, were being honoured at the celebration on May 5, 1955, the fiftieth anniversary of Kelowna's incorporation as a city. They had lived in the district for over 80 years.

101 Eleanor Laurence Saucier was the youngest daughter of Cyprien Laurence, one of the first settlers in Kelowna, and Theresa Laurence, the daughter of old Chief Nkwala and Marie Houghton Brent's great aunt. See Brent's "My School Days" in Part One and "Crossing Lines" in this section for more information on her.

102 White is referring to Matilda Kruger's niece and Mary Kruger's daughter, Jessie Kruger Watson.

103 This letter shows that at least one additional letter has been received from Hester White, which we have not been able to recover, and a visit from White to Republic has taken place before this letter was written.

104 Houghton, leading the 90th (Winnipeg) Battalion of Rifles, fought at Fish Creek and Batoche during the Riel Rebellion of 1885.

105 Brent is probably referring to James A. Teit's "The Salishan Tribes of the Western Plateaus" edited by Franz Boas. It appears in the 45th Annual Report of the Bureau of American Ethnology to the Secretary of the Smithsonian Institution (1927-28). Brent often refers to this work. See also "Indian Lore" in Part One.

106 For more on old Chief Nkwala and Samuel Black, see Brent's "Indian Lore" in Part One.

107 Some of these jottings may have been incorporated in Marie Houghton Brent's "Indian Lore" in Part One.

108 Brent's statements about succession after Nkwala needs some explanation. According to Marie Brent and according to Shirley Louis in Q'sapi, Nkwala had two sons and a daughter from his Okanagan wife (56). Upon his death the chieftainship was passed to his youngest son also named Nkwala who was killed by his jealous older brother (see Brent's "Indian Lore" in Part One) and the chieftainship passed to another relative, his nephew Tsilaxitsa (cəlxicaʔ, Standing-Robe) or Chelahitsa (Chillihitza). A cone of silence around the young Chief Nkwala's death is generally maintained in Okanagan oral history. Perhaps for this reason, James Teit does not mention an elder brother killing a younger brother. However, he does record that Nkwala had a son named Kesaskailex (k̓saʔsqilxʷ, Badman) who killed his wife and her "paramour" near Douglas Lake and then took refuge with one of Nkwala's daughters named Marie who was married to a Peone, probably Louis, in Colville. Teit does not name the "paramour"; however, he reports

that old Chief Nkwala paid blood money of many horses, cattle and robes, to settle his son's deed (259-60). Teit also notes that when Chief Nkwala died he passed on the "head chieftainship" to his nephew and adopted son, Chelahitsa who was chief in the Nicola Valley (Douglas Lake). Chelahitsa's mother, Sapxena'lks (*sʔapxnalqs*- Nez Perce Dress) was Nkwala's "favorite sister" and married Xalekskwailox of Tutekskulox (the name of the place *tucklulaxʷ* near Keremeos) who was from the Keremeos area of Similkameen (Teit 268-71). Chelahitsa, like Nkwala, played a strong role in Okanagan politics, acting as spokesperson in negotiations with settlers and in defense of Syilx land rights without violent confrontation. He died in about 1884, according to Teit (273).

Chelahitsa had two sons with one of his wives, Marie Memi'xsta (*mimiʔxica* or Hanging-loose Robe), from Kamloops: Alexander Chelahitsa and John Celestin or Salista who was based in both *nk'amapəlqs* (Nkamapulks) or Head of the Lake in the Okanagan and Douglas Lake in the Nicola region (Teit 272-77). These are the two sons Brent is referring to in this passage. Alexander Chelahitsa succeeded his father Chelahitsa as head chief in the Nicola Valley, and after he died in 1914 (Teit 274), John ("Johnny") Chelahitsa or Salista acted on the duties of a head Chief, travelling to England and to Ottawa to speak for the Syilx people and their rights. According to historian Peter Carstens, the Chelahitsa family "had been trying for years to take over the Head of the Lake" (121-22). Carstens was referring to an election there in 1912, but rivalry could have taken place later. Brent emphatically states her position in a letter to Ella Clark that Chief Chelahitsa's sons Alexander and John were "successors of Nicola Valley, not in the Okanagan" (October 15, 1956).

9 The stagecoach White refers to left on its Barkerville run from Victoria on May 8, 1958, after parading through town the day before. Mia Reimers notes that the 1958 centennial was a catalyst for the British Columbia provincial government's attention to "heritage and heritage conservation," including the restoration of Barkerville (53).

0 White is no doubt referring to the 100-foot pole carved by renowned Kwakwaka'wakw carver Mungo Martin or Nada'pankam (1879-1962) as a gift to Queen Elizabeth to mark the British Columbia Centennial in 1958. The pole was given a send-off ceremony in front of the legislative buildings in Victoria on May 7, 1958, before it was shipped to England where it was erected and still stands in Windsor Great Park. For a discussion of British Columbia's use of totem poles to promote the province, and Indigenous involvement and opposition to these projects, see Chapter Five of Reimers's thesis, "'British Columbia at its Most Colourful, Sparkling Best': Post-war Province Building through Centennial Celebrations."

1 Following this exploratory trip, Haynes recommended the reduction of reserves in the Okanagan, which took place in November of that year. See Thomson, "A History" 119-20, and the essay "Crossing Lines" above.

2 For more information on Sophie Nkwala, See Brent's "Indian Lore" in Part One, and the headnote on Marie Houghton Brent.

3 The ceremony of rededication for the restored Father Pandosy Mission on Benvoulin Road in Kelowna took place on June 15, 1958.

114 A monument of grey granite was dedicated to Chief Joseph Tonasket, 1822-1891, in Curlew, Washington, on June 21, 1958.

115 This letter is undated, but see following letter dated December 14 referring to "letter received four days ago." As well, White implies that the coming Christmas will be her first without her brother William Haynes, who died in 1959.

116 The 2,500-square-meter Craigdarroch Castle was built by coal magnate Robert Dunsmuir on a hill overlooking Victoria between 1887 and 1890. It was still under construction when Dunsmuir died in 1889. White is no doubt sharing these memories with Brent because Brent's father, C.F. Houghton, married Robert Dunsmuir's daughter Marion. Houghton met Marion Dunsmuir when mobilized in 1877 by the British Columbia government to lead a military force to "restore order" among the striking miners at Robert Dunsmuir's Wellington mine near Nanaimo (Ormsby, *Coldstream* 7).

117 According to White, William Haynes had worked as a cowboy, a constable for the Provincial Police in Hedley (appointed in 1900) and later as an orchardist in Oliver, British Columbia ("William Barrington Haynes" 50-51).

118 After the 1876 Indian Act, systems of band governance were imposed on Indigenous nations in Canada which supplanted the lineage of hereditary or autonomously selected chiefs. These restrictions promoted federal control over leadership in Indigenous communities and thus over land, membership and control of resources and finances.

119 There appears to have been another letter from Hester White here, which we have been unable to locate.

120 Mrs. Ames may mean that Marie Houghton Brent had never registered with the Colville Agency of the Confederated Tribes of the Colville Reservation.

121 Here, Brent had noted in pencil, "Chief Bower."

122 Superintendent of the Colville Indian Agency Elmo Miller later identifies this person as Mattie Hope Kelly. See his letter of February 2, 1960 in this section.

123 Alice Marie Haynes Thompson was the daughter of Valentine Haynes and Elizabeth Runnels.

124 See White's piece "May 1st, 1895, Osoyoos" for more information on the loss of the Haynes estate. Brent, who kept this letter, had underlined from "but it would cost a mint" to "the Haynes Estate which was a steal."

125 It is not clear what ceremony White is referring to here. Peter Carstens notes that a tombstone was placed on old Chief Nkwala's grave at the Head of the Lake in 1959 "in the name of the 'Okanagan Indian Rights Defense League' to mark the 100th anniversary of his death" (47).

126 The envelope for this letter is postmarked August 14, 1962.

127 "And God spake all these words, saying" is from the Bible, Exodus 20:1, and leads into God's delivery of the ten commandments to Moses. This line is preceded by a description of thunder and lightning on Mount Sinai during which God speaks to Moses (Exodus 19:16-19).

128 Richard F. "Dick" Parkinson, Mayor of Kelowna from 1958-1967, was Hester White's nephew, the son of her sister Irene Haynes Parkinson.

129 The Trans-Canada Highway route through Rogers Pass, between Revelstoke and Golden, British Columbia, was begun in 1958 and completed in the summer of 1962. It greatly facilitated transportation between British

Columbia and Alberta, as well as the rest of Canada.

) A letter to Katie Lacey of September 27, 1961, indicates White did make a trip to Republic that month and visited with Mrs. Ames and Marie Houghton Brent.

I White's description of Marie Brent looking like a "warrior chief" may seem to be a stereotype, but it could also show her regard for the strength of this 91-year-old woman, as well as how much White has taken in Marie's history of being a proud descendant of Chief Nkwala and other chiefs. The visit she refers to may have been the unexpected one White writes about to Katie Lacey. White had received a call and heard that "a Vance and Brent" were coming. Anticipating the arrival of two men, she "sat in state . . . waiting." When Marie Houghton Brent and Mrs. Ames arrived, White was "knocked off my equilibrium! I had gone into town Monday afternoon to stock up and the shops were closed—Maria camped on the chesterfield & Mrs. Ames had the cot in the dining room. They left Thursday morning! We drove to Kelowna Wednesday—a lovely day—as Maria wanted to see it—bridge & all there was so much I could have done if I had been prepared! I spent Thursday afternoon and Friday in bed!!" (October 22, [1961]).

Isabel Christie MacNaughton

2 The play was adapted by MacNaughton and Renyi from a story told to MacNaughton by Josephine Shuttleworth. See Isabel Christie MacNaughton's headnote for Elizabeth Renyi's collaboration with Isabel Christie.

3 The greasewood tree (*Purshia tridentata*) is also called antelope-brush and black sage in the southern Okanagan. It grows mainly from Osoyoos to Skaha Lake, and thus near Okanagan Falls, where MacNaughton grew up. Today, it is threatened by agriculture, industry and urban residential growth. Richard Armstrong, Syilx environmentalist, notes in "Spotlight on Species" on the Okanagan Similkameen Conservation Alliance website (osca.org) that the easily combustible plant was used as a fire-starter by the Syilx.

4 These four stanzas, without the "chorus" stage directions, first appeared as the poem "Black Sage" in Isabel Christie MacNaughton's *Wood Fires* (1942).

5 The shooting star is an Okanagan desert flower, *Dodecatheon pulchellum*.

Bibliography

Allison, Susan Louisa. "Account of the Similkameen Indians of British Columbia." *The Journal of the Anthropological Institute of Great Britain and Ireland*, vol. 21, 1892, pp. 305-18.

---."The Big Men of the Mountains: A Legend of the Okanagan Indians Written Fifty- two Years Ago [1875]." *Okanagan Historical Society* (*OHS Report*), vol. 2, 1927, pp. 8-11.

---."The Burial of Quiniscoe." n.d. "Tales of Tamtusalist," Susan Louisa Allison and Family Fonds, Box 001588-0001, Folder 60, BC Archives, Victoria, BC, handwritten manuscript.

---."Early History of Princeton." *Princeton Star*, 5 Jan. 1923, p. 3.

---."Early History of Princeton." *Princeton Star*, 9 Feb. 1923, p. 3.

---."Early History of Princeton." *Princeton Star*, 9 Mar. 1923, p. 3.

---."Emma Hutch or Hutchy." Notes for "Some Native Daughters I Have Known." n.d. Susan Louisa Allison and Family Fonds, Box 001588-0001, Folder 45, BC Archives, Victoria, BC, handwritten manuscript.

---."G-he-nac—Sister of Quiniscoe." "Some Native Daughters I Have Known." n.d. Susan Louisa Allison and Family Fonds, Box 001588-0001, Folder 88, BC Archives, Victoria, BC, typescript.

---."G-he-nac--Sister of Quiniscoe." Notes for "Some Native Daughters I Have Known." n.d. Allison Family Fonds, 1849-1889, MS1-4716, File 5, Penticton Museum and Archives, handwritten manuscript.

---. [Stratton Moir]. "*In-Cow-Mas-Ket, Part One: A Poem of Indian Life.*" *In-Cow-Mas-Ket*. Scroll Publishing, 1900, pp. 4-29, Box 001588-0001, Folder 99, Susan Louisa Allison and Family Fonds, BC Archives, Victoria, BC, photocopy.

---."In-Cow-Mas-Ket: A Poem of Indian Life, Part One." [circa 1890s]. Box 001588-0001, Folder 100, Susan Louisa Allison and Family Fonds, BC Archives, Victoria, BC, typescript.

---."In-Cow-Mas-Ket, Part Two." [circa 1890s]. Susan Louisa Allison and Family Fonds, Box 005188-0001, Folder 101, BC Archives, Victoria, BC, typescript.

---."In-Cow-Mas-Ket, Part Two." 1876. Susan Louisa Allison and Family Fonds, Box 005188-0001, Folder 4, BC Archives, Victoria, BC, handwritten manuscript.

---. Introduction to "In-Cow-Mas-Ket: A Poem of Indian Life, Part One." [circa 1890s]. Susan Louisa Allison and Family Fonds, Box 005188-0001, Folder 100, BC Archives, Victoria, BC, typescript.

---."Kind Penquinac or the Princess Julia." n.d. Notes for "Some Native Daughters I Have Known." Susan Louisa Allison and Family Fonds, Box 001588-0001, Folder 45, BC Archives, Victoria, BC, handwritten manuscript.

---. Letter to Louisa Johnston. 18 Feb. 1930. Private Collection.

---. Letter to Louisa Johnston. 28 Nov. 1930. Private Collection.

---. Letter to Louisa Johnston. [circa 1930]. Private Collection.

---. Letter to Louisa Johnston. 3 May 1932. Private Collection.

---. "Memoirs of a Pioneer [of] The 80s." [circa 1930-32]. Mrs. Susan Allison Fonds, Major Matthews Collection, MS 526-A-7, Folder 4, City of Vancouver Archives, Vancouver, BC, handwritten manuscript.

---. "Memoirs of the 70[s] by a Pioneer of [the] 60[s]."[circa 1930-32]. Mrs. Susan Allison Fonds, Major Matthews Collection, MS 526-A-7, Folder 3, City of Vancouver Archives, Vancouver, BC, handwritten manuscript.

---. "The Monster's Island." 1872. Susan Louisa Allison and Family Fonds, Box 001588-0001, Folder 31, BC Archives, Victoria, BC, typescript.

---. "The Mother of Killeketza." n.d. Susan Allison and Family Fonds, Box 001588-0001, Folder 33, BC Archives, Victoria, BC, handwritten manuscript.

---. "Ne-Hi-La-Kin: A Legend of the Okanagan Indians Written Fifty-two Years Ago [1875]" *OHS Report*, vol. 2, 1927, pp. 6-8.

---. "One Day in a Storekeeper's Life in British Columbia." 1867. Susan Louisa Allison and Family Fonds, Box 001588-0001, Folder 17, BC Archives, Victoria, BC, handwritten manuscript.

---. "The Origin of the Similkameen Indians." *Similkameen Star*, 1 May 1912, p. 4.

---. "Our Louisa." Notes for "Some Native Daughters I Have Known." n.d. Susan Louisa Allison and Family Fonds, Box 001588-0001, Folder 45, BC Archives, Victoria, BC, handwritten manuscript.

---. *A Pioneer Gentlewoman in British Columbia: The Recollections of Susan Allison*. Introduced and edited by Margaret A. Ormsby. U of British Columbia Press, 1976.

---. Preface. "Tales of Tamtusalist" n.d. Susan Louisa Allison and Family Fonds, Box 001588-0001, Folder 55, BC Archives, Victoria, BC, handwritten manuscript.

---. [Stratton Moir]. "Quin-is-coe." *In-Cow-Mas-Ket*, Scroll Publishing, 1900, pp. 32-52, Susan Louisa Allison and Family Fonds, Box 001588-0001, Folder 99, BC Archives, Victoria, BC, photocopy.

---. "Quin-is-coe." [circa 1890s]. Susan Louisa Allison and Family Fonds, Box 001588-0001, Folder 105, BC Archives, Victoria, BC, typescript.

---. "Quiniscoe's Adventure on Mount Chippaco." n.d. "Tales of Tamtusalist," Susan Louisa Allison and Family Fonds, Box 001588-0001, Folder 70, BC Archives, Vancouver, BC, handwritten manuscript.

---. "Sketches of Indian Life." [circa 1870s]. Allison Family Fonds, 1849-1889, MS 1-4716, Penticton Museum and Archives, Penticton, BC., typescript.

---. "Some Recollections of a Pioneer of the Sixties." [circa 1930-32]. Mrs. Susan Allison, Major Matthews Collection, MS 526-A-7, Folder 2, City of Vancouver Archives, Vancouver, BC, handwritten manuscript.

---. "What I Know of Ogopogo." n.d. Susan Louisa Allison and Family Fonds, Box 001588-0001, Folder 85, BC Archives, Victoria, BC, handwritten manuscript.

Alton, Gladys Winnifred "Skip" Christie. Letter to grandchildren. 23 June 1994. Christie family papers, Private Collection, pp. 1-5.

Ames, Ernestine. Letter to Hester White. 9 Jan. 1960. Hester White Fonds, MS 1, Penticton Museum and Archives, Penticton, BC.

Anastasio, Angelo. "Intergroup Relations in the Southern Plateau." Diss. U of Chicago, 1955.

Andrew, F.W. "Dr. R. B. White: An Appreciation." *OHS Report*, vol. 14, 1950, pp. 45-7.

---. "The First Commercial Orchard in the Okanagan Valley." *OHS Report*, vol. 18, 1954, pp. 53-58.

Annual Report of the Department of Indian Affairs, 1883. Gov. of Canada, 1884. Library and Archives Canada, www.bac-lac.gc.ca/ eng/discover/aboriginal-heritage/first-nations/indian-affairs-annual-reports/Pages/item.aspx?IdNumber=3250. Accessed June 15, 2016.

Armstrong, Jeannette C., "Constructing Indigeneity: Syilx Okanagan Oraliture and tmixw Centrism." Diss. Universitat Greifswald, 2009.

Armstrong, Jeannette C. and Lally Grauer, editors. *Native Poetry in Canada: A Contemporary Anthology*. Broadview Press, 2001.

Armstrong, Jeannette C., et al., editors. *We Get Our Living Like Milk from the Land*. Theytus Books, 1993.

Arnold, Laurie. *Bartering with the Bones of Their Dead: The Colville Confederated Tribes and Termination*. U of Washington P, 2012.

---. "More than Mourning Dove: Christine Quintasket—Activist, Leader, Public Intellectual." *Montana: The Magazine of Western History*, vol. 67, no. 1, Spring 2017, pp. 28-45.

Atkins, B.R. "First Federal Election at Yale." *OHS Report*, vol. 15, 1951, pp. 41-43.

Balf, Mary. HWISTESMETXE'QEN. *Dictionary of Canadian Biography*. Vol. 8, U of Toronto/U Laval, 1985. www.biographi.ca/en/bio/ hwistesmetxe_qen_8E.html.

Barman, Jean. "Lost Okanagan: In Search of the First Settler Families." *OHS Report*, vol. 60, 1996, pp. 8-20.

---. *The West Beyond the West: A History of British Columbia*. U of Toronto P, 2007.

Bennest, Jean. "Development of Social Services in the Okanagan:1930-1980." *OHS Report*, vol. 45, 1981, pp. 18-23.

Bouchard, Randy. "Okanagan Legends." 1975. Transcribed by Dorothy Kennedy, BC Indian Language Project, En'owkin Centre, Penticton Indian Reserve, BC.

Boyd, Robert. "Smallpox in the Pacific Northwest: The First Epidemics." *BC Studies*, vol.101, Spring 1994, pp. 5-40.

"Brent's Grist Mill: The Building of a Mill and a Community." Central Okanagan Heritage Society. Virtual Museum.ca, Community Memories, www.virtualmuseum.ca/sgc-cms/histoires_de_chez_nous-community_ memories/pm_v2.php?id=story_line&lg=English&fl=0&ex=0000 0372&sl=2149&pos=1&pf=1.

Brent, Marie Houghton. ["Coyote and Reindeer"], "Indian fables translated by Marie Brent." [circa 1929]. Marie Houghton Brent Papers, MS 203, Greater Vernon and Museum Archives, Vernon, BC.

---. "Indian Lore." *OHS Report*, vol. 30, 1966, pp. 105-113.

---. [Mrs. William Brent]. "The Indians of the Okanagan Valley." *OHS Report*, vol. 6, 1935, pp. 122-130.

---. [Mrs. William Brent], translator. "The Legend of Shuswap Falls." [1929]. *OHS Report*, vol. 12, 1948, pp. 16-17.

---. Letter to Ella E. Clark. 15 Oct. 1956. Ella Elizabeth Clark Papers, Cage 146, Box 1, Folder 9, Washington State University Libraries, Pullman Washington.

---. Letter to Ella E. Clark. 10 June 1957. Ella Elizabeth Clark Papers, Cage 146, Box 1, Folder 9. Washington State University Libraries, Pullman Washington.

---. Letter to Ella E. Clark. 23 August 1957. Ella Elizabeth Clark Papers, Cage 146, Box 1, Folder 9. Washington State University Libraries, Pullman Washington.

---. Letter to Hester White. 8 Sept. 1936. Hester White Fonds, MS 1, Penticton Museum and Archives, Penticton, BC.

---. Letter to Hester White. 24 Feb. 1938. Hester White Fonds, MS 1, Penticton Museum and Archives, Penticton, BC.

---. Letter to Hester White. 13 June 1946. Hester White Fonds, MS 1, Penticton Museum and Archives, Penticton, BC.

---. Letter to Hester White. 20 Oct. 1955. Hester White Fonds, MS 1, Penticton Museum and Archives, Penticton, BC.

---. Letter to Hester White. Xmas night 1956. Hester White Fonds, MS 1, Penticton Museum and Archives, Penticton, BC.

---. Letter to Hester White. 26 Mar. 1957. Hester White Fonds, MS 1, Penticton Museum and Archives, Penticton, BC.

---. Letter to Hester White. 30 Apr. 1958. Hester White Fonds, MS 1, Penticton Museum and Archives, Penticton, BC.

---. Letter to Hester White. 10 June 1958. Hester White Fonds, MS 1, Penticton Museum and Archives, Penticton BC.

---. Letter to Hester White. 14 Dec. 1959. Hester White Fonds, MS 1, Penticton Museum and Archives, Penticton, BC.

---. Letter to Hester White. 8 Jan. 1960. Hester White Fonds, MS 1, Penticton Museum and Archives, Penticton BC.

---. Letter to Hester White. 14 Jan. 1960. Hester White Fonds, MS 1, Penticton Museum and Archives, Penticton, BC.

---. Letter to Hester White. "Do you think [. . . .]" 25 Jan. 1960. Hester White Fonds, MS 1, Penticton Museum and Archives, Penticton, BC.

---. Letter to Hester White. "Please write [. . . .]" 25 Jan. 1960. Hester White Fonds, MS 1, Penticton Museum and Archives, Penticton, BC.

---. Letter to Hester White. [2 ?] Mar. 1960. Hester White Fonds, MS 1, Penticton Museum and Archives, Penticton, BC.

---. "My School Days." [circa 1957-58?]. Marie Houghton Brent Papers, MS 203, Greater Vernon Museum and Archives, Vernon, BC.

---. "The Memories of Marie Houghton Brent, Republic Washington: As told to Dorothea Sophia Sprengel, Republic Washington." Old MSS, F/2/B75. BC Archives, Victoria, BC.

---. [Mrs. William Brent]. "The Name Kelowna." *OHS Report*, vol. 4, 1930, pp. 23-4.

---. "Okanagan Valley Legend." *OHS Report*, vol. 30, 1966, p. 153.

---. "The President, Officers and Members of the Okanagan Historical Society." 25 Sept. 1923. Marie Houghton Brent Papers, MS 203, Greater Vernon Museum and Archives, Vernon, BC. Notebook.

---. [Mrs. William Brent]. "The Priest's House." *Okanagan Historical and Natural History Society Report*, vol. 2, 1927, pp. 26.

---. [Mrs. William Brent]. "The Priest's Valley School." *Okanagan Historical and*

Natural History Society Report, vol. 2, 1927, pp. 27-8.

Brent, William. "The History of the Okanagan." n.d. Marie Houghton Brent
Papers, MS 203, Greater Vernon Museum and Archives, Vernon, BC.

---. Letter to Veterans Administration, Washington. n.d. Marie Houghton Brent
Papers, MS 203, Greater Vernon Museum and Archives, Vernon, BC.

Brown, Alanna K. "The Evolution of Mourning Dove's Coyote Stories."
Studies in American Indian Literatures, series 2, vol. 4, no. 2-3, Summer/
Fall 1992: 161-180. JSTOR, www.jstor.org/stable/20736610.

---. "Legacy Profile: Mourning Dove (Humishuma: 1888-1936)." *Legacy*, vol. 6,
no.1, 1989, pp. 51-8. JSTOR, www.jstor.org/stable/25679050.

---. "Looking through the Glass Darkly: The Editorialized Mourning Dove."
New Voices in Native American Literary Criticism, edited by Arnold Krupat,
Smithsonian Institution Press, 1993, pp. 274-288.

---. "Mourning Dove's Canadian Recovery Years." *Canadian Literature*, vol. 124-
125, Spring-Summer 1990, pp.113-122.

---. "Mourning Dove's *House of Little Men*." *Canadian Literature*, vol. 144, Spring
1995, pp. 49-60.

Buckland, Frank Morgan. *Ogopogo's Vigil: A History of Kelowna and the Okanagan*.
Okanagan Historical Society, Kelowna Branch, 1948.

---. "Settlement of L'Anse au Sable" *OHS Report*, vol. 2, 1927, pp. 16-21.

---. "William Peon." *OHS Report*, vol. 14, 1950, 35-43.

Buell, John. *Travelling Light: The Way and Life of Tony Walsh*. Novalis, 2004.

Candy, Ron. "The History of Coldstream and Lavington." *The Greater
Vernon Museum and Archives*. vernonmuseum.ca/ex_history_of_
coldstream_and_lavington.html.

Cantwell, Margaret, and Mary George Edmond. *North to Share: The Sisters of Saint
Ann in Alaska and the Yukon Territory*. Sisters of St. Ann (Victoria), 1992.

Carlson, Leonard A. *Indians, Bureaucrats, and Land: The Dawes Act and the Decline
of Indian Farming*. Greenwood Publishing Group, Inc., 1981. ACLS
Humanities E-Book, quod-lib-umich-edu.ezproxy.library.ubc.ca.

Carstens, Peter. *The Queen's People: A Study of Hegemony, Coercion and
Accommodation Among the Okanagan of Canada*. U of Toronto P, 1991.
ACLS Humanities E-book, hdl.handle.net/2027/heb. 03538.0001.001.

Cawston, Mary Ann. "Our Wedding Trip from Ontario to British Columbia in
1885." *OHS Report*, vol. 13, 1949, pp. 117-125.

Chance, David H. "Influence of the Hudson's Bay Company on the Native
Cultures of the Colvile District." *Northwest Anthropological Research Notes:
Memoir*, vol. 7, no. 1, part 2, 1973.

---. *People of the Falls*. Kettle Falls Historical Centre, Colville, 1986.

Chase, Cora. "Okanagan Falls—The Christies and Buddie." n.d. Isabel
Christie MacNaughton Files, Oliver and District Heritage Society
Archives, Oliver, B.C.

"Chemawa." *US City Directories, Salem City and Marion County, Oregon, 1896*.
Ancestry.com, U.S. City Directories, 1822-1995 [database on-line]. Provo,
UT, USA: Ancestry.com Operations, Inc., 2011. search.ancestry.ca/
search/db.aspx?dbid=2469

Clark, Ella Elizabeth. *Indian Legends of Canada*. McClelland and Stewart, 1960.

---. Letter to Marie Houghton Brent. 7 August [1956-57?]. Marie Houghton Brent

Papers, MS 203, Greater Vernon Museum and Archives, Vernon, BC.

Cline, Walter, et al. *The Sinkaietk or Southern Okanagon of Washington.* Edited by Leslie Spier, George Banta Publishing, 1938.

Coleman, Daniel. *White Civility: The Literary Project of English Canada.* U of Toronto P, 2006.

Collins, Karen. "Brent Family History." *OHS Report*, vol. 75, 2011, pp. 27-32.

Cumming, Peter, and Neil Mickenberg. "Native Rights in Canada: British Columbia." *British Columbia: Historical Readings*, edited by W. Peter Ward and Robert A. J. McDonald, Douglas & McIntyre, 1981, pp. 185-211.

Daly, Elizabeth M. "Pioneers." *OHS Report*, vol. 28, 1964, pp. 134-35.

Daniells, Laurenda. "ROSS, SALLY (Sarah)." Dictionary of Canadian Biography, vol. 11, 1982 U of Toronto/U Laval,2003-. www.biographi.ca/en/bio/ross_sally_11E.html

"Dan Nicholson." *Kelowna Courier and Okanagan Orchardist.* 15 Sept. 1927, p. 5.

Dawson, George M. 1891 *Notes on the Shuswap People of British Columbia.* Royal Society of Canada, 1891. Interior Early Canadiana Online Ebook Collection, eco.canadiana.ca/view/oocihm.14874/3?r=0&s=1.

"Death Summons Mrs. Nicholson." *Omak Chronicle*, 1 October 1935, p. 1.

DeMeer, Andrea. "The Allisons Are One Family, and We Are a Big Family." The Similkameen Spotlight, 2 Oct. 2017, np. https://www.similkameenspotlight.com/news/the-allisons-are-one-family-and- we-are-a-big-family/

Dewdney, Kathleen. "Driving Cattle over the Old Dewdney Trail." *Penticton Herald*, 27 Sept. 1958, p. 10.

---. "Francis Xavier Richter." *OHS Report*, vol. 25, 1961, pp. 78-101.

Dwyer, M.N. Letter to Hester White. 10 Jan. 1935. Hester White Fonds, MS 1, Penticton Museum and Archives, Penticton, BC.

Eneas, Adam. Genealogy Chart. En'owkin Centre Archive, Penticton Indian Reserve, BC.

Fisher, Dexter. Introduction. *Cogewea, The Half-Blood: A Depiction of the Great Montana Cattle Range*, by Mourning Dove, U of Nebraska P, 1981, pp. v-xxix.

Fisher, Robin. *Contact and Conflict: Indian-European Relations in British Columbia, 1774-1890.* U of British Columbia P, 1992.

Fleming, Thomas, Lisa Smith, and Helen Raptis. "An Accidental Teacher: Anthony Walsh and the Aboriginal Day Schools at Six Mile Creek and Inkameep, British Columbia, 1929-1942." *Historical Studies in Education/revue d'histoire de l'éducation, Spring/printemps 2007*, 2-24. historicalstudiesineducation.ca/index.php/edu_hse-rhe/issue/archive

Fraser, George J. *The Story of Osoyoos: September 1811 to December 1952.* Penticton Herald [publisher], 1952.

Gabriel, Louise. "Food and Medicine in the Okanakanes." *OHS Report*, vol. 18, 1954, pp. 24-9.

G-he-nac. Letter to A. McBride, Esq. 8 Apr. 1889. Transcribed by an unknown writer. Library and Archives Canada, collectionscanada.gc.ca. Accessed 13 June 2018.

Gray, Art. "History in Plenty at Simpson Ranch." *Kelowna Daily Courier*, 4 Dec. 1965, p. 4.

Goodfellow, John. *The Story of Similkameen*, vol. 1, www.goodfellow.mozey-on-inn.com. Accessed 14 June 2018.

Goodfellow, J.C., et al. "An Historical Gazeteer of Okanagan-Similkameen." *OHS Report* vol. 22, 1958, pp. 123-69.

"Government of Canada Designates Susan Louisa Moir Allison as a Person of National Historic Significance." Media Room: News Releases and Backgrounders. Parks Canada. 4 Sept. 2010. www.pc.gc.ca/APPS/CP-NR/release_e.asp?id=1648&andor1=nr.

Haig-Brown, Celia, and David A. Nock, editors. Introduction. *With Good Intentions: Euro-Canadian and Aboriginal Relations in Colonial Canada*, U of British Columbia P, 2006.

Hall, R.O. "Early Days of Fruit Growing." *OHS Report*, vol. 25, 1961, pp. 105-122.

Harris, Cole. *Making Native Space: Colonialism, Resistance, and Reserves in British Columbia*. U of British Columbia P, 2002.

---. "The Native Land Policies of Governor James Douglas." *BC Studies*, Vol. 174, 2012, pp.101-22.

Hayes, Robert M. "Haynes-Moore Story Deserves to be Told." *OHS Report*, Vol. 61, 1997, pp. 80-83.

Hill-Tout, Charles. "Report on the Ethnology of the Okanak'en of British Columbia, an Interior Division of the Salish Stock." *The Journal of the Royal Anthropological Institute of Great Britain and Ireland*, vol. 41, 1911, pp. 130-61. JSTOR, www. jstor.org/stable/2843337.

Hobbs, Janice, editor. "Family Reunion of the Descendants of Helen Catherine Gunn and James Robert Christie held at Okanagan Falls, June 1992." 1992. Christie Family Papers, Private Collection.

Howay, F.W. "The Origin of the Chinook Jargon." *British Columbia Historical Quarterly*, vol. 6, no. 4, 1942, pp. 225-50. www.library.ubc.ca/archives/pdfs/bchf/bchq_1942_4.

Hines, Donald, editor. Foreword. *Tales of the Okanogans*. Ye Galleon Press, 1976.

"Important Canadian Earthquakes." Natural Resources Canada, Government of Canada, www.earthquakescanada.nrcan.gc.ca/historic-historique/map-carte-en.php. Accessed 13 June 2018.

"James Robert Christie." *OHS Report*, vol. 40, 1976, p. 154.

Johnson, Wendy. "Inkameep Art Collection Priceless." *Oliver Chronicle*, 29 May 2002, pp. 1-2.

King, Thomas. *The Truth about Stories: A Native Narrative*. House of Anansi, 2003.

Koch, Frederick H. "Towards a New Folk Theatre." *The Quarterly Journal—University of North Dakota*, vol. 20, no. 3, May 1930.

Koroscil, Paul M. *The British Garden of Eden: Settlement History of the Okanagan Valley*, British Columbia. Simon Fraser U., Dept of Geography, 2003.

Korpan, Cynthia Joanne. "Authentic Culture: The Inkameep Plays as Canadian Indian Folk Drama." Diss. U of Victoria, 2009.

Kroeber, Paul D. *The Salishan Language: Reconstructing Syntax*. Lincoln: U of Nebraska P, 1999.

Kruger, Chrestenza. "Early Days at Osoyoos." *OHS Report*, vol. 6, 1935, pp.76-80.

Kruger, Matilda. Letter to Hester White. 20 Nov. 1934. En'owkin Centre Archive, Kruger Family Folders, Black File, Penticton Indian Reserve, BC.

Lacey, Katie. "The Cascadilla." *OHS Report*, vol. 25, 1961, pp. 145-46.

---. "Chief Tonasket: Chief of the Okanagan Indians." *OHS Report*, vol. 23, 1959, pp. 21-2.

---. "Hoziers." *OHS Report*, vol. 27, 1963, p. 143.

---. "Valentine Carmichael Haynes." *OHS Report*, vol. 27, 1963, pp. 117-18.

Lamb, W. Kaye. Letter to Hester White, 4 Dec. 1936. Hester White Fonds, MS 1, Penticton Museum and Archives, Penticton, BC, Manuscript.

---. "FRASER, SIMON." *Dictionary of Canadian Biography*, vol. 9, 1976, U of Toronto/U Laval, 2003-. www.biographi.ca/en/bio/fraser_simon_9E.html.

Lambley, Mrs. Robert [nee Lucy Postill]. "Early Days at Okanagan Mission." *OHS Report*, vol. 18, 1954, pp. 115-16.

Lawrence, Bonita. "Gender, Race, and the Regulation of Native Identity in Canada and the United States: An Overview." *Hypatia*, vol. 18, no. 2, 2003, pp. 3-31.

---. *"Real" Indians and Others: Mixed-Blood Urban Native Peoples and Indigenous Nationhood.* U of Nebraska P, 2004.

Lejeune, Jean-Marie-Raphael. Letter to Arthur H. McBride. 13 May 1889. Library and Archives Canada, collectionscanada.gc.ca.

Leslie, John F. "The Indian Act: An Historical Perspective." Canadian Parliamentary Review vol. 25, no. 2, 2002. www.revparl.ca/english/issue.asp?param=83&art=255.

Louis, Shirley, author, editor and transcriber. *Q'sapi: A History of Okanagan People as Told by Okanagan Families.* Theytus Books, 2002.

MacKenzie, Evadne. "A Tribute to Grandmother." *In Her Words: Selected Works of Susan Louisa Allison*, compiled by Diane Sterne, Princeton and District Museum and Archives, Princeton, BC, 2010, pp. 81-83.

MacNaughton, Frederick Carleton. "Mr. and Mrs. J.B. MacNaughton Sr. Pioneers." *OHS Report*, vol. 39, pp. 79-81.

MacNaughton, Isabel Christie. *The Crickets Must Sing.* MacNaughton, *Wood Fires* (1942), pp. 9-10.

---. "Deed of Gift." Oliver and District Heritage Society. Isabel Christie MacNaughton Fonds, Oliver, BC.

---. *The Greasewood Tree. Wood Fires*, expanded ed., The Chronicle Publishing, 1948, pp. 23-34.

---. [unsigned.] "How an Ancient Indian Woman Taught Her People Wisdom." *Penticton Herald*, 30 Dec 1937, p. 3.

---. "The Indian folktales. . . ." n.d. Oliver and District Heritage Society, Isabel Christie MacNaughton Fonds, Series 1, Scrapbook.

---. "Indian Paintings." n.d. Oliver and District Heritage Society, Isabel Christie MacNaughton Fonds, Series 2, Hand Drawn Pictographs.

---. [unsigned.] "More Indian Tales." *Penticton Herald*, 11 Aug. 1938, p. 3.

---. "Tribute to a Lady." *Penticton Herald*, 14 Dec. 1950, p. 2.

---. "We have no progress whatsoever to report." [1942-4?]. Okanagan Society for the Revival of Indian Arts and Crafts, OSRIAC, MS 5, Osoyoos and District Museum and Archives, Osoyoos, BC.

---. *Why the Ant's Waist Is Small.* MacNaughton, *Wood Fires* (1942), pp. 17-18.

---. *Wood Fires.* Oliver Chronicle and Osoyoos Observer Print, 1942.

---. and James R. Christie. *The Story of Okanagan Falls*, Okanagan Falls Centennial Committee, 1958.

---. [Isabel Christie], and Elizabeth Renyi. *Why the Chipmunk's Coat Is Striped. The Carolina Play-Book,* vol. 12, no. 4, 1939, pp. 108-10.

Maisonville, Georgina. "Arthur Day . . . Pioneer." *OHS Report,* vol. 18, 1954, pp. 61-65.

Manery, S. "1858—One Hundred Years in the Similkameen—1958." *OHS Report,* vol. 23, 1959, pp. 72-76.

Manuel, Arthur, and Grand Chief Ronald M. Derrickson. *Unsettling Canada: A National Wake-Up Call.* Between the Lines Press, 2015.

Marion County, Oregon, Census 1895, Willamette Valley Genealogical Society. Ancestry.com, search.ancestry.com/search/db.aspx?dbid=2467

Martens, Art. "The Allisons of the Similkameen." *Living Significantly,* 1 May 2015. livingsignificantly.ca/2015/05/01/allisons-of-the-similkameen/. Accessed 14 August 2016.

Martin, Stuart J. "Vernon Street Names." *OHS Report* vol. 13, 1959, pp. 156-60.

Mather, Ken. *Buckaroos and Mud Pups: The Early days of Ranching in British Columbia.* Heritage House Publishing, 2006.

Mattina, Anthony and Madeline DeSautel, editors. *Dora Noyes DeSautel ła? kłcaptikʷł. Occasional Papers in Linguistics,* no. 15, 2002.

McBride, Arthur H. Letter to G-he-nac. 18 Apr. 1889. Library and Archives Canada, collectionscanada.gc.ca. Accessed 14 June 2018.

---. Letter to G-he-nac. 28 May 1889. Library and Archives Canada, collectionscanada.gc.ca. Accessed 14 June 2018.

---. Letter to Joseph W. McKay. 21 June 1889. Library and Archives Canada, collectionscanada.gc.ca. Accessed 14 June 2018.

McKay, Joseph W. Letter to Arthur H. McBride. 13 June 1889. Library and Archives Canada, collectionscanada.gc.ca. Accessed 14 June 2018.

---. Letter to Hamilton Moffat. 4 July 1889. Library and Archives Canada, collectionscanada.gc.ca. Accessed 14 June 2018.

Meldrum, Stu. "Slide Presentation for the Allison Family Reunion, July 30th to August 2, 1999." Allison Family Fonds, 1849-1889, MS I-4716, Penticton Museum and Archives, Penticton, BC.

Millar, Albert. "Okanagan Society for the Revival of Indian Arts and Crafts." *OHS Report,* vol. 12, 1948, 24-28.

Miller, Elmo. Letter to Mrs. Hester E. White. 2 Feb. 1960. Hester White Fonds, MS 1, Penticton Museum and Archives, Penticton, BC.

Miller, Jay. Introduction to the Bison Book Edition. *Coyote Stories,* by Mourning Dove, U of Nebraska P, 1990, pp. v–xvii.

Mills, Charles W. *The Racial Contract.* Cornell UP, 1997.

"Minutes of Council Meeting held on Monday, January18, at the United Church Hall, Oliver, BC." [1942?] Okanagan Society for the Revival of Indian Arts and Crafts, OSRIAC, MS-5, Osoyoos and District Museum and Archives, Osoyoos, BC.

"Minutes of Meeting held March 9th, 1941." 1941. OSRIAC, MS-5, Osoyoos and District Museum and Archives, Osoyoos, BC.

Moore, Cecelia. "'The South as Folk Play': The Carolina Playermakers, Regional Theatre and the Federal Theatre Project, 1935-1939." Diss. U of North Carolina at Chapel Hill, 2013.

Morrie, Thomas. "Southern Interior Stockmen's Association: 1943-1993." *OHS*

Report, vol. 58, 1994, 90-95.

Mourning Dove. *Cogewea, The Half-Blood: A Depiction of the Great Montana Cattle Range*. 1927. With notes and biographical sketch by Lucullus Virgil McWhorter, U of Nebraska P, 1981.

---. *Coyote Stories*. 1933. Edited by Heister Dean Guie, U of Nebraska P, 1990.

---. "House of Little Men." [1930?]. Lucullus V. McWhorter Papers, Cage 55, Series 6, Indian Narratives, Box 45, Folder 433, Washington State University Libraries, Pullman, Washington.

---. Letter to Hester White. 5 Nov. 1934. Hester White Fonds, MS 1, Penticton Museum and Archives, Penticton, BC.

---. Letter to Lucullus Virgil McWhorter. 9 Feb. 1915. Manuscripts, Archives and Special Collections Division, Lucullus V. McWhorter Papers, 1848-1945, Cage 55, Washington State University Libraries, Pullman, Washington.

---. *Mourning Dove: A Salishan Autobiography*. Edited by Jay Miller. U of Nebraska Press, 1990.

---. Preface. *Tales of the Okanogans*. Edited by Donald M. Hines, Ye Galleon Press, 1976, pp. 11-14.

---. "The Red Cross and the Okanogans." 1919. Lucullus V. McWhorter Papers, Cage 55, Series 7, Mourning Dove Correspondence, Box 46, Folder 444, Washington State University Libraries, Pullman, Washington.

---. *Tales of the Okanogans*. Edited by Donald M. Hines, Ye Galleon Press, 1976.

Munroe, Findlay, and Violet Munroe. "Early Day Summerland." Told to Eric D. Sismey. *OHS Report*, vol. 31, 1967, pp. 61-71.

Musgrave, John Brent. "Mourning Dove: Chronicler and Champion of the Okanagan." *Osoyoos Museum and District Archives*, "Exhibits," "Collections—Women of the Okanagan," osoyoosmuseum.ca.

"Native Canadians: A Plan for the Rehabilitation of Indians." Okanagan Society for the Revival of Indian Arts and Crafts, [1944]. Osoyoos and District Museum and Archives, Osoyoos, BC.

Nicholson, Henry. "Early Days in the Similkameen." *OHS Report*, vol. 5, 1931, pp. 13-15.

Nicks, John. "THOMPSON, DAVID." *Dictionary of Canadian Biography*, vol. 8, 1985. U of Toronto/U Laval, 2003-. www.biographi.ca/en/bio/thompson_david_1770_1857_8E.html.

"1910 Memorial from the Interior Chiefs to the Prime Minister Sir Wilfred Laurier," *Shuswap Nation Tribal Council*, shuswapnation.org/to-sir-wilfrid-laurier/. Accessed 30 Jan. 2018.

Niss, Barbara. "Re: Marie Houghton Brent." Received by Lally Grauer, 16 July 2014.

Norris, Leonard. Letter to Marie Houghton Brent. 24 June 1930. Marie Houghton Brent Papers, MS 203, Greater Vernon and Museum Archives, Vernon,BC.

"Okanagan Landmark Burns." *Penticton Herald*, 9 Feb 1950, p.1.

Official Register of the United States, Containing a List of the Officers and Employees in the Civil, Military, and Naval Service, 1897. Vol. 1, p. 802. Government Printing Office, 1897, US Government Publishing Office, GOVPUB-CS1-507a4b2991c4aa6451941ab7c255dc14.pdf

Official Register of the United States, Containing a List of the Officers and Employees in the Civil, Military, and Naval Service, 1901. Vol. 1, p. 983. Government

Printing Office, 1901, US Government Publishing Office, GOVPUB-CS1-4920c6102b5b99e86af84d8294849f59.pdf

Official Register of the United States, Containing a List of the Officers and Employees in the Civil, Military and Naval Service, 1903. Vol. 1, p. 996. Government Printing Office, 1903, US Government Publishing Office, GOVPUB-CS1-b8613e269ff907cfa0819de05bcde57f.pdf

Official Register of the United States, Containing a List of the Officers and Employees in the Civil, Military and Naval Service, 1905. Vol. 1, p. 952. Government Printing Office, 1905, US Government Publishing Office, GOVPUB-CS1-ed32b00a042f89ac511e8c8ccc9580f3.pdf

"100-Year-Old Rancher." *OHS Report*, vol. 26, 1956, pp. 26-27.

Ormsby, Margaret. *Coldstream — Nulli Secundus: A History of the Corporation of the District of Coldstream.* Friesen, 1990.

---. "Directories." *OHS Report*, vol. 6., 1936, pp. 171-76.

---. "HOUGHTON, CHARLES FREDERICK." *Dictionary of Canadian Biography*, vol. 12, 1990, U of Toronto/U Laval, 2003-. www.biographi.ca/en/bio/houghton_charles_frederick_12E.html.

---. Introduction. *A Pioneer Gentlewoman in British Columbia: The Recollections of Susan Allison.* U of British Columbia P, 1976, pp. ix-li.

---. Notes. *A Pioneer Gentlewoman in British Columbia: The Recollections of Susan Allison.* U of British Columbia P, 1976, pp. 86-127.

---. "Some Irish Figures in Colonial Days." *British Columbia Historical Quarterly*, vol. 1-2, 1950, pp. 61-82.

"Our History." Okanagan Indian Band. www.okib.ca/about-us/our-history.

Parsons, Alberta, and Barbara Lawrence. "Keremeos, A History." *OHS Report* 36, 1972, pp. 50-58.

Pateman, Carole. "Race, Sex, and Indifference." Pateman and Mills, pp. 134-64.

---. "The Settler Contract." Pateman and Mills, pp. 35-78.

---. *The Sexual Contract.* Stanford UP, 1988.

Pateman, Carole, and Charles W. Mills, editors. *Contract and Domination.* Cambridge UP/Polity Press, 2007.

Perry, Adele. *On the Edge of Empire: Gender, Race and the Making of British Columbia.* U of Toronto P, 2001.

Peter, Mary. "Reminiscences." 1932. Sisters of St. Ann Archives S.29-350, BC Archives, Victoria, BC.

Phillips, Sallie. "Upcountry Profiles." October 13, 1950. Hester White Fonds, MS 1, Penticton Museum and Archives, Penticton, BC.

Phillips-Wolley, Clive. *A Sportsman's Eden.* Richard Bentley and Son, 1888.

"Pioneer and writer 'Buddie' MacNaughton passes in 88th Year," *Oliver Chronicle*, 12 Nov. 2003, p. 15.

Pratt, Mary Louise. *Imperial Eyes: Travel Writing and Transculturation.* Routledge, 1992.

"Princeton." *Gold Trails and Ghost Towns*, hosted by Mike Roberts with historian and storyteller Bill Barlee, CHBC-TV, Kelowna, BC, 1987. www.youtube.com/watch?v=m9a_eHDVvtE. Accessed 1 May 2018.

"Public Art Heritage Brochure." Westbank First Nation. www.wfn.ca/our-community/culture-language/public-art.htm. Accessed 12 June 2018.

Putnam, Goldie. "Okanogan People Had Rich History." *Republic (Wn.) News-*

Miner, 15 Aug. 1959, p. 3.

Raufer, Maria Ilma. *Black Robes and Indians on the Last Frontier.* Bruce Publishing, 1966.

Ray, Verne F. *Cultural Relations in the Plateau of Eastern Washington and Northern Idaho.* Los Angeles, the Southwest Museum Administrator of the Fund, 1939.

Registre des Noms, Entrées et Sorties des Élèves qui ont fréquente le Convent des Soeurs de St. Anne a Kamloops depuis 1880 jusquà 1930 (Student Register of the Convent of the Sisters of St. Ann in Kamloops). SSA Archives, S.64-9, BC Archives, Victoria, BC.

Reimer, Chad. "Historians of a Genteel Frontier: Margaret Ormsby, Leonard Norris and the *Okanagan Historical Society.*" BC Studies Conference, Kelowna BC, 1994.

Reimers, Mia. "'BC at its Most Colourful, Sparkling Best': Post-war Province Building through Centennial Celebrations." Diss. U of Victoria, 2008.

Rink, Deborah. *Spirited Women: A History of Catholic Sisters in British Columbia.* Sisters' Association Archdiocese of Vancouver, 2000.

Rivère, Edmond. *Father Pandosy: Pioneer of Faith in the Northwest.* Translated by Lorin Card. Midtown Press, 2012.

Robinson, Harry. *Nature Power: In the Spirit of an Okanagan Storyteller, Harry Robinson.* Compiled and edited by Wendy C. Wickwire, Douglas and McIntyre, 1992.

---. *Write It on Your Heart: The Epic World of an Okanagan Storyteller, Harry Robinson.* Compiled and edited by Wendy C. Wickwire, Talonbooks / Theytus, 1989.

Ross, Alexander. *Adventures of the First Settlers on the Oregon or Columbia River.* 1849. Edited by Milo Milton Quaife, The Citadel Press, 1969.

Rubin, David C. *Memory in Oral Traditions: The Cognitive Psychology of Epic, Ballads, and Counting-out Rhymes.* Oxford UP, 1995.

Sacramental Records 1882-1947. Convent of the Sisters of St. Ann, Kamloops, SSA Archives, S.64-16, BC Archives, Victoria, BC.

St. Mary's Mission. *Coyote and the Colville.* Omak School District # 19, 1971.

Saucier, Eleanor. Letter to Hester White. 9 August 1936. Hester White Fonds, MS 1. Penticton Museum and Archives, Penticton, BC.

"Similkameen Day." Similkameen Star, 9 Jul. 1951, np.

"Shuttleworth, Henry [Digby]". Biographical Sheet. Hudson's Bay Company Archives, Winnipeg, MB, www.gov.mb.ca / chc / archives / hbca / biographical / index.html?print

Shuttleworth, Josephine. "Chief Francois, Who Died at 105, Was Notable Old Figure." *Penticton Herald,* 6 Jan. 1938, p. 3.

---. [unsigned.] "The Coyote Lost His Deer Meat and Created a Thirst." *Penticton Herald,* 3 Mar. 1938, p. 3.

---. "The Cranes Herald Spring." *Penticton Herald,* 25 Aug. 1938, p. 3.

---. [unsigned.] "Folk Lore of the Days When Animal People Dwelt Here." *Penticton Herald,* 18 Nov. 1937, p. 3.

---. "He Dreamed—and Died—with the Falling of the Leaves." *Penticton Herald,* 11 May 1939, p. 3.

---. "How Chipmunk Got Markings and Why the Loon Laughs." *Penticton Herald,*

20 Jan. 1938, p. 3.

---. "More Indian Tales." *Penticton Herald*, 11 Aug. 1938, p. 3.

---. [unsigned.] "This Man Died When the Ice Moved off the Lake in Spring." *Penticton Herald*, 23 Mar. 1939, p. 5.

---. When the Coyote Changed the Lives of the Valley Indians. *Penticton Herald*, 25 Nov. 1937, p. 3.

Simpson, George. *Fur Trade and Empire: George Simpson's Journal.* Edited by Frederick Merk, Harvard UP, 1931.

"Sir James Douglas." *BC Black History Awareness Society.* bcblackhistory.ca. Accessed 7 July 2017.

Sismey, Eric. "The Shuttleworths of Okanagan Falls." *OHS Report*, vol. 35, 1971, pp. 136-39.

---. [unsigned.] "Maggie Victor—Wha-hul-kin-malks: An Okanagan." *OHS Report*, vol. 30, 1966, pp. 138-43.

Smith, Donald B. "LONG, SYLVESTER CLARK." Dictionary of Canadian Biography, Vol.16, 2016, U of Toronto/U Laval, 2003-. www.biographi.ca/en/bio/long sylvester clark16E.html

Smith, Lisa-Marie. "Portrait of a Teacher: Anthony Walsh and the Inkameep Day School, 1932-1942." MA thesis, U of Victoria, 2004.

"Some History of the Similkameen Valley." Princeton and District Museum and Archives, Princeton, BC, uncatalogued typescript.

Splawn, Andrew Jackson. *Ka-mi-akin: The Last Hero of the Yakimas.* HathiTrust Digital Library, babel.hathitrust.org/cgi/pt?id=loc. ark:/13960/t9j38wc00;view=1up;seq=9

Splawn, Homer. "Land of Giants." *OHS Report*, vol. 26, 1962, pp. 17-26.

"Spotlight on Antelope Brush." The Okanagan Similkameen Conservation Alliance. osca.org/wp-content/uploads/2017/08/sos_antelope_brush.pdf

Sterne, Diane, compiler. *In Her Words: Selected Works of Susan Louisa Allison.* Princeton and District Museum and Archives, Princeton, BC, 2010.

Swalwell, Eliza Jane. "Girlhood Days in the Okanagan." *OHS Report*, vol. 8, 1939, pp. 34-40.

Teit, James A. "The Salishan Tribes of the Western Plateaus." Edited by Franz Boas, *Forty-fifth Annual Report of the Bureau of American Ethnology, 1927-1928.* Government Printing Office, 1930, pp. 23-396.

Tennant, Paul. *Aboriginal Peoples and Politics: The Indian Land Question in British Columbia, 1849-1989.* U of British Columbia P, 1990.

"Theodore John 'Babe' Kruger Obituary," *OHS Report*, vol. 26, 1962, pp. 161-62.

Thomas, Alfred. "Mountain Pathfinder of Princeton." *OHS Report*, vol. 37, 1973, pp. 27-32.

Thomas, Lori. "Allison, J.F. (1825-1897) and Susan Louisa (Moir) (1845-1937)." *Princeton: Our Valley*, edited by Princeton History Book Committee, Friesens, 2000, pp. 221-26.

Thomson, Duane. "A History of the Okanagan: Indians and Whites in the Settlement Era, 1860-1920." Diss. U of British Columbia, 1985.

---. "PANDOSY, CHARLES." *Dictionary of Canadian Biography*, vol. 7, U of Toronto/U Laval, 2003-. www.biographi.ca/en/bio/pandosy_charles_12E.html.

"To Hester Emily White: A Tribute." *OHS Report*, vol. 28, 1964, p. 136.

"Truth and Reconciliation Commission of Canada: Calls to Action." Truth and Reconciliation Commission of Canada, 2012. www.trc.ca/websites/trcinstitution/File/2015/Findings/Calls_to_Action_English2.pdf

Tunstall, G. C. Letter to H.B. Roycroft, Esq., Provincial Superintendent of Police. 11 Oct. 1886. Library and Archive Canada, collectionscanada.gc.ca. Accessed 14 June 2018.

Turnbull, Elsie C. "Recollections of Marie Houghton Brent." *British Columbia Historical News*, vol. 18, no. 2, 1984, pp. 21-22.

Utley, Terry. "Keen Minded Woman Remembers Century." *Kelowna Daily Courier*, 18 June 1964, p. 3.

---. "Native Kelowna Daughter Still Remembers Past." *Kelowna Daily Courier*, 31 May 1965, p. 2B.

Van Kirk, Sylvia. *Many Tender Ties:Women in the Fur-Trade Society, 1670-1870.* 1980. Watson & Dwyer, 1993.

---. "Women in Between: Indian Women in Fur Trade Society in Western Canada." Historical Papers/Communications historiques, vol. 12, no.1, 1977, pp. 30-46. https://doi.org/10.7202/030819ar

Walsh, Andrea. *Nk'Mip Chronicles: Art from the Inkameep Day School.* Osoyoos Museum Society and Osoyoos Indian Band, 2005.

Walsh, Anthony. "Developing Indian Art and Culture." *The Prospector*, 8 May 1940, p. 4.

---. "The Inkameep Indian School." *OHS Report*, vol. 38, 1974, pp. 14-19.

Wan, LiLynn. "A Nation of Artists: Alice Ravenhill and the Society for the Furtherance of British Columbia Indian Arts and Crafts." *BC Studies*, no. 138, Summer, 2013, pp. 51-70.

Webber, Jean. "Fur Trading Posts in the Okanagan and Similkameen." *OHS Report*, vol. 57, 1993, pp. 6-33.

---. Personal interview with Lally Grauer, 12 Jan. 2009.

"Wedding Unites Pioneer Families." *Kelowna Courier*, 26 Nov. 1936, p. 5.

White, Hester Emily. "Cawston." n.d. Hester White Fonds, MS 1, Penticton Museum and Archives, Penticton, BC.

---. "Camp McKinney." *OHS Report*, vol. 13., 1949, 135-47.

---. "Charlotte Haynes." *OHS Report*, vol. 16, 1952, pp. 37-44.

---. "Chief Pelka-mū Lôx—As told by Maria Houghton Brent to Hester White." n.d. Hester White Fonds, MS 1, Penticton Museum and Archives, Penticton, BC.

---. "First Memory." n.d. Hester White Fonds, MS 1, Penticton Museum and Archives, Penticton, BC.

---. "General Sherman at Osoyoos." *OHS Report*, vol. 15, 1951, pp. 44-66.

---. "Governesses." *OHS Report*, vol. 23, 1959, p. 47.

---. "Jail House No. 2." [1958-61?]. Hester White Fonds, MS 1, Penticton Museum and Archives, Penticton, BC.

---. "Jinney (An Indian Woman)." n.d. Hester White Fonds, MS 1, Penticton Museum and Archives, Penticton, BC.

---. "John Carmichael Haynes: Pioneer of the Okanagan and Kootenay." *British Columbia Historical Quarterly*, vol. 4, no. 3, 1940, pp. 183-201.

---. Letter to Ernestine Ames. [14 Aug. 1962]. Marie Houghton Brent Papers, MS

203, Greater Vernon Museum and Archives, Vernon, BC.

---. Letter to Marie Houghton Brent. 20 Oct. 1955. Marie Houghton Brent Papers, MS 203, Greater Vernon Museum and Archives, Vernon, BC.

---. Letter to Marie Houghton Brent. 11 May 1958. Marie Houghton Brent Papers, MS 203, Greater Vernon Museum and Archives, Vernon, BC.

---. Letter to Marie Houghton Brent. [ca. 8 June 1958]. Marie Houghton Brent Papers, MS 203, Greater Vernon Museum and Archives, Vernon, BC.

---. Letter to Marie Houghton Brent. Thursday [summer 1958]. Marie Houghton Brent Papers, MS 203, Greater Vernon Museum and Archives, Vernon, BC.

---. Letter to Marie Houghton Brent. [early Dec. 1959]. Marie Houghton Brent Papers, MS 203, Greater Vernon Museum and Archives, Vernon, BC.

---. Letter to Marie Houghton Brent. [late Dec. 1959 or early Jan. 1960]. Marie Houghton Brent Papers, MS 203, Greater Vernon Museum and Archives, Vernon, BC.

---. Letter to Marie Houghton Brent. [Feb. 1960]. Marie Houghton Brent Papers, MS 203, Greater Vernon Museum and Archives, Vernon, BC.

---. Letter to Ann Briley. 18 Feb. 1959. Anne Briley Fonds. Okanogan County Historical Society, Okanogan, WA.

---. Letter to Katie Lacey, 18 Oct. [1960]. Katie Lacey Fonds, MS 2, Correspondence 1955-1964, 988.35.15, Osooyos Museum and Archives, Osoyoos, BC.

---. Letter to Katie Lacey. 15 July 1961. Katie Lacey Fonds, MS 2, Correspondence 1955-1964, 988.35.23, Osoyoos Museum and Archives, Osoyoos, BC.

---. Letter to Katie Lacey. "a.m. Wed. [July or Aug. 1961]." Katie Lacey Fonds, MS 2, Correspondence 1955-1964, 988.35.18, Osooyos Museum and Archives, Osoyoos, BC.

---. Letter to Katie Lacey. 7 Sept. [1961]. Katie Lacey Fonds, MS 2, Correspondence 1955-1964, 988.35.24, Osooyos Museum and Archives, Osoyoos, BC.

---. Letter to Katie Lacey. 14 Sept. 1961. Katie Lacey Fonds, MS 2, Correspondence 1955-1964, 988.35.20, Osooyos Museum and Archives, Osoyoos, BC.

---. Letter to Katie Lacey. 27 Sept. 1961. Katie Lacey Fonds, MS 2, Correspondence 1955-1964, 988.35.7, Osooyos Museum and Archives, Osoyoos, BC.

---. Letter to Katie Lacey. 22 Oct. [1961]. Katie Lacey Fonds, MS 2, Correspondence 1955-1964, 988.35.36, Osooyos Museum and Archives, Osoyoos, BC.

---. Letter to Katie Lacey. "Sunday, At last I have been able" [circa 1961]. Katie Lacey Fonds, MS 2, Correspondence 1955-1964, Osooyos Museum and Archives, Osoyoos, BC.

---. Letter to Katie Lacey, "Many thanks for Thursday" [circa 1960-63]. Katie Lacey Fonds, MS 2, Correspondence 1955-1964, 988.35.25, Osooyos Museum and Archives, Osoyoos, BC.

---. "Mail Day." *OHS Report*, vol. 25, 1961, pp. 25-26.

---. "May 1st, 1895, Osoyoos." n.d. Hester White Fonds, MS 1, Penticton Museum and Archives, Penticton, BC.

---. "Nicholson's Creek. . ." [1960-63?]. Hester White Fonds, MS 1, Penticton Museum and Archives, Penticton, BC.

---. "Off to England, Sept. 1890." n.d. Hester White Fonds, MS 1, Penticton Museum and Archives, Penticton, BC.

---. "On Okanagan Lake in 1888." *OHS Report*, vol. 18, 1954, pp. 42-46.

---. "[July 6, 1888] Osoyoos." n.d. Hester White Fonds, MS 1, Penticton Museum and Archives, Penticton, BC, 5 pages, typescript.

---. "Over the Hope Trail." [1958?]. Hester White Fonds, MS 1, Penticton Museum and Archives, Penticton, BC, 3 pages, typescript.

---. "The Pioneer Trail: Reminiscences of Early Days." *Penticton Herald*, 26 June 1947, p. 8.

---. "The Pioneer Trail: Reminiscences of Early Days." *Penticton Herald*, 3 July 1947, p. 14.

---. "The Pioneer Trail: Reminiscences of Early Days." *Penticton Herald*, 10 July 1947, p. 13.

---. "The Pioneer Trail: Reminiscences of Early Days." *Penticton Herald*, 14 Aug. 1947, p. 3.

---. "The Pioneer Trail: Reminiscences of Early Days." *Penticton Herald*, 11 Sept. 1947, p. 3.

---. "The Pioneer Trail: Reminiscences of Early Days." *Penticton Herald*, 2 Oct. 1947, p. 18.

---. "Plymouth Devon 1890." n.d. Hester White Fonds, MS 1, Penticton Museum and Archives, Penticton, BC.

---. "R.L. Cawston." n.d. Hester White Fonds, MS 1, Penticton Museum and Archives, Penticton, BC.

---. "Shuttleworth." n.d. Hester White Fonds, MS 1, Penticton Museum and Archives, Penticton, BC.

---. "Stenwyken." *OHS Report*, vol. 26, 1962, pp. 130-31.

---. "Susap." [1949?]. Hester White Fonds, MS 1, Penticton Museum and Archives, Penticton, BC.

---. "We Cross the Columbia in a Canoe." [1961] Hester White Fonds, MS 1, Penticton Museum and Archives, Penticton, BC.

---. "We Cross the Columbia in an Indian Canoe." *OHS Report*, vol. 25, 1961 , pp. 36- 41.

---. "W.H. Lowe." [1963?] Hester White Fonds, MS 1, Penticton Museum and Archives, Penticton, BC.

Wickwire, Wendy C. Introduction. *Write It on Your Heart: The Epic World of an Okanagan Storyteller, Harry Robinson.* Talonbooks/Theytus, 1989, pp. 11- 28.

---. "'They wanted … me to help them': James A. Teit and the Challenge of Ethnography in the Boasian Era." *With Good Intentions: Euro-Canadian and Aboriginal Relations in Colonial Canada*, edited by Cynthia Haig-Brown and David A. Nock, U of British Columbia P, 2006, pp. 297-20.

"William (Billy) Kruger" obituary. *OHS Report*, vol. 22, 1958, p. 110.

"William Brent Had Adventurous Career." *Vernon News*, 9 Nov. 1939, p. 10.

Woodcock, George. "BLACK, SAMUEL." *Dictionary of Canadian Biography*, vol. 7, 1988, U of Toronto/U Laval, 2003-. www.biographi.ca/en/bio/black_ samuel_7E.html.

Wright, Alice O. A. "Notes on *Some Native Daughters I Have Known*." Susan Louisa Allison and Family Fonds, BC Archives, Victoria, BC, Box 001588-0001, Folder 45.

---. Letter to Major J.S. Matthews. 23 Apr. 1969. City of Vancouver Archives, Vancouver, BC, Box 562-A-7, Folder 1.

Index